THE QUALITY AND QUANTITY OF CONTACT

*African Americans and Whites
on College Campuses*

Edited by
Robert M. Moore III

University Press of America,® Inc.
Lanham · New York · Oxford

Copyright © 2002 by
University Press of America,® Inc.
4501 Forbes Boulevard, Suite 200
Lanham, Maryland 20706
UPA Acquisitions Department (301) 459-3366

12 Hid's Copse Rd.
Cumnor Hill, Oxford OX2 9JJ

All rights reserved
Printed in the United States of America
British Library Cataloging in Publication Information Available

Library of Congress Cataloging-in-Publication Data

The quality and quantity of contact : African Americans and
Whites on college campuses / edited by Robert M. Moore III.
p. cm
Includes bibliographical references and index.
1. College students—Social networks—United States. 2. College
students—United States—Attitudes. 3. College environment—
United States. 4. Education, Higher—Social aspects—United
States. 5. United States—Race relations. I. Title: African Americans
and Whites on college campuses. II. Moore, Robert M., III.

LC191.94 .Q35 2002
378.1'98—dc21   2002024718 CIP

ISBN 0-7618-2277-1 (paperback : alk. ppr.)

∞™ The paper used in this publication meets the minimum
requirements of American National Standard for Information
Sciences—Permanence of Paper for Printed Library Materials,
ANSI Z39.48—1984

Contents

Preface vii

Acknowledgements ix

Introduction xi

Part I. Situational Contexts

Article 1	**Teaching Region, Learning Humility** Larry Griffin	1
Article 2	**Black and White Friendship** Sharon A. Lewis and Sara D. Jonsberg	18
Article 3	**Balancing Academic and Athletic Success: A Chronicle of African American Male Athletes' Involvement in Higher Education** Eddie Comeaux and C. Keith Harrison	34

Article 4	"It's Not About Race:" Making Whiteness Visible in the Interpretation of Rap Music Natalie Fasnacht	48
Article 5	Revisiting African American University Students' Interpersonal Style on Predominantly White Campuses Wanda Collins, Robbie J. Steward, and Douglas Neil	80
Article 6	Don't Stand Too Close to me: Social Distance and College Students at a Northern New Jersey University Gabe Wang and Kathleen Korgen	95

Part II. Social Awareness

Article 7	The History of the Black Student Union at a Professional Institution Joeseph Ruane	109
Article 8	Black and Gay Identity Selection on College Campuses: Master and Subordinate Status Strain and Conflict Tim Baylor	123
Article 9	"Did you hear what that white woman said?" Speaking for Change in Memphis, Tennessee Wanda Rushing	143

Article 10	**Exploring Racial Policy Views of College-Age White Americans: Implications for Campus Climate** Eboni M. Zamani	**160**
Article 11	**African American Male Students at Predominantly White Female Institutions of Higher Education** Amitra Hodge	**186**
Articles 12	**Interaction Patterns Between Black and White College Students: For Better or Worse?** Jas M. Sullivan, Ashraf M. Esmail, and Raymond S. Soh	**204**

Part III. Interaction

Article 13	**Black Professor/White Students: The Unique Problems Minority Professors Face when Teaching Race/Ethnicity to Majority Group Students** George Yancey	**226**
Article 14	**Would but Don't: Reconciling Expressed Willingness to Intergroup Marriage with National Trends** Charles A. Gallagher	**240**
Article 15	**Do Undergraduate College Students Self-Segregate?** Bette J. Dickerson, Kianda Bell, Kathryn Lasso, and Tiffany Waits	**254**
Article 16	**Student Multicultural Tolerance Levels in Relation to Student Rank** Elliot Anderson	**287**

| Article 17 | Understanding the Margins: Marginality and Social Segregation in Predominantly White Institutions
Will Tyson | 307 |
| Article 18 | Race, Gender and Intimacy on a College Campus
Robert M. Moore III | 323 |

Index 345

About the Contributors 348

Preface

The present-day schism or feelings of in-group versus out-group often felt between African Americans and whites in America is fostered by the following: one, unequal political and economic power; two, massive residential segregation; and three, social and psychological feelings of difference, superiority-inferiority, inherited from the legacy of slavery.[1] Points one and two speak to inequities that are related to a class system. The third point speaks to the lingering vestiges of a caste system. It can be argued that all three have interacted with each other in some fashion and continue to do so today. The college campus, hypothetically, should be a place of shelter or "ivory tower," away from the world since the college campus can provide ample opportunities for people to work together.

Colleges and university campuses can introduce and shape the values of their students profoundly by teaching lifelong learning skills. The institutional mandates on campuses have shifted from many decades ago to include an expressed desire to create and maintain multicultural classrooms and campus communities. Although equality between students is stressed, students often feel they occupy different status positions often associated with their race, sex and sexual orientation. A desired goal by many associated with higher education is to enable students to feel a sense of equality to each other as well as recognize and understand why feelings of difference are felt.

---

[1] Portions of the preface and the article written by Robert Moore were given as a paper at the annual meeting of the Southern Sociological Society, New Orleans, 2000. The paper was published in *Sociological Viewpoints*, "An Exploratory Study of Interracial Dating on a Small College Campus," Volume 16, Fall 2000, pp. 46 - 64.

Colleges and universities can act as a microcosm of the real world. But, they can also simulate change, give directions, and show members of the campus community how society could look. Campuses can foster and create opportunities for African Americans and whites to interact in ways that do not often occur in the "real world."

Acknowledgments

As academicians, we often try to create, maintain or have access to a network of colleagues, who have similar interests and who will intellectually push and stimulate us. I was very fortunate to have Ira Blake (Psychology) and Dwayne Williams (History) as colleagues when the three of us taught at Susquehanna University. To the best of my knowledge, Ira Blake became the first African American to receive tenure there, in 2000. Together, Ira and Dwayne challenged me to think more deeply about our world. They remain my friends. We were the only African Americans on the faculty.

Although I have only taught at Frostburg State University a short time, I would like to express my gratitude to my sociology colleagues. They have routinely engaged me in discussions about topics included in this book. Numerous others at Frostburg State University who, without their even knowing it, have stimulated and encouraged me to complete this project.

Attending the annual meeting of the Southern Sociological Society has provided a treasure trove of contacts. The reader will notice that quite a few contributors teach at southern universities and colleges and some of the authors are affiliated with the Society.

My appreciation is given to my family: Mary Beth, Paul, Harry and Timmy. I spent many hours reading and typing at the kitchen table instead of giving more attention to them especially during the holiday season.

My sincere appreciation is given to Patricia Cloward. She spent countless hours editing many of the articles. She has a very busy career at Frostburg State University, but she found time, especially on weekends, to read.

Introduction

Almost thirty authors representing nearly 20 academic institutions have been included in this book about race relations on college campuses. The book is divided into three parts: *Situational Contexts, Social Awareness, and Interaction.*

As many facets as possible of the college experience have been included: faculty-student contact, faculty friendships, social distance research, dating, and much more. Key sociological variables have been considered such as gender, education and socioeconomic status.

The book can be used as a resource for those who are interested in examining race relations on college and university campuses. Although many articles have been written from the perspective of personal experience, numerous references to contemporary, as well as past research are included in most articles.

The overall message of the book is neither one of optimism or pessimism. Rather the authors have attempted to present to the reader in a meaningful, responsible and scholarly way what they believe to be the quality and quantity of contact between African Americans and whites on predominantly white campuses across our nation.

I

Situational Contexts

Article 1

Teaching Region, Learning Humility[1]

Larry J. Griffin

Part One

After graduating from a whites-only public high school in Mississippi in 1965, I entered a small public college in the state--Delta State College (now University)--in its last year of segregated existence. I graduated with a degree in accounting and worked as an auditor for ten months for the U.S. Navy. Because so much was happening in American university and public life in the mid- to late 1960s, and so much was changing in the South, I'll never know exactly why accountancy so quickly escaped my unhappy presence. But I am pretty sure that a man named William Pennington was very much responsible. Bill Pennington was a Methodist minister, a part-time philosophy instructor (later department chair) at Delta State, and the teacher who, in a very gentle but wholly

---

[1] Portions of this essay were first presented at talks at Vanderbilt University and the Southern Sociological Society. I am grateful to the following for their insightful comments on earlier drafts: Karen E. Campbell, Marshall Eakin, Allison Pingree, and Peggy A. Thoits. This essay is dedicated to William A. Pennington.

compelling way, led me to open my eyes, look around, and think about the world around me--my world, Mississippi of the 1960s. And in doing that, Bill Pennington also irreversibly changed my life.

Though Pennington taught me many things of value, the most important was that college teaching itself is a profoundly moral act. By "moral," I do not mean that it is necessarily "good" or has "good" results, only that teaching, "good" or "bad," is rooted in a framework of moral values about self and others, that it is motivated by moral understandings of educational goals, that it is performed with pedagogical practices moral in nature, and thus that it, teaching, inevitably entails moral choice and exerts moral consequence. Because college teachers are culturally and institutionally empowered to impart to students new knowledge and critical perspectives, we are also empowered to alter their moral outlook and standards, to open their eyes, and thereby change forever their lives. College teachers should be humbled by this knowledge, humbled, paradoxically, because most of us both know too well our own intellectual and performative limitations ("was I too simplistic?" "flat wrong?" "boring?"), and, at the same time, know too little about how consequential, even perilous, our classrooms can be for our students. Teaching binds our weaknesses, biases, defensiveness, and egotism to our institutional and interpersonal power, and then it makes us confront this fact, just as it forces many of us to acknowledge that our own accomplishments are as much a matter of luck as merit. Though teaching, then, we learn humility.

All of this was way beyond my comprehension when I graduated from Delta State in 1969. I knew only that I wanted to do for others what Bill Pennington had done for me, and that to do that I had to teach. And teach I have, for almost a quarter of a century in four institutions of higher education, public and private. Though teaching of any sort is inescapably moral in its context and consequence, if not always in its content, college courses about race, gender, sexuality, class, religion, and, for reasons that will become clear, region--to name some of the politically sensitive topics often taught in the social sciences and humanities--deal with issues that are by their very nature moral; that is, with the "rightness" or "wrongness" of the way social arrangements are or were constituted and with the conflictual or challenging strategies advanced to change or perpetuate group relations and privilege. Such courses therefore are more likely to be morally upsetting, even emotionally wrenching, for students and faculty alike.[2] Probing, difficult

---

[2] There is a vast literature in sociology and other disciplines on teaching culturally sensitive/controversial material. See, for example, the following

questions about our purposes in teaching such courses, and about how we should and do teach them, are therefore almost fated to--and indeed, ought--to arise. Those of us who teach such classes should occasionally examine our motives for doing so, reflect on the utility of our procedures in doing so, and worry--worry as a dog "worries" a bone, and also "worry" as in the experience of anxiety--about the consequences, for us and our students, of having done so. Through such worry, we learn humility.

Part Two

My teaching cannot be reduced to the facts of my personal biography-- political and religious beliefs matter, as do intellectual tastes and institutional needs--but why, how and what I teach nonetheless do significantly reflect biographical experience. Born and reared in what historian James Cobb has called "the most Southern place on earth," the Mississippi Delta, at just about the time Strom Thurmond and the Dixiecrats bolted the Democratic party in 1948, I am the grandson of hardscrabble Mississippi hill farmers/ sharecroppers, and the son of non-unionized, small-town New South factory and office workers who often labored at minimum wages and suffered periodic bouts of unemployment.[3] I have argued elsewhere that for Jim Crow-era southerners of my parents' and grandparents' generations, race was the basis of their personal and group identities, channeling their ambitions for themselves and their children, establishing their patterns of sociability, defining their "duty," their moral sensibility, and their legal and cultural "place," and privileging whiteness with a degree of political presence, economic advantage, and honorific obeisance unparalleled by

---

articles from the journal Teaching Sociology, published by the American Sociological Association: Susanne Bohmer and Joyce L. Briggs, "Teaching Privileged Students About Gender, Race, and Class Oppression" 19 (April, 1991): 154-63; Amy B. Lusk and Adam S. Weinberg, "Discussing Controversial Topics in the Classroom: Creating a Context for Learning" 22 (October 1994): 301-08; Mark Beeman and Robert W. Volk, "Challenging Ethnic Stereotypes: A Classroom Exercise" 24 (July, 1996): 299-304; Frances V. Moulder, "Teaching About Race and Ethnicity: A Message of Despair or a Message of Hope?" 25 (April, 1997): 120-27.
[3] James Cobb, *The Most Southern Place on Earth: The Mississippi Delta and the Roots of Southern Identity* (New York: Oxford University Press, 1992).

all else that socially constituted women and men in the South at the time. I suppose this is true also of my generation, those of us who came of age in the region in the 1950s and 1960s: race was the window through which we saw our world, the ground upon which we walked, the air we breathed. Past, present, and possibility were all interwoven with race, and all were interpreted, vitally if not exclusively, in racial terms. In a culture premised on and organized by racial meanings and practices, in which literally no facet of human existence escaped profound racial coloration, explanation, and trajectory, race became the primary way southerners, black and white, knew our selves and our situations, articulated our hopes, and envisioned our futures.[4]

Given the confluence of biography, history, and disciplinary endorsement, then, I have always taught race (and class, to an extent), whether my course happened to be introductory sociology, or social problems, the sociology of work or education or one explicitly designed around race relations. After leaving Indiana University for Vanderbilt in 1990, a move motivated in part by a desire to return to the South, I continued to teach race, now combined, though, with teaching region. To teach is to learn, and committed college teachers are always learning--learning about the topics we teach, about our students, about what higher education can and cannot do, about ourselves--but I took a crash course in learning-by-teaching in all of these ways by having to prepare a public lecture on teaching I was required, as a recipient of a teaching award, to deliver to interested Vanderbilt faculty in 1997. What happened was that I had to acknowledge in my teaching what "the South" was and what the region meant to the world, to America, to my students, and to myself. What I learned was humility.

For the public lecture, I chose to speak on "Teaching Controversial Material" because my award was in part based on the perception of the awards committee that though I usually taught such material, and did so from a frank, if not dogmatic, political stance, I did not unduly offend or anger most students. To get a better sense of what the students thought of my presentation of such material and to learn, from their perspective, how it might be improved, I read in a single sitting all of my Vanderbilt course evaluations, about six years worth of commentary. Despite their well-publicized weaknesses and abuses, student course/instructor evaluations do indicate something of import about courses and those who teach them, so I have always taken them seriously. But I have never read

---

[4] Larry J. Griffin, "How Do We Disentangle Race and Class? Or Should We Even Try?" Work and Occupations 22 (February, 1995): 85-93.

so many at one time, or read them so single-mindedly fixated on the criticisms of my teaching. And there were criticisms aplenty: I seemed too anxious to defend liberal "preconceptions" from conservative attack; did not warn students of the emotional weight of the reading/discussion early enough in the semester for them to drop the class; harked too much on the problems of racism and spoke too little about its solutions; used books (especially Andrew Hacker's pointed *Two Nations: Black and White, Separate, Hostile, Unequal*, 1992) that were unfair and unbalanced.

Having taught similar material for years, and having heard many of the complaints before, I was somewhat dispirited, though not particularly surprised. What I read from an anonymous student about my first "Sociology of the South" course, however, shocked me. It read, verbatim: "Blacks, slavery and CR [civil rights; my insert] are important but not total. What about our culture?" Because every student in that inaugural "South" offering was white and most from the South, the word "our" in the student's course evaluation could have had only one meaning. Simply put, a student had left my class on the South believing, despite what were then my best efforts, in the reality of segregated black and white histories that most certainly did not converge in the American South, believing in the existence of a white regional culture having nothing to do with—and therefore innocent of--African Americans, or slavery, or the black freedom struggle.

Teaching about the region to the region's own was one reason I had moved to Vanderbilt, and the "South" course already elicited more investment of self and emotion than any I had ever taught. So what I read hurt, humbled. That only one student out of twenty or so openly voiced the complaint did not matter: to my mind, the statement painfully signified my failure and that of the course, failure as judged not by some abstract or external standard but in the very terms and language I held dearest. Whatever my success as a teacher, it was obvious in that class that I had done things I should not have and left undone things I should have attended to. I had little reason for hubris.

My failure on this signal point was not really due to the materials I used in that first class, wonderful books and essays by C. Vann Woodward, Jacquelyn Hall, Michael Schwartz, Doug McAdam, James Oakes, and others.[5] True, each of these scholars is white, but the fault did not rest

---

[5] C. Vann Woodward, "The Search for Southern Identity," pp. 3-25 in Woodward, *The Burden of Southern History*, rev. ed. (Louisiana State University Press, 1968); Jacqueline Hall, "Disorderly Women: Gender and Labor Militancy in the Appalachian South" Journal of American History, 73

with excessively racialized reading on my part. I had, independent of class, read and grieved over Richard Wright's *Black Boy*, understood and agreed with Martin Luther King, Jr's impatience in *Why We Can't Wait*, and devoured and passed along to many Anne Moody's searing autobiography, *Coming of Age in Mississippi*. Instead, the problem was that despite such reading my comprehension of what the region really was--its ontological being, as it were--was filtered through a racial lens so profoundly and subtly distorting that I evoked in class, and thereby gave license to others to evoke, an implicit identity between "the South," on the one hand, and "the white South," on the other, between "southerners," on the one hand, and "white southerners," on the other. Referring to Woodward's still important but deeply flawed interpretation of "southern identity," for example, I would say (or, what is worse, triumphantly lead my students to conclude) that its basis lay in "the South's" defeat in the Civil War and its guilt for racial crimes. As an inference about white southerners, or the white South, such a claim offers genuine purchase: as a valid statement about "southerners," or about "the South," it is absurd. As I have come to realize, and since written about in a different venue, "southerners," generally speaking, could not have been guilty of racial tyranny because *black southerners* were its victims, not its perpetrators. "Southerners," moreover, did not lose the Civil War: the Confederacy lost the War, even as some southerners, *black southerners*, won it and thus their legal freedom.[6] At the time of the award, though, I "knew" this only intellectually; I did not *know* it as an existential, orienting truth.

Such formulations of "southern identity," reproduced and valorized in my course, are similar in their logic to the mode of thought Roger

---

(September, 1986): 354-382; Michael Schwartz, *Radical Protest and Social Structure: The Southern Farmers' Alliance and Cotton Tenancy, 1880-1890* (New York, Academic Press, 1976); Doug McAdam, *Political Process and the Development of Black Insurgency* (Chicago: University of Chicago Press, 1982); James Oakesci (New York: Alfred A. Knopf, 1990).

[6] Larry J. Griffin, "Southern Distinctiveness, Yet Again, or, Why America Needs the South" Southern Cultures 6 (Fall, 2000): 47-72. Roger Cunningham, "Appalachianism and Orientalism: Reflections on Reading Edward Said," Journal of the Appalachian Studies Association 1: 125-32. On southern cultures and a bi-racial southern culture, see, for example, Richard Gray, "Negotiating Differences: Southern Culture(s) Now," Pp. 218-27 in *Dixie Debates: Perspectives on Southern Cultures*, Richard H. King and Helen Taylor, eds. (New York: New York University Press, 1996), and Mechal Sobel, *The World They Made Together: Black and White Values in Eighteenth-Century Virginia* (Princeton: Princeton University Press, 1987).

Cunningham called "Appalachianism" (and before him Edward Said labeled "Orientism"), a way of thinking about Appalachia (or the "Orient") that is "a discourse of power, a way of seeing and talking about things which is conditioned by domination and which tends both to perpetuate itself and to perpetuate that domination. It is a way of organizing perceptions into a closed self-referential system which takes on a life of its own, shaping assumptions and perceptions even among those who are unaware of any motivation to oppress." Coming back to discussions of the South, the consequences of thinking and teaching thusly are harsh indeed: by defining and framing the South largely, if unknowingly, in terms of *whiteness*, this and similar interpretations make--conceptually, semantically, morally--racially plural southern *cultures* unimaginable, make a bi-racial South impossible, make a syncretic southern culture arising from black and white together inconceivable.[7]

By uncritically parroting the formulations of Woodward and others, I had rendered myself incapable of thinking not only about what "the South" was, or who a "southerner" was, but also about why these questions mattered, intellectually and morally.[8] My white students could hardly be expected to open their eyes under my tutelage, as Bill Pennington had helped me do under his, if I myself was unable to open my own and search for this undetected and unwanted cynosure implicitly structuring the entire course. My failure to absorb and digest the elemental truth that black southerners were *southerners* and, consequently, that "the South" belonged as much to them as to whites' was a failure of vision and empathy, an act of moral blindness more troubling still because my student critic's easy, seemingly natural use of the phrase "our culture" implicated me as a member of his or her whites-only southern culture. All of these realizations--cognitive epiphanies, and perhaps moral ones as well--one after another in a tightly sequenced

---

[7] My Vanderbilt colleague, and fellow Mississippian, Jimmie Lewis Franklin insightfully explored this theme in his 1993 Presidential address to the Southern Historical Association. See his "Black Southerners, Shared Experience, and Place: A Reflection," Journal of Southern History 59 (February 1994): 3-18.

[8] The most influential sociologist of the U.S. South, John Shelton Reed, has an uncanny knack for doing this with humor and great intelligence. For an appreciation of Reed's accomplishments and a discussion of the sociological relevance of the region, see Larry Griffin, "The Promise of a Sociology of a South," Southern Cultures 7 (Spring, 2001): 50-75.

pattern were humbling indeed. They also spurred change, both in how I thought and in what I taught.

Part Three

In the spring of 2002, I teach the "South" course for the seventh time, and I am, finally, reasonably satisfied with it. The course continues to draw on southern history to raise questions about power, inequality, race, protest, and stereotyping that transcend any particular place or time. Because I believe that by obsessing about regional particularity we put human flesh on the sociologically general, and, simultaneously, that by wrestling with the general we grasp more firmly that particularity. Fittingly for a course now titled "The South in American Culture" and cross-listed with African American Studies and American/Southern Studies, however, it is now framed as much by the region's conflicted, and too often sorrowful, relationship to America as by overtly "sociological" concepts. It has become much more interdisciplinary over the years, now extensively employing fiction, music, film, and autobiography created by blacks and whites, women and men. The course increasingly draws minority students, so it is now much more multi-hued than when I first taught it. All of this is exactly right, I think: the South is too big, too contradictory, and too diverse to teach aided by only one or two disciplines, mediums, perspectives, representations, or voices.

To the extent that the course works as it should, it resembles in important ways a conversation of sorts between the South and America, a dialogue in which the region's meaning to and significance for the nation are the primary subjects. Rather than view the region as something exotic and separate from nation, the course presumes precisely the opposite, namely that the South, even in its peculiarity and distinctiveness, historically has been tightly bound to "America," and that the definitions of region and nation have always been co-dependent, each making and remaking the other.[9] This is made clear to students in their very first assignment: fitting the region into the "America" so powerfully evoked by Gunnar Myrdal in the introductory chapter ("American Ideals

---

[9] One of most insightful discussions of how "the South" has repeatedly altered the course of U.S. history is Carl Degler, "Thesis, Antithesis, Synthesis: The South, the North, and the Nation." Journal of Southern History 53 (February, 1987).

and the American Conscience") of his *An American Dilemma* (1944), and analyzing how the South might have thwarted, or paradoxically furthered, what Myrdal defined as "The American Creed." Though such readings, hearing (not reading, not watching, but *hearing*) speeches such as Martin Luther King's "I Have A Dream," and through confronting texts such as King's magisterial "Letter from the Birmingham Jail," in which he evinces a South with no place in a morally just United States, my students learn that in studying the South, one also inevitably studies America.[10]

The conversation between nation and region is the course's scaffolding, so to speak, sometimes deliberately left bare, more often woven into considerations of how race, gender, and class made the South what it has become today. Through the late C. Vann Woodward's influential history, *The Strange Career of Jim Crow* (3rd rev. ed., 1974), students come to see that race has largely defined the South as something separate from the nation. First published in the mid-1950s, *Strange Career* was described by Martin Luther King, Jr. as the "bible of the Civil Rights Movement" because it argued that Jim Crow, as a relatively recent (i.e., post- Reconstruction), deliberately created "invented tradition" rather than what was euphemistically called a "time-honored practice," could be undone by moral agency. The novelty of this has probably faded with time, but Woodward's corollary, that white southerners could have organized a humane racial order in the 1890s but instead *chose* the path of white supremacy in part because of the class interests and power of the region's so-called "better elements," remains an eye-opener.

Seeing how children learn of the rules and restrictions of Jim Crow, and then observing what they do with this information and what it does to them, is quite instructive for students who, themselves, may be encountering the South's racial apartheid for the first time as a serious topic of study. So by using the hurt or angry or puzzled or arrogant voices of southerners close in age to those of the students in the course, several of the assigned books on race and region have a "coming of age," eye-opening feel to them. The story in Harper Lee's still poignant *To Kill a Mockingbird* (1960) is, of course, told in Scout Finch's young white (and increasingly horrified) voice, and much of Anne Moody's *Coming of Age in Mississippi* (1968) powerfully recounts Anne's childhood and teen years in the 1940s and 1950s, when she suffered from lacerating poverty and grew to know and despise its main cause for black

---

[10] Pp. 76-95 in Martin Luther King, Jr., *Why We Can't Wait* (New York: Mentor, 1964).

Mississippians, white supremacy. Though one is fiction, the other autobiography, both texts deal with how young girls, one black and one white, experienced the Jim Crow South in the pre-*Brown* days. There are some commonalties deriving from a shared southern culture, gender, and rurality, but mostly students see that differences in class and race gave rise to vast, unignorable differences in what it meant to be southern.

Anne Moody's experience, moreover, can be very usefully contrasted with that of Melton McLaurin. In his memoir of growing up in a very small town in North Carolina, *Separate Pasts: Growing Up White in the Segregated South* (1987), McLaurin, today a historian of the region (see below) and almost exactly Moody's age, describes a "South" that is about as racist as Moody's Mississippi, but one lived, through the double privilege of white skin color and economic comfort, as its opposite. It is also an obviously conflicted South, and McLaurin has his grandfather, "Lonnie Mac," serve as the repository of the racial contradictions of many southern whites--racist, paternalistic, and oddly egalitarian, all at the same time. *Separate Pasts* is especially illuminating when McLaurin uses the rituals of adolescent males to demonstrate how unfathomably insecure whites' were in their dominance and how truly captive they were to their self-created constructions of African Americans. These and other points are driven home, I think, by having students read a portion of Moody and then a chunk of McLaurin, returning again to Moody, then back to McLaurin. Black and white together, though separate: the South before the Second Reconstruction.

By demonstrating just limited and ineffective white liberalism in the region was, Lee's *To Kill a Mockingbird* also offers painful lessons in how white southerners were imprisoned by jails of their own making. The question of whether Atticus Finch was a racial paternalist--well-meaning, perhaps, but hardly a friend of racial equality--sparks a lively (and unresolvable) class debate.[11] but what is clear is that for all his undoubted personal decency and devotion to law, Atticus could not save Tom Robinson. The very best the white South had to offer in the mid-1930s, then, was not good enough. Nor, frankly, was it ever good enough. Southern whites did not, en mass, "rescue" or "save" African Americans in the region. Blacks, of course, "saved" themselves through sustained, non-violent collective militancy a generation later. My students learn a good bit about the Civil Rights Movement from Woodward's *Strange Career*, from the documentary series "Eyes on the

---

[11] This is the argument of Joseph Crespino in is article "The Strange Career of Atticus Finch," Southern Cultures 6 (Summer, 2000): 9-29.

Prize," and from a number of essays analyzing the Movement in such communities as Nashville and Birmingham.[12] but they encounter it most directly and richly in Moody's *Coming of Age*. Much of Moody's autobiography describes her years as a dedicated activist in Mississippi. *Coming of Age* is especially good on the always tense, often harrowing, day-to-day experiences of African Americans immersed in the Movement and on what intransigent white resistance to freedom cost Moody personally. Students in the course thus learn that "southern heritage" is more complex, both for worse and for better, than they might have thought, including, as it does, both another, less honorable, "southern" tradition and its exact opposite, a marvelous emancipatory gift from the region to the world, the Civil Rights Movement.

Emancipatory collective action did end Jim Crow in the region--at least as a system of state-sanctioned, state-mandated segregation--but it only set the stage for, rather than guaranteed, real racial equality. After the Movement's initial legal successes in the mid-1960s, the South's meaning was even more contested, more uncertain, more in flux than ever, with black southerners continuing to struggle to make their voices heard and to secure in daily practice what was theirs in law. Ernest Gaines's absorbing novel, *A Gathering of Old Men*, about a 1970s killing on a Louisiana sugarcane plantation and its galvanizing effect on a group of elderly African American men, wonderfully captures this sense of new world hesitantly, painfully coming into existence with no template as to what it will become. Initially, the text is confusing, opaque, even-off-putting: readers must process page after page before they have a handle on what's going on, or who the characters are and how they are related, a narrative device I suspect Gaines deliberately employed to symbolize the very real confusion about identity and place and action in the immediate post-Civil Rights South. In important particulars, Candy, the paternalistic white plantation owner who ultimately loses her power to speak for "her" blacks in Gaines's novel, is strikingly similar to Atticus and Scout finch, both of whom were also in the habit of speaking and acting for African Americans.

---

[12] Linda Wynn, "The Dawning of a New Day: The Nashville Sit-Ins, February 13-May 10, 1960." Tennessee Historical Quarterly 50 (Spring, 1991): 42-54. Martin Luther King, Jr., "Letter from the Birmingham Jail." Aldon D. Morris, "Birmingham Confrontation Reconsidered: An Analysis of the Dynamics and Tactics of Mobilization." American Sociological Review 58 (October, 1993): 621-636.

By contrasting *A Gathering* with *To Kill a Mockingbird*, therefore, students learn important insights about authorial voice, representation, and perspective. More than mere technical conventions in the art of narrative, these story-telling devices also convey a moral sensibility about race and hence can be productively exploited to raise vexing questions about whether the region's whites could ever "speak" for, or even genuinely know, its African Americans. *A Gathering* also beautifully shows that only by speaking for themselves--by acting in concert and autonomously--did southern blacks achieve self-determination, a form of equality, to return to the overarching theme of the conversation between region and nation, not so commonly articulated in idealizations of "America."

My students learn, too, that race is inseparable from gender in the making of the region. Gaines's novel, for example, is very much about masculinity, really the gendered meanings of racial existence in the South: through their actions, the "old men" of the title become, fully and for the first time, "men," *black* men. Another assigned text is Melton McLaurin's *Celia: A Slave* (1991), an extraordinary history of an enslaved African American female who, in 1850, was purchased by her owner for reasons of sex and who later killed him for repeatedly raping her. Using the killing and Celia's subsequent trial as interpretive vehicles to explore the practice and contradictions of slavery, McLaurin concludes that the white jurors deciding Celia's fate could not have defined her action as "protecting her honor," and thereby absolve her for the killing, because to do so would have created an intolerable inversion in the region's racialized sexual hierarchy: it would have given enslaved African American women a right white males withheld from their own legally free wives, the right to rebuff, with violence if necessary, unwanted sexual advance from their "masters" (or husbands).

Gender also is central to the section of the course that I find the most emotionally exhausting to teach, that about lynching. This is a sorry story indeed, but one that must be told to convey just how discrepant the region was from the rest of America. If students do not squarely confront both the motivating/exculpatory (and hideously inaccurate) constructions of race and gender, they cannot understand why white southerners for fifty years or more after Reconstruction resorted so willing to lynching. The white justification for lynching rested on the self-serving mythology that white women were (or were to be) pure, asexual, and defenseless. As "southern ladies" of this sort, they were thus thought dependent on the protection of white men from African American males, who, in the sick collective psychology permeating much of the white South at the time, were thought to be continually lusting after white women.

Harper Lee very deliberately unmasks this pathology in *To Kill a Mockingbird*. During Mayella Ewell's testimony against Tom Robinson, she declares that she had been "violated" by Tom and then added that "if you fine fancy gentlemen don't wanna do nothin' about it then you're all yellow stinkin' cowards, the lot of you. Your fancy airs don't come to nothin'...." (p. 188). The allegation of black-on-white rape elicited such outrage from southern whites because the act did not simply "defile" what were thought to be defenseless white "ladies": it also contaminated the purity of the white blood line--the "white race" could be preserved only by white women--and hence was the ultimate taboo in the Jim Crow South. The only winners in all of this, of course, were white men, who, by manipulating the gender constructions underpinning racial lynching, were able to turn privilege into "necessity" and thereby perpetuate their dominance over African Americans of both sexes and white females.[13]

Most students are uncomfortable (as am I) with the lynching statistics and accounts they read or see (of the lynching of Emmett Till, for example) in the *Eyes on the Prize* documentary series. I sense also that some white men in the class have not agreed entirely with the inference about how the entire process worked to perpetuate the privilege of their racial and gender identities. I would not have done so either at their age; indeed, I did not even have the bald facts from which such inferences are drawn. This, too, is humbling and leaves me little room for self-righteousness or even excessive impatience.

Like gender and race, class is everywhere in the making of the modern South. My students see its racially decisive (and usually toxic) operation in Woodward's *Strange Career*, in Moody's *Coming of Age in Mississippi*, in Gaines's *A Gathering of Old Men*, and in Lee's *Mockingbird*, where Atticus Finch, surely a member of the white South's "better element," defends Tom Robinson against the depredations of Bob Ewell and other (typically) lower-strata "rednecks." Perhaps the single

---

[13] Some of the class readings on this and similar points include J. William Harris, "Etiquette, Lynching, and Racial Boundaries in Southern History: A Mississippi Example," American Historical Review 100 (April 1995): 387-410; Stephen Whitfield, A Death in the Delta: The Story of Emmett Till (Baltimore: Johns Hopkins University Press, 1988); and Sara Evans, "Myth Against History: The Case of Southern Womanhood," Pp. 149-154 in Patrick Gersten and Nicholas Cords (eds.), Myth and Southern History, vol. 2. 2nd ed. (Urbana, Ill. : University of Illinois Press, 1989).

most provocative reading in the entire course, in fact, is an unorthodox class analysis of the region's rednecks by Will Campbell, a native white Mississippian, civil rights activist, and Southern Baptist preacher. Campbell depicts southern rednecks as both victimizers and victims, scapegoated by a self-satisfied, "enlightened" America for the racial privileges accorded more advantaged, liberal, whites.[14] "What must be understood," Campbell says:

> "is that *all* whites...are racist because racism is the condition in and structure under which we live and move and have our being....[Racism] has nothing to do with how liberal or radical or enlightened or educated or good I am. Nor does it have to do with how reactionary, conservative, ignorant or bad I am. It just has to do with *being white within these structures*" (p. 93, emphasis in original).

Yes, "rednecks" have, Campbell readily admits, too often acted on their bigotry, suspicion, and frustration. They have done so though--at least in his analysis (one surely unusual for a man of the cloth)--because they too deeply drank the intoxicating brew known as evangelical Protestantism, a mind-numbing elixir the South's white elite used to entice those on the bottom rail from union with even more oppressed blacks and one therefore ultimately addicting poor whites to a self-defeating, burning religion of hate.

By depicting, often with first-hand accounts, gender, class, and racial differences in what Richard Wright once called "living Jim Crow," all of these texts help insure that students leave the course knowing that there is no totalizing "southern heritage," no essentializing "southern experience," no single "southern identity."[15] Students learn also that race has indelibly shaped the region's economy, polity, its cultural appetites in religion, food, music, and leisure, and even its religious beliefs and practices, and, finally, that "our" culture is not a white culture at all, but a *southern* culture, the syncretic accomplishment of two races, never really equal in principle, never fully separate in practice, each always looking to

---

[14] Campbell, "Used and Abused: The Redneck's Lot," pp. 90-104 in Dudley Clendinen (ed.), *The Prevailing South: Life and Politics in a Changing* Culture (Atlanta: Longstreet Press, 1988). Once the Chaplain at the University of Mississippi, Campbell migrated to Nashville in the mid-1950s. When I asked him why he left the state, he said, simply, "They would have killed me if I had stayed."

[15] Richard Wright, "The Ethics of Living Jim Crow." Pp. 9-22 in Wright, Uncle Tom's Children: Five Long Stories. (Cleveland: World Publishing, 1938).

the other for place and definition. Students now realize that to study the South is to study race.

Part Four

"Relative satisfaction" with the course is not to suggest that it be beyond improvement. Despite the addition of material on the Southern Appalachians in recent offerings· the reading list probably continues to concentrate too much on the "Deep South" and on black-white relations. Other geographic sub-regions and the ethno-racial complexity stamping the region today (e.g., in the late 1990s, there were an estimated 50,000 Hispanics in Nashville alone) get too little attention, as do the South's original inhabitants, Native Americans.[16] Issues of social class permeate the course, but most often when configured with race, making me unsure if my students, my *Vanderbilt* students, appreciate as fully as they should just how meaningful class is to the region's history and culture. Rick Bragg's *All Over But the Shoutin'* (1997), his memoir about growing up abjectly poor and white in the region, might work wonders here. Also too little represented in the course is the South's religious traditions and practices. The writer Flannery O'Connor once referred to the South as "Christ-haunted," a sentiment echoed in Will Campbell essay I assign. Nonetheless, there is need for more on the topic, perhaps Donald Matthews's *Religion in the Old South* (1977), with its incendiary final chapter on the awesomely redemptive power of what had once been the slavemaster's tool, now appropriated and transmuted by African Americans, evangelical Christianity. Gender, clearly, figures prominently in the very design of the course, but I occasionally think about using Lillian Smith's autobiography, *Killers of the Dream* (1949). Smith was a novelist (*Strange Fruit* is her most famous), an authentic white southern radical on matters of race and sex, and a feminist, lesbian and Christian, who beautifully metaphorized racial segregation to bodily "avoidance

---

[16] Included here is the stunning documentary, *Stranger With a Camera*, made by Kentuckian Elizabeth Barret. The film tells the story of the 1967 murder of a Canadian film-maker who, having gone to eastern Kentucky to portray the poverty of southern mountain whites, was killed by a native of the area apparently incensed by the barrage of unflattering (if sympathetic) images of hungry children, pinched faces, and squalid living conditions. It does not rationalize thekilling, but Stranger does provoke wide-ranging questions about how and why "the downtrodden" are represented by "outsiders" and about the ownership of these images.

rites." Speaking of autobiographies, one by an African American male with roots in the South, Richard Wright's *Black Boy*, say, or Henry Louis Gates's *Colored People: A Memoir*, would prove an insightful gender (and for Gates, who grew up in West Virginia, geographic) juxtaposition to Anne Moody's *Coming of Age in Mississippi*. Each of these works, and much more, deserve to be taught in the course. That I've no room for them–the syllabus is stuffed now (7 books, 25 essays)--does not mask the fact that I've a long way to go before the course is what it ought to be. Humbling.[17]

I will also confess that though I conclude with Peter Applebome's *Dixie Rising: How the South is Shaping American, Values, Politics, and Culture* (rev. ed., 1998)--an interpretation of the region's present-day tensions, identities, inequalities, and national import by an experienced *New York Times* reporter--there is no doubt that the discussion of the South of today is too hurried. Still, history is essential to any serious study of the region. The region's past is a tragically rich repository of social institutions and cultural practices of perennial moral urgency--arrangements voicing death and desire, exploitation and exclusion, class and courage, and fanaticism and freedom, to name a few—and that past persists in, haunts, the South's present, more so than is seen in any other region of the country. Even to pose the question of continuing southern distinctiveness, or of the region's "otherness," necessarily pushes the class (and its instructor) to chart the extraordinary changes in the region's laws, racial practices, migration patterns, economic and political institutions, and ethnic composition that have occurred in just one generation.

Despite all of these changes, the "South" continues to this day to function as a prism, filtering how Americans, northern and as well as southern, evaluate the moral grounding of our communal life and so refracting, always, our vision of such essential matters as freedom, equality, justice, and guilt.[18] To teach about life in the South, past or present, then, is to teach about human horror and pain, human yearning and possibility. To teach the South, finally, is necessarily to make moral commitments to oneself and to ask for moral reasoning from others. And

---

[17] The fine movie, "Mississippi Marsala," which I should show more frequently, makes the point about racial and ethnic complexity with a rare sensitivity.

[18] In "Southern Distinctiveness, Yet Again, or, Why America Needs the South," I explore several of these themes in greater detail, including the "pastness" in the South's present and what "the South" might mean today.

this, most assuredly, teaches the teacher--himself indelibly of the region--humility.

Article 2

Black and White Friendship

Sharon A. Lewis and Sara D. Jonsberg

Setting the Stage: Where They Teach

Montclair State University (MSU) occupies a 200-acre campus in Upper Montclair, New Jersey. Fourteen miles west of New York City, the Township of Montclair is unusual among New Jersey towns of metropolitan New York suburbs for its racial and socioeconomic diversity. Originally a farming village and then artists' colony, the town is today marked by extremes of wealth and poverty. Yet one high school, with a study body approximately 51% black, serves the entire population. Though MSU's teacher education program enjoys a productive relationship with the Montclair schools, and indeed a handful of MSU faculty live in the town, there is in fact little interaction between the university and the town.

MSU was established in 1908 as the New Jersey State Normal School, became Montclair State Teacher's College in 1927, Montclair State College in 1958, and Montclair State University in 1994. Today, MSU consists of three Colleges and two Schools, offers 44 undergraduate and 31 graduate majors, and has just launched a unique doctoral program in Pedagogy. Until the mid-1960s, all graduates were eligible for certification as public school teachers in the State.

The University is part of the second tier of New Jersey's higher education system, one of nine of state colleges and universities. Self-named a "teaching" university, to separate itself from the state's three public research institutions -- Rutgers, the State University of New Jersey; the New Jersey Institute of Technology; and the University of Medicine and Dentistry of New Jersey -- Montclair State offers faculty incentives that foreground teaching. "Scholarship of pedagogy" is considered as worthy as the traditional "scholarship of discovery." In addition, teacher education continues to be significant in the curriculum and in the allocation of resources. In a total student body of approximately 13,500, there are almost 700 students in early childhood and secondary education programs at any given time.

In 1997, students enrolled in New Jersey's colleges and universities were 69.2% white; 10.6% Black; 10.6 Latina/o; 4.3% Asian; and 0.4% American Indian. These figures more or less imitate national totals of 73.9% white students enrolled in higher education institutions and 26.1% minorities; or, more specifically, student enrollment at four-year public institutions in 1997 was: 70.1% white; 11.3 Black, 11.4% Latina/o, 5.9% Asian/Pacific Islander, and 1.2% American Indian/Alaskan. MSU's racial and ethnic distribution is similar to state and U.S figures: currently, 11% of the students identify themselves as African American, 5.6% Asian, 16.5% Hispanic, and 66.5% white. As of the Spring 1999 semester, of the 452 full-time English majors, about 8% are Black, 9% Hispanic, and 2% Asian. The Fall 1993 MSU Freshman Profile suggests socioeconomic diversity in the student body which has remained relatively the same in the ensuing seven years. Approximately 30% of MSU students came from families whose incomes ranged from $25,000 to $50,000; slightly more than a quarter came from families with incomes over $50,000; and, about 15% lived at or below the poverty level. Students reported that more than 50% of their mothers and more than 40% of their fathers had not attended college

Most of MSU's students are commuters; only about one-fifth of the student body lives on campus. Students frequently live on campus their freshman year, and then become commuters. The vast majority of MSU students are the first in their families to attend college. Most view higher education as primarily a means to upward mobility. Many work more than one job in order to help pay for their education (tuition, books, and transportation). Almost all MSU students are from New

Jersey towns, and because of New Jersey's de facto segregation, few students have had experience in multicultural environments before they arrive on campus.

Full-time MSU faculty, in 1998, were 80% White; 6% Black; 6% Latino/a; and 8% American Indian/Asian/Pacific Islander. In terms of faculty rank, as of Fall 1998, 42% of full professors are white and 21% "of color"; 27% of associate professors are white and 31% of color; 30% of the assistant professors are white; 44% of color; and, 1% of the instructors are white and 3% are of color. These figures echo state and national percentages, and it is clear that, despite its official affirmative action posture, Montclair State does no better than average in bringing faculty of color to its campus.

In 1993, when Sara and Sharon met as new members of the English Department, the University hired six Black Americans, or 11.9% of those hired that year, and thirteen women, or 48.1% of the new hires. Sara is white, Sharon is Black. Sara, at 54, had just completed an Ed.D. at the University of Massachusetts, Amherst. Before coming to MSU, she had been a school teacher and worked in college administration. She was hired originally on a one-year temporary line and had to reapply for her assistant professorship in the fall of 1994. Her position continues to be half teaching, half administering the teacher education program in English.

Sharon was hired to a full-time, tenure-track position at the rank of assistant professor. When she joined the faculty, Sharon was 38 years old and ABD in the Ph.D. program in English at Rutgers University. Two years later she successfully defended her dissertation and took on an administrative role in the department as Associate Coordinator of the Freshman Composition Program. Whereas Sharon considered herself a fledgling in the profession; Sara viewed this position as her last (and best!) job before retirement. It should be noted as well that Sharon's Ph.D. commands higher status in academic circles than Sara's Ed.D.

Besides differences in age and job perspective, Sara and Sharon are, more importantly, divided by race. Upon her arrival to the position, Sharon saw herself as something of a trailblazer in the English Department. Before 1993, two Black American men and one Black woman had occupied full-time positions in the English Department, but Sharon would be the first African American to teach Black writers.

Presently, of the 33 full-time Department faculty, seventeen are men and sixteen are women. The faculty includes one Asian woman, one Black American woman, and one Latino male. Committed to teaching film, writing, and literature from a diverse range of theoretical and critical approaches, the English Department demonstrates an array of progressive and traditional scholarship and teaching practices. The University claims approximately 650 undergraduate English majors. Of that number, about 20% are enrolled in the Teacher Education Program.

Who We Are: Speaking for Ourselves

We were drawn together initially just because we were new at MSU and in the English department at the same time. Also, despite a tradition of distrust between the races, a distrust that would seek to resist instinctive friendship, a mutual respect and a will to trust sprang up between us immediately. We share a philosophy of teaching that decentered "the teacher" and suggested the classroom as a site for students to construct their own knowledge by means of reading and writing. In any course, we both intend to persuade students to generate and pursue their own questions and to experience the amazing "high" that comes of making discoveries as one writes. We hope by our teaching to send students out as confident and inquiring life-long learners, willing and able to see their college education as something other than merely a vehicle for climbing the socioeconomic ladder.

What's more, we are both invested in helping students who have grown up in the segregated New Jersey world figure out how to live in a diverse society. We insist that our students speak to each other with respectful curiosity, and we try to guide them in learning about each other so that they will be able to live together harmoniously and generously. Over time, this covenant, coming at it as we do from quite different angles, has become the center of our collaborative scholarship and teaching. It is not all that we share, but it is the core of what we share.

Getting Here from Where I Began: Sara

Born in 1939, I was raised in a tradition of what I would call passive Southern racism. I don't recall anyone in my family or community ever uttering an overtly racist remark; certainly no one engaged in cruel or rude behavior. I never questioned, or even noticed, the level of my "white privilege" (McIntosh); indeed I was encouraged to accept as given (if not divinely ordained!) the hierarchical arrangement of black and white in our culture. How things are is the way they are supposed to be.

Yet somewhere along between one and twenty-one, I began to understand that what I had been taught, by my Virginia-born father as well as by the segregated and inherently racist culture in which I lived, was dead wrong -- not only wrong in the sense of incorrect but wrong in the sense of evil.

Years of reading and listening and struggling to unlearn had brought me, by my mid-50's when Sharon and I met, to a reasonably advanced level of sensitivity and active anti-racist behavior. I had come far, but I still had much to learn. Indeed, it is my sad conviction that white people in western culture may never be able to fully unlearn; trying to do so is at the least a lifelong project and process.

I am increasingly certain-and Sharon has been my primary teacher in this -- that the hardest part of unlearning racism is facing and coming to understand the enormous rightful anger of Black people in this country. It is, as bell hooks has said, a "killing rage." James Baldwin reiterates: to be Black in America is to be angry all the time. For white people, no easy disclaimer is allowed: "but I didn't do it, so don't be mad at me." Just walking around white is participation.

This is the hardest thing of all for our white students. They want it to be enough to say they are "color blind." They do not want to hear me say to them that to be "color blind" in a racist culture is to participate in racism. Coming to the kind of boldness that lets me say these words to students is in very large measure the result of my friendship with Sharon. She has helped me to that kind of courage, I think most of all by insisting that I see and swallow all that anger.

Because my particular scholarly interest focuses on how schools (and the myth of educational opportunity) have functioned in American culture, I am confronted continually with the realities of systemic racism. Our American educational system promises but withholds hope. By its foundation as a middle class institution, it is grounded in European traditions which privilege certain kinds of discourse and language styles; it is inherently discriminatory, favoring certain kinds of "cultural capital" (backgrounds and previous experiences) over others. Inequitable distribution of resources, both material and human, uneven expectations for academic success, and the liberal conviction that access is enough --these are a few of the factors which perpetuate educational abuse. I try to help future teachers become aware of these issues without inviting a sense of despair at the impossibility of genuine reform.

Getting Here from Where I Began: Sharon

Born in 1955, I grew up in a predominantly white seaside resort community off the southern-most coast of New Jersey and came to racial consciousness relatively late in life. Even as an undergraduate, I had not awakened to the United States' social order. I was oblivious to the way in which power is unevenly and unjustly disseminated in this country, to the country's history of imperialism, colonialism, and slavery, and to the entrenched and pervasive ramifications of that history. The doctoral program afforded me the first opportunity to read Black feminist and Black Marxist literature and theory. Through these bodies of imaginative and intellectual works, I realized the degree to which I had internalized white, patriarchal, Judeo-Christian, Anglo-European, heterosexist, and bourgeois ways of seeing, knowing, and being. My "textbook" learning occasioned my examination and exploration of my past, helped me to re-see and rethink my experiences and identity in a wholly different context.

By the time I met Sara, I was well aware, through study and experience, of the degree to which race matters, even determines life and life chances in America. I did not come to trust in our relationship quite so easily as Sara might imagine. I saw our connection as fragile and complicated. First, there was the matter of trust. Black women claim a collective memory - and subsequent fear - of betrayal by white women during the 19th century abolition/suffragist movements, during the Civil Rights Revolution, and during the resurgence of mainstream feminist activism in the 1960s and 70s. Given Black women's empirical and entrenched distrust of white women, I had been on guard, maybe, as popularly charged, paranoid, of establishing a friendship with Sara.

Second, much to what I perceived as Sara's initial dissatisfaction, I deemed it crucial to foreground our racial differences. I remembered the idea of Patricia J. Williams, legal and critical race theorist, that "...for Black people, the systemic, often nonsensical denial of racial experience engenders a sense of split identity attending that which is obvious but inexpressible; an assimilative tyranny of neutrality as self-erasure" (27). While Sara acknowledged, on a philosophical level, the differences attributed to race, I struggled to make known to Sara that the repudiation, misnaming, or appropriation of my Black experience was a categorical denial, annihilation of mySELF.

So much of what we had in common as scholars and teachers, was ever so slightly shaded by the difference of race. Audre Lorde had demonstrated for Sharon how "the entrapments used to neutralize [her] and [Sara] [were] not the same" (63). For example, although I was hired on a tenure-track line and Sara on a one-year line, and although, theoretically, my degree carried more status than hers, I knew that Sara's whiteness was ready currency anywhere she went in the United States and certainly within the borders of a predominantly white -- staffed and administered -- university.

Finally, Sara acknowledges that I have "aided" her self-examination on matters of race. She sees me as her facilitator, as an ally who helped her see how to speak in what she perceives as anti-racist and activist tones. All the while, however, I was heedful of Lorde's admonition to Black women not to be consumed, distracted, and depleted by white women's working to un-learn racism. It is one thing to commend and encourage, to fuel the endeavor. It is quite another to find oneself not only diverted from one's own personal and intellectual pursuits but debilitated by the effort of edifying white people about white supremacy.

So, when, as we confronted differences of perception in an early conversation, I asserted myself, a dissonance was sounded. On the one hand, Sara is hardly representative of a white America seeking to eradicate racism. There is no national campaign against racism. Sometimes, it feels as if Sara is on a solo mission, claiming few white American compatriots in her conscientious struggle to cure herself of white supremacy. On the other hand, gaps of unknowing, coupled with Sara's confession of "unlearning racism," became for me a verifiable, unequivocal reason to withhold trust. Though weary, unnerved, and vigilant, I somehow perceived that I could trust Sara to HEAR and believe my scholarly and experiential relationship to race and racism.

One summer, upon returning home from an extraordinary trip to Bali, Indonesia - a graduation gift from a generous, wealthy friend -- I called Sara to ask for her feedback and assistance on a course I was framing around questions of money. Quite by accident, Sara had been reading Michelle Cliff's novel, *Free Enterprise*, and she recommended that I include the novel on my course reading list. Through its characters and multiple story lines, the book interrogates the sources and uses of wealth in 19th Century slaveholding America. I had read the novel and discussed it briefly in my doctoral dissertation, a text that examined the ways in which Black women novelists fictionalized "the paradox of money" in capitalist America.

What Happened Next With Us

Rereading *Free Enterprise* together launched us into the project that continues to drive our collaboration: can Black and white women in our culture truly be friends? Doubts already present about the trustworthiness of our connection to each other prepared us for the question that caught us in this text, raised in an exchange between the white character Alice Hooper and the Black woman, Mary Ellen Pleasant. Hooper has included Pleasant among those who will, after an elegant dinner at Hooper's Boston home, be treated to an unveiling of J.M.W. Turner's painting, *Slave Ship, Throwing Overboard the Dead and Dying, Typhon Coming On*. Hooper's advisors have purchased the work partly for its value as investment, but also because it appears to support her abolitionist opinions. Pleasant not only finds the painting almost too painful to observe, but is offended by Hooper's gaffe in asking her to explain its history. Aware of her error, Hooper sends a lengthy and effusive note to Pleasant at the Parker House Hotel apologizing for misunderstandings of the evening before. Pleasant replies in a cool tone:

August 6, 1874, 9 A.M.

Dear Miss Hooper,

I hold nothing against you. I wish for you all the best. I think the difference between us may be reduced to the fact that while you focus on the background of the Turner painting, I cannot tear my eyes from the foreground. It is who we are.

Yours sincerely,
Mary Ellen Pleasant (80)

For us, this particular epistolary moment is the novel's most chilling. Pleasant strikes us as unyielding in her conviction that Black and white women -- because of their radically different collective and individual, present and historical experiences, as well as the power differential marking them, can never hope to cross the border of race - for friendship, unity, alliance. Pleasant is not doubtful; she's convinced, her position final: the difference of race determines difference in SEEING. According to Pleasant, the commonalities ascribed to gender-and indeed to class, for both women are wealthy--are undermined by differences attributed to race.

Wondering if Pleasant speaks for Cliff, wondering if Cliff is avowing a hopelessness of disconnection as thematic message, we decided to go SEE the novel's storied painting for ourselves. On a small research grant from MSU, we traveled to New England and the Boston Museum of Fine Arts. Seeing the painting, we were dumbstruck. It is large, and something about it, some force, pulls the viewer right up to the scene and inside. Much of the painting's field is a dark, raging ocean, and in contrast a glaring white storm, is centered. For Sharon, the painting spoke violence and destruction, but what's most visible is the natural or environmental destruction -- one can hardly see the endangered slave ship. Sara was struck by the glaring white typhoon at the center of the picture. She read the painting as Turner's notion of what Conrad calls "the benign indifference of the universe."

At first, Sharon sat down and gazed at the piece from a distance. She remembers watching, hearing Sara, gazing at and exclaiming the glaring white at the picture's center. Remembering how Hooper and Pleasant are described as focusing on different components of the painting, Sharon got up from the bench and walked up to the painting. She wanted to see details that, from a distance, are scarcely visible. She wanted to see what Pleasant had focused on, the foreground, the limbs and torsos thrown overboard. She remembers seeing the iron chains around amputated limbs, bodies half submerged in the tossing sea which was surely about to claim them. No faces, she recalls thinking -- no faces. Then, Sharon began to speak an interpretation. For Turner, she thought, nature is far more destructive than self-interested, profit-fueled mankind. The brutality of the slave trade, for Turner, I read, is far less significant, less consequential, than nature.

How nearly the same but how different our four eyes saw. Sara saw Turner saying that nature ignores in the end all human effort, all human pain. He is not denying the horror of slavery. Indeed, he focuses eyes upon it, calling attention to its worst abuse, but he seems to be saying that in the end all will be wiped away, kind and cruel, evil and blessed alike. Sharon read Turner as attempting to convey the notion that nature and the artist's act of depicting nature are more significant than human cruelty; that humans and their "foibles" (such as greed and enslavement of one another) are trivial in light of the power of nature; and that nature matters more as a subject than any vision of human behavior. The storm dominates, erases the bodies, erases the human atrocity, erases responsibility as well as torments.

Our differences in seeing extend into the novel, echoing perhaps the differences between Hooper and Pleasant. Though Sharon continues to be most engaged by recurring questions on the entanglements of race and money, Sara puzzles over what Cliff may be saying about gender. Clearly, Cliff's novel wonders where money comes from, where it goes, whether it can ever be "clean" considering its generation always, it seems, at the expense of human life. In particular, Sharon thinks, *Free Enterprise* seems to point to American chattel slavery as the origin of capitalist wealth, and over generations, to the current power differential between races in America.

Though Sara does not disagree with this analysis, she also sees Cliff raising questions, through mystery about Pleasant's source of funds, about women and heterosexism as exploitable sources of wealth. Ever the optimist, Sara continues to believe the Cliff may also be saying something about the ways in which women may be able to connect in order to resist exploitation in all its forms. Sharon reminds Sara that the novel "ends" with a powerful re-connection between Pleasant and Annie Christmas - a bi-racial Jamaican who identities Black - and an empathetic dialogue between Annie and Rachel, a Jew.

Our Working Friendship

In the aggregate, women's cross-race friendships are quite uncommon on our campus. Sheer numbers. Because of the white/Black disparity of faculty, Black faculty are forced into work and social interactions with white faculty - a condition unfamiliar to white faculty. In other words, white faculty can choose not to involve themselves with Black faculty. On a daily basis, Black women at our University associate with more white women than white with Black, and white women have a smaller pool of Black women with whom to form coalitions. What white women frequently take for granted is their ability to pick and choose and craft friendships and alliances from among a variety of white female colleagues.

Consequently, Sharon's and Sara's "friendship" is not singular for Sharon. Like Black professionals all over America, Sharon's occupational realm (with the exception of her literary research and scholarship) - her classrooms, workshops, committee work, outside consultations, board memberships -- which occupy a good portion of her livelihood - is white.

What others refuse to see as "cloning," and what Sharon calls "racial nepotism," functions as well. If the vast majority of empowered white people hail from and run in social, occupational, and educational spheres predominantly white, most (not all) licenses, favors, decisions wielded are likely to benefit other whites. Such is a reality that Black people never forget, but which white people ignore.

One of the political ramifications of their friendship, of course, is what Sara has been calling "the power differential." If we agree that we live in a racist society, and if we agree that MSU is a microcosmic mirror reflection of the society in which it exits, then it is safe to say that racism prevails at MSU. In the most subtle and unseen -- to white people - registers, racism affords Sara manifold evidence of her professorial legitimacy, access to knowledge, and a trust to which Sharon would not be privy. What's more, at MSU, from faculty positions up the institution's chain of command, power is shared equally between white women and white men.

Nevertheless, we hope that, on campus, we -- Sara and Sharon -- are perceived as "a united front." Over the years, over the course of our friendship as faculty on a college campus, we have, with foresight and deliberation, teamed up to achieve several common goals. For one, together, we join Department Personnel Committees to ensure tenure applicants a fair hearing. We join Search Committees to insist on the hiring of faculty from traditionally overlooked cultures and language communities. Recently, our University's President conceived -- and is in the process of instituting -- innovative and provocative tactics for overcoming past-wrongs in hiring and, therefore, promotions, throughout the University. In layperson's terms, she offers faculty-hiring committees a two-for-one model that, fundamentally, guarantees two new openings if one of the hires represents a group not represented in the staffing department. While Sara feels some discomfort in utilizing perhaps reproachful employment tactics, Sharon applauds the President's resourcefulness, her clever use of power to correct past mistakes.

We are busy. We have conceived and orchestrated workshops for high school teachers -- collaborative writing and brainstorming workshops that seek to get Black and white teachers in meaningful dialogue about and across the barrier of race. We participate in any campus initiatives which center discussions of race and racism and which offer new pedagogical and methodological strategies for including race, in knowing and sensitive ways, in course offerings. Together we attend "industry" conferences where we present workshops which insist on teaching the "truth" of America's history of white supremacy and, consequently, on conceptualizing more effective ways of annihilating racism throughout the institution of education and higher education.

We are learning to swiftly identify those moments and occasions when it is more effective for Sharon to remain silent and for Sara to speak. After a few harrowing collisions and resulting awkward silences, squabbles and battles of mishearing and misunderstanding, Sharon is learning to ask -- rather than to kneejerk into assumptions - to ask Sara for her so-called "insider's insight" into certain behaviors and procedures taking place in their workworld.

Our Intensive-Writing Literature Course

We offered our co-taught special topics literature course, "Black & White Women Writers," during the Spring 1999 semester. The majority of the 44 students enrolled in the course were English majors, most women and most white. The class met twice a week, three hours per week, for fifteen weeks.

In written narratives accompanying the syllabus, we told the students about the origin and foundations of the course. We invited the students to join us in reading selected fictional and non-fictional works by Black and white women writers. Together we would examine the texts to determine what these women writers have to tell us about the nature, history, and future of the relationship between white and Black American women. We sketched what we deemed the course's central questions:

How are the writers defining "friend"? What are the markers or characteristics of "friendship?" What does "friendship" entail, require? Why is it that so much of the imaginative and theoretical writing by both Black and white women cast doubt on the possibility of women's friendships across race? What is it about race or racial identity that thwarts or renders impossible meaningful relationships between White and Black women? How are these writers defining "race"? According to the writers, in what ways, if any, does "race" relate to friendship? What is it about American history and/or culture that worries or forestalls women's cross-race relationships?

We wanted students to share not only their personal experiences but also their impressions, questions, uncertainties, and analyses of the course reading material. We told students that we expected them to advance the critical and interpretive skills of all class members. They were charged with pointing us in the direction of congruent and fresh avenues and angles of pursuit.

Preparing and entering the course, we claimed two objectives: 1) to ensure that students' questions would underpin and inform the course in its entirety; and 2) to help students develop their skills as critical interpreters of complex texts. In terms of authorship, it was important to us that the reading list consist of an equal number of Black and white women writers, of lesbians and heterosexuals, across history, and across form - novel, poetry, film, biography, essay, personal narrative, short fiction.

Most of all, we insisted that student writing determine the course. In addition to peer critiques, reflective writing, and the journal-exchange exercise, coursework included class discussions, group work, a guest lecturer, and a trip to the Newark Museum to see the Jacob Lawrence exhibit.

We tried to structure the course in order to reflect the way in which our thinking about cross-race friendships had been developing. Thus, we began the course with the novel *Free Enterprise*. We would go on to read Nell Painter's biography, *Sojourner Truth: A Life, A Symbol*; selections from Adrienne Rich's poetry collection *A Wild Patience Has Taken Me This Far*; short fiction from *Skin Deep*, an anthology; Shirley Anne Williams's novel, *Dessa Rose*; a film, *The Long Walk Home*, which is based on the Montgomery bus boycotts; Lillian Smith's *Killers of the Dream*, a powerful self-exploration of whiteness; and a selection of personal narratives and critical essays by Audre Lorde, bell hooks, Peggy McIntosh and others.

It is impossible to recreate, in writing, the course we experienced. Writing is not a videotape. The best we can manage are some highlights preceded by a truth: triumph! Our "Black and White Women Writers" was a huge success by any constructivist teacher's standards. Every night, we left class dizzy with ideas -- challenged, stimulated, and surrounded by students who were breathlessly hungry for more. Class never ended on time - we always ran over without complaint. Frequently, students begged to open class with a story, specifically, telling us how what they were reading, wrestling with, learning was being received by their circles outside our classroom, usually beyond the boundaries of the campus - at home and at work.

Rarely, if ever, did either of us lecture. Sometimes, as within the hour conditions permitted or encouraged, one or both of us told stories: stories about our travels, about the development of our own friendship, about our fears, anxieties, crash-ups, about our surprises, victories, discoveries, rapture -- for instance, of riding our bikes together beside the sea on Martha's Vineyard-- anecdotes and incidents, individual, duet, occupational. Indeed, we demonstrated some of the very issues and problems under interpretive and critical scrutiny. Students witnessed critical dialogue, disputes, debates, disagreements, diverging perceptions, love, compassion, trust, and improving listening skills. There was provocation and confrontation as well as moments of overwhelming joy and laughter.

All members of the community, we're convinced, underwent personal and intellectual growth. The course enrollment diversity figures omit so much. The class consisted of returning students, students who boldly and shamelessly proclaimed colorblindness, of students who had never traveled across State borders. Sara remembers most vividly Carrie, the Black woman about her own age who told stories of driving through the South in the bad old days of segregation. Most of the white students entered the class with feel-good, romanticized, uninformed, and misinformed opinions about the history of race relations in America. Finding their experiences of racism confirmed by the texts, many of the Black students were astonished, incredulous upon perceiving white women writers and classmates who named themselves racist and who were actively and self-reflexively seeking to unlearn, to purge themselves of racism. We watched friendships develop across sexuality, gender, race, religion, ethnicity, and geographic region. From the very beginning of the semester, we insisted that students learn to work collaboratively, in respectful, fair-minded, and democratic ways. Consequently, we observed groups of students leaving the course determined to find sites where they could take resistant action.

Upon reflection, Sara and Sharon recognize that they modeled critical inquiry for the students. They believe that what was electrifying and meaningful for the students was the tension manifest in cross-race friends interrogating and investigating the feasibility of a cross-race friendship. The visibility sensitized students to inter-racial relations that, prior to the course, were not always explicit for them.

Students were exposed to new language, to a more precise, concise, thoughtful language in which to speak across boundaries, to speak their questions and concerns about race and oppression in America. We performed the permission to speak about race in mixed company with sensitivity and grace. We are sure students would say that we demystified so many of the misconceptions about race/gender they toted with them into the university. We are sure we gave students the gift of inquiry -- a language and position of wonder, curiosity.

We left the course with our own new questions, our own new agendas for action. We have worked diligently, with steadfast commitment-- Sara to accept that differences of race exist, prevail, and signify and may never be erased; Sharon to accept that racial difference does not necessarily impede meaningful, gratifying friendship. Both of us have had to undergo difficult, agonizing awakenings in order to step over the racial divide. Our friendship means doing for and learning from each other. As teachers, our friendship means that our teaching is richer and therefore, our students are enriched. As our friendship matures, we are learning something about license and abandon, informality in friendship.

References

Baldwin, J. "The Language of the Streets." *Literature and the Urban Experience: Essays on the City and Literature.* Michael C. Jane and Anne Chalmers Watts, eds. New Brunswick, NJ: Rutgers University Press, 1981, 133.

Cliff, M. *Free Enterprise.* New York: Penguin/Plume, 1993.

Conrad, J. *Heart of Darkness*: *Complete, Authoritative Text With Biographical and Historical Contexts, Critical History and Essays from Five Contemporary Critical Perspectives.* Ed. Ross Murtin. New York: Bedford St. Martin's Press, 1996.

Golden, M. and S. R. Shreve. *Skin Deep: Black Women and White Women Write About Race.* New York: Anchor Books, 1995.

hooks, bell. [sic] "'Where Is the Love?': Political Bonding Between Black and White Women." *Killing Rage, Ending Racism.* New York: Holt, 1995.

Jonsberg, S. "Grounds of Seeing." Unpublished paper. *Long Walk Home (The).* Dir. Richard Pearce. Miramax Films, 1991.

Lorde, A. "Age, Race, Class, and Sex: Women Redefining Difference." *Sister Outsider: Poems and Speeches*. Freedom, California: The Crossing Press Feminist Series, 1984.

_____ "The Uses of Anger: Women Responding to Racism." *Sister Outsider: Poems and Speeches*.

McIntosh, P. "White Privilege and Male Privilege: A Personal Account of Coming To See Correspondences Through Work in Women's Studies." *Working Paper 189*, Wellesley College Center for Research on Women, 1988.

Montclair State University. Fall 1999 Semester Enrollment Report, Office of Institutional Research.

Painter, N. I. *Sojourner Truth: A Life, A Symbol*. New York, W. W. Norton, 1996.

Rich, A. *A Wild Patience Has Taken Me This Far: Poems 1978-1981*. New York: W.W. Norton, 1981.

Silvera, M. "Her Head A Village." *Her Head A Village & Other Stories*. Vancouver: Press Gang Publishers, 1994, 11.

Smith, L. *Killers of the Dream*. New York: W. W. Norton, 1949.

Turner, J. M. W. *Slavers Throwing Overboard the Dead and Dying: Typhon Coming On*. 1840. Boston Museum of Fine Arts, Boston, Massachusetts.

Walker, A. "Advancing Luna and Ida B. Wells." *Black-Eyed Susans, Midnight Birds: Stories by and about Black Women*. Ed. Mary Helen Washington. New York: Anchor, 1989.

Washington, M. *Narrative of Sojourner Truth*, (ed). New York: Vintage Books, 1993.

Williams, P. J. *Seeing A Color-Blind Future: The Paradox of Race*. New York: Noonday Press, 1998, 27.

Williams, S. A.. *Dessa Rose*. New York: Berkley Books, 1986.

Article 3

Balancing Academic and Athletic Success: A Chronicle of African American Male Student Athletes' Involvement in Higher Education

Eddie Comeaux and C. Keith Harrison

> "From Willis Ward (early African American male on athletic scholarship at the University of Michigan) to James Hall (contemporary African American male professional athlete and University of Michigan 1999 graduate) black athletes at the University of Michigan have gone through many individual battles on and off the field. The more things change the more they stay the same. Over time things have changed from generation to generation but the game remains the same. Universities, for financial gain and athletic status in the media, continue to use black athletes, but it is up to *us* to use our opportunities to the fullest and not take them for granted."—James Hall, 1999

In recent years, the relationship between higher education and African American male involvement in college athletics has been a highly debated topic. While African Americans constitute 13% of the United

States population and approximately 9% of the student population at the National Collegiate Athletic Association (NCAA) Division 1 institutions, they constitute about 25% of the student-athletes who are on scholarship at these institutions (NCAA, 1995a). Approximately 1 of every 9 African American males on campuses of the 302 Division 1 universities are scholarship athletes as opposed to only 1 of every 50 white male college students that are scholarship athletes (NCAA, 1995a). Intercollegiate athletics, clearly, has become an important vehicle toward upward mobility for some African American males.

Many African Americans are recruited to play football and basketball in big-time university athletic programs, which are increasingly business-like operations that make the term "student-athlete" more approximate to a paradox (Eitzen, 1999). According to Eitzen (1993), the average budget for an athletic program in the 106 football schools (presently 117) in Division 1A is $12.5 million; the NCAA's 1990-1991 budget was $106.6 million; CBS agreed to pay the NCAA $1 billion over seven years for the television rights to the men's basketball tournament; the University of Florida rents sky boxes at its football games for $30,000 a year, with a minimum five-year lease, and each year supporters of university athletic programs donate about $400 million. This is to suggest that the system creates economic imperatives that lead colleges to make business decisions that supersede educational considerations. Nevertheless, student-athletes are required to maintain a high-level of productivity in the classroom, balance the incredible amounts of time demanded from coaches (for practices, meetings, travel, videotape and playbooks), and cope with the physical exhaustion and mental fatigue that comes with being a student and an athlete. (Eitzen, 1999). Thus these patterns show that a large-scale entertainment enterprise is embedded into higher education, which is antithetical to their goals.

In an effort to reinforce the relevance of academics in higher education to more African Americans, increased initial eligibility requirements and programs geared to develop student athletes academic talents have been implemented. This venture has heightened the trajectory of those willing to use sport as a tool to enhance their academic prowess. The five-year graduation rate for all student-athletes has grown from 45.7% in 1990 to 58% in 1995. African American male student-athletes also have exhibited an improvement in their graduation rates. In 1991, the NCAA reported that only 24.8% of the African American male student-athletes who entered school in the fall of 1984 had graduated five years later (Liederman, 1991). Four years later, the five-year graduation rate for African American male student-athletes had climbed to 42% (NCAA, 1995b). Interestingly, African American male student-athletes actually graduate at a significantly higher rate than African American non-athletes, who graduate at a rate of 34%(due to better support services for student-athletes).

In several ways the patterns and trends of today's students-athletes are similar to previous generations in terms of their efforts and commitment to balance their academic and athletic success. The structure of this analysis is to identify distinct time periods that highlight African American males' participating in higher education and college athletics from the latter part of the nineteenth century onward. Based on this framework, we will examine societal changes within the context of time, shifts in higher education accessibility to African Americans, and also how African American male student-athletes have benefited from opportunities to higher learning despite environmental factors that have worked to disengage many African American student-athletes from their academic pursuits.

Early African American Scholar-Athletes

African Americans first appeared on predominantly white universities during the latter part of the nineteenth century when intercollegiate sport was evolving from an unorganized to a highly structured activity (Wiggins, 1991). For most African Americans, admission into predominately white institutions meant being from the upper-middle class echelon, of superior athletic ability, and with high regards for education at that time (Harrison, working manuscript). These individuals usually prepared for various careers in law, medicine, and other professions by first attending a private academy in New England, a known public school, or a black college in the south. After completing this stage of their education at one of the aforementioned institutions, they would move to a more racially liberal college in the north to participate in intercollegiate sport while obtaining a quality education. Several were competing in athletics at prestigious universities such as Nebraska, Williams College, Oberlin, Amherst, and Harvard. Others took advantage of the Second Morill Act of 1890, which provided public supported colleges for African Americans. States would have to set up separate but equal facilities if they were to deny admissions to colleges on the basis of race (Cohen, 1998). Also, the Freedman Bureau, according to Lucas (1994), was another agent on behalf of the War Department that was instrumental in founding black schools; civic and religious groups along with the Bureau took part in developing ventures for African Americans.

Many African American scholar athletes took this path to gain access to higher education because of their interest to participate in either baseball or football in the latter part of the nineteenth century. For example, Moses Fleetwood Walker was one of many African Americans at a predominantly white institution. Playing catcher for Oberlin College in 1878, he later attended the University of Michigan Law School. Probably the most gifted individual during this period was William Clarence Matthews. Matthews was born in Selma, Alabama in 1877. Early on Matthews was educated at the Tuskegee Institute under the direction of Booker T. Washington. Matthews showed promise and Washington arranged for him to go to Phillips Andover Academy. At Andover, Matthews played three sports- baseball, football, and track. Academically, Matthews was the Class Historian, and was the only African American to graduate in the class of 1887. After graduating, Matthews entered Harvard in 1901. There he played both football and baseball. Matthews preferred baseball and spent four years with the team as a shortstop. While participating in baseball, Matthews was the best player on the best collegiate team of that time. Despite a racially charged atmosphere, which often led to Matthews being held out of games, Harvard surmounted a record of 75-18 during his four years. By 1905, Matthews entered Boston University Law school. To continue with his career pursuit, he supported himself through law school as an athletic instructor. Graduating in 1907, Matthews became an Assistant U.S District Attorney, appointed by President Taft. He went on to be special counsel for New York, New Haven and Hartford Railroad from 1915 through 1919. In 1924, Matthews was chosen by William M. Butler as the chief organizer among African American voters of the country in the Republican Campaign for Calvin Coolidge which subsequently led Coolidge to receive a few million votes by African American to win the election. Indeed, he was an extraordinary man who took advantage of his opportunities in both academics and athletics.

William Henry Lewis was another student-athlete who benefited from his time on university campuses. As a participant, football was a game of intellect to him. Lewis felt that this sport was the best game for developing the mind. According to Lewis, "Men could gain quick conception, cool judgement, and are of rapid and accurate judgment" (Harrison, working manuscript).

Born to a Baptist minister and former slave in Berkeley, Virginia in 1868, Lewis left home for Boston after graduating from high school. In order to get to Boston, he worked as a Congress errand boy to earn money, and worked in restaurants and hotels to earn college funds. Later, Lewis enrolled At Amherst College in 1888 where he distinguished himself as a star football player, class orator, for which he won several debate prizes, by his sophomore year. As a result, Harvard and Yale pursued him intensely. He, eventually, decided on Harvard where he continued his football career while a student in the Harvard Law School. There, Lewis was selected as an All-American center in 1892 and 1893, and in 1895, he graduated from Harvard Law School. Lewis eventually went on to practice law and an active figure in politics.

The experiences of Mathews and Lewis are remarkable. Using their physical gifts to obtain freedom through intellect, these scholar athletes were visible role models of their time. They were able to withstand the "separate, but equal " treatment on campus in order to enhance their individual, upwardly mobile in society.

While African American athletes were being excluded from various levels of white organized sport during the racially oppressive years of the early twentieth century in the Jim Crow America, African Americans would continue to find their way on to campuses of large northern universities. However, to attend a black college before attending a white institution was not unusual for African American athletes. Black college competition grew as the decade came to an end in spite of poor facilities, few coaches, underdeveloped leagues and conferences, and the lack of funding from colleges. In fact, black colleges preferred spending funds on educational books, hiring teachers, and improving facilities. Despite these setbacks, the trend toward increased participation of African Americans in black colleges grew along with predominately white institutions.

Robeson and the Fight for Legitimacy

The rivalry between the north and south was the most immediate event during the early years of the twentieth century. Although a large number of African Americans migrated to the north during the First World War, the majority of them still lived in the South at the end of the 1920s. A young African American would be lucky to finish the seventh grade before being forced by economic necessity to work. The migration northward, however, allowed many African Americans an opportunity to pursue various sports because of access to public school buildings and resources that assisted new arrivals. But, with these accommodations, life for African Americans was not recognizably better.

Two events during the 1920s occurred that heavily affected sports for African Americans. One was the stock market crash that pushed America into the Great Depression. The other was the Carnegie Report that highlighted widespread abuse of rules in college sports programs. The report, according to Ashe (1983), recommended a deemphasis of sports on campuses which meant that for the already underfunded black land grant colleges, decision-making was extremely difficult.

While African Americans were greatly impacted by intense circumstances, this decade was remarkable for its productivity. There was a growing trend in higher education occurring in the 1920s. According to Aptheker (1968), enrollment in colleges and normal schools totaled 355,215 in 1910, 597,682 in 1920, and 1,188,532 in 1930. Also, in 1920, a total of 396 black youths received bachelor's degrees (118 in northern colleges), in 1925 the total number had reached 832, and by the end of 1929 the figures were at 1,903. Perhaps more interestingly, graduates from black colleges had increased six times in ten years, and graduates from northern colleges had increased three times.

Among the African American student-athletes during the early twentieth century were Frederick Douglass "Fritz" Pollard, the first black All-American running back, from Brown University in 1916 and Paul Robeson from Rutgers University. Robeson was only the third African American to attend Rutgers University since its founding in 1766, and the only black at the school in 1915(Harrison, working manuscript).

Born the youngest child of an escaped slave later turned minister, Paul Robeson grew up in Somerville, New Jersey, where he was a distinguished student who participated in several sports receiving accolades for various achievements in both academics and sports. At Rutgers, he was one of ten men in the university's history who won letters in four sports as an undergraduate. He was also an outstanding debater, and a Phi Beta Kappa scholar. It has even been noted that Rutgers has been remembered for two reasons: Rutgers and Princeton playing the first official intercollegiate football game on American soil, and it was at Rutgers were Paul Robeson helped to build the greatest football team in school history.

The experiences of Robeson and many other African American scholar athletes at predominately white universities were very antagonistic. As a first year member of the Rutgers football team, Robeson had already received word from racist teammates that if he continued to play, they would boycott. Realizing the seriousness of his commitment to play football at Rutgers University, Robeson continued to participate as he recalled:

> On my first day of scrimmage, they set about making sure that I would not get on their team. One boy slugged me in the face and smashed my nose-an injury that has been a trouble to me as a singer ever since. And then as I was down, flat on my back, another boy got me with his knee.... partially dislocating my right shoulder (Edwards, 1980, p.208).

After being sidelined for two weeks because of the injuries, Robeson, to a certain extent, won his teammates over with his strong resiliency, courage, and superior athletic ability. Rather, he was accepted as long as the team maintained their winning streak due to his immense contributions. The white challenges to the legitimacy of Robeson's participation continued throughout his career at Rutgers University as his teammates and coaches did not learn from their racist behaviors (Edwards, 1980).

Robeson, despite the racial prejudice and endless dehumanizing remarks, refused to lash out violently in the fear of being dismissed from sport participation, losing educational support, and the chance of being labeled as an athlete with a "bad attitude." This demonstration was a major component of his responsibility of representing the masses in hopes of bridging the gap of current ideological practices at predominately white institutions. His strategic mission set him apart as a human who possessed integrity, political awareness, intellectualism, and physical ability.

Edwards (1980) stated:

> Robeson was not just an outstanding athlete; or just a premier actor; or just an orator of proven brilliance. He was a complete man- not because of the racism, degradation and humiliation that have historically been the burden of all blacks in America. Paul Robeson conquered the obstacles, and accomplishments that few of even the most fortunate, gifted, and privileged of Americans ever approximate- he actualized his inherent potentials for creativity, manhood and humanity (p. 210).

The sacrifices made and the insights gained are relevant inquiries into the social and political climate of this period. Robeson's life and accomplishments along with others during this decade revealed a need for not only protest demonstrations, but also a further investigation into the sports' dynamic relationship with higher education and society as a whole (Smith, 1988). The efforts made by these individuals are benchmarks to the development of the modern civil rights struggle and the protest movements on various college and university campuses.

Pre-World War II and the Black Athlete in Intercollegiate Sports

Often overlooked by scholars in their investigation of the civil rights movement, big-time intercollegiate sport was an important arena of protest in the pre-war years (Spivey, 1983). An increased number of African American college students who migrated to the north had a greater sense of political and social activism concerning issues from the international politics to higher education. Despite a growing concern for consequences of participating in protests by African Americans, many students across the country were active in improving discriminatory practices against college athletes and non-athletes in higher education. For example, at the University of Kansas, "a state institution that may have led all its peers in the number of African Americans students enrolled, with some 175 African Americans in a student population of approximately 5,000," protests on campus were widespread (Wiggins, 1991). African American students on campus were disallowed any rights to extracurricular activities, involvement in campus events, and admittance to facilities on campus; the only right, for the most part, was an opportunity to attend classes. This subsequently led to a committee investigation on the schools exclusionary policies because of pressures from active students. As a result, the University of Kansas continued its policy to exclude African Americans from participation in intercollegiate sport, signifying an unwillingness to support their movement on campus.

During this period, other protests at state institutions challenged social discrimination practices as well. The love-hate relationship of predominately white institutions was widespread as they celebrated and praised the athleticism of African American scholar-athletes since the latter part of the twentieth century, but despise any commitment to equality academically and outside the playing fields (Harrison & Lawrence, working manuscript). According to Ashe (1993), student unions and co-operatives were frequently off limits, invitations to dances were not forthcoming and interracial dating was at the top of the list of "no-no's."

African Americans irrespective of the fates of Jim Crowism in college sports, were successful contributors to their schools. Student-athletes such as Jesse Owens of Ohio State University, Ozzie Simmons of Iowa, Jerome Holland of Cornell University, Johnny Woodruff of Pittsburgh, Bernie Jefferson of Northwestern, William Watson of Michigan University, Charles Drew of Amherst College, and Lou Montgomery of Boston College, among others were visible leaders.

One of the most notable of these "scholar-ballers," for example, who suffered racial abuses and discrimination at the hands of opponents, teammates, fans, coaches, the student body, and the wider sports establishment was Jerome Heartwell Holland (Harrison, working manuscript). Born in Auburn, New York in 1916, Holland was one of thirteen children. Understanding his indigenous background, he knew that education was his quickest way out of poverty, subsequently attending Cornell University. There he gained numerous academic and athletic honors. Academically he was an Omega Psi Phi, Sphinx Head, Aleph Samach, and a Scarab. Athletically he was a member of the football club, the freshman team, and the varsity football team from his sophomore through his senior year. He eventually became an All-American defensive end in 1937 and 1938 and team captain in his senior season. In 1939, he graduated from Cornell with a degree from the College of Agriculture.

Holland became an instructor of sociology at Lincoln University in Pennsylvania from 1939 through 1942. When the war concluded, Holland went back to Cornell, and earned his Master's in agriculture. In 1950, he earned his Doctorate from Pennsylvania University in sociology. By 1953, Holland was named president of Delaware State College. While at Delaware State, Holland improved his status by taking the institution from the verge of closing to a fully accredited member of the Middle States Association. And in 1960, Holland became the 9th president of the Hampton Institute where he planned and directed various fund raising events.

Holland was clearly committed to academic excellence. This is evident from the five books he published, his activism in Civil Rights toward the advancement of African Americans in education, his involvement in the United Negro College Fund, and his various roles in the academy.

In sum, the climate had not changed much on university campuses since the beginning of the century, as student protests were still visible, yet ineffective in changing the dominant paradigm. Several extraordinary scholar-athletes, however, were able to endure the context of their time while improving their scholarship and athletic skills. As the contemporary era of sport after World War II emerged, historic changes and breakthroughs occurred in higher education and larger society that strengthened the African American accessibility to higher education, thus improving their academic and athletic pursuits.

Securing Respect and Dignity

Several events took place during the 1940s and well into the 1970s that changed the trajectory of African American student-athletes in higher education and larger society. These events had major significance on access to higher education and athletic opportunities to compete for and against predominately white institutions. As the fight for full citizenship and equal economic opportunity expanded, the persistent effort of many advocates of change became more evident and convincing.

Congress, for instance, passed the Servicemen's Readjustment Act of 1944, in fear of a disproportionately high number of servicemen increasing the unemployment rate. The act, also known as the GI Bill, provided funding that allowed veterans an educational opportunity. The benefits included a year of unemployment insurance, medical care, counseling services, tuition, books, and living expenses (Cohen, 1998). The bill also allowed entrance to hundreds of African American veterans willing to take advantage of higher learning and individual upward mobility. Athletically gifted African Americans as well followed the route of non-athletics in pursuit of a college education and athletic competition, particularly at black colleges.

In the 1950s, the early civil rights movement had not responded well to African American student-athletes at predominately white institutions. There were no establishments that supported these student athletes other than their white counterparts, which was minimal at best. It was not until the 1954 United States Supreme Court decision in *Brown v. Board of Education*, which ruled that separate-but-equal public school systems for blacks and whites were unconstitutional, that the current patterns shifted to accommodate *all* Americans. This meant that African Americans had access to better institutions, athletic facilities, and a broader range of other resources to enhance their upward mobility. Also, as equal opportunity emerged, more African Americans were also being recruited to play at predominately white institutions in the south (Martin, 1998).

As concerns over civil rights issues heightened in the 1960s, active protest against discrimination became a long, dedicated, uncompromising struggle. Many African American student-athletes took part in the struggle to improve their position in society. According to Wiggins (1997), "they tried to come to grips with their conflicting role demands as athletics and black Americans by continuing to distinguish themselves in sport while at the same time combining with others in the black community to denounce everything from the lack of black executives in professional sport to racial exploitation in college athletics" (p.105). Reflected in the protest movement in intercollegiate athletics in the 1960s was Harry Edwards.

Harry Edwards, a former scholar-athlete at San Jose State, was an instrumental advocate for change. Edwards attempted to organize a boycott by African American athletes of the 1968 Summer Olympic Games in Mexico City as protest against obvious inequalities in both college and professional athletics. Although the boycott never materialized, Edwards was credited with encouraging several athletes to publicize their political beliefs during the Olympic medal ceremonies.

Several institutions felt the shock of the Olympic Movement: the University of Texas El Paso, University of Wisconsin, San Jose State University, University of California at Berkeley, University of Washington, San Francisco State University, and the University of Kansas. Edwards, in fact, along with several protesters, caused the cancellation of San Jose State versus the University of Texas El Paso football game in 1967. Their sole purpose was for academic institutions and larger society to recognize specific discriminatory practices that affected various groups of students on campus.

Harry Edwards, the embodiment of a true scholar-athlete legacy, was the mouthpiece of the athletic rebellion whose activism and intellectual strategy transformed the pattern of *all* participants in college athletics. Currently, a professor of sociology at the University of California at Berkeley, where he has taught since 1970, he continues to be a leading pioneer in the sociological examination of sport and society. More importantly, his presence in the 1960s and 1970s set a precedent for further reforms to improve the conditions of student-athletes in higher education.

Conclusion

For African American student-athletes who traverse the educational terrain, it is clear that reconciling the dual roles as student and athlete are difficult. Early African American scholar athletes who gained access to predominantly white institutions in spite of selective admission policies experienced an uphill battle during the oppressive years of Jim Crowism. However, these individuals were "transcendents," enduring various obstacles in pursuit of noteworthy athletic careers and upward mobility through their academic commitment. Furthermore, similar experiences and pressures of Paul Robeson in the 1920s during the emergent growth years of higher education had a profound impact on others as he sacrificed himself in order to help redefine the purpose of higher education and society. His academic and athletic responsibilities were essential in shaping the years that followed.

In the 1930s and continuing well into the 1960s, while African American students were gaining a greater sense of political activism and a slightly higher access to colleges, many protested discriminatory practices. Several pressures transformed the nature of society marking the end of segregation and greater opportunities for all Americans to higher education.

With immense environmental factors: discrimination, exploitation, cultural adaptation, and the rigorous demands and business-like enterprise of college athletics currently, African American student-athletes are constantly placed in inherently contradictory positions. The wherewithal to overcome these barriers is a reflection of their dedication and commitment to balancing the roles of academics and athletics. It is anticipated that we will continue to advance educational reforms to meet the needs and interests of all student populations. In doing so, we can expect a better today and tomorrow.

Acknowledgements

Both authors would like to thank the University of Michigan for their support and resources for this article and specifically Dr. Lester Monts, Senior Vice-Provost for Academic Affairs, the Division of Kinesiology, Department of Sports Management and Communication, and Dr. Earl Lewis (Dean of the Rackham Graduate School) that supported this project with the Distinguished Graduate Faculty Award for the 3rd Annual Paul Robeson Symposium: The Past is the Present (2000), held in Ann Arbor, Michigan. Thanks to Dr. Arthur Cohen (professor of education at UCLA) for his comments (the first author wrote an earlier version of this paper for Cohen's graduate class on the history of higher education). We would also like to thank student Brad Kenna and archive assistants Quentin Love and Khaliah Burt at the Paul Robeson Research Center for Academic and Athletic Prowess at the University of Michigan, Ann Arbor.

References

Aptheker, H, "The Negro College Student in the 1920's," *Science and Society* 33 (Spring 1969): 150-67.

Ashe, A. (1993). *A Hard Road to Glory: a history of the African American Athlete, 1919-1945*. In 3 vols. New York: Warner Books.

Cohen, A. (1998). *The Shaping of American Higher Education: emergence and growth of the contemporary system*. San Francisco, CA: Jossey-Bass Publishers.

Edwards, H (1980). *The Struggle that Must Be*. New York: Macmillan Publishing Co., Inc.

Eitzen, S. (1993). Racism in college Sports: prospects for the year 2000. In D. Brooks & R. Althouse (Eds.), *Racism in College Athletics: The African American athlete's experience* (pp. 23-49). Morgantown, WV: Fitness Information Technology, Inc.

Eitzen, S. (1999). *Fair and Foul: beyond the myths and paradoxes of sport*. New York: Rowman & Littlefield.

Hall, J. (1999). From Willis Ward to James Hall. Unpublished document in the Paul Robeson Research Center for Academic and Athletic Prowess.

Harrison, C.K. (Working Manuscript). *Paving the Way, Early African American Males on Athletic Scholarship: Scholars and Ballers*. The Paul Robeson Research Center for Academic and Athletic Prowess, Ann Arbor, Michigan, the University of Michigan.

Harrison, C.K. and S. M. Lawrence. (working manuscript). Student-Athletes' perceptions of career transition in sport: An mixed methodology and visual investigation. Unpublished document.

Lederman, D. (1991, March 27). College athletes graduate at higher rate than other students, but men's basketball players lag far behind, a survey finds. *Chronicle of Higher Education.* 37, 28, A1, A35-38.

Lucas, C. (1994). *American Higher Education.* New York: St. Martin's Press National Collegiate Athletic association

Martin, C. (1998). *Journal of Sport History. NCAA division I graduate-rates report* (1995). Overland Park, KS: National Collegiate Athletic Association (a).

National Collegiate Athletic Association (1995). NCAA research report 93-01: *Cohort trends in college academic performances of 1984-88 freshman student athletes.* (ERIC Document Reproduction Service No. Ed 381045) (b).

Smith, R. (1988). *Sports and Freedom.* Oxford: Oxford University Press.

Spivey, D, "The Black Athlete in Big-Time Intercollegiate Sports, 1941-1968," *Phylon* 44 (June 1983): 116-25.

Wiggins, D. (1991). Prized performers but frequently overlooked as students: the involvement of black athletes in intercollegiate sports on predominantly white university campuses, 1890-1972. *Research Quarterly for Exercise in Sport.*

Wiggins, D. (1997). *Glory Bound: black athletes in a white America.* Syracuse, New York: Syracuse University Press.

Article 4

"It's Not About Race:" Making Whiteness Visible in the Interpretation of Rap Music

Natalie Fasnacht

Beginning in the 1970s, Hip-Hop culture gained a voice in rap music that slowly gained popularity in mainstream music. Originating from the unique culture found in predominantly African-American, urban, and poor communities, the music drew attention to many social issues found there that were ignored or exacerbated by public policy. Rap music quickly became the fastest growing and selling genre of music in the United States. Over the past three decades, Hip Hop has gone global, increasing in popularity in other countries as various groups adopted the rapping style to express their own local concerns and cultures (Bennett 1999). While rap is considered an African-American musical genre, it has never been an exclusive club. White working class artists such as Beastie Boys and Eminem have found their home in the Hip Hop tradition, not to mention artists such as Limp Bizkit and Kid Rock who integrate the rapping style with their heavy metal and rock and roll tradition. Ultimately rap music has shown itself to be a versatile, cutting edge genre that resonates with today's youth and has never shied away from controversy.

Alongside the evolution of Hip-Hop, critical White studies was growing during these decades. This perspective studies White people as raced individuals, working to deconstruct the image of Whites as the "norm" or the universal human subject. The literature places White culture within a racial dialogue and uncovers the ways Whiteness shapes everything from history, government policy and laws, to values, norms and interpersonal relations.

These two perspectives, while seemingly unconnected phenomena, were shaped by the same historical events within the racial context of American society. This paper will bring these two perspectives together to gain an understanding of the impact Hip Hop has on today's White youth. Through qualitative interviews this paper will examine the impact rap music has on the way White listeners construct their racial identities and whether rap music effectively communicates a message of resistance and oppositional culture. Depending on the social position of the listener, many interpretations of rap music are possible. The purpose of this paper is to uncover what meanings and actions are possible, and which are rendered impossible, by the subject due to their various interpretations of rap music and Whiteness. It will also explore other factors that influence how race is constructed in the early twenty-first century.

This project was conducted at a small, predominantly white, private, liberal arts university in a suburban area located in the southern United States. The "Core Values" which shaped the goals of the university heavily encouraged social responsibility and activist work. There were numerous organizations dedicated to giving back to the community such as a service fraternity, an environmental organization, and various organizations committed to educating and mobilizing students around sexuality, gender, race and other social justice issues. There were also numerous religious organizations, including a sorority and fraternity for Christian worship. A Greek system that stressed social interaction was also strong on campus. As with most colleges, opportunity for social interaction was a major component of the undergrad experience.

Interestingly, many white, upper class students often referred to the university as a "bubble," where they were protected from the "real world." For students of color, who comprised 12% of the student body, attending this school did *not* protect them from the "real world."

It actually exposed them to numerous interactions with people who came from very sheltered environments, often leading to hurtful or enraging interactions based on stereotypes and subtle racism. However, there were populations of students who worked together to create integrated spaces dedicated to education and communication about social justice issues. Thus, students had numerous options regarding what groups they wanted to join and what types of interactions they wanted to have with other students on campus.

Being introduced to an atmosphere of challenging intellectual engagement, a newfound independence and interactions with other students from different backgrounds, the college experience is a time of radical change in a student's outlook as well as identity. Many students may start to rethink their racial identities due to attitudes and experiences they've never been exposed to before. This research will provide one snapshot of the college experience in order to explore differences between the racial identities of some White students, and how these identities are constructed in relation to Hip Hop, a musical genre that specifically targets young people.

Methodology

The material for this research was collected through 6 qualitative interviews selected from a purposive sample of 1200 undergraduate students. When I discussed my research with fellow students, the question almost every White person asked was, "What's Whiteness?" This indicates a low level of racial awareness among the majority of the white student body and the fact that Whiteness was significantly invisible and dominant at this Methodist university.

I sent a campus wide e-mail to 1200 students asking anyone who was a fan of Tupac Shakur to respond to the e-mail. I received 25 e-mails back, a response rate of 2%. After eliminating four students I knew were Black or Asian-American, I sent out another 11 e-mails asking respondents to volunteer to be interviewed and to set up appointments. The first four people to respond were interviewed. The last two interviewees were purposefully chosen for their demonstrated awareness of racial issues in order to get a more well-rounded collection of viewpoints. The data collected from these interviews are in no way generalizable. However, trends were discovered that merit further study, and other research possibilities are discussed.

Methods for effective interviewing skills were taken from Kleinmann and Copp's (1990) *Emotions and Research*. Due to the grounded theory approach used in this research, the questions asked during the interviews evolved over time. The list of questions that I used is shown in Appendix A. Grounded theory is best used for exploratory research since it begins with the data collected from open-ended questions and draws patterns, themes or relationships among the data. This technique is not set up to test specific hypotheses but does allow room for unexpected findings (Babbie 1998: 283).

The six participants in the qualitative interviews all identified themselves as White and answered open-ended questions regarding their gender, socioeconomic standing, sexuality, age, year in school, major, religion and ability/disability. Gender equity was maintained with half the participants male and half female. One participant identified as working class, one middle class, the other four were upper-middle class. Only one stated her sexual orientation as bisexual, the rest were heterosexual. Ages ranged from 19 to 21 and from sophomore to senior year in college. Their majors came generally from the social sciences, with one in the fine arts. The religions ranged from one person who did not label her religion, to one Mormon, one Lutheran, two Catholics and one self-labeled Christian. Two participants had disabilities.

During the course of this research the questions that were explored changed numerous times. The main goal of this research was to find out what impact rap music had on White racial identity. If no effect were to be found then what strategies were used to distance the subject from the messages in the music and/or from their own racial identity and privilege? How was the invisibility of Whiteness maintained while listening to the vocalized resistance to systems of oppression found in many types of rap music that often directly implicate Whites? These questions were clarified and further broadened to include an analysis of the way rap music is understood by the White participants. How do White people conceive of rap music in the process of preserving the invisibility and dominance of Whiteness?

Figure 1: Continuum of White Racial Identity

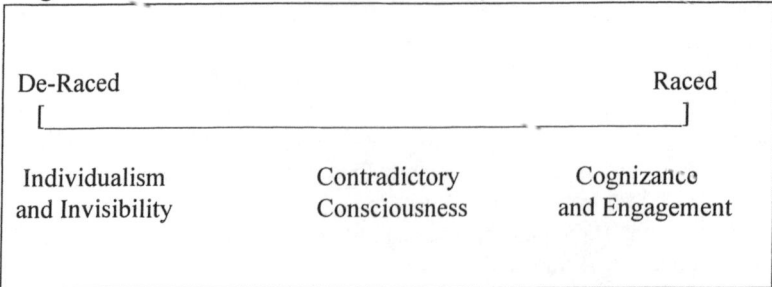

```
De-Raced                                                  Raced
[_____]

Individualism          Contradictory          Cognizance
and Invisibility       Consciousness          and Engagement
```

Throughout the interviews a range of constructions of Whiteness were found. The graph above illustrates more clearly the continuum on which Whiteness exists. Each subject occupied a specific position on the continuum, a position that could change at any time, depending on how identities, ideologies or ideas about race are constructed. Individuals are able to move back and forth along the continuum depending on how they construct, evaluate and interpret their own identity and the interactions they have with those around them.

A "de-raced" identity is constructed when privileges are utilized without awareness or evaluation and when ideologies that maintain or perpetuate white supremacy or other structural inequalities are accepted as true. De-raced viewpoints are unquestioned, unchallenged and constructed as invisible, unimportant or "normal." "Raced" identities occur when individuals are aware of how their own race and racism shapes their lives. They are aware that racism is always a force in their lives, especially when there are no people of color around.

Maggie, Jenny, Chris, Hank, Fred and Casper each occupy specific positions along the continuum between raced and de-raced, and their interpretation of rap music reflects these various positions. The six interviews were placed in a general progression from de-raced to raced identity constructions in order to illustrate a very abbreviated range of possibilities in White racial identity construction and interpretations of rap music. However, each person can move back and forth along the continuum. The study of Whiteness must encompass this specificity in order to find the areas of potential change.

Results and Discussion

Individualism and Invisibility

<u>Maggie</u>

The first subject, Maggie, started listening to rap music when she worked at a summer camp for urban, predominantly African-American children in New York City. This interview illustrates how a negative interpretation of rap music maintains the invisibility and dominance of whiteness. Here is an excerpt from her interview:

> NF: So when you listen to rap music do you ever think about the lyrics in the song or the message that that specific song is trying to get across?
> Maggie: Yeah, definitely. With music in general I didn't pay attention a lot. But when our kids (at summer camp) were listening to these kinds of songs that were explicit and obscene, I was definitely aware of that. A lot of times the kids would have to decode the lyrics for me. They knew a lot more about it than I did.
> NF: What were a lot of the themes that were running through the songs?
> Maggie: Crime, drugs, sex, stuff like that.
> NF: Did it give you any kind of new perspective on those issues?
> Maggie: Just the fact that these kids at this young age felt such a connection to those issues and those celebrities.
> NF: So why do you think there is so much crime and drugs and sex, why do you think those kids have to deal with those issues?
> Maggie: Because they're growing up in an environment that fosters those kinds of issues. A lot of these kids are in single parent families with young parents and way too many siblings. They're hanging out with older kids. A lot of my girls have talked about having sex with their boyfriends back home and they're 12 and 13.

This discussion of rap music and its connection to the daily lives of children could have been taken right out of an article on the negative impact of rap music. "The corruption frame emphasized the music's corrupting effect on young listeners" (Binder 1993: 758). By describing the lyrics as explicit and obscene, Maggie dismisses any positive, constructive or beneficial content within the song lyrics. At another point in the interview she described the impact this music had on the children when she described a girl who built a shrine to Tupac Shakur on her bed everyday. Here we see a conflict between two ideologies in the construction of rap music. Using the language "explicit and obscene," Maggie prioritizes her own viewpoint, or rather the viewpoint of hegemonic society that she has adopted.

Antonio Gramsci's concept of "cultural hegemony" illustrates the political functions served by cultural symbols. Clashes over definitions of what is obscene and ideologies regarding race, poverty, crime, drugs, etc. are played out over cultural symbols, such as rap music. While language is commonly understood to describe cultural symbols, it actually conceptualizes and confers meaning onto these symbols. Thus, the language used by Maggie marks the boundaries of permissible discourse, placing any messages found in rap music outside of that discourse (Lears 1979: 14). Through her interpretation of rap music and the social issues it brings attention to, she demonizes single Black mothers while effectively ruling out structural factors which detrimentally affect poor people and people of color while privileging white people and the wealthy. These are ideas that rap music itself often draws attention to.

If Maggie's interpretation, or a similar one, is accepted as legitimate and natural by groups who are subordinated by this ideology, hegemony has been established. Hegemonic ideologies operate on the unconscious level, seeming 'natural,' 'spontaneous,' instantly recognized and commonsensical. Ideologies explain, through the mechanics of common sense and recognition, where things fit into the existing social structure without revealing the premises on which they are based or whose interests they serve. Ideology has no history, thus appearing immutable and constant. It maintains itself by winning the consent of groups whose interests are not served (Hebdige 1979: 7).

Hegemony is never permanent and is often unstable, because members of the dominant and subordinated groups can always abrogate consent. This clash between hegemony and resistance is often fought on the battleground of cultural symbols (Hebdige 1979: 11-16).

Almost in a direct response to Maggie's interpretation, Valerie Lehr states, "The inability to see people not as individuals but as members of groups, who face differing circumstances because of how the groups of which they are a part have been and continue to be defined and treated, means that issues are not going to be defined as political" (Lehr 1995: 39). This interpretation was further supported when Maggie said she did not personally see rap music as political, even though she acknowledged that it could be viewed that way.

Many writers (Feagin 1995; Mitchell 1995; Stuckey 1987; Scott 1990; Cross 1993; Denisoff 1972; Gilroy 1993; Dyson 1996; Kuwahara 1992; Lusane 1993; Martinez 1993; McDonnell 1992; Rose 1991, 1994, 1998) have developed a foundation of research and theory showing how rap music and, more specifically hip-hop culture, is a form of oppositional culture that creates strategies for hegemonic resistance. Oppositional culture "embodies a coherent set of values, beliefs and practices which mitigate the effects of oppression and reaffirms that which is distinct from the majority culture" (Mitchell and Feagin 1995: 65). Rap artists expressing the day-to-day realities of living in poor and working class inner cities implicate the political, economic, and social processes that combine to institutionalize inequalities in the social structure. Rap in general, and gangsta' rap specifically, is an ardent form of resistance and a political expression of oppositional culture. "The voices within rap are able to effectively bridge the gap between popular culture and social criticism by means of a potent form of oppositional culture" (Martinez 1997: 3, 11).

Through the utility of her interpretation, Maggie executes the privilege to disengage from the realities of life for these children and other possible explanations about what creates this reality. By interpreting the music as valueless, corrupt, and dangerous, she resists a new reading of not only the music but of the structures that shape these childrens' lives as well as her own. By drawing attention to the size of families, rather than being open to a different cultural construction of the family unit that is shaped by specific structural determinants, she constructs as normal her own cultural understanding of what a proper family size is and assumes anything larger is deviant and ultimately criminal.

By refusing to see the value in the music she does not see the meaning this music brings to the lives of these children. In not seeing this, she also does not see the forms of resistance developed by the children, nor how necessary it is for them to celebrate this expression of Hip Hop culture, an expression that includes them. By normalizing her experience of being protected from these issues and by choosing to be exposed to these issues by becoming a counselor at a summer camp for children who do not have the same freedom of choice, Maggie exercises her privileges. Thus, her Whiteness remains invisible, dominant and "normative" while Blackness remains criminal, dangerous, dysfunctional and irresponsible.

In addition to this, policy changes regarding increasing aid to poor families, increasing equal access to resources, eliminating the racism of the War on Drugs and many other issues become useless and unimportant within this conceptualization.

> NF: The only other question I had was what do you think of when you hear the word white? What does that mean to you to be White?
> Maggie: To tell you the truth, I don't think about it a lot. I think that because I'm White it means I'm privileged in ways that other people aren't. I think it means that I have advantages in a lot of situations.
> NF: How often do you think about those privileges?
> Maggie: Not a lot.

I counterpose this quote with the above discussion for a couple of reasons. First, Whiteness is continually being constructed. While some privileges of Whiteness are institutionalized and have assumed an almost permanent status, race is and always will be a social construction. This construction can be changed and recreated, sometimes by simply listening to the lyrics of a song. It can transform daily interactions and manifestations of Whiteness. The potential for change always exists. Identity and ideology construction are never permanent or finished, nor clear cut and rigid. There are always points of potential change. There is also complexity in the interaction of discursive paradigms and cultural symbols. Finding these contradictions, making them visible, and prying them open allow resistance ideologies to surface and gain power. Interpretations of rap music prevent or allow for the dissemination of the resistant messages found in Hip-Hop culture. While I have picked certain sections of these interviews to illuminate the interaction between Whiteness and rap music, in reality the complexity of this interaction cannot be overemphasized.

Secondly, the phrase "I don't think about it a lot" occurs frequently in these interviews. While this was always said very casually among those I interviewed, I do not want to underestimate the political significance of this statement. Within this context, the fact that these individuals have not thought about these issues reflects a lifestyle that has been insulated from difference to the point where their value systems, opinions, and viewpoints have not been challenged in any significant way, but have been constructed as normative for everyone. The ability to walk through life without having intimate contact with people who have vastly conflicting understandings of the world, and to not have to self-reflect or internalize these understandings, reflects a privileged existence that can only exist with societal, cultural and historical support.

Jenny

Jenny has a much more positive interpretation of rap music when she was asked if she could identify with anything in the lyrics. However, this interview shows the colonizing dangers of relying on an individual interpretation rather than a larger social critique.

> Jenny: I think I can identify with things in the sense that everyone could. Like I didn't grow up in the ghetto or anything. But I had friends who did and I had friends who died from guns or whatever. But it never seemed quite as hard-core as it did in the rap songs. I guess what I was identifying with was more of the rebellion thing. It seemed like rappers were rebelling, and they were loud and they were saying things that weren't accepted by society, like my mother. And I'm also a psychology major and I'm really interested in people and it interested me in that way too. I was wondering why they're like this, what's wrong, they're not happy.

She makes sense of the messages and meanings in rap music by interpreting them through her own life experience. While this is a strategy of empathy, it is actually quite limited in its potential for significant change. In order to interpret this music through her own experiences, she has to de-racialize and de-contextualize it. Equating the messages in rap with teenage rebellion, she infantilizes it and removes the serious meaning being communicated. It becomes a phase they go through, as she did, and not something to take seriously.

In this interpretation her experiences are the norm for everyone. In this way, rap music is contained and controlled through the ideology of rebellion. While the messages found in rap music may be heard outside the context of structural oppression, the voices of the rappers are given less significance and weight, thus not heard at all. Her comment indicating her psychological interpretation of the issues found in rap shows that the artists' words are not being connected to the larger social structures in society and are still being interpreted as the problems of the individual artist, not problems that may be experienced by anyone belonging to the same social, or cultural group.

While Jenny's interpretation is more liberal and positive, finding universal meanings in rap music, it is still interpreted through her own individual viewpoint. While she chose to encounter this different environment more often than Maggie did, she still was not cognizant of the significance of that choice and how that influenced her interpretation of events and lyrics. When asked about how she thinks about whiteness she replied:

> Jenny: I don't think White has anything to do . . . I mean it's me, but that has nothing to do with it. Maybe the different ethnicities got me to where I am, like learning about those, I can say I'm proud to have come from this guy. But see, I don't even really like that. What I do with my life is what I can be proud for. I'm not going to take credit for what other people have done. Being White is just what I look like. It kind of put me in my class, in the sense that I was adopted and the adoption agency chose someone that was... My mother would be similar to this girl in the sense that she was White, the somewhat same class and just things like that so I would fit as well as I could. Does that make sense?
> NF: But the fact that you're White, it only has a limited...?
> Jenny: Yeah, I don't think that has a whole lot to do with it. It has kind of affected me, like, in how I've grown up and how people have treated me which can affect who I am. But the whole sense that I am White does not... I'm not proud of being White, I'm not proud of having brown eyes. That doesn't make sense to me. I'm proud of having a fingernail, it doesn't...

Here Jenny chooses not to "take credit" for what her ancestors have accomplished. In this instance "privilege is not visible to its holder; it is merely there, a part of the world, a way of life, simply the way things are" (Wildman and Davis 1996:316). Not taking credit for what they have done also allows her to not acknowledge the benefits she receives from her White heritage and from the historical processes her ancestors were a part of that still continue today. By only being proud of what she accomplishes, she maintains a focus on her own individual efforts and erases the historical and structural privileges that also helped her achieve her goals.

In the next sentence, Jenny simultaneously acknowledges structural factors and dismisses their importance in her life. Equating her position in the middle class as the place where she would best 'fit,' she constructs Whiteness as equivalent with a middle class status and by default equates Blackness with a working class status. By marginalizing the importance of being placed in an upper middle class home, she again de-contextualizes her position of privilege with respect to those living in the "ghetto." This allows her to interpret her experiences with rap music and the "ghetto" through her own life experience, since the structural forces that shape housing options are no longer significant. If it is not a force in her life, neither can it be a force in the lives of inner city residents, since her interpretation of rap music only uses her life experience as a reference. Residential segregation is no longer a structure that can be implicated in the existence of social problems discussed in rap music.

This interaction allows Jenny to construct her Whiteness as invisible, insignificant, and individual, while rap music is depoliticized and individualized. These co-constructions reinforce each other. It is here that rap music loses its ability to create change. Since Jenny is living within a residentially and educationally segregated environment, these dominant ideologies become probable and 'common sense' for her, while the meanings expressed in the oppositional culture of Hip Hop become impossible and are subverted into an 'individual' interpretation.

Chris

The interview with Chris shows the complex relationship between Whiteness, cultural appropriation and multiculturalism within a capitalist economic system.

> Chris: I'm sure it appears that way, like I'm trying to be Black, to act Black. But its just, because the rap music is on television, it's portrayed as a cool thing to be, I don't think it has anything to do with racial identity. I just think it's become popular and it's become part of mainstream America now. It's becoming more mainstream, therefore it's okay to talk like that, more than it used to be.

This statement was prompted by the retelling of an instance when Chris was called 'wigger' by some friends, presumably as a way of enforcing racial boundaries and letting Chris know he had crossed them. Rather than questioning how race is defined, Chris de-racializes rap music and Hip Hop culture. While incorporating Hip Hop into American culture may seem positive, he equates consuming the cultural products of Hip Hop, i.e. CDs, clothing, mannerism, and forms of speech, with multicultural awareness. This de-contextualizes the history of Hip Hop that expresses the many ways African-Americans have been excluded from the benefits of mainstream America.

A musical piece's social significance within a capitalistic economy is determined by who performs it, who listens to it, and the circumstances under which it is heard and performed. These factors determine whether a musical piece is an organic cultural performance or a super organic spectacle. Music as a cultural performance, whether performed before a crowd or on a compact disc, speaks of political issues that are very significant to a social group. The music serves to re-center the audience around a "shared, reciprocal identity." It expresses a commonality within a cultural group and embodies symbolic power for that group (Pena 1999: 6, 24).

Music as spectacle, however, has lost all sense of community and awareness. Since Chris became interested in rap music by watching MTV and listening to the radio, his socialization to rap music subsumed the importance of race and class in its formation and made it appear as an alternative form of "normal" (White) American culture. This musical spectacle replaces social relations with consumption and strives to represent that which must be lived. As an individual spectator Chris remains detached and uncommitted. Rather than expressing a commonality, this spectacle satisfies personal desires and perpetuates the separation of those desires from larger social influences. It 'preempts valid social discourse,' thereby allowing dominant hegemonic conceptualizations of reality and norms to go unchallenged (Pena 1999: 6, 10). Listening to rap music under these conditions, with no contact with people of color, eliminates the possibility of conceptualizing the social relationships and community in which Hip-Hop developed.

By de-racializing the mannerisms, Chris appropriates the culture, which then loses its ability to be oppositional. As a White man trying to be "cool," he subverts its ability to make a political statement about alternative ways of being and reinstates it as a type of White ethnicity. Due to the invisibility of a racial identity for most White individuals, ethnicity is one axis around which identity is constructed by Whites.

Mary Waters (1990) illuminates the social implications of Whites having ethnic identities that are voluntary, costless, and symbolic. Since racial and ethnic heritage is constructed as biological or blood related, the amount of choice involved in having an ethnic identity is obscured. The appeal of celebrating an ethnic identity reveals the privilege of Whiteness. "Having a symbolic ethnicity combines individuality with feelings both of community and of conformity through an exercise of personal choice" (Waters 1990: 151). Appropriating Hip Hop culture allows Chris to belong to a costless, voluntary, and symbolic community that makes him more unique but does not threaten his individuality. In this way it satisfies his personal desires while separating those desires from the influence of larger social structures, like capitalism and white supremacy.

With the invisibility of privilege, Whites are able to consider themselves and other Whites "individuals," without acknowledging the benefits they receive or extend to each other due to their White skin. As the dominant group, they have access to resources, and thus more freedom of choice over how their ethnic identity is defined, without having that identity defined for them. By not acknowledging the mandatory, costly, and material effects of being racialized as a person of color in America, Whites maintain an individualized and merit-based analysis of success and failure, again obscuring any benefits that people of color do not have access to.

Once again, rap music loses its ability to be oppositional and resistant as it is appropriated into a "raceless" form of rebellion. When maintaining its oppositional quality, Hip Hop culture serves to question mainstream White culture. When these questions and deconstructions are eliminated, the music is simply appropriated in one more example of the colonization of another culture's resources for monetary or personal gain.

> Chris: I just don't think, I have a feeling like race isn't a big deal. I'm sure it is to a lot of people, people who are racist who think that there's a big difference between Blacks and Whites and others. But I don't think it's a big deal, I think that everyone's, we're made up the same, it's just how people treat each other. That's the only difference.
> NF: So you think race is only an issue for people who are really racist?

Chris: Not who are really racist, but for people who encounter race and treat it like it's a big deal. Like, for example, Black people who go into a White environment, White people who go into a Black environment. For them it's a big deal, if they live in that, it's a big deal because they're the minority.

Here Chris summarizes the color-blind point of view that asserts a value system of essential sameness. Since the concept of race places individuals in a hierarchical system, the best solution, according to the color-blind paradigm, is to ignore race altogether. By acting like race does not matter, the effects of racism will supposedly go away. Once we have color-blind policies, programs and laws then any failure to achieve success becomes the fault of those individual people of color (Frankenberg 1993: 14). Another result of this paradigm is the erasure of any cultural differences, constructing White culture as the invisible norm. The only racism that gets confronted is blatant, obvious discrimination executed by individuals, which is then pathologized as something normal White people would not do.

Institutionalized oppression cannot be conceptualized within this paradigm, as indicated by Chris's comment where he naturalizes and perpetuates the idea of segregation in order to justify and normalize his own experience of White-only neighborhoods and schools. He compartmentalizes the impact of race which maintains the dominance and invisibility of his Whiteness. This is also enacted by defining racism as an individual act of discrimination with intent and malice. By ignoring the benefits Chris has personally received from segregation, regardless of whether he has personally discriminated or not, the color-blind strategy allow Chris to maintain and perpetuate systems of domination. All these mechanisms construct his racial identity in such a way as to allow very limited interpretations of rap music and a very limited understanding of race relations.

While his life experience is normalized due to the historical forces of segregation, White flight, and privilege, few avenues are left open for him to learn alternative ideas. Hegemonic dissemination is made more effective when it is exercised through 'private,' i.e. non-political organizations of the state like schools, neighborhoods, and the family (Lears 1985: 570). Surrounded by people who also hold this viewpoint and with one of the few expressions of dissent found in rap music already subverted, Whiteness is constructed as invisible and dominant through the discursive paradigms of color-blindness and the use of his privilege.

Within this section we've seen the interaction between de-raced racial identities and rap music that has been interpreted as an apolitical expression of the problems and lives of individual rap artists. This relationship was created through various strategies. By dismissing the possibility of any value within rap music, outside of its ability to help her form a connection with her campers, Maggie protects herself from any alternative explanations for the social problems found in inner cities. Prioritizing her own interpretation of rap music above the childrens' interpretations allows her to maintain her privileged viewpoint. While Jenny was able to identify with the messages in rap music, her ability to only interpret rap music through her own experiences placed a limit on what messages could be heard within the music. Interpreting rap music as a form of rebellion also limited the challenge rap music presents to mainstream culture.

While Whiteness illustrates the structural position of social privilege and power that is the "invisible" result of systems of oppression (Hartigan 1997), it has also been conceptualized as the cumulative effect of race on the lives of White individuals and a standpoint from which privileged individuals see and construct issues of race (Frankenberg 1993: 14). Dominant racial ideologies, constructed by Whites, develop meaning around the visibility of domination and subordination while erasing the existence of benefits received from structural oppression. It also serves to individualize issues of discrimination and obscure the existence of a system. Whites define racism as the result of the personal actions of individuals with the intent and the means to discriminate. This obscures the cultural and structural forces that support the individual behavior, and simplifies the complex ways racism interacts with forms of domination along other axes of identity, such as class, gender and sexuality. Privileged individuals can avoid seeing the system that coordinates individual actions in efficient ways and incorporates them into the existing structure (Wildman and Davis 1996: 315).

Chris illustrated the value Hip Hop culture holds in presenting White youth with an alternative, costless, symbolic, and voluntary ethnicity in the beginning of the twenty-first century. As the substance and meaning of White ethnicity becomes diluted over time, and as Americans form more and more interracial unions, Whites will depend more and more on the mass media, stereotypes and popular culture to tell them, not only what it means to be Italian, Polish, or Irish, but also what it means to be Black, Hispanic, or Asian-American. Chris's acceptance of the status quo is then guaranteed due to the weight he gives to the means of communication controlled by the dominant social classes. De-racializing and de-contextualizing rap music allows White youth to appropriate various cultural products of Hip Hop and mistake it for multicultural awareness. The next section will take us further along the racial continuum as individuals become more aware of race and class issues.

Contradictory Consciousness and Complexity:

Hank

Hegemonic conceptualizations can be subverted by subordinate groups if the members of these groups are able to claim plausibly that their interests are those of society at large (Lears 1985: 571). If this successfully occurs, hegemony can also be subverted by members of the dominant social group when they become aware of the damage the ideology inflicts on members of subordinate groups. Since the line between subordinate and dominant groups is always permeable, it is always possible to form new social groups based on more inclusive and powerful definitions of identity. Hank's interview reveals the complexity experienced when one is aware of his or her own position within a matrix of oppression and analyzes rap music from a social/political perspective. Here we have an excerpt that illustrates this dynamic:

> NF: Do you think rap is political?
> Hank: Definitely, there's no question rap is political. I think that the social issues that are covered by rap music and the conditions that rap musicians portray are largely issues that should be addressed by politics. And really this is speaking more from the older era of rap when the economy was worse. There is a close bond between general national economics and rap music and the veins that are in them. With the boom 90s, we've had people talking about how great things are and how they've got all this money, and you really didn't see that in the recessed, or really for urban America, the depressed early 90s... It's always been about coming up and getting over. It's

something I can identify with, to try and defeat a situation that is difficult.

Moving away from the de-politicized individualization of rap music, Hank immediately connects it to larger social and economic forces. Discussions of class dynamics permeate Hank's interview, forming a common bond between Hank's experiences and the messages he hears in rap music. The messages in rap are plausible to Hank because of the similar class based identity that has always shaped Hip Hop music.

While Hank's interpretation of rap is more complex, he emphasized class dynamics and focused little attention on racial impacts and the interaction of race and class:

> I don't have any problems with my racial identity. I'm proud of my heritage and where I come from. I more closely associate myself with the plight of White ethnics than I do with the victory of WASPs. Because my family, we have not had the benefits of the WASP setting, the WASP privileges.

Here he is associating himself with working class Whites, thereby drawing attention to his experience of class oppression. Again, the focus is on domination and subordination, making the privileges he receives as a White man invisible. By choosing to engage with this form of oppression, Hank utilizes his racial privileges unknowingly, thereby masking the privilege of being able to choose to confront racial oppression at all. It is at these interactions between race and class and other identity axes where the ability to see privilege gets blurred. While Hank has had to deal with classism, these experiences blur the racial privileges that have aided him in his accomplishments as far (Wildman and Davis 1996: 318).

> Hank: When I hear White racial identity, I instantly trigger the Aryan nation prison gang sort of images. I don't think of a White heritage or a White culture. I think more along the lines of an Italian-American culture, an Irish-American culture, things like that.

Here, two more strategies are used to deflect attention away from Whiteness. By associating Whiteness with extreme radical groups, racism is interpreted as individual acts by deliberately malicious individuals. This image allows White Americans to dissociate themselves from racial issues and deny any complicity or benefits they receive from the structures that support White supremacy. While Whites often choose to be cognizant of White ethnicity, rather than seeing the structural benefits all Whites receive, they focus on the symbolic differences embodied in ethnic identities that used to hold political import, but do not any longer.

The struggle for hegemony and the formation of a new social group based on a common class identity does not always end in a clear victory. One result is contradictory consciousness. This is a form of dual consciousness within individuals when the values and ideologies they believe contradict their daily experiences or behaviors. This contradiction is often dealt with by dividing the consciousness into boxes that maintain mental equilibrium while creating contradictory behavior, attitudes, and language. Here is an example of the contradictory consciousness that can be caused by the conflation of race and class:

> NF: Do you believe we live in a meritocracy?
> Hank: No. Yes, No. I mean, people who work hard do get rewarded.
> NF: Do you think anyone who works hard is going to be rewarded for that work?
> Hank: No. There's no question. We have, there's a social system that reinforces the existing social system.

Here, we can see the conflicts that can occur from the disparate messages individuals receive about what they can accomplish versus what they experience. As a White man, Hank is told that he can achieve the American Dream if he just works hard enough. For him this is probably true; however, the ideology of the American Dream leaves out all the assistance he will receive along the way, and there are many cultural forces making it easy for him to ignore his privileges. Yet, at the same time, growing up in a working class environment and being able to identify with poor, urban, Black oppositional culture, Hank also knows this simple message is not all that simple.

Finally, we reach the point where Hank discusses his first exposure to the idea of racial privilege at the hands of a member of the Nation of Islam in London. The Muslim tells him that "White people are not necessarily responsible for the sins of their father, but that they need to recognize they have special privileges as a result of their birth into a certain skin color and to offer assistance to those who do not have that kind of advantage." Clearly, direct communication with a person of color brought this message home in a way that Hank was able to agree with completely. This openness to contact with people of color and the *opportunity* of contact makes all the difference when dealing with issues of race and identity construction.

Lest we end this interview with an overly simplistic, happy ending, Hank's last comment further illustrates the complexities of Whiteness. After the tape recorder was turned off, we start to talk about capstone papers that are term papers required in order to graduate. He tells me he only spent three hours working on his capstone paper. This comment illustrates two things. Although he has thought a lot about the political, economic, and social implications of race and class, he has yet to realize the daily benefits he receives from his White skin. Our discussion on the ways race and class interact to determine who gets rewarded for hard work was somehow distanced from his own experience of not working hard and not getting penalized for it. He did not seem to be aware of how his privileges as a White man worked to his advantage to construct his behavior and intentions as worthy and legitimate, regardless of how hard he worked at his studies.

A privilege that is often hidden in affirmative action debates is the ability of privileged individuals to be mediocre or to just get by in their work and not have it interpreted as a result of their race or gender. In fact, to be rewarded regardless of how their performance compares to others shows that they were given the benefit of the doubt due to their race or gender. Hank's casual statements reflect a life experience that has never been exposed to blatantly unfair judgments based solely on skin color and not on performance. While some people of color must work twice as hard to be considered equal, many White men are given the benefit of the doubt since they are predominantly judged by other White men, who may see a similar value system, work ethic, or individual worth reflected in the faces of other white men.

Fred

While Fred was also very cognizant of the direct connection between Hip Hop and larger social forces, he also focused on the humanity found in rap music and emphasized its "appeal to the rhythmic nature in people." Fred described the ability of rap music to communicate the specific realities of life for African-Americans in a different socioeconomic position than he, while putting forth a cultural critique about "the meanings of humanity . . . what it means to be American and [a] different way of looking at the overall American culture, that can really reach you."

Historically contextualizing Hip Hop as one of many results of cultural and political domination, Fred discussed the results of racial inequality in terms of domination and subordination, without making any reference to the third result: privilege. While he did mention that rap music made him "think differently about the car that my parents were driving, the house that I had, things like that," when asked directly about what it meant to him to be White, he replied:

> I don't, it's not the aspect of my background that I emphasize in my self-formation. It's a badge issue, you know, where in certain circles it's a benefit and in others it's a curse. Obviously more of the former than the latter. At some levels being White is considered a bad thing, the whole guilt factor. You worry about the things you control and I can't control my race for better or for worse, so I try to emphasize the beliefs that I have that can help improve things.

Here, we see the limits of focusing solely on the domination and subordination aspects of race. The ability for Whites to choose whether or not to emphasize their race is a privilege that remains invisible when focusing solely on the dominating aspects of race relations. Seeing race as a badge issue reaffirms it as concrete and real, not constructed. This allows for the inadvertent reaffirmation of racial difference, even as Fred strives to draw attention to human commonality. By stating that he cannot control his race, he relieves himself of any responsibility for the benefits he receives from his race. In the next phrase he uses the privilege he has to be judged without reference to his race. As a White man, he is rarely affected by negative stereotypes that could detrimentally shape the way his ideas are interpreted, as often occurs with rap music. With a dominant conceptualization of White as "normal," Fred is able to discuss controversial issues without appearing to be threatening to other Whites and without having his views attributed to his race or socioeconomic status. Meanwhile people of color often have to negotiate what they say, how they say it, whether or not they say it at all, based on the environment they are in.

In this section, Fred and Hank very effectively connect the issues discussed in rap music to social factors that are relevant across all sectors of life in America. By connecting the music to larger structures, they are able to place themselves and their lives in dialogue with the various issues raised in rap music. Hank interprets rap music through his experiences growing up working class. However, by focusing on class and ethnicity, the ability of rap music to elicit contemplations of Whiteness is constrained. Similarly, Fred focuses on aspects of domination and subordination to the detriment of the third result, privilege. This limits the type of actions possible to create change. While various social problems that are the results of domination can be eliminated, they will always manifest in new ways, creating new social problems until the third result of privilege is also eliminated. Focusing only on domination will inadvertently reaffirm some negative outcomes, regardless of good intentions.

Cognizance and Engagement:

Casper

Similar to Hank and Fred, Casper is very aware of the detailed political history that has shaped the formation of Hip Hop culture. The difference is that Casper has also understood her privileges. Casper was always aware of her Whiteness when listening to rap music with her group of Black friends. This awareness influenced her to begin questioning the cultural norms that dictated appropriate behavior for her. When accused of being a "poser," rather than de-racializing Hip Hop as Chris did, Casper began questioning the very concept of race itself:

> If I'm a White person that's considered Black because I can move that way (when dancing), then what is race in general? Like what is it if it's just a bunch of characteristics that I can take on, I can learn how to dance, I can learn this music, what is race?

Here Casper distinguishes between cultural differences that can be learned by anyone within a specific environment, and the biological assumptions underlying racist ideologies. Understanding that race is not a biological component, and yet seeing that it still shapes individuals' daily lives, she deconstructs the social and cultural mechanics that construct race. Through her relationships with her Black friends, Casper becomes cognizant of the differences that do exist and how these differences are created. With this knowledge, Casper learns about the impact race has on her life.

> There were a lot of times where I felt like I had no idea where they were coming from because obviously I've never been discriminated against like that based on my race... Like race wasn't a big part of it to me. I had never seen it like that because I was so ignorant of my privilege.

This statement illustrates a lot about race cognizance. Race cognizance signifies the conceptualization of difference along cultural lines while also understanding the different life experiences and values that have resulted from the institutionalization of social inequality. As opposed to seeing difference as innate and hierarchical, it reflects the reality of discrimination, colonization, and oppression. Race cognizance allows commonalties to exist between cultural groups and allows for the understanding of difference within cultural groups. While this paradigm complicates the idea of race and identity, it also provides strategies for anti-racist action and implicates Whites in the course of race relations (Frankenberg 1993: 14).

Casper's comment shows that the true difference between the races occurs from the very real effects these ideas have on laws, policies, values, and interpersonal relations that construct racial difference through disparate treatment and differential access to resources. Being discriminated against or seeing the very damaging effects of racial stratification creates a perspective on the world that cannot be ignored or erased, as it is in the color-blind paradigm. Being cognizant of the many ways social forces shape lives, both positively and negatively, allows strategies to be developed that effectively create change by confronting the ideologies that seem "common sense" until the values they rely on are revealed.

> Even though I don't consider myself a racist, there are things about me that I don't realize, like that I've been born with or that I've been raised with, my own privilege, my own ignorance and those are all racist things even though I try as hard as I can not to be a racist.

This comment brings home some of the ramifications of White privilege. Racism is a structural phenomenon, not necessarily just the result of deliberate acts by malicious individuals. White people receive benefits from their White skin regardless of whether they ask for them. White people are bound together by the viewpoints, privileges and constructions of daily experience that are broadcast as "normal." The ramifications of these factors affect every person in this country. Once you are cognizant of what exactly race is, which is predominantly a construction based on the historical structure of oppression and privilege, then the place that White people hold with respect to taking responsibility for the state of race relations becomes clear.

For Casper, listening to rap music was a way of reaffirming the community she had built with Black friends in high school and later in college. This influence exposed her to the political and social issues dealt with in rap music and also shaped her conceptualization of her Whiteness. Through this music she constructed a community based on anti-racist sentiments and a deep questioning of society and identity. In this way, rap music was able to maintain its symbolic power, remaining a cultural product and not becoming merely a spectacle to satisfy personal desires and prevent significant discourse on social issues. Reciprocally, Casper constructed a White racial identity that took into account the results of domination, subordination, and privilege, thereby creating effective resistance to hegemonic conceptions of race.

Each of these interviews illustrated a complex relationship between how each subject interpreted rap music and conceptualized their own racial identity. Since there was no way to measure the causal relationship between these two variables, the next section will explore an antecedent variable that heavily influenced each subject's position along the continuum.

Segregation:

Since awareness of Whiteness and the interpretation of rap music were interrelated, both influencing each other and changing over time, I decided to look for an antecedent variable that could possibly explain the differences among interviewees. Except for Maggie, who only began listening to rap music a few months ago, each interviewee brought up issues surrounding their upbringing, schools, neighborhoods and friends that influenced the way they thought of rap music or their Whiteness. Consistently for each person, the level of segregation in his or her childhood had a strong impact on how rap music was interpreted.

> Jenny: I went pretty much to an all White school and most of my friends were White. My best friend in high school, she was White also, but she lived near the ghetto.

For Jenny, while she had many experiences and friendships with people of color in inner city neighborhoods, her school was predominantly White. She discusses her interest in Hip Hop as growing out of a desire to fit in at her lower middle class school and to detach from the stereotypes and sheltering associated with her upper middle class background. She was introduced to Hip Hop and friends of color through her White girlfriend.

> Chris: The suburb I grew up in was a suburb northwest of Houston and it was pretty much all White. Not because there was a lot of racism involved but just because that was the way the place was made up, it was just the fact that a lot of White people lived in that area, not many Blacks did.

Chris got into rap music through MTV and the radio and did not mention the influence of any people of color. Due to this avenue of introduction, Chris sees his lifestyle as normal, never questioning any of the forces that have created the all-white environment he grew up in. He attributes it purely to chance, which is another ideology that draws attention to individual attributes and away from the effects of historical patterns or government policies.

> Fred: Some of my friends, and it was a pretty ethnically mixed group. We didn't have any African-Americans in the class but some of my best friends that I grew up with had really strong Indian cultures and Middle Eastern cultures. And it wasn't so much as, their race never mattered but, it didn't really, I'm trying to explain how [I] just grew up respecting a wide variety of cultures and seeing, probably getting a much deeper look into that sort of thing than I should have about the situation.

Fred was introduced to the music by a multicultural group of friends who imbued him with an exploratory interest in music. While Dallas was also divided into "White environments and Black environments,"[1] Fred questioned the construction of the racial social geography he experienced when traveling from his house to his friends' houses.[2]

> Hank: At the age 11, 12, I was confronted with the same sort of things they would talk about. The drugs, the violence, we would have drive-bys at the junior high, we had drugs, we had mysterious fires... everybody knew it was arson, stuff like that. It was definitely a working class school. It was probably a third, a third, a third, Hispanic, African-American and European-American. There was a lot of segregation [but] my particular group was intermixed. I've always found my self a person who is drawn toward multiethnic sorts of groups and environments.

Due to the environment that Hank grew up in, Hip Hop music was something he could identify with on a class level. Many of the issues dealt with in rap music were manifested in his daily life at a multicultural, working class school. In addition, his friends who were Latino and White introduced him to the music, making the racist and class implications of the music very salient. Rap music also helps Hank connect his working class background and the life experiences of rap musicians to larger social structures. His college studies in political science have served to reinforce this connection and deepen his understanding.

> I'm in Houston... a suburb of Houston. However, it's not a White suburb. It's a place filled with every kind of race you could probably imagine, every kind of class income level, I mean, just anything you could imagine, that's what we had. So, coming from a place like that really affected my perception of race in general. My parents were always very aware of racism and always wanted me to stay away from that... And that's why we moved to where we moved because we were

---

1. Described in the interview with Chris.
2. Frankenberg, 44. "This concept refers to the racial and ethnic mapping of environments in physical and social terms. It illuminates the ways racism shapes the daily environments of individuals and allows us to view the historical, social and political forces which brought these environments into being."

gonna move to the Woodlands but that's like White flight over there, so my parents were like, no, we're gonna move here.

Casper had the benefit of being educated about racial issues by her parents. Rather than finding all White spaces "normal" and unquestionable, Casper and her parents sought out integrated spaces. Casper was educated at an early age about White flight, segregation, and anti-racism. She was also introduced to rap music by a group of Black friends. Rather than an alternative (rebellious) form of identity construction, or another way to be different but still an individual, listening and dancing to rap music created and reaffirmed a sense of community with her group of friends across race and class lines. Casper found it much easier to reject dominant ideologies because her family, school and neighborhood provided an alternative language for conceptualizing race and rap music.

As segregation is created by a White supremacist value system, so it perpetuates this system. Once this structural factor was removed, rap music was found to have a large impact on the viewpoints of the participants who grew up in integrated spaces. It gave Fred an alternative construction of American history and a new viewpoint on what it means to be American. It challenged Casper to question the construction of race and step outside her comfort zone. And it helped Hank connect his college studies on social structures to the lives of urban, poor, African-Americans.

Conclusion

After interviewing 6 White students at a predominantly White private university, inductive reasoning and grounded theory methods uncovered a complex relationship between the interpretation and construction of rap music and how each subject conceptualized their Whiteness. "The interpretation of the material world and the ways we explain and understand it 'generates experience' and, therefore, the 'experience' of lived Whiteness is something continually constructed, reconstructed and transformed for White people" (Mahoney 1995: 331). For those who never thought about their racial identity or had a very rudimentary understanding of it, rap music was interpreted as a non-political expression of an individual rapper's experiences. It was also seen as similar to teenage rebellion, an obscene product with no positive message and as a musical type outside any racial context. Hip Hop culture became for some an alternative ethnic identity that youth could assume and consume in order to be more unique.

With the pop music explosion of White, working class rap artist Eminem, the ease with which suburban White youth can adopt Hip Hop as an ethnic identity can only increase. Racial ideologies that essentialize what it means to be White or Black do not take into account the complex relationship between class, race and place when determining identity. White fans of Hip Hop only see a White guy modeling, not only how best to "act Black," but also that it is okay for a White person to appropriate Hip Hop culture no matter where they come from. Eminem is a very complex figure who deserves to be studied in his own right. However, the complexity that he represents in American culture is not maintained by the fans who only see him as a model for how to belong to a costless, voluntary, and symbolic community that does not infringe on their individuality.

For those who saw rap music as a political and cultural critique of dominant society, rap music drew their attention to class issues, gave them a different perspective on the ways domination and subordination manifested themselves and caused them to think about their own ethnic identity. However, by being able to focus on these issues, the privileges that are also a result of systems of oppression remained invisible.

Once these privileges became visible then the personal experiences described in rap music were seen as indicators of larger social structures that shaped the lives of Whites as well as people of color. Discrimination and prejudice were understood to be aspects of a system of oppression in which each person was accountable for the benefits and privileges they received as White Americans. Rather than racism being a deliberate act by an individual, it was understood to be culturally, socially, and historically created and perpetuated. Privilege was understood to be the structural result of this system for White Americans and a major component of Whiteness.

The antecedent variable that seemed to predict how each subject would interpret rap and construct their racial identity was the level of segregation experienced in childhood schools or neighborhoods. The more segregated environment the subject came from, the less cognizant of race, privilege and Whiteness they were and vice versa. Thus, when race was supported by structural factors that resulted from a White supremacist value system, that system was perpetuated.

College campuses are one of the primary spaces where many of today's youth are exposed to new people and ideas. It is also the place with the highest rate of hate crimes. Hip Hop and rap music can create some wonderful opportunities to bring people together, regardless of their reasons for listening to the music, and create dialogues about issues such as racism, classism, sexism, media representation, cultural appropriation, crime, drugs, the criminal justice system, institutional discrimination and many others.

White people who listen to Hip Hop for social justice oriented reasons can be a valuable resource on college campuses striving to integrate and educate students about multicultural issues. For those who are sensitive to the complex issues dealt with in rap music, this can create numerous opportunities to form new social groups based on more inclusive ideologies and powerful identities.

However, for those Whites who deracialize or individualize rap there are also risks involved regarding the stereotypes and essentialistic ideas that they may have about African-Americans that can seriously impact how they interact with or treat other African-American students. At this private university, there were numerous occasions of White students casually calling African-American students the N-- word. One explanation was that since White students heard the word used often in rap songs and did not have to understand the history or politics surrounding use of that word, they created serious hurt and anger among Black students without taking responsibility for their behavior or acknowledging the racism inherent in such behavior. While interpreting the dialogue for their fellow White students, they used their privilege of glossing over the racialized content of these interactions, stating that Black students were too sensitive and did not understand the casual manner in which it was meant. It can be very hard to create a dialogue with those White people who are not aware of how racial privilege or larger social structures shape their lives. Since it is not possible to tell at first glance why an individual is listening to rap music or what they are getting out of it, it is important not to make assumptions and instead to take advantage of every opportunity to create dialogue.

While none of this data is generalizable, it indicates important trends in White racial identity construction and other areas of research in race relations. Rather than continuing to study domination and subordination in systems of oppression, it is also necessary to explore the techniques and strategies used to construct the invisibility and dominance of Whiteness. Until privilege is deconstructed and de-normalized, structural and cultural racism will continue to exist.

Appendix A: List of Qualitative Questions

1) When and how did you first become interested in rap music? Through friends, the radio, a concert, etc.?

2) How often do you listen to rap music now?

3) What artists do you listen to?

4) What about rap music do you specifically like?

5) Do you think rap music is a reflection of reality or entertainment or both?

6) What are your favorite songs? Why? Can you describe them?

6) Are you able to identify with anything in hip hop music or culture?

8) Does listening to rap music make you think differently about who you are, what you have, where you came from or anything else?

9) People say rap music is very sexist and violent. What do you think about that?

10) Does hip-hop make you think about your whiteness? Why or why not?

11) Are there situations in general that do make you think about your whiteness? How did that make you feel?

12) Do you think rap music reinforces stereotypes or deconstructs stereotypes about Black people?

13) What do you think of when you hear the word white? What does it mean to you to be white?

Additional questions added later:

14) Do you think rap is political?

15) Does listening to rap music lead you to be concerned about social issues or does your concern with social issues lead you to listen to rap music?

16) In those situations where you are aware of your whiteness, have you ever thought before today about how those experiences give you insight into what black students must feel attending a predominantly white campus? If not, why not?

17) Do you think we live in a meritocracy?

References

Bender, A. 1993. "Constructing Racial Rhetoric: Media Depictions of Harm in Heavy Metal and Rap Music." *American Sociological Review* 58: 753-767.

Bennett, A. 1999. "Rappin' on the Tyne: White Hip Hop Culture in Northeast England - An Ethnographic Study." *The Sociological Review* 47(1): 1-21.

Binder, A. 1993. "Constructing Racial Rhetoric: Media Depictions of Harm in Heavy Metal and Rap Music." *American Sociological Review* 58: 753-767.

Frankenberg, R. 1993. *The Social Construction of Whiteness: White Women, Race Matters*. Minneapolis, MN: University of Minnesota Press.

Hartigan, J. 1997. "Establishing the Fact of Whiteness." *American Anthropologist* 99(3).

Hebdige, D. 1979. *Subculture: The Meaning of Style*. London: Methuen.

Kleinman, S. and M. Copp. *Emotions and Fieldwork*. Newbury Park: Sage Publications, Inc.

Lears, T. J. J. 1985. "The Concept of Cultural Hegemony: Problems and Possibilities." *American Historical Review* 90:567-593.

Lehr, V. 1995. "Redefining and Building Community: The Importance of Anger." *Women and Politics* 15(1): 37-63.

Mahoney, M. 1995. "The Social Construction of Whiteness," pp. 330- 333 in *Critical White Studies: Looking Behind the Mirror*, edited by Richard Delgado and Jean Stefancic. Philadelphia: Temple University Press.

Martinez, T. 1997. "Popular Culture as Oppositional Culture: Rap as Resistance." *Sociological Perspectives* 40(2): 265-286.
http://wilsontxt.hwwilson.com/pdfhtml/00630/MH4EE/HSN.htm.

Mitchell, B. and J. Feagin. 1995. "American's Racial-Ethnic Cultures: Opposition Within a Mythical Melting Pot." Pp. 65-86 in Toward the Multicultural University, edited by Benjamin Bowser, Terry Jones and Gale Auletta Young. Westport, CT: Praiger.

Pena, M. 1999. *Musica Tejana*. College Station, TX: Texas A&M University Press.

Waters, M. 1990. *Ethnic Options: Choosing Identities in America*. Berkeley, CA: University of California Press.

Wildman, S. and A. Davis. 1996. "Making Systems of Privilege Visible," pp. 314-319 in *Critical White Studies: Looking Behind the Mirror*, edited by Richard Delgado and Jean Stefancic. Philadelphia: University Press.

——. "What Kind of White Person Are You?"
http://euroamerican.org/editor/Edit0499.htm.

Article 5

African American University Students: Revisiting African American University Students' Interpersonal Style "Switching" on Predominantly White Campuses

Wanda Collins,[1] Robbie J. Steward, and Douglas Neil

African American university student populations make up from as few as 3% to as many as 15% of the large, state, predominantly White institutions of higher education in the USA today. As early as 1991, Jones' survey indicated that as many as 75% of Black Americans

---

[1] During the process of moving this work to publication, Wanda Collins passed from this earth. She was a dear, precious, and outstanding individual who was committed to making the world a more positive place for those who were less fortunate. Wanda brought joy to all with whom she worked and maintained a spirit of perseverance and a strong professional commitment until the end of her very short existence among us. At the time of the research, she was a third year doctoral student enrolled in the Michigan State University Counselor Education program. Her primary area of interest was multicultural counseling training. We dedicate this work to Wanda and her family as we continue to miss her physical presence among us.

attending college attend predominantly White universities in spite of consistent reports in the literature indicating higher attrition, higher alienation, and a greater number of experiences of racism than Whites and members of some other racial/ethnic minority groups in such settings (Griffin, 1991; Henderson, 1988; Steward, Germain, & Jackson, 1992; Steward, Jackson, Sr., & Jackson, 1990). Better understanding of the issues uniquely related to African Americans' interpersonal adjustment to this setting is the focus of the works of many researchers, scholars, and practitioners.

Interpersonal Style

Interpersonal style is defined as the manner in which individuals perceive others and view themselves in interactions (Schutz, 1978). Minority students' interpersonal styles have been significantly correlated with increased academic retention, effective coping, ethnic identity, self-esteem and psychological adjustment and well-being (Cantrall & Pete, 1990; Kazaleh, 1986; Martinez, 1987; Pertusali, 1988). Specifically, African American university students' on-campus interpersonal style has been empirically linked with the experience of alienation (Steward, Jackson, Sr., & Jackson, 1990). African American students' interpersonal style while in predominantly White on-campus settings was found to be significantly related to students' reported experience of alienation. Findings from this study indicated that the more students reported wanting close intimate ties with Whites, the greater degree of reported alienation. Given all of these significant relationships, it would seem imperative that researchers revisit the examination of African Americans' means of engaging the predominantly White university campus setting.

One phenomenon that complicates the study of racial ethnic minorities' interpersonal styles in predominantly White settings is interpersonal style switching based upon the racial composition of a setting at any given time. The alternation model of second-culture acquisition assumes that it is possible for individuals to know and understand two different cultures and that they can alter his or her behavior to fit a particular social context (LaFromboise, Coleman, & Gerton, 1993; Ogbu & Matute-Bianchi, 1986; Ramirez, 1984). This hypothesis implies that individuals who alternate their behavior appropriate to two targeted cultures will be less anxious than one who does not (Saville-Troike, 1981). Some scholars (Garcia, 1983; Rashid,

1984; Rogler, Cortes, & Malgady, 1991) speculated that individuals who have the ability to effectively switch their interpersonal styles might well exhibit higher cognitive functioning and mental health status than people who are monocultural, assimilated, or acculturated.

Willie (1981) and Loo and Rolison (1986) hypothesized that Black students actually have different interactional styles when interacting in an all-White environment than in an all-Black environment. Loo and Rolison (1986) proposed that Black students might experience a two-world existence within which two different interactional styles are required and for which two different comfort levels are experienced. In addition, Anderson's conceptual and empirical work (1990,1999) supports the existence of interactional style switching among African Americans even within all-Black community settings. He proposes that individuals' ability to shift in interpersonal styles within African American communities, or "code-switching", is an important part of Black socialization. Whether within White or Black settings, it appears critical that research continues to explore the phenomenon of 'interpersonal style switching' among African Americans.

Steward, Jackson, & Jackson (1990) found support for the combined hypothesis that interpersonal style switching among the most academically prepared minorities does occur. Findings from this study of the most successful African American students on a large predominantly White campus indicated that students behaved differently when in an all White campus environment than when in an all Black campus environment. Rashid (1984) defined this type of biculturalism for African Americans as the ability to function effectively and productively within the context of American's core institutions while retaining a sense of self and African ethnic identity. The finding of this study was particularly noteworthy given that significant differences in styles based on racial composition situation were not found in a subsequent study of the most academically prepared Asian and Hispanic American students in the same setting (Steward, Germain, & Jackson, 1992).

Supporting earlier and current literature, participants' explanation for this switching was attributed to their perception of a necessity to consciously adjust their interpersonal style to more effectively manage negative incidents and daily race-related hassles (Griffin, 1991; Henderson, 1988; Jones, 1991; Thompson, Anderson, & Bakeman, 2000). Consequently, it might be concluded that shifting interpersonal style among some minorities might not be solely an issue of shifting due to cultural differences between majority and minority populations, but as a means to mediate and rise above the toxicity and barriers present in the predominantly White setting due to racism. Continual examination of this tendency to shift or to avoid shifting might be particularly important given that in general, even among the most academically successful students, Black students' interpersonal styles tended to reflect a tendency toward social isolation. It appears that for the general population student, success is positively correlated with the degree of integration into the academic and social systems of the university (Baumgart & Johnstone, 1977; Pascarella & Terenzini, 1986), for African Americans on predominantly White university campuses, this may not completely be the case.

Purpose of this Study

Although the above literature review alone presents a strong enough rationale for the preponderance of literature addressing African American students' interpersonal styles and experiences on predominantly White universities, the results of the early works discussed above must be read with some caution. In many ways, the university is a microcosm of the general society, reflecting aspects of its cultural norms and values (Burbach & Thompson, 1972; Loo & Rolison, 1986), and the world has changed, along with the university setting in a number of ways within the last two decades. First, most state universities have made concerted efforts to increase and maintain the presence of racial/ethnic minority faculty, staff, and students. With a more visible presence of persons of color, today's African American students may not experience the same degree of hopelessness, haplessness, and normlessness as those in the past (alienation). Second, given bussing and the more extensive racial integration of both urban and suburban communities, many African American and White students may be admitted to predominantly White campuses with more social exposure to one another and, therefore, with higher levels of inter-racial comfort. Consequently, both major societal changes may result in a diminished press to switch interpersonally based on the racial composition of the setting. These general cultural shifts may result in interpersonal styles that are both more social than the 'loner' found in the earlier studies and in interpersonal styles that are consistent regardless of the setting. The African American experience on predominantly White campuses might have changed significantly within the last twenty years.

The objective of this study is to partially replicate the earlier study of Steward, Jackson, & Jackson (1990). The following research questions are addressed: Do today's Black students change interpersonal styles to accommodate predominantly White or predominantly Black campus situations? Do today's Black students' interpersonal styles significantly differ from the interpersonal styles found in Steward et al (1990)? Do today's Black students' interpersonal styles reflect a greater degree of social integration than those found in the earlier study? Given the societal changes discussed above, it is hypothesized that: a) today's African American students' interpersonal styles will not be significantly different based on the racial composition of the setting; b) today's African American students' interpersonal styles will be significantly different from those in the earlier study; and, c) today's African American students' interpersonal styles will reflect a greater degree of social engagement than those in the earlier study.

Method

Participants

Participants were 68 African American undergraduate students, having a mean age of 20, and enrolled in a large predominantly White Midwestern University (n = 45,000) with an African American student population of approximately 7%. Participation in the study was strictly voluntary and students were debriefed about the study after survey completion. Participants were conveniently selected from several undergraduate courses within the College of Education and African American student organizations on campus. Participants completed packets that contained the following: a consent for research participation, demographic data sheet, and two copies of Fundamental Interpersonal Relations Orientation-Behavior Scale (FIRO-B)(Shultz, 1967).

Instruments

Demographic data Sheet consisted of 12 items concerning participants' personal and academic background. The items requested were age, sex, major, grade classification, grade point average, familial residency, family education, and area of study will be requested from each student. In addition, participants completed two Schultz's

Fundamental Interpersonal Relations Orientations Questionnaires (FIRO-B) measures. To determine participants' interpersonal styles in a predominately White and in a predominately Black campus environment, the researchers requested that participants complete one FIRO-B, marked W, as they have behaved in an all White campus setting, and complete the second FIRO-B, marked B, as they have behaved in an all Black campus setting.

Schultz's Fundamental Interpersonal Relations Orientations Questionnaire (FIRO-B). The FIRO-B is a self-administered written measure that assesses individuals' interpersonal style. It consists of 54 Likert items reflecting three behavioral dimensions: inclusion (the degree to which one associates with others; control (the extent to which one assumes responsibility, makes decisions, or dominates people); and affection (the degree to which one becomes emotionally involved with others)(Shultz, 1978).

There are two scores, symbolized by 'w' and 'e', are obtained for each dimension. The 'w' score represents what the individual wants from each other people. The 'e' score represents the person's expressed or manifest behavior. It is the overt, observable behavior. There are 18 Likert scale items composed of each dimension, with scores ranging from 0-9. Combining the scores of the six scales (adding and subtracting) six additional scores may be obtain (two for each of the three interpersonal needs) indicating the overall amount of interaction. Higher expressed scores indicate higher frequency of behaviors is related to inclusion, control, and affection. Scores of 0-1 are considered extremely low; 2-3, low; 4-5, medium; 6-7, high; and, 8-9, extremely high. The instruments' content validity is based on factor analyses; the reliability estimate is .94 for all six scales. The range of mean coefficients of stability for the six scales is .84-.88.

Results

Table 1 presents the means and standard deviations of each FIRO-B subscale by situation. T tests were used to examine the mean differences existing between FIRO-B component scores. No significant (p = .05) differences were found between the interpersonal styles between the all Black and all White situations.

Table 1. T-test results for comparison of FIRO-B Interaction Components in an All-White Situation and in an All-Black Situation (N = 68).

Variable	M	SD	
Variance		t	

Expressed Inclusion				
White	3.29	2.45	6.00	1.73
Black	3.96	3.05	9.01	
Expressed Control				
White	2.21	2.09	4.38	1.33
Black	2.65	2.70	7.28	
Expressed Affection				
White	2.50	2.08	4.34	1.85
Black	3.16	2.80	7.84	
Wanted Inclusion				
White	2.38	2.94	8.66	1.88
Black	3.26	3.52	12.41	
Wanted Control				
White	1.68	1.68	2.82	.00
Black	1.68	2.28	5.18	
Wanted Affection				
White	3.46	4.04	16.31	.42
Black	3.66	2.91	8.47	

* No significant differences were found between situations.

Table 2 presents the results of the current and past studies' FIRO-B subscale results by score categories. In the current study, components of interpersonal style categorized as low were expressed inclusion with Whites, expressed control with Whites and Blacks, expressed affection with Whites and Blacks, wanted inclusion with Whites and Blacks, wanted control with Whites and Blacks, and wanted affection with Whites; components of interpersonal style categorized as medium were expressed inclusion and wanted affection with Blacks. There were no subscale scores that could be categorized as extremely low, high, or extremely high.

We believed that there were also noteworthy points in the comparison between the results of the past and current studies. In interpersonal styles within all Black situations, participants' scores indicated greater expressed inclusion (low to medium), greater wanted inclusion (extremely low to low), greater wanted affection (extremely low to medium), and lower wanted control (extremely high to low) in the current study than in the past.

Table 2. FIRO-B Interaction Component Scores by Category comparing current and past studies

Interaction Component	All Black Past	All Black Current	All White Past	All White Current
Expressed Inclusion	Low	Medium	Medium	Low
Expressed Control	Medium	Low	Medium	Low
Expressed Affection	Low	Low	Low	Low
Wanted Inclusion	Extremely Low	Low	Low	Low
Wanted Control	Extremely High	Low	Extremely High	Low
Wanted Affection	Extremely low	Medium Low	Extremely	Low

In interpersonal styles within all White situations, participants FIRO-B scores indicated lower expressed inclusion (medium to low), lower expressed control (medium to low), lower wanted control (extremely high to low), and higher wanted affection (extremely low to low) in the current study than in the past. FIRO-B subscale scores remained the same in the following areas across studies: expressed affection in both White and Black situations (low); and, wanted inclusion in White situation (low).

Discussion

First, no significant differences were found between participants' interpersonal style based on the racial composition of the on-campus setting. At first glance, findings suggest that today's African American students are somewhat consistent in behavior regardless of the setting. One possible explanation for the absence of a significant difference between the two situations is societal changes and campus climate changes that have occurred over the past 2 decades. However, given the literature, another possible explanation is that these students were not the 'most academically prepared' seniors who were included in the prior study. Given that behavioral switching has been associated with higher cognitive functioning and academic preparedness, targeting only a general population of students may have resulted in a 'washing' out of differences that might have been apparent otherwise.

Second, all FIRO-B scores were 'low' except in expressed inclusion and wanted affection when in the all-Black situation (medium). Low scores were also consistent with those found in the prior study in expressed affection in both situations and wanted inclusion in the White situation. Participants in this study appear to have assumed somewhat of a social 'hesitancy' interpersonal style. Though there is some indication of some movement toward other African Americans while in an all-Black situation (medium expressed inclusion scores), there is also some indication that there is a wish for closer intimate relationships while in these same situations (medium wanted affection) than what they express (low expressed affection). All other scores indicate hesitancy for self-involvement (low expressed scores) and a heightened selectivity with whom they want to be in involved (low wanted scores) regardless of the situation. It appears that African American students, in general, continue to assume what Steward et al

(1990) referred to as the 'loner' style as a means to mediate their experiences within the predominantly White campus environment.

However, another explanation for finding the 'loner' style in this student population on predominantly White campuses is that students may have arrived on campus with a style of interpersonal hesitancy. Those African Americans who are most competitive for admissions to a large, predominantly White state institution may have already acquired a 'loner' stance prior to admission in order to most effectively pursue academic excellence. This possible explanation has sometimes been addressed tangentially in the literature addressing the association between academic success and 'Whiteness' among some urban African American students. Consequently, students are most academically prepared and most ready for college might be those who are already somewhat isolated. However, regardless of the etiology of the 'loner' interpersonal style, the association between success and being alone may have a significant impact on future social functioning, lifestyle, and psychological well-being.

It would appear that this consistent finding would certainly warrant greater attention in the literature for a number of reasons. Often student development literature purports the notion that college life is most successful for students who are engaged socially within the university settings (Tinto, 1982, 1985; Pascarella & Terenzini, 1986). Consequently, academic success may be erroneously associated with the social competence and psychological well-being. However, this may not be the case for high achieving African American university students. Such students may, in fact, experience greater degrees of unattended alienation and isolation than Whites and other racial/ethnic minorities on campus (Steward, et al, 1990; Steward, et al, 1992). This outcome becomes increasing more problematic given findings from an earlier study that identified a significant and positive relationship between wanted friendship when with Whites (FIRO-B I Affection subscale) and reported feelings of alienation on campus. So any efforts on the part of African American students in predominantly White campus settings to mediate feelings of alienation may exacerbate the 'problem' instead of making it better. It would seem important for student affairs staff to provide orientation that normalizes this 'sense of isolation' for some students, including the most academically prepared, and develop campus services and programs that will specifically attend to this aspect of university student development.

Third, the results suggest one population behavioral shift found over time that these authors believe to be noteworthy. One most stark change was related to the Control FIRO-B subscale. Given these results, African American students appear to be moving toward greater avoidance of leadership opportunities (shifting from medium to low expressed control scores) and greater independence in decision-making (shifting from extremely high to low wanted control). This trend is particularly important given that it was found to occur in both the all White and all Black campus situations.

This first shift is easily explained by the comparison between a population of lower academic status group in this study (freshmen and sophomores) and seniors in the prior study. It would make sense that seniors would be more apt to move comfortably into the role of leadership than freshmen and sophomore. However, this explanation also highlights the potential problematic outcomes of the second shift. It would appear even more critical that given their stage of development, freshmen and sophomores would actually want more or at least as much guidance and assistance (wanted control) than seniors. The opposite was found to be the case. The findings from this study indicate a possible premature 'foreclosure' in information gathering that may have severe, negative implications on the process of career development and decision-making. Future research in this area is certainly warranted.

A post-hoc analysis was performed to explore the possibility of gender differences among African American students within this setting. Given the most recent wide-spread media that highlights the plight of African American men and their limited presence on university campuses, this analysis appeared warranted. African American women were found to have significantly higher FIRO-B scores than African American men on two subscales: wanted Affection in an all Black campus situation ($F = 4.20$; $p = .04$); and, expressed Inclusion in an all White campus situation ($F = 4.22$; $p = .04$). Black women had a mean wanted Affection score in the Black campus situation of 4.16 (sd = 2.98); whereas Black men had a mean score of 2.64 (sd = 2.54). Black women had a mean expressed Inclusion score in the White campus situation of 3.86 (sd = 2.62); whereas, Black men had a mean score of 2.60 (sd = 1.71). Findings indicate that: African American women in an all Black campus situation tend to want more intimacy than African American men; and, African American women in an all White campus situation tend to actively pursue interpersonal engagement moreso than African American men. No other significant gender differences were found. It is unclear at this point if these differences are due to differential treatment within settings or due to differences in socialization or an interaction of both. For example, we do not know if African American men wanted less empathy while in the all Black situation because their needs are automatically met to a degree to which they are satisfied and those of African American women are not, or that African American men have fewer needs for empathy in that setting than African American women. Likewise, we do not know if African American women pursue interpersonal engagement moreso within an all White situation because Whites approach them less often than they approach African American men, or if African American women see greater importance in approaching others in these settings than African American men, or if African American women are received more positively within these settings than African American men and consequently move toward social engagement more often. These are questions that might fuel additional empirical study. Future research examining the underlying cause of these gender differences and the academic outcomes would lead to our better understanding the phenomenon of differential attrition rates between African American men and women on predominantly White campuses. In addition, these findings suggest the need for gender-specific student development services designed to meet the unique experiences of both African American men and women on predominantly White university campuses.

In summary, each university campus must assume some responsibility in monitoring population trends and the psychosocial and career development implications of the trends identified. Program development must be updated to serve the most recent population and not rely solely on the literature that may be periodically outdated presenting findings that are suitable for a population of students that no longer exist. Given the already significantly higher attrition of African American students on predominantly White campuses, it would seem particularly critical that this would occur for this population. Future research in this area is strongly suggested and encouraged.

References

Anderson, E. 1990. *Street Wise: Race, class, and change in an urban community.* The University of Chicago Press: Chicago, IL.

_____ 1999. *Code of the Street: Decency, violence, and the moral life of the inner city.* W.W. Norton & Company: New York, NY.

Baumgart, N. L., and J. N. Johnstone. 1977. Attrition at an Australian university: A case study. *Journal of Higher Education*, 48, 553-570.

Burbach, H. J., and M. A. Thompson. 1972. Development of a contextual measure of alienation. *Psychological Reports*, 33, 273-274.

Cantrall, B., and L. Pete. 1990, April. *Navajo culture: A bridge to the rest of the world.* Paper presented at the annual meeting of the American Educational Research Association, Boston.

Garcia, H. W. 1983. Bilingualism, biculturalism and the educational system. *Journal of Non-White Concerns in Personnel and Guidance*, 11, 67-74.

Griffin, J. T. 1991. Racism and humiliation in the African American community. *Journal of Primary Prevention*, 12, 149-167.

Henderson, P. L. 1988. The invisible minority: Black students at a southern White university. *Journal of College Student Development*, 29, 349-355.

Jones, E. P. 1991. The impact of economic, political, and social factors on recent overt Black/White racial conflict in higher education in the United States. *Journal of Negro Education*, 60, 524-537.

Kazaleh, F. A. 1986. *Biculturalism and adjustment: A study of Famallah-American adolescents in Jacksonville, Florida.* Dissertation Abstracts International, 47, 448A. University Microfilms No. DA8609672.

LaFromboise, T., Coleman, H. L. K., and J. Gerton. 1993. Psychological impact of biculturalism evidence and theory. *Psychological Bulletin*, 114, 395-412.

Loo, C. M., and G. Rolison. 1986. Alienation of ethnic minority students at a predominantly White university. *Journal of Higher Education*, 57, 58-77.

Martinez, A. R. 1987. *The effects of acculturation and racial identity on self-esteem and psychological well-being among young Puerto Ricans.* Dissertation Abstracts International, 48, 916B. University Microfilms No. DA8801737.

Ogbu, J. U. and M. A. Matute-Bianchi. 1986. *Understanding sociocultural factors: Knowledge, identity, and social adjustment.* In California State Department of Education, Bilingual Education Office, Beyond language: Social and cultural factors in schooling (pp. 73-142). Sacramento: CA: California State University—Los Angeles, Evaluation, Dissemination and Assessment Center.

Pascarella, E. T., and P. T. Terenzini. 1986. Informal, interaction with faculty and freshmen ratings of academic and non-academic experiences of college. *Journal of Educational Research*, 70, 35-41.

Pertusali, L. 1988. Beyond segregation or integration: A case study from effective Native American education. *Journal of American Indian Education*, 27, 10-20.

Ramirez, M. 1984. Assessing and understanding biculturalism-Multiculturalism in Mexican-American adults. In J. Martinez & R. H. Mendoza (Eds.), *Chicano psychology* (pp.77-94). San Diego, Ca: Academic Press.

Rashid, H. M. 1984. Promoting biculturalism in young African-American children. *Young Children*, 38, 13-23.

Rogler, L. H., Cortes, D. E., and R. G. Malgady. 1991. Acculturation and mental health status among Hispanics. *American Psychologist*, 46, 585-597.

Saville-Troike, M. 1981. *The development of bilingual and bicultural competence in young children.* Urbana, IL: Clearinghouse on elementary and early childhood education. ERIC Document Reproduction Service No. ED 206376.

Schutz, W. C. 1967. *The FIRO scales.* Palo Alto, CA: Consulting Psychologists Press.

Schutz, W. C. 1978. *FIRO awareness scales manual.* Palo Alto, CA: Consulting Psychologists Press.

Steward, R. J., Germain, S., and J. D. Jackson. 1992. Alienation and interactional style: A study of successful Anglo, Asian, and Hispanic university students. *Journal of College Student Development*, 33, 149-156.

Steward, R. J., Jackson, Sr., M. R., and J. D. Jackson. 1990. Alienation and interactional styles in a predominantly White environment: A study of successful Black students. *Journal of College Student Development*, 31, 509-515.

Thompson, C. P., Anderson, L. P., and R. A. Bakeman. 2000. Effects of racial socialization and racial identity on acculturative stress in African American college students. *Cultural Diversity and Ethnic Minority Psychology*, 6, 196-210.

Tinto, V. 1982. Limits of theory and practice in student attrition. *Journal of Higher Education*, 53, 6, 687-699.

Tinto, V. (1985). Dropout from higher education: A theoretical synthesis of recent research. *Review of Educational Research*, 45, 89-125.

Willie, C. V. (1981). *The ivory and ebony towers*. Lexington, MA: Heath.

Article 6

SOCIAL DISTANCE AND COLLEGE STUDENTS AT A NORTHERN NEW JERSEY UNIVERSITY

Gabe T. Wang and Kathleen Korgen

If you look at the typical cafeteria on a college campus today, you will find racial segregation. Black students and white students tend not to mix in campus dining areas. Even on campuses with relatively high percentages of nonwhites, the picture remains the same. Most students claim, however, that this separation of the races does not indicate any hostility between the two. It appears, however, to indicate a rather large degree of social distance between black and white college students. When a high degree of social distance between groups of persons exists, a lack of empathy and even possible anatagonism may exist between members of the two groups.

Previous research indicates that social distance may be influenced by several factors, including the degree of diversity in society (Goldberg and Kirschenbaum 1989; McCallister and Moore 1991; Netting 1991) and world events (Bogardus 1968; Owen et. al 1978). Social Learning Theory facilitates our understanding of how such factors can affect social distance. According to Social Learning Theory, people determine their behavior based upon what they have learned and what they believe will be the consequences of their actions (Bandura 1977). Therefore, it makes sense that persons who grow up in multiracial communities will have more experience interacting with people of other races, and therefore a higher comfort level and willingness to do so, than those raised in monoracial settings. The theory also helps to explain why social distance between members of different nations is high when tensions exist between the respective countries. For instance, during World War II, social distance between Americans and Japanese was great (Bogardus 1946) and in the early 1980s, shortly after the hostage crisis in Iran and in the midst of the US and Iraq war, white Americans desired a great deal of social distance from Iranians and Iraqis (Nix 1993). During periods of hostilities between nations, the citizens of each are taught to regard one another as enemies and often even subhuman (Keene 1986).

Lack of social interaction and messages of inferiority that influence levels of social interaction between members of different countries also holds true among various groups within nations. The United States, with its diversity of races, provides a good example. Following the logic of Social Learning Theory and considering the history of slavery and legal segregation in the United States, it is no surprise that the greatest social distance among the various racial groups in the US exists between whites and blacks (Bobo and Zubrinsky, 1996).

As suggested above, and as much research has indicated, social distance is most likely to be overcome when physical proximity exists (Festinger, Schachter, and Back, 1950; Bersheid and Walster, 1969; Vela-McConnell 1999; Verkuyten and Kinket 2000). In most areas of the United States, blacks and whites are spatially separated, with little chance of interaction (Massey and Denton 1993; Sigelman, Bledsoe, Welch, and Combs 1996).

However, at the university from which our data comes, more than 28% of the student body describe themselves as African American, Asian, Latino/a, or Native American. Similar to the percentage in the overall US population, African Americans comprise almost 12% of the undergraduate student population.

Moreover, students are actively taught to understand and respect other cultures. All students are required to take a Racism and Sexism class and a course selected from a list of specifically Non-Western classes. Diversity among the student body and openness to other cultures is promoted and highlighted. This is not a school where it is possible for white students to avoid sharing classrooms with black students or avoid hearing the message that diversity is good.

Nonetheless, aside from the apparent self-segregation in the cafeteria, the overall social distance that exists between white and black students on campus has been unclear. This study was undertaken to provide at least a partial answer to this query. We sought to determine 1) the degree of social distance and 2) the factors that contribute to the level of social distance that white students seek to maintain from their black classmates.

Method

Data and Measurement

Data were collected from students through a survey in a comprehensive university in northern New Jersey in 2000. The University has approximately 10,000 students and is located in a suburban area near New York City. The survey was administered in Social Problems and Principles of Sociology classes containing students from a variety of majors. Respondents were told that the survey was for a culture research project and their participation was voluntary. They were also told that the questionnaire was anonymous. About 97 percent of the sampled students fully completed their surveys.

Since this research specifically focused on the degree of social distance white students desire from black students, only 90 of the 127 respondents, those who identified themselves as Caucasians, were included in the data analysis. Among the selected students, 42.2% are males and 57.8% are females, and their average age is 21. The distribution among years in school are similar to those of the university students' population, 26.7% freshmen, 21.1% sophomores, 22.2% juniors, 20.0% seniors, and 10.0% graduate students. The average family income is approximately $65,000, which is typical in the Northeast coastal area but higher than the national average.

Five items were used to measure white students' social distance from black students. These five items are:

1. Are you willing to sit next to a black student in a classroom?
2. Are you willing to sit next to a black student in the cafeteria?
3. Are you willing to go to a school dance with a black student?

4. Are you willing to be roommates with a black student?
5. Are you willing to date a black student on campus?

The development of the five levels of social distance measurement was based on Bogardus social distance scale, which is a well-developed and frequently used technique for determining the willingness of people to participate in social relations with other people. The clear differences of intensity suggest a structure among the items (Babbie, 2000).

Data Analysis

The primary purpose of the study was to measure the level of social distance white students hold towards their black schoolmates. Simple frequency percentages were used to indicate the level of social distance and to determine the degree to which the white students are willing to associate with black students in different settings, from sitting next to one another in class to dating. After considering each level of white students' willingness to associate with black students, we recoded the five levels of measurements into a comprehensive one to determine the overall willingness of the white students to associate with black students. Specifically, if a respondent marked "Yes" to answer all five questions, this respondent would have an overall value of 1. If a respondent marked "No" to answer one or more or five of the questions, this respondent would have an overall value of 3. Similarly, if a respondent checked "Uncertain" to answer one or more of the five questions, this respondent would have an overall value of 2. The last line of Table 1 reveals the results of this recoding.

We used Spearman's r to determine the level of correlation between variables. The variables examined for possible correlation with the social distance scale were gender, college status, family income, and belief in the importance of understanding other cultures. Table 2 illustrates the results of the correlation analysis.

Finally, we ran cross-tabulation analyses to determine if there is a relationship between 1) gender, 2) college status, 3) family income, and 4) belief in the importance of understanding other cultures and the white students' overall social distance from black students. In order to simplify the presentation of the findings, we recoded the respondents college status, family income and the variable "belief in the importance of understanding other cultures" into three categories. In recoding family income, we put those respondents whose last year's annual income was up to $30,000 in the low income group, those between $30, 001 and $70,000 in the middle income group, and those more than $70,000 in the high income group. Table 3 reveals the results of this analysis.

Results

Table 1 presents the percentages of the white students' willingness to associate with black students on campus in different circumstances. It appears that the five questions utilized to measure social distance do form a good measurement scale. While all the white students are willing to sit next to a black student in a classroom, only 94.4% are willing to sit next to a black student in the cafeteria. This willingness continues to decrease when the association gets closer. While 76.7% are willing to be roommates of black students, 68.9% are willing to go school dance with a black student, and only 48.9% are willing to date a black student on campus.

When these five levels of measurement are combined, only 44.4% of the white students would have no problem in associating with black students in all five of the occasions. Except for sitting next to a black student in a classroom, 23.3% of the white students are uncertain whether they would be willing to associate with black students in at least one of the settings, and 32.2% are not willing to associate with black students in at least one of the proposed scenarios.

Table 2 presents the levels of correlation between the variables gender, college status, family income, belief in the importance of understanding other cultures and the social distance scale. Females who are more willing to associate with blacks also attach greater importance to understanding other cultures than do other females. Also, family income, which, rises with college status is positively related to willingness to associate with blacks. White students who come from families with higher incomes desire less social distance from blacks than do those who come from poorer families. The importance of understanding other cultures indicates the strongest relationship with the social distance scale. Those white respondents who attached great importance to understanding other cultures are much less likely to hold social distance from black students.

Table 1: White Students Social Distance Toward Black Students

Social distance variables	Percent of students who answered Yes Cases (%)	Percent of students who answered Uncertain Cases (%)	Percent of students who answered No Cases (%)	Total percent Cases (%)
Are you willing to sit next to a black student in a classroom?	90(100)			90(100)
Are you willing to sit next to a black student in a cafeteria?	85(94.4)	1(1.1)	4(4.4)	90(100)
Are you willing to be roommates with a black student?	69(76.7)	11(12.2)	10(11.1)	90(100)
Are you willing to go to a school dance with a black student?	62(68.9)	14(15.6)	14(15.6)	90(100)
Are you willing to data a black student on campus?	44(48.9)	20(22.2)	26(28.9)	90(100)
Five levels of measurements combined	40(44.4)	21(23.3)	29(32.3)	90(100)

Table 2: Spearman Correlation Coefficients

1. Gender	-.1966 N(90) Sig. 063			
2. College Status	-.1838 N(90) Sig. 083	-.0315 N(90) Sig. 768		
3. Family Income	-.2205 N(80) Sig. 049	-.1143 N (80) Sig. 313	.3906 N (80) Sig. 000	
4. Importance of Underst. Other Culture	-.5402 N (90) Sig. 000	.2968 N (90) Sig. 005	.1572 N (90) Sig. 139	.0962 N (80) Sig. 396
	1. Scale	2. Gender	3. Colsta	4. F.Income

Table 3 illustrates that gender, income, college status, and belief in the importance of understanding other cultures impact the levels of social distance white students seek from their black classmates. Fifty percent of the white females compared to only 36.8% of the white males answered "yes" to all the questions on the social distance scale. Fifty percent of all the white students from families with high incomes but less than half of those from low and middle-income families answered in the affirmative to all the questions asked on the social distance scale. When college status was considered, 77.8% of the white graduate students were willing to associate with black students at any of the five settings measured while less than half of the undergraduate students are willing to. Among the undergraduate students, the juniors and seniors (44.7%) are more willing to associate with black students than are the freshmen and sophomores (37.2%). Over 73% of respondents who believe that understanding other

Table 3: Relationships Between Gender, Family Income, Importance of Understanding Other Cultures and White Students Social Distance From Black Students

Variables	Social distance variables	Percent of students who answered Yes Cases (%)	Percent of students who answered Uncertn Cases (%)	Percent of students who answered No Cases (%)	Total percent Cases (%)
Gender	Males	14 (36.8)	9 (22.7)	15 (39.5)	38 (100)
	Females	26 (50.0)	12 (23.1)	14 (26.9)	52 (100)
Family Income	Low Income	1 (20.0)		4 (80.0)	5 (100)
	Middle income	15 (40.5)	10 (27.0)	12 (32.4)	37 (100)
	High income	19 (50.0)	10 (26.3)	9 (23.7)	38 (100)
College Status	Fresh/Sophomore	16 (37.2)	9 (20.9)	18 (41.9)	43 (100)
	Jun/Senior	17 (44.7)	11 (28.9)	10 (26.3)	38 (100)
	Graduate	7 (77.8)	1 (11.1)	1 (11.1)	9 (100)
Import. of understan other cultures	Not important	1 (4.8)	5 (23.8)	15 (71.4)	21 (100)
	Important	17 (46.3)	12 (30.8)	10 (25.6)	39 (100)
	Very important	22 (73.3)	4 (13.3)	4 (13.3)	30 (100)

cultures is "very important," while only 46.3% who believe understanding cultures is merely "important," would be willing to interact with black students in situations ranging from sitting next to them in a classroom to dating. Finally, among those respondents who believe that understanding other cultures is "not important," only 4.8% would be willing to interact with black students in situations ranging from sitting next to them in a classroom to dating.

Discussion

The results indicate a traditional, Bogardus-like decrease in the comfort levels of the white respondents to increased contact with their black classmates. As noted above, while all of the students would be willing to sit next to a black student in a classroom, only 44.4% of the white students indicated that they would have no problem associating with a black student on all five of the occasions studied in this research. This lack of willingness to be a roommate or date across races seems rather high in light of such recent headlines as "Teen-age Dating Shows Racial Barriers Falling" in USA Today and the quadrupling of interracial marriages over the last three decades (Peterson 1997). Importantly, though, the increase between black and white dating and intermarriage has been slower than other racial combinations. The taboo concerning interracial relationships between blacks and whites, while beginning to crumble, still remains somewhat intact (Korgen 1999).

The fact that white males favor greater social distance than do white females is consistent with past research (Hoxter and Lester 1994; Verkuyten and Kinket 2000). The female students who are more willing to associate with black students than are the male students also attach greater importance than do the male students to the understanding of other cultures. This may indicate that females are more open-minded to other cultures and therefore more willing to associate with people of other races. This could be due to the fact that women are socialized to be more caring and interested in the needs of others and have faced discrimination themselves (Nix 1993). Females' interest in other cultures may also encourage them to understand people with different racial backgrounds better, leading to their increased willingness to associate with people of other races.

The relationship between family income level and degree of social distance also follows evidence from much past research (e.g. Wirth 1938, Wilson 1985, and Agnew et al. 2000). As income levels, which are usually closely related to education levels, rise, desire for social distance from other races decreases. This fact often is attributed to the increased mobility and interaction with a wide range of people that usually comes with high levels of education and wealth. It makes sense, then, that those white students at this institution who come from families with relatively high incomes have less desire for social distance from blacks than those who come from less financially well-off homes of origin.

College status may indicate increased education and awareness of other cultures. Graduate students or junior and senior students' higher level of willingness to associate with black students suggests, like other past research, that education does contribute to the reduction of prejudice (Nix 1993; Guthrie, King, and Palmer 2000). Increased awareness of other cultures may also enable the students to see the merits of other cultures and races, therefore increasing their willingness to associate with students of other races.

The findings concerning the influence of believing in the importance of learning about other cultures also make common sense. The fact that white students who believe that learning about other cultures is important would seek less social distance from black students than those who do not think that learning about other cultures should be a priority is not surprising. Moreover, just as evidence in past research indicates that persons who are prejudiced towards one group of people are likely to be prejudiced toward other outgroups as well (Allport 1954, Ray and Lovejoy 1986, Agnew, Thompson, and Gaines 2000), it seems likely that students who desire low levels of social distance toward blacks will also be open to associating with students of other minority groups.

The influence of belief in the importance of understanding other cultures also gives colleges the most obvious clue in the effort to determine how to combat social distance between races on college campuses today. Consistently and persuasively stressing the importance of learning about cultures outside of one's own can lead to reducing levels of social distance among college students. Clearly, if one is interested in increasing interaction among college students of different races, the trend over the past two decades on campuses across the U.S. to emphasize a multicultural education and respect for diversity makes sense.

Conclusion

This research, at a university in northern New Jersey, reveals a desire among almost half of white undergraduates for social distance from their black classmates as the degree of interaction increases from sharing dorm rooms to dating. While the level of social distance appears high in light of the relatively heterogeneous student body at this university and the increased levels of interracial dating among U.S. teenagers, the variables influencing the levels of desired social distance are consistent with both common sense notions and past research. White males indicate higher levels of social distance than white females while students from families with relatively high income have less interest in maintaining social distance from their black classmates. Among all students, desired social distance decreases as years in school increase. Most significantly, students who maintain that understanding other cultures is important have the least levels of social distance. This provides evidence that the emphasis on multiculturalism on many campuses across the United States today may be an effective means of decreasing social distance among students of different races.

References

Agnew, C.R., Thompson, V.D. and S. O. Gaines, Jr. 2000. Incorporating Proximal and Distal Influences on Prejudice: Testing a General Model. *Personality and Social Psychology Bulletin.* Vol. 24, 4:403-418, April.

Allport, G. 1954. *The Nature of Prejudice.* Reading, MA: Addison Wesley.

Babbie, E. 2000. The Practice of Social Research (9th Edition). Belmont, CA: Wadsworth.

Bandura, A. 1977. *Social Learning Theory,* (ed). Englewood Cliffs, NJ: Prentice-Hall, Inc.

Bobo, L. and C. Zubrinsky. 1996. "Attitudes on Residential Integration: Perceived Status Differences, Mere In-group Preference, Or Racial Prejudice?" *Social Forces.* 74 (3):883-900.

Bogardus, E. 1946. *Introduction to Social Research.* Los Angeles: Suttonhouse Ltd.

----------- 1968. "Racial Distance Changes in the United States Duringthe Past Thirty Years." *Sociology and Social Research.* 43 (2):127-135.

Festinger, L., Schacter, S., and K. Back. 1950. *Social Pressure in Informal Groups: A Study of Human Factors in Housing.* New York: Harper and Brothers.

Goldberg, A. and A. Kirschenbaum. 1989. "Black Newcomers to Israel: Contact Situations and Social Distance." *Sociology and Social Research.* 74 (1):52-57.

Guthrie, V. L., King, P., and C. Palmer. 2000. "Higher Education and Reducing Prejudice: Research on Cognitive Capabilities Underlying Tolerance." Diversity Digest.
http://www.inform.umd.edu/diversity web/Digest/Sp.Sm00/tolerance.html#top

Hoxter, A.L. and D. Lester 1994. "Social Distance Evaluations in White and African American Students: Gender Differences in Prejudice." *Perceptual and Motor Skills* 79:1666.

Keene, Sam. 1986. *Faces of the Enemy.* San Francisco: Harper & Row.

Korgen, K. 1999. *From Black to Biracial.* Westport: Praeger.

Massey, D.S. and Denton, N. A. 1993. *American Apartheid: Segregation and the Making of the Underclass.* Cambridge: Harvard University Press.

McAllister, I. and R. Moore. 1991. "Social Distance Among Australian Ethnic Groups." *Sociology and Social Research.* 75 (2):95 - 100.

Netting, N. 1991. "Chinese Aloofness from Other Groups: Social Distance Data from a City in British Columbia." *Sociology and Social Research.* 75 (2):101-104.

Nix, J. V. 1993. "Assessing the Existence of Social Distance and Factors that Affect Its Magnitude at a Southern University."
http://www.sspp.net/archive/papers/nix.htm

Owen, C., Eisner, H., and T. McFaul. 1977. "A Half-Century of Social Distance Research: National Replication of the Bogardus Studies." *Sociology and Social Research.* 66 (1):80-98.

Ray, J.J.and F. H. Lovejoy. 1986. "The Generality of Racial Prejudice." *Journal of Social Psychology*, 126:563-564.

Sigelman, L., Bledsoe, T., Welch, S. and M. W. Combs. 1996. *Making Contact? Black-White Social Interaction in an Urban Setting. American Journal of Sociology.* 101:1306-1032.

Vela-McConnell, J. 1999. *Who is My Neighbor?: Social Affinity in a Modern World*. Albany, NY: State University of New York Press.

Verkuyten, M. and B. Kinket. 2000. "Social Distances in a Multi-Ethnic Society: The Ethnic Hierarchy among Dutch Preadolescents." *Social Psychology Quarterly*. Vol. 63, 1:75-85, March.

Wilson, T.C. 1985. "Urbanism and Tolerance: A Test of Some Hypotheses Drawn from Wirth and Stouffer." *American Sociological Review*. 50:117-123.

Wirth, L. 1938. "Urbanism As a Way of Life." *American Journal of Sociology*. 44:1-24.

II

Social Awareness

Article 7

History of a BSU at a Professional Health Science University

Joseph W. Ruane

Initiating a Black Student Union at a white professional college proved challenging even after the Civil Rights movement. The changes over time in the eventual development of the Black Student Union at a university chartered for health sciences are worth mentioning. Coming out of the civil rights era of the 1960's, the college, which at that time predominantly prepared pharmacists, had no association on campus for African Americans. In 1971 a group of 12 African American men and women approached a new white sociology professor on campus and asked him to be an advisor to a Black Student League. The professor checked with the Student Government, which funded all of the student organizations, and he checked with the Faculty Council, which granted permission to student groups to organize under the banner of Student Affairs and Student Government. Faculty Council, he was told, would not likely grant permission for a "Black Student League" and its presumed radical agenda to exist on campus in 1971.

This was a college which had experienced no civil rights protests, nor anti-Vietnam War protests, and was supported and led by a conservative Board of Trustees and a three-person administrative staff who were also officers of the corporation. Liberal faculty would joke that the college did not know there was a war going on, let alone protest actions in Vietnam. The only black faculty member on campus was a Jamaican chemistry professor who did not identify as African-American, and declined to be the advisor to any such group. There were no more than fifteen black students on campus at that time.

The black students were, for the most part, working class street smart students who wanted a voice in how they might be treated in an all white school. The purpose was "to form a helpful and informing union for the black people (students) at the Philadelphia College of Pharmacy and Science."[1] Together with the professor they decided that if academics were what was important to the faculty, then academics would get them recognized. The black students called their organization the Black Academic Achievement Society (BAAS), and formally petitioned the Faculty Council to recognize them as a student organization.

The faculty, of course, favored academic achievement, and any group that would work toward that end should be recognized in a college setting. The group proposed a constitution which fostered a tutoring system to assist black students in remaining students at the college; encouraged BAAS officers to locate and obtain scholarships for black students to attend the college; informed incoming students what to expect academically upon entering the college; fostered a closer relationship among the black students on campus; provided a means for the expression of black opinions on issues on campus; and to achieve academic excellence above all. Membership in the organization was not to be interpreted as separation from the rest of the college.

Faculty Council approved BAAS after a bit of discussion. Who could object to "mom and apple pie?" The black students had their organization, and they interacted with the Black Student Leagues of other schools. In the early stages of the organization most of the activities were social. The group sponsored a men's basketball team in the intramural league and all the non-players turned out to cheer for them. In years when the number of men interested was insufficient, a couple of the women joined their team. As the population of the school shifted from 70% male to 60% female the interest in having a team in the league waned. Most of the social activities were parties; they never waned.

The organization was most active during Black History Month, and always presented the work of prestigious African Americans in a prominent setting, the center hall of the main college building.

During the 1980's they tried to change the name to Black Student Union, but an African American administrator insisted they keep the name BAAS. However, in 1993, the organization voted to change its name in order to be uniform with similar associations in other colleges.

The students wished the organization to be known as BSU/BAAS, the Black Student Union/Black Academic Achievement Society, giving them both current acceptance, and bowing to their historical beginnings, as well as allowing that academic excellence was still part of their goals. Coincidentally, during the twenty years since their beginning, the organization was usually two organizations in one. All of the students were members of the Student National Pharmaceutical Association, the African American pharmacy student component of the National Pharmaceutical Association, once called the Negro Pharmaceutical Association. Further, since the college student government rules declared all student organizations open to all and any students who desired membership, on occasion a few white students, often of Latino background joined the group. In 1997 there were enough Latinos on campus that a Latino Student Association was organized, but the original Latino students maintained their membership in both groups until they graduated. Now the two organizations occasionally hold joint projects.

The ease with which the 1993 change of name was approved by the administration demonstrates the change that had come over the college by that time. The support staff had become integrated through the work of a president who came from industry, and through his newly appointed Human Resource manager who was an African American woman. Jobs which once came only to whites by word of mouth, now were openly advertised, and today in the twenty-first century, all jobs are advertised and both black and white networks of family and friends, inviting people to apply for open positions. This change in personnel helped shift the mentality of staff and students to accept the competency of peoples of color. While students may have little or no interaction with some of the staff generally, the whiteness on campus had changed noticeably for African American students with the addition of black secretaries and administrators.

The African American Human Resource manager contributed immensely in another way to the BSU. She met with the group on several occasions to make them aware of their black consciousness.

Too often the students saw the world from the perspectives of the white majority, and did not look deep enough to their African roots to understand their present position as an African American minority which was beginning to stand tall to gain their proper role as equals in a white dominated society. Some African American students were even advised by their parents not to get involved in the BSU for fear they may might get involved in black vs. white politics, and consequently get themselves in trouble in school. Fortunately, fewer students, if any, give this as a reason for not joining today.

With the presence of more African American staff on campus the students attempted to enlighten more of the campus about black involvement in American culture by bringing in professional stage productions such as a history of popular music put on by Freedom Theater. Sadly, while the production was great, the attendance was poor. Only the members of the Student association, a few of their parents, and some staff were present. Similar experiences followed with dancers from Philadanco. Here were two world-renowned Philadelphia groups receiving no attention on this white campus. The only consolation the students had was knowing that at that time during the late 1980's even had the groups been white, the apathetic attention would have been no different. Such was the narrow focus of the students and, for the most part, the science-minded faculty.

Things did begin to change in the 1990's, however. A Black History presentation on Black Ancestry and Black Inventions co-sponsored by BAAS and Student Government succeeded immensely. Also, one of the most popular multicultural dinners annually attended by all students is that provided by the BSU. Ribs, cornbread and yams seem liked by all.

A bigger change in BSU is the background of the students. Today's generation at the millennium comes from city and suburbs, and depending on parents' background, the difference in attitude may be profound. The founders of BAAS were mostly from the inner-city and had street smarts, and the street demeanor, complete with defensive attitudes. Today it is different. Most black students studying for a professional degree in a health science field today are at least a step up from the poorest neighborhoods, if not more. Some of their parents were professionals, teachers, or physicians, but many are still the first generation in their families to go to college. The life of the African American students in a professional health science university calls for dedication to one's career. Students of any color who graduated from the university know that they had earned their degree. No one, black or white, was given a free pass to get by.

After teaching at the university for a year, a colleague wrote:

> So far, my experiences with students have been my main point of reference. I tend to be student-centered to begin with, and I have spent a lot of time with students, since the visiting professor role has meant four courses each semester. I have not yet made as systematic or detailed a view of USP as an institution as I'd like, so please interpret my initial impressions in that light. From my perspective so far, USP seems to function as a school for good students, many of whom are from working-class or immigrant families who actively aspire toward upward mobility, even as they struggle with its meaning and implications. Paying for their education and balancing its costs with other claims on family resources seem to be major issues for a considerable number of students. Many students seem to have neighborhood-based urban, rural, or small-town rather than suburban or more cosmopolitan urban backgrounds. In relation to our geographic location, I think we have very few African American or Latino students. A good number of students seem to be first or second generation immigrants, especially from India or other parts of Asia. Even though our students embody racial/ethnic diversity, in its dominant ethos, USP seems oriented toward the kinds of values typically associated with white upwardly mobile males. The natural sciences function as carriers for values of logic, rationality, supposed neutrality, emotional inexpressiveness, assertiveness within the bounds of deference to authority, professional identity, and hard work (meaning putting in long hours and meeting externally imposed demands). Given this context, these are some reflections on its implications for two groups of students.

African Americans

> Other than the efforts of individual faculty, I don't see much recognition of the problem of institutional racism or the difficulties faced by African American students throughout their careers as students. (I had been impressed that USP sponsored the DuBois conference each year, but I see that the financial commitment will be reduced.) White and Asian students sometimes assume that African Americans benefit from Affirmative Action, as if other groups rely more on individual achievements perceived without reference to social support of various kinds. A number of white and Asian students have difficulty acknowledging the extent to which racism colors every facet of life now, especially in its institutional

and deep cultural forms and especially as directed toward African Americans.

Asian Americans

The stereotypical Asian student would seem at first glance to be a good match for the dominant ethos of USP: good at science, hard-working, focused, reserved. However, a number of Asian students struggle with oral and written expression, for reasons rooted in language barriers and in cultural values. While USP makes some resources available to students, the requirements of their major subjects, the values of the dominant ethos of the school, and the stigma attached to seeking help of any kind seem to discourage students from taking full advantage of resources such as the writing or tutoring centers.

In general, I think all students at USP, and especially minorities, are affected by trends in higher education. Traditionally, higher education has been more content than student-oriented, as if students were passive receptacles of knowledge rather than creative agents with much to share from their diverse cultures and the potential to help transform institutions and disciplines. More recently, higher education is experiencing pressure to identify more directly with corporate business interests. This identification can have some positive implications, such as the call for competencies beyond the technical, which could include an appreciation of cultural diversity. There are also negative implications such as the reinforcement of tendencies to reify all students in relation to monetary and status objectives of faculty, administration, donors, and others. For minority students especially, this focus can mean a negation of their experiences, perspectives, values, and senses of connection to their families and communities."[2]

The university has held diversity workshops for staff and faculty, and the student government has held successful multicultural nights and weeks, all of which have positive effects. However, while students enjoy the new food experiences and listening to the music and poetry of distinct cultures, such activities are layered over the existing structures without truly changing or integrating the dominant ethos of the university. Individual attitudes may be challenged by such events, and for now, that must be seen as growth as prejudices are questioned. Summer programs which exist to recruit minority and disadvantaged students through preparatory courses do assist in forming friendships among those working together in such programs.

University records indicate that 54% of the faculty is male, and 88% of faculty are white. Ten percent of faculty is Asian and 2% African American. Two of the faculty claim American Indian ancestry in their mixed backgrounds. There are three Latino faculty. The university at the undergraduate level has a 42% minority student body, however, only 6% are African American. Thirty-two percent are Asian. The families of the majority of the minority students come from India or Korea. There are also several Chinese and Vietnamese students in that minority. Thirty-seven students identify as Latino, barely 2%. These figures represent a change from a white population of 69% in 1996. There are 67% women in the undergraduate population. Each of the groups appear to segregate themselves from the other as well as from the whites, although many individual minority students integrate organizations and social groups comprised predominantly of whites. From the African American perspective many of the Asians students seem to see themselves as "almost white," thereby denying their own personhood as a people of color. These 2000 figures are interesting when one reflects on the population of the city of Philadelphia where the university is located. The city is 43% African American, 45% white, 4% Asian and 8% Latino. A large number of the students of Indian parentage live in New Jersey.

Student experiences and reactions to the white campus vary according to their own background, and the actual incidents occurring in their own history on campus.[3] One African American student from Connecticut found his time here exciting and stimulating. He made good friends and got a good education and a profession. He will go home with good memories of campus life, and even an appreciation of stressful classes. He, however, never joined the Black Student Union since when he was a first year student, he found them intellectually shallow and only concerned with intramural sports or partying. His distance from them remained even after a major turnover left intramurals behind and the BSU students became more service oriented. He lived in neighboring housing with a Peruvian, two Koreans, and a student from India and spent much of his time off campus working when not in class.

Another student of black and white parentage, and a native of the local area, had a sour taste in his mouth as a result of what he saw as an unfair treatment. He can't forget the poor resolution of a discipline problem in which he was unfairly targeted in a complaint, and the lack of understanding of his family financial problems when his parents lost work. He carried a good GPA but received no tuition aid to help him out. He will be happy to shake the dust of the school off his feet at graduation. He, however, had no difficulty making friends on campus, and found having grown up locally gave him the option of enjoying campus or his own neighborhood.

Experiences of African American athletes gives another perspective of campus life. One shy All-American graduate basketball star notes that he felt comfortable at the university since his own home suburban community was only 15 minutes away. While the university is in a mixed inner-city area surrounded on one side by relatively affluent predominantly middle class and upper middle class university faculty and staff intermixed with working class families, the other side of the campus borders a poorer section of the city. The neighborhood presence of African Americans gave him the ambiance of an African American community even though he knew none of those neighbors. However, being one of a small minority of black students on a white campus, he always knew that he could simply go home to his community to feel more comfortable.

This same athlete said that his high school had a large African American population, but also was predominantly white, so coming to a school 70% white (five years ago) did not bother him. He had a white roommate in his campus apartment, and met a white student who became his best friend over the course of his career at the school. He now as a pharmacist spends much time with his white friend and the friend's girl friend in his social life outside of work. His own girl friend is an African American athlete still at the university.

One observation the male athlete said about the curriculum is echoed time and again by other students, black and white. Namely, they note that the science curriculum is so difficult that classmates begin to work together across racial lines in the struggle to get through their courses. No one hesitates to give another student help in learning a subject. This male athlete credits this joint struggle as an important element in overcoming any racial biases. The fact that students see that one another has succeeded for a year or two in the curriculum signals that the classmate is serious about graduating, so each is willing to help the other.

Another black male athlete had a similar experience with classmates. However, he understood his success at school in slightly different terms. He had gone to a high school in which he was the only African American except his brother who was the year ahead of him. When he arrived at this university, there were about fifty African Americans on campus, so it was that much less of a problem, and it was aided by the fact that his brother was also here a year ahead of him.

Comparing the two brothers is interesting, however. The younger brother found it difficult to date the females on campus. Dating is a persistent problem when there is a small number of African Americans on campus. Once a person dates a student on campus and then breaks up with the student, there is an awkwardness in meeting each other in class or in the cafeteria when most are likely to see each other daily. Workers who date someone at the job find similar awkwardness. The younger brother preferred to date off campus in the community. He commuted from home for the first couple of years then moved into a house of athletes with his brother. His older brother, on the other hand, rarely dated African American women, but often dated the Asian and white women on campus, and eventually lived with an Asian woman after graduation.

A memorable student who came to the university on a basketball scholarship but then contracted cancer in his second year also dated a white woman. He overcame the illness and returned to school to graduate. Throughout his ordeal students and faculty befriended this personable young man. He could be found hanging out with the basketball team even though he no longer played on the team, or he could be found with black or white groups in conversational circles on campus. His ease in either black or white company might be explained by his interracial background. Sadly, he died after seven years of marriage to the same woman who stuck with him through his college illness. His cancer had returned. At his funeral just eight years after graduation his many friends, black and white filled an overflow Greek Orthodox church, the church of his mother and him, in a ceremony jointly officiated with his father's Baptist pastor and the Greek Orthodox priest.

The history of another African American athlete was very different, however. Unlike the previous student, he came to the Philadelphia school from New York City. Far from his Bronx setting of black neighbors he found himself in a strange city on a mostly white campus expecting to play basketball. The struggle to be a good student and to give time to playing on the men's basketball team worked against him, so he gave up basketball to be a student in the pharmacy program. While he had a few black friends on campus, a certain insecurity about the friendships stayed with him. They still were students and played on the varsity basketball team. The isolation of being an obvious minority student, and possibly being seen as a basketball player who didn't make the team left him in a predicament that lasted until he graduated. He did have a few classmates who were friendly with him, but it would be difficult to say who were really friends. He readily accepted the friendly encounters with other students and faculty, black or white, but those who knew him well still considered him somewhat of a loner since he was often seen by himself. Of course, the perception could have been wrong. He saw himself as independent of any of the cliques on campus, but longed for the comfort of a black community like the neighborhood at home.

A student from Africa found that all of the students were politely friendly as far as aiding one another in class work, and also in extending invitations to fraternity and social parties. Nevertheless he said that even at the parties there was a certain distancing that inhibited getting to know someone. He found this among both the white and African American students. Consequently, many of the African students seemed to group together in social circles on campus.

The response from a Bermudan student showed similar distancing from African American students. Her interview noted:

> Although I am a black student, I am not an American. My background has more of a British influence as my country is a British colony and for this reason I find myself placed in a rather unique position.
>
> During my early years at USP, I often felt that I could not connect with the African American students on campus because my background/ my experiences were different. I could not understand their jargon, i.e. the Ebonics. I could not relate to their struggles as a black person living in America, because back home, blacks and whites lived, worked and played side by side. It was okay for black children to play with the white children. Interracial dating is not so much frowned upon in my country. My brother has dated white women for years, not because there is a lack of quality black women to date, but because my brother grew up working in a white dominated profession. My brother is an equestrian instructor/show jumper. Our country depends on tourism and international business for its survival, so we are much more tolerant and accepting of other races. However, yes there is racism in my country, but it takes on a different form. There is corporate racism, for example. The whites have the better paying jobs; however, I will say that educational opportunities for minorities are excellent. However, we have to fight a bit harder to get to the top.
>
> So when I came to the United States, I did not have the attitude or express the bitterness that I've seen expressed among the African American community. I did not really understand their struggle

because I come from such an affluent society. Please don't get me wrong, I don't want to sound arrogant, but I am just saying that when I came to the United States, I did not understand what all the bitterness was about. Yes there was slavery in my country; however, I believe that my country has learned to put the past in the past and move on whereas here in the United States, African Americans still choose to hang on to the past.

It has only been this past year that I have did a lot of thinking. I felt that I needed to connect more with my African American sisters in order to find out what all the hype was about. Boy have I learned a lot. In addition, I have experienced acts of racism toward me while here in the United States. This has prompted me to really get in touch with who I am as a person because I realize that my identity is so fragile and could easily be taken away if I did not stand firm and believe in where I came from and where I was going. That is so important.

One of the sad things I have experienced is a lack of acceptance from the African American students. As a person of a British background, I tend to have a formal nature about the way I speak and the way I carry myself. To me I have a very proper personality and I think that for people, who have not taken the time to get to know me, this may turn some people away. Other black people would stare at me or have this attitude and I could not understand it. I have been told that many of them have the perception that I think that I am better than them and that is not the case at all. So this year I have taken an extra effort to connect with my African American sisters and so far, things have gotten better. I am particularly committed to finding out more about their struggles in America and in doing so, it has reaffirmed my identity as a black person. I realize that it takes a lot more to be able to find one's place here in this society and so I think it is important for me to stand firm for who I am. Back home I could relax a bit, but here it's different. I don't mind it though because it will definitely make me a stronger black woman.

How do I feel among so many white students? It's not intimidating at all. I just wish that the black students on campus would come together more as a unit. We are so divided and that, I think, is where the major problem is. It is clearly evident that the black students from Africa have something against the black students from America. I could understand that to some degree, but when you really put things in perspective, we all share a common bond, regardless of our background, regardless of our history. My background was a bit different, and I too felt isolated for a while but like I said, I have matured enough to know that I must bridge the gap by finding out more about their background and that is something I have made a commitment to do. I believe that if we as a black people want to get ahead in this world and make things better for future generations, we've got to stop feeling like victims. We must start forgiving one another and realize that we have the power and the potential to make great things happen for ourselves. We as a black people like to complain when things are not going our way, but what are we doing to change it? That is a question I'd like for every black person to think about. If we continue to sit back on our "toosh" then nothing will get done. Yes, we'll have to fight and fight hard. But haven't we fought all our lives, so what is the big deal? So once again, I don't feel intimidated by a large white presence on campus, but I feel isolated because the black students are not united.

Yes, I can be myself but it has not been easy. Being myself meant being a black person with a British influence and that came across strange to students here. Just my friendly manner was foreign so I stopped being so friendly just to fit in a bit. I would smile and say "Hi" and people would look at me like I was stupid! But for the most part I am myself. I believe that being as independent as I am has made it easier for me to be myself.

Do I have white friends? No not really. I speak to them and we may exchange a few words but that is as far as it goes. There is quite a difference between American whites, Canadian whites and British whites. The white students here on campus can be a bit snobbish but I've gotten used to that. They treat me with respect, and I try to do the same. Sometimes, other black students treat them better than they treat me. This is particularly evident with the black cafeteria staff. But I refuse to stoop to their low level.

Do I mind interracial dating? Not at all. Who knows, I may have a white sister-in-law in the near future, It doesn't bother me, but I know that interracial dating is a big taboo among the African American community! When I listen to the reasons for it, sometimes I have to smile. Other times, I try and put myself in their shoes and that's when I understand their view point. Don't get me wrong, interracial dating is frowned upon by some cultures in my country, in particular the Portuguese, but on the whole, interracial dating is much more accepted in Bermuda.

Did I come here with an attitude? Yeah I did. I was told before coming here that Americans are not as friendly as Bermudans. I was told that I had to watch my back and not be so trusting of others. I was told that Americans are more direct in their approach and that I had to be careful what I said and how I said it.

Did USP give me an attitude? No, not really. In fact, being here has opened my eyes a lot. WOW! I have learned a lot.

Are African Americans treated any differently from other minority students on campus? Most definitely. I can't really tell who is Chinese or who is Korean or who is Indian. I call them all Asians. They do treat us differently. Some of them act like they are scared of us. There is definitely an academic disparity. They are clearly more gifted in the natural sciences, computer sciences and mathematics. And what makes a lot of other students angry is that they, majority of the time, will get the better grades because they have access to the back tests. But definitely, we are treated differently.

Another female wrote

> Well, ever since you've mentioned this I thought a lot about it, so I think that what I have to say will be of some value. This situation isn't anything new to me. I'm from Williamsport PA, and the black population there isn't really significant. The black population has grown enormously from the time I was in elementary school till the time I graduated but still, the blacks were definitely the minority. I guess it's because of this that I don't really have a hard time here at all. I'm used to being the only black girl in a classroom a lot of times, and honestly, on most days it doesn't bother me that much. Both my roommates are white, and one of them, I consider my best friend here. No matter what the situation, I'm still true to who I am. I don't put on masks anywhere that I go. I still do find that, on those rare opportunities where I'm not the minority anymore, for example BSU meetings, the cheerleading squad, which is predominantly black now, it feels really nice. Just to be able to talk and not to be asked to repeat myself, or to come in with hair extensions, and not be asked "how did my hair get so long?", or to be around other black girls who have the same body type as me and be proud of it and not think that they're fat. But, in the real world I know I will rarely be in situations like those so I've learned to answer the stupid questions and not get irritated, and in a way, I've taken the questions and stares as compliments. Every time I walk into a room where there is no one else like me, I become the center of attention and I've learned to love it. But for those of us who just want to "fit in" I could see where everyday life on a white campus might be too much for someone to handle.

Her comment about the cheerleading squad is significant. The cheerleaders were always white women, with an occasional black woman joining them, and the men's basketball team was always the same. A historic change came in the 1994-95 season when the college first started five black players. It came so naturally that the white coach was not aware of it until afterwards. It is not often that the team has had enough black players that they could put an all black team on the floor. All of the players were active in the BSU, as well as the

Association of Student Pharmacists, the new name of SAPHA. Two of the players today manage pharmacies in major hospital medical centers. During that same era another Bermudan black woman, four white women, and four African American women formed the first student dance team to perform at the basketball games. The interracial group was almost as popular as the basketball team as some fans came to see the dancers rather than the game itself. The group has continued to be interracial, with members of the BSU now to be found either on the dance team, the cheerleaders, or as leaders in student government.

The institutional racism occurs infrequently, usually as the result of an administrator taking the complaint of biased students at face value rather than investigating the prejudice first. However, today thirty years later, no longer a ready scapegoat, the BSU leadership is strong enough to defend its position as an outstanding organization on campus, and is itself a source of leadership training for tomorrows leaders in several health fields. Sometimes being black the BSU is the center of attention, but as the student above put it, "they have learned to love it."

Notes

1. Black Student Union Constitution

2. Barbara Hogan, Ph.D., Assistant Professor of Sociology, e-mail note, 5 July 2000.

3. Students were promised anonymity in interviews or e-mail communications that follow.

Article 8

Black and Gay Identity Selection on College Campuses: Master and Subordinate Status Strain and Conflict

Tim Baylor

It would be naive, or perhaps hopeful at best, to believe that college campuses are "ivory towers" where society's ideals find fertile ground and flourish in terms of lived experience. Rather it must be realized that student interaction on college campuses does not occur in a vacuum. The social patterns, structures, norms, values, and beliefs of the surrounding society are more often than not replicated within the boundaries of educational institutions. This does not mean that there are not any observable differences between college campuses and the surrounding social milieu, or that there is not greater space for seeking alternative social relations than those weighing on one in the larger society. However the ability to shrug off, even if only for a few years, some of these burdens and constraints on social interaction varies greatly from campus to campus. Variables such as the degree of selectivity in student admissions, residential or commuter campuses, the social class make-up, coupled with the racial and ethnic mix of the student body each affect campus dynamics. From published stories and informal conversations with colleagues, it appears that even the most highly selective college with a high degree of social class homogeneity cannot avoid the fact that we live in a racialized society. Even where class differences are absent the color of one's skin still acts as one filter through which the world is seen and understood. I suggest this is even more typical for the average, less prestigious educational institution where most students are educated. For instance, I recently read a student journal in which the student, who was white, related overhearing a conversation between some black[1] students following the World Trade Center bombings. One of the black students said something to the effect that, "he didn't care what happened to the people in New York since his forefathers were brought here against their will." This thought reveals so much about how race acts as a filter through which we see things. I'm sure that this was not a common reaction among black students. However, it does show how one black student from the Midwest could not perceive that there were numerous black people who were inside this symbol of power and economic influence in New York City who also lost their lives. This essay is concerned with how this filter of race interacts with an equally pervasive and problematic filter – sexual orientation,[2] especially when the person is both black and gay.

College campuses are often the first place where young people begin to escape some of the constraints of family, explore, and begin to make choices for themselves. Certainly, this is true regarding sexual orientation. As someone who found greater freedom, space, and support on a college campus to come to terms with my own sexual identity, I have maintained an interest in the struggles students undergo in coming to terms with their own sexual orientation. This concern has led me to serve as a faculty advisor to gay, lesbian, bisexual student groups on two different college campuses. Interaction on a college campus between students having a shared identity (sexual orientation) but also different identities (black-white) provides an interesting space from which to think about black-white relations in the larger society, because as suggested earlier, these larger patterns are often replicated in smaller microcosms like the college campus. While my thoughts are based on my own experience as a college student and my role as faculty advisor to two different student groups, and is therefor limited, I still think my experience reflects a much wider and common pattern of student interaction; or more accurately, the lack thereof.

Student's of color lack of involvement in gay student groups on campuses struck me as unusual as I began to consider this piece and reflected on my own experience over the years.[3] Indeed, I could only remember two black students, one black male during my own student days and one black female in one of the groups for which I served as faculty advisor. Yet from my attendance at gay dance clubs and bars and online in computer chat rooms, it was clear that black-gay college students existed in greater numbers than their representation in the gay student groups which I had experienced. As an academically trained professional sociologist, I began to ask myself "Why?" this was so. The answer that I would like to suggest, rest on the sociological distinction between what is called our "master" verses "subordinate" statuses.

Hughes (1945) observed that each of us has multiple statuses, i.e., social defined positions within a large group, or society in general. For instance I have the status of "son" in relationship to my family, the status of "professor" in relationship to my employment, and the status of a "White male" in relationship to my society overall. Attached to each status is also a set of socially constructed "roles" which define ways individuals are supposed to act. Hughes (1945) also observed that a process occurs whereby a society, subculture, or social group selects one or more of these different statuses as being more important, what he called one's "master status."[4] Compared to our "master status," our remaining statuses become subordinate in their consequences and social significance. This process of status sorting is often an area of contention between the individual and society as there is sometimes disagreement about which status should serve as one's master status and what roles are appropriate for each status. Much is at stake since it is our master status that determines how most people relate to and interact with us.

Many of our potential statuses are obvious in that we cannot escape other people being aware of them, such as our sex or race. While the attempt to avoid having one's sex or race determine one's master status, if one was female or non-White, led to the very interesting phenomenon of "passing" where one attempted to assume another status, notably male or white because these statuses enhanced one's social position, these were less frequent although theoretically important responses to status discrimination.[5] Some statuses, however, such as sexual orientation are not so obvious and present the bearer of such a status with a choice of whether to make this status known to others. In revealing an unobvious status, the potential revelation must be weighed in terms of whether it enhances or detracts from one's position in society at large or other groups to which the individual belongs. Something akin to a cost-benefit analysis occurs. A person must ask oneself, "What do I gain, and what do I loose by revealing my unobvious status? I will argue that from the perspective of a gay black student, revealing one's sexual orientation in a public manner by becoming involved in a gay, lesbian, or bisexual student group is perceived as having more costs than benefits. Due to these greater costs, black-white gay, lesbian, and bisexual student interaction is decreased.

The costs of being an "out" gay black student on a college campus come from several sources. Many of these costs are tied to the prejudice and discrimination due to a general climate of racism, homophobia, and heterosexism existing at-large in society.[6] Another major cost is tied to the heterosexism and homophobia within the black community itself. The interaction between these two potential sources of prejudice and discrimination, one external to and the other internal to the Black community, creates some powerful forces reducing the likelihood of social interaction and support between black and white gay, lesbian, and bisexual students. Examining the source of these costs demonstrates some of the complexities involved in intra-racial and interracial group relations.

No one would argue that the college campus is devoid of racism. Indeed conflicts sometimes emerge that are significant enough to gain the attention of national news outlets. Behind these high profile examples of racial conflict and tensions are many more common and ongoing debates regarding the consequences of race on college campuses. Some of these debates and areas of contention reflect attitudes and beliefs about groups students bring with them from their prior socialization experiences. For example national surveys asking respondents "Are blacks treated less fairly than whites?" consistently display major disconnects between blacks and whites regarding discriminatory treatment in the workplace, while dinning out, shopping, or while driving, with blacks agreeing that discrimination takes place at a rate 2-3 times higher than white respondents.[7] Even if these responses only reflected "perceptions" and not the actual state of affairs, perceptions still matter as they make people apprehensive or cautious, or in some manner complicate social interaction that occurs or doesn't occur on campus between students.

Minority students I have interviewed report "divided campuses" with "boundaries" separating groups from each other, "They were here and we was over there." Crossing these boundaries took extra effort. One black student reported, "I learned that I have to initiate things. White kids will not come to me, I have to come to them. It's like I have to show them it's okay to talk to me, or something like that."[8] However, white students are not only ones constructing boundaries. One multiracial student described how she was ostracized from a black student campus group after she joined an all-white sorority.[9]

On college campuses, minority students report being discriminated against or victimized at increasing rates the longer they have been on campus. For instance in one study, fourteen percent of incoming minority (black, asian, and hispanic) freshman reported being victimized, twenty-eight percent for those having completed between one and four semesters, while forty-one percent of minority students who attended at least five semesters reported being victimized.[10] Faced with such discrimination many minority students, including black students, especially on integrated campuses, often seek support in largely racially segregated student organizations such as Greek fraternities and sororities or Black Student Unions, etc. The observation that people subject to prejudice and discrimination often seek social support within their own community is nothing new in the study of racial and ethnic relations. It does though, for purposes of this essay, emphasize the role of the black student community as an important support mechanism for black students. Therefor, for a gay, lesbian, or bisexual (GLB)[11] black student, outing one's self by participating in a racially mixed gay, lesbian, or bisexual student support/educational organization jeopardizes an extremely important source of social support in the form of the black student community itself. This assumes of course, that a GLB black student would loose much support from the black student community because of its own homophobia and heterosexism, a point considered latter in this essay.

The potential loss of support from the black student community, besides the additional prejudice due to having one's status as a GLB person known, obviously represents another substantial cost, especially if the loss of black community support is not compensated for by support from the GLB community. The degree of support and other benefits from participating in the GLB student community, however, is also dependent on the absence or at least negligible presence of racism in the GLB student community; a problematic assumption to make. Let's consider each of these issues in turn.

That GLB individuals are subject to prejudice and discrimination in the U.S. is obvious. For instance, during 1999 a total of 7, 876 "bias-motivated" crimes were reported to the Federal Bureau of Investigation by various local law enforcement agencies. Of those crimes, seventeen percent (1, 317) were based on sexual orientation.[12] In addition, although general societal attitudes towards GLB people have improved, approximately fifty-nine percent of the U.S. population still respond that "sexual relations between two adults of the same sex" is "always or almost always wrong."[13] A 1993 report for the Massachusetts Governor's Commission on Gay and Lesbian Youth found that 97% of public school students reported regularly hearing various anti-gay remarks, while a 1997 study of Des Moines, Iowa high school students reported students hearing about 25 anti-gay epithets per day.[14] High profile hate crime murders like that of gay student, Matthew Shepard, at the University of Wyoming on October 6, 1998, only add to this general climate of prejudice and discrimination and therefor concern on the part of GLB people regarding being open about their sexual orientation. Given this general social climate towards GLB persons, the black GLB student would have to be pretty secure about the support available from the GLB community to risk the loss of support from the black community in the face of racism, homophobia, and heterosexism. Unfortunately, such secure compensating support from the GLB community is not the case as racism also affects black-white GLB relations.

Perhaps it is not surprising that white GLB persons have also been conditioned by the general racism present in society. Given that white GLB persons come from all social and economic levels, they too have been socialized with either overt or subtle aspects of racism present in the groups and families to which they belong. Just because they may understand what it is to be discriminated against due to their sexual orientation, does not mean that they have become what sociologist Robert Merton called the "all-weather liberal," i.e., someone who lacked any prejudicial attitudes and therefor did not engage in any form of discrimination.[15] Indeed, Mandy Carter, a black lesbian activist, has said, "I think –bottom line– even though we're queer, we can still be racist" when commenting on both black and white racism within the GLB community.[16] Within the GLB community, claims of racism from people of color are common. Decades ago the well-known black gay writer James Baldwin articulated his observation that "The gay world as such is no more prepared to accept black people than anywhere else in society. It's a very hermetically sealed world with very unattractive features, including racism."[17] The black GLB community's claims of racism by the white GLB community have been articulated, again and again, most recently by Keith Boykin.[18] Boykin documents either from his own experience or stories he has heard, numerous examples of racism within the white GLB community. Other sources confirm the existence of racism and the difficulty of black & white GLB people working cooperatively, even in the form of interracial relationships. In one computer message board, one person wrote:

> This is all beautiful and stuff... but come on! Love has no color, but the world does. Our society does. And everyday that race prejudice is made manifest. I am in an interracial relationship and it is the best one I have ever been in simply because we don't hee and haw about "Love knowing no color". We acknowledge that we are from different cultures and try to grow with and in each other by learning and understanding those differences. We also try to make sure we understand internalized racial oppression and inferiority and internalized racial superiority because that tears a relationship up worse than anything in my experience. Love sees no color, but we do.[19]

Racism in the white GLB community represents one more cost the black GLB person, including students, must weigh in terms of "coming out" by participating in something like a GLB college campus group. Given the potential loss of black community support discussed earlier and racism within the white GLB community, it is not surprising that few black GLB students choose to participate in GLB student organizations, further reducing black-white interaction on college campuses and preventing mutual systems of support from forming. For instance I remember having one online conversation with a black student whom identified himself as bisexual. He vehemently denied and got angry when I suggested some similarities existed between the black community and the GLB community when it came to our mutual experiences with prejudice and discrimination. He saw no common ground at all.

Perhaps, the greatest cost though affecting a black GLB student's choice of whether to interact with white students in a GLB student organization, is the probable loss of support from the black community due to its own homophobia and heterosexism. The black community's homophobia and heterosexism, however, must not be seen in isolation from the homophobia and heterosexism in the larger, dominant white community. Indeed, I will argue that black-white issues exacerbate the prevalence and degree of homophobia within the black community, increasing the costs for black GLB students, especially male students.

Homophobia and heterosexism within the black community can be seen as similar to the homophobia and heterosexism within the white community, except it is more complicated due to a history of subordination, discrimination, and differential treatment by the white community. As an ethnic subculture within the dominant white culture, the social norms and values of the white community have influenced the black community This includes attitudes towards GLB persons. Some of this influence is seen among the black intelligentsia and leadership of the black church.

A number of contemporary black intellectuals, such as Frances Cress Welsing, Molefi Asante, Amiri Baraka, and Robert Staples have argued that homosexuality was unknown in Black African cultures. Contemporary occurrences reflect European decadence and corruption, or it is the result of white racism which has weakened the black family and emasculated black men.[20] For instance, Cress (1991) states:

> The black male does not arrive at the effeminate bisexual or homosexual stance from any deeply repressed sense of genetic weakness, inadequacy or disgust . . . instead, the black male arrives at this disposition . . . as the result of the imposed power and cruelty of the white male and the totality of white supremacy social and political apparatus that has forced 20 generations of Black males into submission.[21]

A young black male expressed the same idea more simply, "Even though there are a lot of black homosexuals, a lot of blacks do not want to accept that fact . . . . [To them the] homosexual thing is a white thing."[22] It is interesting to note that the idea of no indigenous expressions of homosexuality in the black community is also found among some African intellectuals and political leaders who also identify white colonialism as the culprit responsible for introducing homosexuality and emasculating black men.[23] While the assertion of no same-sex sexual behavior among black Africans is historically and anthropologically inaccurate, the connection between homosexuality and emasculation is a substantive idea that needs closer examination.[24]

As Harlon Dalton, an Associate Professor of Law at Yale Law School has observed, "My suspicion is that openly gay men and lesbians evoke hostility in part because they have come to symbolize the strong female and the weak male that slavery and Jim Crow produced . . . . Thus, in the black community homosexuality carries more baggage than in the larger society."[25]

For the black gay or bisexual male student the gender construction of black male masculinity presents yet another cost to both "coming out" and interacting in a racially-mixed GLB student organization. To "come out," especially if one then interacts in a racially mixed GLB student group, is to fail to live-up to culturally prescribed standards of masculinity and bring upon the black community shame by "airing" one's homosexuality or bisexuality which are stigma bearing statuses. As one multiracial heterosexual student related, "Maybe some of it is African-Americans are themselves trying to be so accepted in general in the whole society, that to say within that particular community, 'okay we accept this [homosexuality and bisexuality],' and since this isn't a worldwide norm, they are losing some of the ground that they are trying to gain . . . ."[26] At the same time, a black student who "outs" himself must confront some ostracism from the black community in addition to potential racism from the white community with fewer resources and support than he would have otherwise had available. Cools (1998) has described black gay men as being "doubly 'othered': by race and by sexual preference and gender assumptions." Cool continues:

> The black homosexual comes to embody a condition of aggravated psychic unease. His skin color exposes him to racism and his gender exacerbates the anxiety he causes the white community. Compounding this marginalization is the fact that these men are 'othered' because of their sexuality. Unlike black men who subscribe to the heterosexual definition of black masculinity the black male homosexual finds little solace from the pressures of racism in his community for there is little or no acceptance of him in this community. This is because he makes more precarious, a masculinity which the black community has always 'engaged in a never-ending battle' to possess in the wider American community . . . . Thus the seeming loss of his masculinity isolates the black gay male and he is left with virtually no community to which to turn.[27]

While it might be argued that gay white students also face similar demands of masculinity because of stereotypical gender ideas about homosexual men, such standards of masculinity are not constructed and standing counterpoised to those of another ethnic group as in the case of black male masculinity. The white gay male student by "coming out" does not risk opening himself to racism whether from his own ethnic community or one outside his own community. As Boykin (1996), who is a gay Black man, has observed, "For black lesbians and gays, unlike straight blacks, our sexual orientation does not insulate us from the oppression of homophobia, and unlike white lesbians and gays, our skin color does not insulate us from the oppression of racism"[28]

The situation for black lesbian and bisexual female students does not seem to be as oppressive compared to black gay and bisexual male students. While black lesbian and bisexual women still face similar issues in respect to potential racism, and some loss of support from the black community, gendered expectations are not constructed in such a juxtaposed manner in relationship to "race." Less emphasis is placed on female "femininity" than male "masculinity," according to Cools.[29] However, black lesbian and bisexual women still face prejudice and community sanctions for not conforming to general gender expectations, even if these expectations don't compromise their ethnic identity. Boykin (1998) cites the comment of Tony Brown, who hosts the television show *Tony Brown's Journal*, that "No lesbian relationship can take the place of a positive love relationship between black women and black men," as representative of homophobia based on the belief that women-women relationships endangers the black family.[30] Still, from a sociological perspective, other factors contribute to less attention given lesbians than gay men. Besides the general sexism existing in both the black and white communities, studies of "marriage markets" might also provide another reason why black lesbianism and bisexuality is seen in a different light than black male homosexuality and bisexuality.

Numerous social researchers, including one of the foremost sociologist of the black family, Robert Staples (1985), have argued there are simply not enough black men for black women to marry, especially black men capable of providing economically for a family.[31] For instance, Jaynes and Williams (1989) have calculated that at age twenty-six, black women with less than a high school education are in a marriage pool that has 651 men per 1,000 women. For the twenty-six year old black woman with some college education the pool grows to 772 men per 1,000 women.[32] This means that there are many more black women who will have to remain single or find alternative social relationships. I am simply suggesting that the oversupply of black women as it were, could lesson the social sanctions attached to black lesbians and bisexuals, whereas the opposite is true for black gay and bisexual men in a situation where marriageable black men are already in short-supply. Such an assertion seems to have face validity. Dr. Alvin F. Poussaint, an Associate Professor at Harvard Medical School, commented in an article in the black magazine *Ebony* that:

> Many Black women in America's major urban centers, including New York, Chicago, Washington, D.C., and Atlanta bemoan the fact that finding "a good Black man" for the purpose of marriage or a committed relationship has become increasingly difficult, if not impossible. Justifiably or not, they blame this situation on what they perceive as a rapidly increasing number of upwardly mobile-looking, educated Black males who can be seen in upscale neighborhoods living obviously gay lifestyles.[33]

Given the dynamics described in the preceding paragraphs, it is not surprising that black GLB students remain closeted, which prevents them interacting with white GLB students. Besides the constraints based on gender expectations, including those that are ethnically specific, homophobia and heterosexism is further reinforced through popular culture and organized religion. While these sources of homophobia are not unique to black students, they may have equal or greater importance because they originate from their own community.

Boykin (1996) has suggested that black figures in popular culture may be the "worst offender" among all the sources of homophobia and heterosexism in black institutions. Among black musicians and singers the list would include Buju Banton, Tone Loc, Snoop Doggy Dogg, Brand Nubian, Lench Mob, Chuck D, Ice-T, Ice Cube, Queen Latifah, Shabba Ranks, Donna Summers, etc. Comedians and film stars such as Arsenio Hall, Eddie Murphy and the Wayan brothers regularly contribute to stereotypical notions of GLB persons.[34] Some of the material of black entertainers can be interpreted as historically and culturally reactive. Outlaw (1995) argues that the lyrical content of some black entertainers should be seen as a reaction to centuries of struggle in which black male masculinity has been assaulted. " . . . the queer is the worst kind of freak. He is not a real man, he's more of a bitch than any 'ho' could ever be."[35] Given the role and importance of popular culture, especially for youth, popular culture must be seen as a significant force constraining the expression of sexual identity among black adolescents and young adults. Even where black homosexuality is pictured somewhat positively, as in the case of the character "Carter" on *Spin City*, he is still not fully "masculine." For instance, in one show he artificially tries to appear more athletic to impress a boyfriend. In addition, different ethnic viewing habits mean that this show is less likely to be viewed by a wide black audience.

Another significant agent of heterosexism and homophobia in the black community is the black church. In this respect, the black church is not any different from the non-black church where heterosexism and homophobia have been a part of its message. While this is decreasingly true of some denominations[36] strong strands of homophobia and heterosexism are prominent in Catholic and Protestant Christianity.

Boykin (1996) has argued that in relationship to the black church, church dogma is more homophobic than the church community.[37] One black student I interviewed for instance, related how she knew of one black male couple who attended a black Baptist church together where people were aware of their relationship.[38] Yet they were "in church" and that mattered more than their sexual orientation, although one should not assume that black GLB persons receive warm messages of welcome from black church pulpits. Unlike many white Christian denominations which are more centralized and hierarchical in structure and have "official" church statements or positions on homosexuality, the largest black or mostly black denominations (National Baptist Convention, USA Inc., Church of God in Christ, and African Methodist Episcopal Church) have no such statements. However, most black churches tend to disprove of homosexuality and bisexuality even though many acknowledge the presence of GLB people. As one Church of God in Christ pastor put it, " . . . it is no secret that gays and lesbian are in the church from the highest levels on down."[39] Still, the overall attitude one is more than likely to encounter was expressed by a National Baptist Convention pastor who said, "All the ministers in the churches that I know of believe that God can change anyone. First, you must admit that you are wrong, that what you are doing is sinful, and then ask for change."[40] Thus one has a difficult time characterizing the black church as a supportive institution for GLB persons, a point which certainly upsets many black GLB Christians. "I find it despicable and a desecration," according to Jewelle Gomez, a black lesbian writer, "that our spiritual beliefs are perverted and used against Black gay people. Anyone who understands what the spirit of Christianity is supposed to be, would never use it against gays."[41]

It is also possible to see the homophobia and heterosexism in the black church as a product of white racism. Bishop Carl Bean, a black gospel singer provides an interesting viewpoint.

> All oppressed people try hard in that whole idea of assimilation to prove to the oppressor that they're okay. . . . If you tear that [assimilation] away and just look at the community, you'll find that the other side of the coin is great acceptance. There is no one in the church who doesn't know who's gay and lesbian. Everyone knows. . . . There is not a community, black, that I've ever known of where homosexuals were not living. Real honest-to-God, broken-wristed, twisting sissies don't get thrown out of the black community. That white phenomenon does not happen in our community.[42]

For the GLB black student, such an understanding is beyond her/his ability to comprehend these potential racial dynamics on her/his own. All that he/she knows is that another institution which has historically provided support indicates that it is wrong to be a GLB person. He/she learns it is better to keep one's sexual identity hid, preventing participation and interaction in a GLB student group. What options then do black GLB students have available?

Options for the gay black student, and gay black persons in general, are those any gay person must choose from, although within a different qualitative and quantitative structure of benefits, constraints, and costs. It is clear that black homosexuals, male and female, when contemplating their own master status from the various statuses they possess, identify with their ethnic background before their other statuses.[43] One study found 81.4% of GLB online users identified themselves as "gay" when asked, "Do you identify more strongly with your ethnicity or your sexual orientation?". Important for this essay, however, were the differences between ethnic groups. Among white respondents, eighty-five percent (85%) identified more strongly with their sexual orientation than ethnicity, whereas sixty-three percent (63%) of blacks and fifty-five percent (55%) of Korean Americans identified more strongly with their ethnic backgrounds rather than their sexual orientation." While these results were of a select group of GLB people, for instance almost eighty-nine percent (89%) had attended college, I would predict that ethnic group identification over sexual orientation would be more skewed among less educated minority group individuals, including blacks since homophobia tends to decrease with more education.[45] Less educated individuals would have even fewer resources to weather racism and homophobia and therefor seek greater support from their ethnic communities. I would predict that this would be especially true of black gay students since it appears that actual or perceived incidents of racial discrimination increase the longer one has been in college which increases the need for community support.[46]

Selecting ethnicity as one's master status because it carries with it more benefits than costs, does not however mean that "sexual orientation" is absent from one's subordinate statuses. It is still there but gaining the benefit of support from the black community cost the subordinating of one's sexual orientation. As one black lawyer and educator put it, "In exchange for inclusion, [black] gay men and lesbians have agreed to remain under wraps, to downplay, if not hide, their sexual orientation, to provide their families and friends with 'deniability.' So long as they do not put the community to the test, they are welcome. It is all right if everybody knows as long as nobody tells."[47] This response or social adaptation has been neatly summed-up by one black lesbian writer in the phrase, "Play it, but don't say it," an idea striking familiar to the United States' military policy of "Don't ask, Don't Tell."[48]

Another status/identity choice that appears more prevalent among black males is "bisexuality" as several studies have shown.[49] One member and observer of the black community referred to bisexuality as "black America's best kept secret" and ". . . a larger closet than homosexuality."[50] It is easy to see why self-identifying as bisexual rather than homosexual happens so frequently, especially within the black male community. Given the emphasis on "masculinity" within the black community, partially conditioned by white racism as described earlier, in addition to the other sources of homophobia and heterosexism as also described earlier, bisexuality reduces some of the potential costs. One can still claim to fulfill masculine gender expectations because of one's relationships with women, and since one still keeps one's same-sex relations discrete, one can continue to rely on the black community for support. But again for the black male and female student these benefits are conditioned on remaining politically inactive and relatively "invisible" when it comes to sexual orientation, something which involvement in a ethnically mixed GLB student group precludes.

The greater likelihood of young black men self-identifying as bisexual rather than gay holds several important implications for black students and the black community as a whole. First, some of those self-identifying as bisexual reflect cases where individuals have not been able to come to terms with their homosexual orientation due to societal and community prejudice and fear of discrimination creating some degree of internalized homophobia in these individuals. One respondent in a study related how his friends saw themselves as "bisexual" even though they were only sexually attracted to men, but since they talked to women in clubs and flirted a little, they maintained their bisexuality.[51] This inability to accept one's sexual orientation is often manifested by secondary social, physical, and psychological problems.[52] Whether it is alcohol or drug abuse, stress and anxiety disorders, or a greater likelihood to engage in unsafe sex, internalized homophobia coupled with lack of community acceptance increases the occurrence of dysfunctional consequences.

Black men who are actively bisexual, report a higher proportion of female sexual partners than their white male bisexual counterparts.[53] At the same time they are less likely to disclose their homosexual activity to their female partners, an outcome predicted by arguments advanced in this essay.[54] The Centers for Disease Control (CDC) has indicated that black women account for sixty-four percent (64%) of new HIV/AIDS cases among women even though blacks make-up only 12-13% of the U.S. population. Seventy-five percent (75%) of these new cases are attributed to black women having unprotected sex with men. Further, health researchers estimate that sixty percent (60%) of these men are bisexual or living an alternative "secret" sexual life called "down low."[55] Another study by Ross and Rosser (1996) found that HIV seropositive men were less likely to publicly identify as being gay and less likely to be comfortable with other gay men, including belonging to a gay or bisexual group.

If we extrapolate the above findings to black students on a college campus, there should be a great deal of concern. The picture that research paints is of black women at greater risk of contracting AIDS through unprotected sex with "down low" black men who identify and act bisexually, although often secretively, in an attempt to mediate societal and black community homophobia and heterosexism and live up to community standards of masculinity, all of which is made more complicated by white racism. Research by Waldner, et. al. (1999) has also found that black university students scored higher on a measure of homophobia than white and hispanic students. At the same time, they also had the lowest levels of AIDS knowledge among the three ethnic groups, including knowledge about means of transmission, etc.[56] Since AIDS education and prevention is usually one of the activities of GLB student organizations, black GLB students lack this important informational source. Getting involved with an AIDS Awareness student organization if they exist on campus appears even less likely given the stigma surrounding AIDS and "fear of AIDS" which is greater among black students than white students.[57]

Examination of black-white GLB student interaction demonstrates campus patterns of black-white relations that replicate those found in the surrounding society. It also reveals the struggles centered about "identity" and the potential conflict within oneself in deciding on one's "master and subordinate" statuses, in addition to the conflict between the individual and society over status recognition and determination. While this study has primarily thought about these issues within the context of a racially mixed campus, it would be interesting to consider some of these issues at historically black colleges. A preliminary, informal examination of web pages at some of the better known historically black colleges revealed only one campus which had a student group that was clearly represented and identified as a GLB organization and that was at a historically black women's college.[58] It would also be desirable to hear the voices of black GLB students at both racially-mixed and historically black colleges to determine what identity dynamics are similar or dissimilar when it comes to status choices. Finally, we need to think about ways in which bridges can be built over the chasms that currently exist between black and white students, black and white gay, lesbian, and bisexual students, and between heterosexual and GLB students whatever one's ethnicity. Because as it is now, managing one's multiple identities, trying to find some balance or compromise between different statuses creates incredible role strain and conflict in many cases. As one multiracial student put it, and something which would be equally true for black GLB students, "It's almost like you have to divide yourself, and that's just too much work."[59]

Notes

1. I will use the terms "Black" and "White" or "Black community" and "White community" rather than African-American or European-American for two reasons. First, the latter terms are more cumbersome. Second, and more important, I do not think that the real issue which causes so much conflict is tied to nationality as much as it is "skin color" and all the social baggage that gets attached to that variable.

2. The concept "sexual orientation" is used to represent the idea of an "identity" that goes beyond simple same-sex behavior. For purposes of this essay it does not matter whether one thinks this identity is established through nurture during the process of socialization or through nature in some form of fixed genetic biological predisposition. In either case, the emphasis is placed on the lack of a conscious choice regarding what one feels inside in a cognitive-emotional sense although choice may still exist in terms of whether an individual acts on these feelings.

3. One study of gay men at a college campus found that fifty-four percent (54%) of gay men who responded to the survey indicated that they participated in the campus gay and lesbian student organization. This figure may be high, however, since the sample was not random but selectively recruited. See D'Augelli, Anthony R. 1999. "Gay Men in College: Identity Processes and Adaptions." *Journal of College Student Development* 32: 140-146, p. 143.

4. See Hughes, Everett. 1945. "Dilemmas and Contradictions of Status," *American Journal of Sociology*, 50 (March):353-359.

5. For a recent discussion of "passing," see Sanchez, Maria Carla and Linda Schlossberg, eds. 2001. *Passing: Identity and Interpretation in Sexuality, Race, and Religion.* New York: New York University Press.

6. In this essay, "homophobia" refers to an "irrational and distorted view of homosexuality and of homosexual individuals." "Heterosexism" refers "an institutionalized enforcement of heterosexual 'normality' that is assumed by our culture." See Owens, Robert E., Jr. 1998. *Queer Kids: The Challenges and Promise for Lesbian, gay, and Bisexual Youth.* New York: The Haworth Press, Inc., pp. 7-8.

7. Gallup poll results cited in Schaefer, Richard T. 2000. *Racial and Ethnic Groups.* Upper Saddle River, New Jersey: Prentice Hall. P. 59.

8. Personal interview of 22 year old African-American college senior. 2001. Interview by author. Tape recording. Saint Joseph, MO, October 31.

9. Personal interview of 22 year old multiracial college senior. 2001. Interview by author. Tape recording. Saint Joseph, MO, October 29.

10. Smith, T., R. Roberts, and C. Smith. 1997. "Expressions of Prejudice Among College Students Over Three Assessments." *College Student Journal* 29(2): 235-237.

11. For brevity's sake "gay, lesbian, and bisexual" will simply be abbreviated "GLB."

12. Statistics are from the FBI National Press Office. Http://www.fbi.gov.pressrel/pressrel01/hate021301.htm

13. NORC. General Social Surveys, 1972-1998; Cumulative Codebook. Chicago: National Opinion Research Center, 1999, P. 236.

14. Studies cited in "Families & Educators Partnering for Safe Schools," by Parents and Friends of Lesbians and Gays (PFLAG). Http://www.pflag.org.

15. Merton, Robert K. 1949. "Discrimination and the American Creed," in Robert M. MacIver, ed., *Discrimination and National Welfare*, Pp. 99-126. New York: Harper & Row.

16. Cited in Boykin, Keith. 1996. *One More River to Cross*. New York: Anchor Books, P. 224.

17. Ibid. P. 228.

18. Ibid. and Boykin's various columns archived at http://www.gay.com under "Channels" subsection "News."

19. Gay.com Interracial Relationships message board, Whimsy75, (#6 of 35) Sept. 21, 2000.

20. See Welsing, Frances Cress. 1991. *The Isis Papers.* Chicago: Third World Press, Asante, Molefi, 1989, *The Afrocentric Idea*, Philadelphia: Temple University Press, Amiri Baraka, 1965, *American Sexual Preference: Black Male*, reprinted in Baraka, Imanm Amiri. 1998. *Home: Social Essays.* Hopewell, NJ: Eco Press, and Staples, Robert. 1982. *Black Masculinity: The Black Male's Role in American Society.* San Francisco, CA: Black Scholar Press.

21. Ibid. p. 86.

22. Sears, J. T. 1991. *Growing Up Gay in the South: Race, Gender, and Journeys of the Spirit.* NY: Harrington Press, P. 68.

23. For a discussion of these ideas within the context of Zimbabwe, see Epprecht, Marc. 1998. "The 'Unsaying' of Indigenous homosexualities in Zimbabwe: Mapping a Blindspot in an African Masculinity." *Journal of Southern African Studies* 24(4): 631-651.

24. For a brief discussion regarding same-sex behavior among the Azande, see Herdt, Gilbert. 1997. *Same Sex, Different Cultures: Exploring Gay and Lesbian Lives.* Boulder: Westview Press, Pp. 76-80.

25. P. 217 in Dalton, Harlon L. 1989. "AIDS in Blackface." *Daedalus* 118(3): 205-227

26. Personal interview with 22 year old multiracial college senior. 2001. Interview by author. Tape recording. Saint Joseph, MO, October 29.

27. Cools, Janice. 1998. "The (Re)Construction of African-American Masculinity." *African American Male Research.* 3(1). Retrieved November 22, 2001 (http://www.pressroom.com/ ~afrimale/cools.htm).

28. Boykin, Keith. 1998. *One More River to Cross: Black and Gay in America.* New York: Anchor Books, p. 22.

29. Cools, Janice. Op cit. p. 4.

30. Boykin, Keith. Op cit, p. 164.

31. Staples, Robert. 1985. "Changes in Black Family Structure: The Conflict between Family Ideology and Structural Conditions." *Journal of Marriage and the Family* 47:1005-13. See also, Bennett, Neil G., David E. Bloom and Patricia H. Craig. 1989. "The Divergence of Black and White Marriage Patterns." *American Journal of Sociology* 3:692-722 and Kiecolt, K. Jill and Mark A. Fossett. 1995. "Mate Availability and Marriage among African Americans." Pp. 121-142 in *The Decline in Marriage among African Americans: Causes, Consequences, and Policy Implications*, edited by B. Tucker and C. Mitchell-Kernan. New York: Russell Sage Foundation.

32. Jaynes, Gerald D., and Robert M. Williams, Jr., eds. 1989. *A Common Destiny: Blacks and American Society.* Washington, D.C.: National Academy Press, p. 539.

33. P. 126 in Poussaint, Alvin F., M.D. 1990. "An Honest Look at Black Gays and Lesbians." *Ebony* 45(11):124, 126, 130-131.

34. Boykin, Keith. Op cit. p. 181.

35. Outlaw, Paul. 1995. "If that's your boyfriend (he wasn't last night)." *African American Review* 29(2): 347-350.

36. For a recent report and summary of the position towards homosexuality and GLB persons, see Bennett, Lisa. 1998. "Mixed Blessings: Organized Religion and Gay and Lesbian Americans in 1998." Washington, D.C.: Human Rights Campaign Foundation. (http://www.hrc.org/ publications/index.asp)

37. Boykin, Keith. Op cit. p. 126.

38. Personal interview of 22 year old African-American college senior. 2001. Interview by author. Tape recording. Saint Joseph, MO, October 31.

39. Bennett, Lisa. Op cit. p.18. Similar acknowledgments are found in Boykin, Keith, Op cit. Pp. 126-128 and Zulu, N. S. 1996. "Sex, Race and the Stained-glass Window." *Women and Therapy* 19: 27-35.

40. Ibid. P. 16.

41. P. 53 in Smith, Barbara. 1990. "Talking About It: Homophobia in the Black Community." *Feminist Reviews* 34: 47-55

42. Cited in Boykin, Keith Op cit. P. 132.

43. For example one black lesbian related how most of the black lesbians she knew identify as "black women first and lesbians second." In Poussaint, Op cit. p. 131.

44. Garber, Jeffrey S. 2001. "2001 Gay/Lesbian Consumer Online Census." A Syracuse University, OpusComm Group, GSociety Study. Retrieved 10/22/2001. (http://www.glcensus.org)

45. Kim, Bryan S.K. Michael J. D'Andrea, Poonam K. Sahu, and Kiaka J.S. Gaughen. 1998. "A Multicultural Study of University Students' Knowledge of and Attitudes Toward Homosexuality." 36(3): 171-182.

46. Smith, T., R. Roberts, and C. Smith. Op Cit.

47. Dalton, Harold L. Op cit. P. 215.
48. Black lesbian writer Ann Allen Shockley cited in Gomez, Smith Op cit. P.49.
49. See Doll, L., and Beeker, C. 1996. "Male Bisexual Behavior and HIV Risk in the United States: Synthesis of Research with Implications for Behavioral Interventions." *AIDS Education and Prevention* 8: 205-225, Stokes, J.P., Vanable, P.A., and McKiman, D.J. 1997. "Ethnic Differences in Sexual Behavior, Condom Use, and Psychosocial Variables among Black and White Men who have Sex with Men." *Journal of Sex Research* 33: 373-381.
50. Rhue, Sylvia and Rhue, 117-130 in Blumenfeld, Warren J. 1992. *Homophobia: How We all Pay* Thom. 1992. "Reducing Homophobia in African-American Communities," Pp. *the Price*. Boston: Beacon Press.
51. Stokes, Joseph P. and Miller, Robin L. 1998. "Toward an Understanding of Behaviorally Bisexual Men: The Influence and Context of Culture." *Canadian Journal of Human Sexuality* 7(2): 101-113.
52. See Chapter 6 "Outcomes for Sexual-Minority Youths," Pp. 101-122 in Owens Jr., Robert E. 1998. *Queer Kids: The Challenges and Promises for Lesbian, Gay, and Bisexual Youth*. New York: Harrington Park Press and Szymanski, Dawn M., Y. Barry Chung, and Kimberly F. Balsam. 2001. "Psychosocial Correlates of Internalized Homophobia in Lesbians." *Measures and Evaluation in Counseling and Development* 34: 27-38.
53. McKirnan, David J. and Stokes, Joseph P. 1995. "Bisexually Active Men: Social Characteristics and Sexual Behavior." *Journal of Sex Research* 32(1): 65-76.
54. Ibid. P. 72 and Ballard, Scotty R. 2001. "Why AIDS is Rising Among Black Women." *Jet* July 23. Retrieved 10/27/2001. (http://www.findarticles.com/cf_0/m1355/6_100/76800067/ print.jhtml)
55. Ballard, Scotty R. Op cit. P.1.
56. Waldner, Lisa K., Anjoo Kikka, and Salman Baig. 1999. "Ethnicity and Sex Differences in University Student's Knowledge of AIDS, Fear of AIDS, and Homophobia." *Journal of Homosexuality* 37(3): 117-133. See also, Dilorio, C., Parson, M., Lehr, S., Adame, D., and Carlone, J. 1993. "Knowledge of AIDS and Safer Sex Practices among College Freshman." *Public Health Nursing* 10: 159-165.
57. Ibid. P. 124.
58. An informal review of nine historically black college web pages conducted by the author.
59. Personal interview of a twenty-two year old multiracial college senior. 2001. Interview by author. Tape recording. Saint Joseph, MO, October 29.

Article 9

"Did You Hear What That White Woman Said?" Speaking for Change and Chance in Memphis, Tennessee

Wanda Rushing

Growing up female in rural North Carolina I learned that certain things are not to be talked about. Southern girls are taught "the world is full of secrets.... The better part of valor is to accept these secrets and never try to find out what they are" (Smith 1994, 88). In my experience, any mention of sex and pregnancy (with or without benefit of marriage); disability, disease, or death; or racial difference, provoked threatening looks and impervious silence from adults at home, at school, and in church. I learned to be a good girl and keep quiet. In other words, I became invisible, but I could not be insensitive to cycles of birth and death, and evidence of racial tensions in the world around me. I yearned to know the secrets behind the silence.

My upbringing as a "good" Southern girl did not prepare me to deal with the challenges of growing up in a rapidly changing South. White flight from nearby Charlotte, and the dislocations of Southern economic expansion changed my serene rural community into a suburban thoroughfare between Charlotte and Monroe. Poised on the western boundary of North Carolina's Cotton Belt and the southeastern boundary of the state's jewel of the New South, my community became a laboratory experiment in social change. Leaving home at the age of 18, seeking education and life experience, I wanted to understand the processes of social change. Eventually, but not immediately, I reached a point where my search for knowledge made it impossible for me to ignore the conundrum of social inequality and remain silent. As a student I learned that as we break silence, speak the unspoken, uncover the hidden, and make ourselves visible, we "begin to define a reality which resonates to *us*, which affirms our being..." and allows us to discover knowledge of ourselves and the world (Rich 1979, 245). As a scholar and a teacher, I find it essential to break the silences about race, class, and gender, not only to help me rethink basic social science concepts (Collins 1990, 222) as I try to understand social change, but also to advance my search for knowledge about myself.

In 1998, my quest brought me to the University of Memphis where I have taught an upper division undergraduate racial inequality course for six consecutive semesters. In class, we work to break the silence about race and inequality by studying macro-theoretical perspectives, historical processes, structural connections, and their links to racial identity. In so doing, we learn a great deal about the subject matter, each other, and ourselves. A theoretically and historically grounded course in racial inequality might be expected to generate good results anywhere in the United States, but I find it rewarding to teach the class in Memphis. My adopted home is a unique American (and Southern) city alternately described as standing at a cultural and social crossroads, or positioned in the margins. Memphis is "an inland river city where cultures, rich and poor, black and white, urban and rural, Northern and Southern, did not so much converge as collide" (Childers 1998, 100). Noteworthy historical symbols of the cultural collision include the National Civil Rights Museum, built on the site of the Lorraine Motel where Dr. Martin Luther King, Jr. was slain, and Beale Street, home of the blues and once the center of a vibrant African American community in the segregated South. Other symbols include Graceland and Sun Studio, which commemorate the birthplace of rock 'n' roll.

Current Memphis institutions reflect old paradoxes regarding politics, race, geography, and wealth. Today, Memphis is an African American-controlled city in a white southern state (Wailoo 2001, 232). It is represented by two mayors, a black city mayor and a white county mayor; two school systems, a large, predominantly black city school system and a smaller, predominantly white county school system; and two economic and social landscapes, suburban sprawl and affluence outside the expressway with urban poverty and prosperity within it. Racial matters continue to be dichotomized as black and white despite the presence of a small but active Native American community, increasing numbers of Asians and Africans, and dramatic growth in the Latino/Latina population.

At the University of Memphis, once an all-white campus, minority students now comprise about one-third of the student body, but this particular class enrollment ranges from 50% African American and 50% European American to 100% African American. The class sometimes includes Native Americans, Asian Americans, Middle Eastern Americans, and foreign students. Most students in the class originate from Memphis and the Mid-South region, and most of them are women. The majority of these students are not sociology majors, but many take the course for credit toward a major or minor in African and African American Studies.

Many white students, not only in Memphis but also throughout the United States, who find it unsettling to examine the contradictions between our nation's ideological commitment to equality and the persistence of inequality may elect not to take a course that probes two hotly contested subjects -- race and inequality. Frequently, white students who do take my class find it disturbing to examine their own individual assumptions about racial identity and privilege. Minority students who take the course hoping to validate their own experiences from living in a racially divided society may be shocked and disturbed to learn the complicated ways that white students think about race and racism, or how they deny it (Suter and Schweickart 1998, 129).

Just as these assumptions about race and inequality influence student decisions to take the class, they affect student understandings of class readings, interactions with classmates, and expectations of faculty. All students carefully scrutinize the professor who teaches the class, expecting to find evidence of academic competence along with personal credibility. All faculty, especially if they are white, must demonstrate believability and trust (Hendrix 1998, 749). Students often express surprise to find me, a white Southern woman, teaching both graduate and undergraduate sociology courses on racial inequality at the University of Memphis. My own race and regional background may raise credibility issues at first, but readings and discussions convince even the most skeptical students to question their stereotypes about white Southerners. I like to think that my love of literature and references to the work of Toni Morrison, Zora Neale Hurston, and Richard Wright, my Baptist upbringing and citations from old hymns and scripture, as well as my Southern accent and accounts of discrimination on the basis of speech also make me more credible. It helps that I am a woman and that many readings focus on race, class, and gender.

In my class students develop trust for each other and for me through readings, class discussions, personal journals, and individual student-teacher conferences. From the outset we acknowledge that members of all racial groups, including whites, have racial identities (Tatum 1992). We work at understanding how racial identities relate to gender and class identities, and how these identities relate to historical and global processes. We discredit scientific racism and demystify white privilege. Students quickly learn to engage in discussions of power and privilege and the social construction of race and gender. White students often say, "I never thought a course about race would say anything about white people." They add, "I didn't realize how much I benefit from white privilege," or "I didn't think I was a racist until I read this." Black students often express surprise that white people don't "know" this information. Both men and women learn to see race and gender differently. Through these candid exchanges, students learn to trust each other, which makes it possible for us to discuss sensitive issues. My class offers students a "safe" and respectful environment to learn about each other while grappling with complicated theoretical and historical issues (Cannon 1990).

Students keep personal journals to write about class discussions, readings, videos, speakers, and other activities. At some point in the journal, many minority students comment on their initial reaction to me. Some apologize for misjudging me. At first they cannot believe a white southern woman can speak convincingly about white privilege, racial identity, and institutional racism. They quickly change their minds and their expectations for the class.

Interestingly, white students are more likely than students of color to drop the class, and students of color are more likely to add the class during the drop-add period at the beginning of the semester. Typically, students who add the class tell me they are acting on the recommendation of a friend. Some students who drop express dissatisfaction with my refusal to adopt their view that racism is in the past, i.e., an historical artifact. Some criticize the class as "negative," presumably because it rejects an "orientation" to whiteness

(Frankenberg 1993), while others leave without any explanation. Drops are more likely to occur when the ratio of white enrollment to black enrollment is low, presumably because white students feel uncomfortable being a minority in this class.

My experiences sharply contrast with those of sociologist Lewis Killian, a white Southern man, who taught a race relations course at the University of Massachusetts, 1969-1970, and observed that black students frequently dropped his class. His autobiography states, "I will always wonder how many of the drops occurred when students discovered that I was not black but a 'honkie' with a Southern accent" (Killian 1994, 168). I wonder, however, how many drops occur when white students in Memphis discover that I am a white southern woman who works to demystify white privilege and represent "other" perspectives on most racial issues. In both experiences, Killian's and mine, perhaps some students perceive the lack of convergence between the message and the messenger to be as problematic for them as the actual course content about race (Moulder 1997). But gender, regional, generational, and course content differences are factors that may account for our different experiences.

Course Overview

In Sociology 4420, Racial Inequality, the objectives are: to develop a macro-theoretical perspective on racial inequality, to become aware of one's own racial identity in a theoretical context, to understand whiteness as a form of racial and social identity, and to understand that race is given meaning through historical and social contexts and is not a natural or biological category. This course is not a social psychology course about attitudes nor is it a social problems course about the nation's most disadvantaged ethnic and racial groups. It is not a regional studies course about the South as a bastion of racism. My course shifts away from personal attitudes, group pathology, and regional backwardness to concentrate on historical processes, macro-theoretical perspectives, and structural connections to racial identity.

A number of class readings acknowledge and demystify the privileges of whiteness to show the flip side of racism. Peggy McIntosh's "White Privilege and Male Privilege: A Personal Account of Coming to See Correspondence Through Work in Women's Studies," Abby Ferber's "What White Supremacists Taught A Jewish

Scholar about Identity," and Ruth Atkin and Adrienne Rich's " 'J.A.P.' Slapping: The Politics of Scape-Goating," open up discussions of the complexities of white racial identity. Readings from W. E. B. Du Bois, David Roediger, Gunnar Myrdahl, Joe Feagin, William Julius Wilson, Gerald Horne, and others analyze the complexities of structured inequality. We also address current and historical issues about foreign immigration to the United States as well as historical migration patterns within the United States.

Results of the Class

My racial inequality class offers students the opportunity to broaden their understanding of the theoretical complexities of race, while helping them find ways to analyze their own experiences. All of us in the class, especially me, learn from their personal accounts. A young African American man, a Gulf War veteran, discussed his military experience in the context of one of our readings about the "double-consciousness" of African American soldiers in the Gulf War. A Native American woman brought her tribal enrollment papers to class in connection with readings about Native Americans and the federal government. An Arab American woman from the Middle East relayed her frustrations as a devout Muslim woman in America, and in Memphis. An African American mother spoke with me privately about tragically losing two sons through violence. White students often talk about how it feels to a minority in the class. Students openly discuss being stopped for driving while black, being followed in stores, or being instructed by employers to follow minorities in stores in the context of class readings. Many students remark that the course validates their own experience. Others express shock and alarm at the correspondence between readings and class discussions. A student from France, a black woman, contrasted her own experiences in France with her life in the United States. Her European perspective on race revealed an entirely new world to her classmates.

Semester after semester, I am amazed at the courtesy and concern shown by class members for each other, efforts at conflict negotiation and resolution within the class, the composition of study groups that emerge, and long-term friendships that blossom. Only ten percent of our students live on campus. Many students relate that they just do not get to know people in most classes. Yet they form bonds in a class addressing subject matter that many Americans feel uncomfortable talking about. Student course evaluations indicate that students find readings and class discussion to be vigorous and enlightening. They rate me as an effective teacher and often recommend that every undergraduate should be required to take the class.

I find that I get to know students better in this class than in any other class I teach. Students are more likely to seek one-to-one conferences with me during the semester, and they are more likely to stay in touch with me afterwards. At my urging, one former student applied for the University of Memphis Martin Luther King, Jr. Award and received it for scholarship and activism. Last year, I marched with former students in the city's Martin Luther King, Jr. holiday parade, and I attended a professional Black Repertory Theatre production starring a former student. By all indications, the class is a success. I attribute this success to the students and to the strategies discussed below.

Six Strategies for a Successful Racial Inequality Class

- Acknowledging that black students and white students view the subject of racism differently and allowing each group to learn the "other" perspective.
- Situating the "problem" of racism within mainstream institutions and ideologies, both past and present, rather than dismissing it as a preoccupation of fringe groups.
- Introducing interdisciplinary materials to support social scientific analyses.
- Intervening or responding to potentially confrontational remarks, not only to defuse them, but also to use them to enhance class discussion.
- Requiring students to keep journals reflecting their own thoughts about their experiences and their understandings of class readings and discussions.
- Using exam reviews and group projects as methods of teaching collaboration.

Acknowledging that Black and White Students View Racism Differently

The class rejects an "orientation" to whiteness (Frankenberg 1993) as well as the notion that a color-blind society is attainable or desirable. Readings include Noel Jacob Kent's article, "The New Campus Racism: What's Going On?" Kent writes that white students and students of color speak entirely different languages when discussing racism. These differences not only contribute to a lack of understanding of racism in larger society, but also lead to conflict on college campuses. Whites see racism as peripheral and as an historic artifact, but Blacks see it as central to present society; consequently, white students may become defensive about black student organizations and critical of them (Kent 1998). Our class discusses Kent's article in terms of campus life at the University of Memphis where membership in black sororities and fraternities and participation in black student activities such as Friday afternoon Step Shows sometimes provokes controversy. Often our discussion of campus organizations expands to include debates about black and white spring breaks in Florida, black and white football weekends in Memphis, and other racially divided college-related events.

Situating the "problem" of racism within mainstream institutions and ideologies, both past and present

Many students came of age in a time when official sources denied the existence of inequality and celebrated the virtues of colorblindness (Davis 1992). In fact, many official sources continue to make these claims. In class discussions about racism, however, students of all races agree that public expressions of overt racism may have declined in recent years, but covert racism continues. New forms of racism emerge, partly in response to economic uncertainty. Omi and Winant (1986) explain that a "rearticulation of racial ideology" occurred in the post-civil rights era; using code words, conservatives treat white males as the victims of reverse discrimination in an era of economic restructuring. In reality, however, African Americans, Latinos/Latinas, and Native Americans continue to be over-represented at the bottom of the scale of income and other valued resources. Bonacich (1989) argues that mainstream ideologies endorse inequalities of wealth and privilege as "justifiable and desirable" in a capitalistic society and capitalism depends on inequality. In discussions of mainstream ideologies about race and inequality, students struggle to reconcile the contradictions between popular and official denials of inequality and scholarly analyses of its impact on all Americans (Killian 1998).

Situating the "problem" of racism within mainstream institutions focuses attention on issues of racial justice. Topics such as the over-representation of young black men in the US criminal justice system, the practice of racial profiling, and harsher penalties for possession of crack cocaine than powder cocaine, interest students. Recently, I showed a video for the first time, The Greensboro Massacre. It documents the 1979 murder of five Communist Worker Party activists, both black and white, in Greensboro, NC by members of the Ku Klux Klan. News cameras captured the Klan attack on the CPW parade in broad daylight. Much to the disbelief of the students, the trial of the Klansmen resulted in "not guilty" verdicts. The verdict, and media coverage of the trial proceedings, demonstrated the entrenchment of institutional discrimination. After watching the film, many students felt moved to do something to prevent future tragedies.

Introducing interdisciplinary materials to support social scientific analyses

Interdisciplinary materials support social scientific analyses both directly and indirectly. Directly, I use one history book as a text, David Roediger's *The Wages of Whiteness*. I also hand out Adrienne Rich's poem that maps our country from *An Atlas of A Difficult World* and Benjamin Zephaniah's poem, "White Comedy." Consistent with theoretical readings, these materials help shape student perspectives on race. Indirectly, I frequently cite examples from African American literature such as Toni Morrison's *The Bluest Eye* and *Beloved*, Zora Neale Hurston's *Their Eyes Were Watching God*, Richard Wright's *Native Son*, and Ralph Ellison's *The Invisible Man*, to support sociological readings. These citations resonate with students who have read the works and spur others to read them. They vividly illustrate the importance of race, class, and gender in the sociological analysis of inequality, oppression, and internalized oppression.

I also use religious teachings as an interdisciplinary, multicultural resource not only because religion bridges the racial divide in the religious South, but also because it establishes common ground for Christian, Jewish, and Islamic students. For example, one of our readings examines the historical and political significance of the self-selected name change from African, to Colored, to Negro, to Black, to African American (Grant and Orr 1998). I ask students to think of examples of name changes associated with transformative experiences from Christian, Judaic, or Islamic religious teachings. Soon, students begin to call the roll for Abram-Abraham, Jacob-Israel, Saul-Paul, and Simon-Peter. They also think of Malcolm X and Mohammed Ali. Then I ask them about Dr. Martin Luther King, Jr. Occasionally, someone knows that he was first named Michael Luther King, Jr., but most students admit surprise when I recount the story of Michael Luther King, Sr.'s 1934 tour of Europe, Africa and the Holy Land and his decision to legally change his name, and his son's name, to Martin in honor of the founder of the Protestant faith (Branch 1988, 44-47). This exercise permits students from diverse backgrounds to share a cultural understanding of the power of self-definition and personal transformation. It reveals "the power dynamics underlying the very process of definition itself" (Collins 1991, 38) and validates links between individual identity and social change processes.

Intervening or responding to potentially confrontational remarks, not only to defuse them, but also to use them to enhance class discussion

One semester a young African American man announced: "Black people have *been* knowing this. I don't know why we find it more acceptable coming from the mouth of a white man at Harvard." The student's remark occurred during a class discussion of Stephen Jay Gould's video – Evolution and Human Equality. The video and assigned readings discredit 19th century scientific racism and argue that there is no scientific basis for racial inequality. Gould's video traces all human origin to Africa and shows that the recency of human evolution could not have produced alleged biological racial differences. Generally, students respond positively to the video, especially African American students. I show it early in the semester following discussions of the social construction of race, white privilege, and inequality.

The student continued his criticism of white authority adding that his mother doesn't believe him when he tells her his "natural hair" (i.e., long and braided) is healthy. Looking directly at me, he said scornfully, "Maybe if you told her, she would believe you." His comment was partly a response to Stephen Jay Gould's video. It was also a direct challenge to me. In effect, he challenged the class to question my authority. He implied: "Why are we so accepting of a white person teaching something that we would be less willing to accept if it came from a black person?"

I chose to respond to the student's remark as a challenge to scientific knowledge, and took the opportunity to ask who produces "scientific" knowledge, who controls its production, and who benefits from it (Harding 1991). It kept us focused on the issue of scientific racism, power, and privilege. It acknowledged and helped define the student's role as a class leader and defused a potentially damaging confrontation. I ignored the challenge to the authority of white male Harvard professors, white female University of Memphis professors, and mothers.

Faculty will manage student challenges to authority more effectively when they do not undermine their own authority and discredit themselves. Before moving to Memphis, I taught this class once at the University of Tennessee in Knoxville to mostly white students. The sociology course was cross-listed with African American Studies. At the end of the semester, an African American female student told me that she and another student knew each other from earlier African American Studies courses. She confessed that they exchanged questioning looks with each other the first day of class when I stepped into the room. In a previous course the white teacher walked in and said: "I guess you are wondering why a white woman is teaching a course in African American studies." The student claimed that she did not question the professor's race or her qualifications to teach the class until asked to do so. Afterward, she never felt comfortable in the class, and never perceived the teacher as competent. She expected all white faculty to begin an African American Studies course raising questions about his or her qualifications or right to be there. When I did not bring up the subject, she decided that my race must not be a problem for me, or for her. Initially, she gave me the benefit of the doubt. At the end of the semester she felt good about her experience in the class.

Requiring students to keep journals reflecting their own thoughts about their experiences and their understandings of class readings and discussions

Students are required to keep weekly journal entries and each week's assignment appears on the syllabus. Assignments vary and students choose their own topics some weeks. The first assignment is: write your reaction to the first week of class and explain your expectations of the course. The journal helps students work through personal and interpersonal issues and teaches them how to write academic critiques of readings and presentations. I assure students that I will protect their privacy, and I encourage candor. Some students choose to write poetry about their reactions to class and their life experiences, but most write narrative accounts of economic difficulties, encounters with the criminal justice system, neighborhood conflicts, family stress, and personal loss. Many students reveal strong personal feelings about their experiences with racial issues. Some students comment on class discussions and explain their reasons for remaining silent in class. Others air grievances with their classmates.

Minority students who are the first in their family to attend college often write about their ambivalence toward higher education. Some receive criticism from friends and family who accuse them of "trying to be white." Others write about their frustrations with school but their desire to honor family wishes and fulfill high parental expectations. Much to my surprise, I find that many students share their journals with people outside the class. Readers include parents, friends, and significant others who sometimes question whether it is safe to disclose true feelings with a white faculty member. One student took her journal on visits with her mother who was undergoing chemotherapy. She said that her mother looked forward to reading her journal and hearing accounts of what happened in class that week. Another student reported that her father complained: "Aren't you taking anything else at that university?"

Using exam reviews and group projects as methods of teaching collaboration

Reading assignments in my racial inequality course are rigorous. I give three essay exams per semester, including the final, and I assign one group project. One week prior to each exam I distribute a review list of possible essay questions and terms for identification. These questions are designed to help students review the material and identify major themes. I select two or three of the essays and five or six terms for the exam. I encourage students to use all readings and notes and to study with their classmates prior to exam day. The group projects usually focus on a particular racial controversy, or group, and students select groups according to their interests. Occasionally, I give them a few minutes of class time to talk to group members and plan meetings outside of class.

These instructional tools benefit students in many ways. First, students learn how to study, subsequently, most students learn a great deal. Second, students learn to collaborate. Often the composition of study groups changes from one test to another. If the class is racially diverse, study groups tend to be less racially segregated by the end of the semester. Interestingly, students seem to be more comfortable speaking in class after working in groups. Frequently, group discussions continue outside of class even when there is no exam or project to prepare.

Course Problems – Missing Persons

The number one complaint from black and white students concerns the racial composition of the class. Every semester students comment on the small number of white students, particularly white males, who take the class. "If only more white men took the class and talked with us about race, things would be different" they say. I imagine that white students, particularly white males, are underrepresented in similar classes in other universities in the United States. Based on my observations, I offer four explanations for this phenomenon related to racial identity, denial, victim ideology, and fear.

Typically, white students do not think of themselves as having a racial identity, but minority students certainly do (Suter and Schweickart 1998, 129). Because whiteness is taken for granted, white students are less likely to choose an elective course in racial inequality or any explicit "race" topic based on identity issues or subjects deemed to be of personal relevance. Similarly, men are less likely than women to take courses in gender or Women's Studies. Students in my course learn to question taken-for-granted assumptions about race and gender, and they long for the opportunity to bring more white students, especially white males, into class discussions.

The common misperception that race concerns "other" people relates to "a general denial among white Americans, male and female alike, that black Americans face serious problems with racial discrimination" (Feagin 1992, 404). Denial means that "white Americans, especially middle-class and upper-class white men with power," do not have to take "responsibility for the widespread prejudice and discrimination that generate rage and protest among black women and men..." (Feagin 1992, 405). Denial also allows white students to continue to assume that classes about racial inequality are not for or about white people.

Some white students may consider a course about reverse discrimination to be more relevant for them. In America since the 1980s, with the "rearticulation of racial ideology," popular discourse now places whites, particularly white males, in the role of victims of racial discrimination (Omi and Winant 1986). Students who internalize this victim ideology are unlikely to take an inequality class. They are unlikely to confront evidence showing that whites may find themselves as targets of oppression on the basis of sexism, heterosexism, classism, religion, or region, but they are not at the mercy of systematic racial oppression that demeans, disenfranchises or ignores them (Rose 1996, 36). Moreover, the ideology of white victimization obscures the present and past reality of institutional racism in the United States, and encourages white people to scapegoat people of color for economic and political shifts that negatively affect their lives.

It is possible that white male students, or any student from an advantaged background, avoid inequality courses for fear of being cast in the role of victimizer vis-à-vis students from disadvantaged backgrounds (Davis 1992; Bohmer and Briggs 1991; Cannon 1990). The fear of being blamed or held responsible for centuries of injustice creates defensive or evasive behavior; consequently, it is essential to structure inequality courses to avoid dividing the class into victims and victimizers. Discussions of individual, institutional, and symbolic racism at the beginning of the course help allay fears.

The Future of Teaching Racial Inequality

W. E. B. Du Bois identified the problem of the color line a century ago, but racial divisions are as real today in our society, on college campuses, and in classrooms. Finding strategies to build alliances across those lines and divisions offers us not only means of understanding the world, but also means of discovering knowledge about ourselves. I find teaching Racial Inequality courses to be a challenging but a meaningful way for students and faculty to address sensitive issues and build strong alliances across the color line.

No doubt, teaching or taking a class in racial inequality involves risks, both personal and political. For Du Bois, "education...always has had, and always will have, an element of danger and revolution, of dissatisfaction and discontent" (Du Bois 1994, 20). But educational environments can offer courses where it is safe to ask tough questions, break silence, and overcome fear of the "other." Through education and experience we can engage in discussions of sensitive issues without being hindered by crippling denial and feelings of victimization. Instead, knowledge about inequality may arouse discomfort with the status quo. Feelings of dissatisfaction and discontent mount when our comfortable and familiar ideas about the world, and about "us," no longer fit our knowledge and experience. But dissonance and discontent may motivate us to seek knowledge, claim the power of self-definition, become visible, and speak "for change and chance" (Hurston 1991, 37).

References

Bohmer, S. and J. Briggs. 1991. "Teaching Privileged Students about Gender, Race, and class Oppression." *Teaching Sociology* 19:154-163.

Bonacich, E. 1989. "Inequality in America: The Failure of the American System for People of Color." *Sociological Spectrum* 9:1:77-101.

Branch, T. 1988. *Parting the Waters: America in the King Years 1954-63.* Simon and Schuster, Inc.

Cannon, L. W. 1990. "Fostering Positive Race, Class, and Gender Dynamics in the Classroom." *Women's Studies Quarterly* 1 & 2:126-134.

Childers, T. 1998. "Memphis." *American Heritage* (October), pp. 96-115.

Collins, P. H. 1990. *Black Feminist Thought: Knowledge, Consciousness, and the Politics of Empowerment.* New York: Unwin Hyman.

Collins, P. H. 1991. "Learning from the Outsider Within: The Sociological Significance of Black Feminist Thought." Pp. 35-59 in *Beyond Methodology*, Mary Margaret Fonow and Judith A. Cook, Eds. Bloomington and Indianapolis: Indiana University Press.

Davis, N. J. 1992. "Teaching About Inequality: Student Resistance, Paralysis, and Rage." *Teaching Sociology* 20: 232-238.

Dubois, W.E.B. 1994. *The Souls of Black Folk.* Dover.

Frankenberg, R. 1993. *The Social Construction of Whiteness: White Women, Race Matters.* Minneapolis, MN: University of Minnesota.

Grant, R. W. and M. Orr. 1998. "Language, Race and Politics: From 'Black' to 'African American.'" Pp. 117-132 in *Sources: Notable Selections in Race and Ethnicity* by Adalberto Aguirre, Jr. and David V. Baker. Dushkin/McGraw Hill. Second Edition.

Harding, S. 1991. *Whose Science? Whose Knowledge?* Ithaca, NY: Cornell University Press.

Hendrix, K. G. 1998. "Student Perceptions of the Influence of Race on Professor Credibility." *Journal of Black Studies* 28:6:738-763.

Hurston, Z. N. 1991. *Their Eyes Were Watching God.* Urbana and Chicago: University of Ilinois Press.

Kent, N. J. 1998. "The New Campus Racism: What's Going On?" Pp. 189-197 in *Sources: Notable Selections in Race and Ethnicity* by Adalberto Aguirre, Jr. and David V. Baker. Dushkin/McGraw Hill. Second Edition.

Killian, L. 1994. *Black and White: Reflections of a White Southern Sociologist.* Dix Hills, NY: General Hall.

Killian, L. 1998. "Race Relations and the Nineties; "Where Are the Dreams of the Sixties?" Pp. 133-145 in Adalberto Aguirre, Jr. and David V. Backer, Sources: *Notable Selections in Race and Ethnicity.* Guilford, Connecticut: Dushkin/McGraw-Hill. Second Edition.

Moulder, F. V. 1997. "Teaching about Race and Ethnicity: A message of Despair or a Message of Hope?" *Teaching Sociology* 25:120-127.

Omi, M. and H. Winant 1986. *Racial Formation in the United States from the 1960s to the 1980s.* Routledge.

Rich, A. 1979. *On Lies, Secrets, and Silence.* New York: W.W. Norton.

Rose, L. R. 1996. "White Identity and Counseling White Allies About Racism." Pp. 24-47 in Benjamin P. Bowser and Raymond G. Hunt, Eds. *Impacts of Racism on White Americans.* Second Edition. Sage.

Smith, L. 1994/1949. *Killers of the Dream.* New York: W.W. Norton.

Stassen, M. L. A. 1995. "White Faculty members and Racial Diversity: A Theory and Its Implications." *The Review of Higher Education* 18:4:361-191.

Suter, D. and D. Schweickart. 1998. "The Biology and Philosophy of Race and Sex: A Course." *NWSA Journal* 10:2:117-136.

Tatum, B. D. 1992. "Talking about Race, Learning about Racism: The Application of Racial Identity Development Theory in the Classroom." *Harvard Educational Review* 62:1:1-24

Tatum, B. D. 1994. "Teaching White Students about Racism: The Search for White Allies and the Restoration of Hope." *Teachers College Record* 95:4:462-476.

Wailoo, K. 2001. *Dying in the City of the Blues.* Chapel Hill: University of North Carolina Press.

Article 10

Exploring Racial Policy Views of College-Age White Americans: Implications for Campus Climate

Eboni M. Zamani

> In the 1960s the Congress amended the Constitution to extend suffrage to Blacks, passed four major civil rights bills, and funded numerous social welfare programs, including the War on Poverty. These efforts to improve the situation of Blacks were successful: the economic status of Blacks improved, poverty declined, and on many indicators differences between races became much smaller. Will this racial progress continue? Or, just as the advances made by Blacks after the Civil War were largely eliminated in the period following Reconstruction, will the gains of the 1960s and 1970s disappear in the coming decades? (Farley, 1984, p. 203)

INTRODUCTION

More than fifteen years ago the above quote questioned a national commitment to equalizing opportunities, fostering greater participation and advancement of African Americans in American life. Although there were gains in social welfare for African Americans during the 1960s and 1970s, efforts toward ending this period of civil unrest and racial divide were made through legal motions to ensure equality across racial/ethnic groups. Racial inequities intensified as growing numbers of minorities criticized institutionalized racism, asserting policy and program demands for change in housing, employment, and education. As the country enacted legislative mandates to redress discrimination, college campuses were not immune to the racial crises as many "ivory towers" were microcosms of the larger society manifesting hate, rage, and bigotry (Chang, Witt, Jones, & Hakuta, 1999).

As racial diversification and policy implementation slowly approached becoming one of several national priorities, the promotion of equality for all was not widely accepted as systems of segregation, prejudice and discrimination continued. During the Kennedy administration, Executive Order 10925 was issued later evolving into Executive Order 11246 enacted by President Lyndon Johnson. Hence, a series of policy programming commonly referred to as affirmative action was originated to eradicate previous discrimination and its present day effects toward African Americans.

Affirmative action was instituted to hold institutions accountable for fostering diversity and to promote the inclusion of other disadvantaged/underrepresented racially/ethnically diverse groups (i.e., Asian American, Hispanic American and Native American). Likewise, affirmative action sought to address the concerns of the economically disadvantaged and women who also had been treated unfairly and experienced barriers to upward mobility (Crosby, 1994; Fleming, Gill, & Swinton, 1978; Trent, 1991). By 1971, the formulation of affirmative action plans and programs were required at institutions of higher learning, particularly targeting predominately White institutions (Fleming, Gill, & Swinton, 1978). During this time, affirmative action programs at colleges and universities were beginning to examine the disparate treatment of African American students in particular, with regard to access, recruitment and support services.

Since its inception, affirmative action, particularly in higher education has been continually challenged. In attempting to foster greater educational access and equitable outcomes for those previously not served by society, affirmative action programs are often thought of as a form of preferential treatment or tokenism and used as a euphemism for reversed discrimination (Chideya, 1995; Clegg, 2000;

Feinberg, 1996; Dovidio & Gaertner, 1996; Tierney, 1997). Given the current period of retrenchment relative to racial policy programming, the future of affirmative action as a mechanism to diversify American institutions hinges on the social acceptance of the majority (i.e., White Americans). Therefore, this chapter seeks to address three objectives: 1) to discuss the framing of affirmative action as it relates to public support or disfavor; 2) to examine the extent literature on college enrollment patterns, institutional type and collegiate responses to race matters on campus; and 3) to explore traditional-college age Whites racial policy views and discuss what receptivity or lack thereof to affirmative action efforts possibly suggest for campus climate. In view of that, the following research questions guide this exploratory study: (a) To what degree are gender, highest year of school completed, parent's highest year of school completed, subjective class identification, annual family income, political party affiliation, and political ideology significantly associated with views regarding compensatory assistance specifically geared toward African Americans? (b) Are there differences between males and females between the ages of 18-24 in stance toward affirmative action targeting African Americans? and c) Is there a shift in responses to affirmative action among White American respondents on the General Social Survey (GSS) from 1994-1998?

BACKGROUND

Framing of Affirmative Action: Economic, Race-blind or Race-based?

As an undergraduate, I had the opportunity to participate in two summer internships that made lasting impressions on me in that both solidified my desire to pursue post-baccalaureate training. The summer following my sophomore year in college I was selected to take part in the University of Colorado at Boulder's SMART Program (Summer Minority Access to Research Training Program). The next summer I was a research intern at Notre Dame University in a program very similar to UC-Boulder's referred to as PMEGS (Promoting Minority Education in Graduate School). The goal of each program was to increase the number of students of color attending graduate school, particularly in fields with an underrepresentation of minorities and women. While at UC-Boulder, I had my first exposure to the term affirmative action and its framing. A fellow intern majoring in Chemistry expressed her frustration regarding comments made by one of the graduate assistants in the department. She was told, "You are only here because of affirmative action. It must be nice to be Black; if I were I would get a free ride as well". In my naiveté I did not know what she was referring to and she explained to me "That graduate student thinks that I don't deserve to be here despite my grade point average being a 3.9 on a 4.0 scale". The graduate students' inflammatory remarks reflect one end of the continuum with regard to how affirmative action is perceived.

One common misconception of affirmative action is that it is a form of preferential treatment which provides opportunities and for unqualified persons (Chideya, 1995; Feinberg, 1996). Unfortunately, the discontents of diversity have become even more pronounced. Since that time, Notre Dame's funding for PMEGS was cut completely and UC-Boulder has had funding restrictions limiting the program to only those in the physical sciences and engineering. This has resulted in fewer student interns in other fields of study where the participation of underrepresented/disadvantaged groups is not on par with that of majority counterparts.

Current debates about the framing of affirmative action have included whether or not members of groups that have suffered historical discrimination and institutional racism may be targeted by the policy (Boris, 1998; Crosby, 1994; Feinberg, 1996). If affirmative action is presented solely in terms of race, then the anti-sentiment (i.e., negative stereotypes) that Whites may harbor toward people of color could manifest itself through opposition to race-targeted programs. Public opinion on social policies is often formed by how the issues are framed and presented to society-at-large (Bobo & Smith, 1994; Kinder & Sanders, 1990).

In recent years, an alternative form of affirmative action has been proposed. Economic/need-based affirmative action is thought to be a potential compromise by some because policies would no longer target just racial minorities and women but extend to persons who illustrate economic need from all racial backgrounds (Chatman & Smith, 2000). Feinberg (1996) argued that race- and gender-based affirmative action addresses three moral issues that need-based affirmative action policies do not adequately meet. Those three are 1) historical debt, 2) equality of opportunity, and 3) economics and the distribution of societal resources.

Affirmative action is often viewed as a burden imposed on modern-day society in compensating or correcting historical discrimination and its present-day effects (Clegg, 2000; Tierney, 1997). A great deal of conflict arises when present-day Americans do not feel a sense of obligation for previous discrimination although all modern-day citizens of the majority have benefited from grievous acts of the past as they supported, sustained and stabilized this country's economy (Bonacich 1975; Bonacich, 1989). Because American institutions could not·be trusted to voluntarily consider women and applicants of color, affirmative action was necessary. Thus, traditionally equal educational opportunity has eluded many citizens who were not White, male, and middle class.

Advocates of race-based/race-targeted forms of affirmative action assert that the majority of African Americans and other underrepresented groups are not equivalent with Whites regarding educational and employment opportunities. On the other hand, economic/need-based affirmative action supporters argue that ideas of fairness are addressed more appropriately by setting low socioeconomic status as the targeting criteria due to the unequal distribution of income in the United States (Chatman & Smith, 2000). The majority of Whites are comfortable with the socioeconomic gap between themselves and African Americans (Kluegel, 1990). Economic/need-based affirmative action presumes that inequities for all persons should be addressed and can be remedied. This perspective only entertains the economic factors of affirmative action while not acknowledging previous injustices to people of color and women in addition to insufficiently addressing the contemporary ramifications of former subordination of marginalized groups.

Within the last few years, various foundations and public institutions of higher learning have been struck with lawsuits challenging the use of affirmative action in awarding fellowships, scholarships and internships for students of color (Barnes, 1996; Wright, 1997). Several states have debated the use of affirmative action, weighing whether to dismantle it altogether (Grahnke, 1999). Attempts to dismount affirmative action in the state of Washington received support as voters passed Initiative 200 by state referendum in a 54 to 46 decision (Tharp, 1998). Very similar to its predecessor Proposition 209 in California, I-200 ended affirmative action practices by the state and local government.

Washington State interestingly is not very culturally diverse unlike California given that 83 % of Washington's 5.6 million population is

White and no racial/ethnic group exceeds 6% (Tharp, 1998). Although race and ethnicity will no longer be considered in the admissions process at the University of Washington, increasing attention will be drawn to factors such as socioeconomic status and personal disadvantage as a means of addressing diversity. The Office of Financial Management in Washington State compiled information from four-year institutions finding that the key beneficiaries of special and/or alternative admissions as well as hiring at Washington State's four-year institutions were White (Kelly, 1996). Kelly (1996) reported the following:

> Special/alternative admission standards have long been derided by critics of affirmative action as a "lowering of standards" which diminishes academic excellence and limits opportunities for those who are better qualified. To the degree that alternative admission standards can be viewed as lowering the bar, Whites are jumping that bar far more often than African Americans in Washington's four-year schools. (p.78)

In sum, Whites have been receiving opportunities of access under affirmative action in public higher education at greater rates than underrepresented students of color were prior to or following the installation of I-200.

Race and Institutional Attendance Patterns of Collegians

The challenge to affirmative action has far-reaching consequences for students of color across institutional types from state to state. In the midst of the affirmative action dispute unfortunately, African American and Hispanic students are entering higher education at lower rates than their White and Asian American counterparts (Rendon & Hope, 1996). Due to various factors such as academic preparation, financial need, low socioeconomic status (SES), and family obligations, many students are locked out of attending four-year institutions of higher learning, particularly disadvantaged and underrepresented students of color. Four-year colleges and universities may find it increasingly difficult to successfully admit students of color in large quantities (Gillett-Karam et al., 1991; Lederman, 1997; Rendon & Hope, 1996). Given this fact, continued support of diversity initiatives and opportunity enhancement (i.e., the use of race as one of several factors in admissions decisions) may aid in bridging the educational attainment gap.

By 1994 two-year institutions enrolled 39% of all collegians while nearly half of all students of color in higher education attend two-year institutions (Cohen, 1998; Rendon & Garza, 1996). Given the threat of affirmative action retrenchment in college admissions, coupled with the disproportionate enrollment of African Americans and Hispanics in community colleges, two-year institutions may face the possibility of serving a larger segment of first generation students of color. And so given the shifting demographics of this country's populace, continuance of special efforts to recruit from two-year colleges and assist students of color in their transition to senior level institutions are particularly germane.

At various postsecondary institutions, increasingly diverse campuses bring forth conflicts regarding race, particularly as it relates to whether racial background is considered as one of a myriad of factors in determining college admissions. Research addressing attitudes toward affirmative action in college admissions suggests that the majority of White students disfavor endeavors to diversify when race-based or race-neutral (Meader, 1998; Sax & Arredondo, 1999; Smith, 1996; Zamani, 2001). As college campuses are merely microcosms of the larger society, additional studies have shown that among the general population, White Americans agree with affirmative action in theory but not in practice (Dovidio, Gaertner, & Murrell, 1994; Dovidio, Mann, & Gaertner, 1989; Kluegel & Smith, 1986). The majority of Whites contend that they are egalitarian in their views and support opportunity enhancing programming. However, a paradox exists in levels of support for affirmative action when it is race-specific (Dietz-Uhler & Murrell, 1993).

Campus Climate

The composition of American college students has been significantly altered since the enactment of affirmative action. For example, undergraduate enrollment of African Americans has increased by nearly one-third over the last ten years while the enrollment of Hispanic collegians has risen by 98% in contrast to a decline of 1% among White undergraduates (Nettles & Perna, 1997). However, underrepresentation still persists and is more pronounced at the four-year level despite increases in attendance of traditional college-age non-Asian students of color. As such, the boost in African American and Hispanic undergraduate enrollment has not remedied continual underrepresentation or lower bachelor's degree conferment for these groups as it relates to the general population of traditional college-age students (Perna, 2000).

Clearly the institutional climate at colleges and universities are of ever-increasing importance given the slow but growing rates of attendance among students of color in a post-Proposition 209 era. The sum of the daily environment that surrounds students can be defined as campus climate (Chang, Witt, Jones, & Hakuta, 1999). More broadly, campus climate refers to the level of comfort (i.e., academic, social, and interpersonal contentment) experienced by majority students, students of color, faculty, administrators, and staff (Hurtado & Carter, 1997; Ponterotto, 1990). Conversely, how campus climates are transformed as attempts to foster diversity and equalize participation rates across different racial/ethnic groups is increasingly challenged. It is not surprising that many higher educational institutions have reached a stalemate in terms of making concerted efforts in providing a campus community fully inclusive of students from all racial/ethnic groups.

Research has found when the campus climate is inviting and inclusive of minority students, their collegiate experience is greatly improved relative to their adjustment, matriculation, degree completion and overall satisfaction (Cabera, Nora, Terenzini, Pascarella & Hagedorn, 1999; Hurtado & Carter, 1997; MacKay & Kuh, 1994; Schwitzer et al., 1999). In a study addressing campus climate, a telephone survey of 1,170 African American, Hispanic and White respondents' ages 15-24 concluded that these youth are cynical about improved race relations (Collison, 1992). Fifty percent of those surveyed viewed race relations as "generally bad". According to Ancis, Sedlacek and Mohr (2000), making inquiries into student perceptions of campus climate and culture is valuable because students do not hold monolithic views and racially/ethnically diverse collegians commonly experience campus life that is not akin to majority students.

While greater proportions of students of color attend predominately White two- and four-year institutions, campus climate is largely suited to the majority student (Ponterotto, 1990; Riordan, 1993). Campus climate can positively or negatively affect students of color as they may feel unwelcome in predominantly White settings whereby the quality of interaction with faculty and peers is adversely impacted (Schwitzer et al., 1999). The climate at various colleges and universities often mirrors the degree to which there is interethnic exchange and harmony. Mack and colleagues (1997) examined the campus climate at five colleges by assessing the relationship between students from diverse ethnic groups. Their findings suggested that White and Hispanic students were more comfortable with cross-race socialization than were African Americans or Asian students. Research has suggested that White students most frequently describe campus climate as very positive and inclusive while ethnic students reportedly felt hostility and exclusion exists on campus (Hurtado, Dey, & Trevino, 1994; Mack & Pittman, 1993).

Studies addressing cross-cultural contact among college students have shown that interethnic exchange is valued by the majority of collegians though there is a lack of consensus as to whether the necessary climate for fostering positive socialization between racial/ethnic groups exists (Arnold, 1995). The American Association of Community Colleges (AACC) conducted a climate assessment and found a relationship between administrator perceptions of campus climate and minority faculty or student presence. More specifically, campuses with less than 20% minority faculty and enrollment reported having the least harmonious campuses. Interestingly, institutions with 60% of minority faculty and/or 40% of minority student enrollment reported the most harmony (Kee, 1999). AACC's results illustrate one component of creating the necessary climate for positive cross-cultural communicating is linked to having more than a dearth of faculty and students of color on campus.

In investigating faculty perceptions of campus climate for diversity, Conley and Hyer (1999) surveyed over 1300 faculty. Their survey instrument asked respondents opinions regarding institutional culture, attitudes toward affirmative action, and experiences with discrimination. The findings demonstrate that majority faculty members' perceptions and experiences differed from faculty of color and furthermore, majority faculty members (similar to majority students) were unaware of these differences regarding institutional climate.

In sum, understanding cross-cultural contact and responses to affirmative action is central to grasping issues surrounding campus climate. Moreover, cross-racial exchanges are less apt to occur in a racially charged and tense campus environment. As affirmative action is contested, the grave reality is that fewer students of color are gaining access to higher education at senior level institutions. Down the pike, affirmative action dismantling could also translate into fewer administrators and faculty of color who can assist all students in more fully integrating socially and academically into the campus community. Research has noted that the driving force of American race relations is the degree to which Whites and people of color differ on social policy issues due to their values and beliefs about inequality (Bobo & Kluegel, 1993; Bobo & Smith, 1994; Collison, 1992). Therefore, examining public opinion on social policy issues and assessing the overall climate both in and out of the classroom should be of critical concern to educators (Riordan, 1993).

METHOD

Data Source and Analysis

In providing a portrait of background characteristics and public opinion of traditional college-age White Americans, the 1994, 1996 and 1998 General Social Survey (GSS) data was utilized. The GSS contains social indicator items pertaining to public policy concerns. The National Opinion Research Center (NORC) at the University of Chicago administers the GSS to national samples almost annually (Davis & Smith, 1994). For the purposes of generating information on Whites that are of traditional college age, attention was restricted to White respondents between 18-24 years old yielding a total net sample of 553 which is inclusive of respondents from GSS surveys administered during 1994-98. The survey contains several questions that gauge support for programs aimed at assisting African Americans.

GSS Items of Interest

Demographic variables from the GSS were selected for this study based on their utility in previous research. Traditional measures such as age (as a selection variable), gender, social class (i.e., as measured by annual family income and subjective class standing), highest year of school completed and parents' highest level of education were used. Variables such as these can provide important information regarding the differences between groups (i.e., low or high social standing, male/female, and rich/poor).

Aside from pulling demographic information, two items regarding political party affiliation and political ideology were of interest.

Gathering a general sense of political leanings was important as Republicans are considered conservative while Democrats are typically liberal in their political views. More specifically, literature has noted that conservatives generally echo preference of the status quo, while not challenging the distribution of societal resources or the stratification of their group's positioning in the present social order (Shingles, 1992; Van Dyke, 1995). In contrast, liberals are considered to be individuals who question unequal participation of all citizens, advocate for governmental intervention in assuring equity and at the same time maintaining a basic belief in economic, political and social reform (Feldman & Zaller, 1992). In turn, political affiliation and ideologies may act in accordance with how individuals justify or rationalize their stance on social and political matters such as race-based or need-specific affirmative action (Hinich & Munger, 1994). Previous studies have illustrated a convincing degree of association between racial attitudes and political views that may assist in explaining attitudes people hold toward affirmative action (Sears & Jessor, 1996; Sniderman, 1993).

Of primary interest, six items were selected for the purposes of this study that referred to affirmative action efforts earmarked for African Americans. The first item was anchored on a Likert scale from 1 (strongly support preferences) to 4 (strongly oppose preferences), coded *affrmact* asked, "Some people say that because of past discrimination, Blacks should be given preference in hiring and promotion. Others say that such preference in hiring and promotion of Blacks is wrong because it discriminates against Whites. What about your opinion -- are you for or against preferential hiring and promotion of Blacks"? The second item indicative of views regarding race-based social policies coded *wkwayup* questioned, "Do you agree strongly, agree somewhat, neither disagree nor agree, disagree somewhat, or disagree strongly with the following statement? Irish, Italians, Jewish, and many other minorities overcame prejudice and worked their way up. Blacks should do the same without special favors". This item was on a five-point Likert scale with responses ranging from 1 = disagree strongly to 5 = agree strongly.

Third, coded *blksimp* asked on a three-point scale (1 = improved, 2 = gotten worse, 3 = about the same), "In the past few years, do you think conditions for Black people have improved, gotten worse, or stayed about the same"? A fourth item regarding whether the government should aid Blacks coded *helpblk* stated, "Some people think that

(Blacks/Negroes/African-Americans) have been discriminated against for so long that the government has a special obligation to help improve their living standards. Others believe that the government should not be giving special treatment to (Blacks/Negroes/African-Americans). Where would you place yourself on this scale, or haven't you made up your mind on this"? This item was on a five-point scale from 1 = government help for Blacks to 5 = no special treatment. Next, *discaff* assessed whether Whites feel hurt by affirmative action on a scale where 1 = very likely to 3 = not very likely. The item read, "What do you think the chances are these days that a White person won't get a job or promotion while an equally or less qualified Black person gets one instead? Is this very likely, somewhat likely, or not very likely to happen these days? Lastly, *racpush* asked respondents to reply to the following statement: "Blacks shouldn't push themselves where they're not wanted: anchored on from 1 = strongly agree to 4 = strongly disagree.

Descriptive Findings and Correlations

The descriptive statistics provided will be discussed in two parts, first aggregating responses for 1994-98 and second highlighting selected information garnered for each GSS subsample separately reflective of affirmative action attitudes. Relative to the total sample pulled from GSS 1994-98, half of the respondents were female (50.3%). The average age of White respondents of traditional-college age was 21.6 years old. With respect to total annual family income 14.4% of those responding indicated incomes under $14,999, 10.7% between $15,000 and $19,999, 9.7% had annual family incomes from $20,000 to $24,999, while 39.5% reported total family incomes of $25,000 or more. Correspondingly, in reporting subjective class identification, roughly 6% stated lower class, 52.3% working class, 39.4% responded that they were middle class and 2.4% upper class.

Approximately 39% of respondents' mother's and 33% of father's highest year of school was the 12th grade, with 24.8% of mothers and 22.8% of father's having completed some college. Just fewer than 14% indicated their mother's highest level of educational attainment was 16th grade (i.e., completion of a bachelor's degree); similarly, roughly 18% of father's finished college.

The modal response to highest year of school completed by those surveyed was 12th grade (29.9%). Interestingly for this 18-24 subsample drawn from the general population, 21% reported having 6th through 11th grade as the highest year of school completed. In addition, nearly 16% completed one year of postsecondary, 12.5% finished the 14th grade, 9.2% completed 15th grade, almost 11% completed four years of college and little over 2% complete one year of postbaccalaureate work.

In response to political party affiliation, 22% identified themselves as democrats, 15.4% as independent near democrat, 21.6% as clearly independent, almost 12% as independent near republican, 28% republican and less than 2% indicated other. With respect to political ideology, 33% acknowledged that they were either slightly liberal, liberal or extremely liberal; 37% stated moderate and 29.8% referred to themselves as slightly conservative or conservative.

With regard to the items corresponding with views regarding racial policies or programs solely assisting African Americans, the overall figures suggest disfavor for race-based efforts. In reference to race targeting in hiring of African Americans, roughly 13% support or strongly support preferences while 31% responded opposing views and 55% strongly opposed the use of race in hiring African Americans. Approximately 75% agreed strongly or agreed somewhat that African Americans should overcome prejudice without favors, 11.5% neither agreed nor disagreed and 13% disagree somewhat or strongly with the same sentiment. In examining whether this White college-age subgroup felt conditions for African Americans improved, well over half (57.6%) felt that times had gotten better, 9% felt it was worse and one-third thought is was about the same.

In terms of government aid designated for African Americans, few responded in support for race-specific assistance. However, interesting to note is nearly one-third agreeing with both government help and no special treatment. When asked if Whites are hurt by affirmative action, 22% felt that it is very likely to threaten them, just over half thought it may be somewhat harmful to Whites, and 27% did not perceive threat by affirmative action. Lastly, approximately 28% agreed strongly or slightly with the sentiment that Blacks should not push themselves where they are not wanted.

With respect to the general responses of males and females, well over one-third of each reported family incomes of $25,000 or more. Over one-quarter of males and females reported being republican. However there were dissimilarities as over one-quarter of females reported being democrat and while the same amount also clearly identified with independent political party affiliation. In contrast, around 15% of males were reportedly democrat while fewer than 25% were independent. Also noteworthy among this cohort of collegiate age Whites there was a greater leniency of women to be independent but near democratic. Not so analogous to party affiliation, the political ideologies of this subgroup also suggest that for those responding there was approximately the same amount of each associating themselves with liberalism. Additionally, of females, nearly 20% connect with conservatism in contrast to their male counterparts (about 30%).

In terms of favoring preference in hiring African Americans, White male and female respondents have parallel views in some respects. Well over 80% of females and males oppose or strongly oppose race-targeting in hiring. But there were slightly higher percentages of men espousing support or strong support for preferences than females (about a 4% difference). In replying to whether African Americans should overcome prejudice without favors, approximately 70% of women and little over 70% of men agreed strongly or somewhat. On the opposite side, 10% of males and females disagreed strongly or somewhat with the same statement.

More women (64%) than men (55%) felt that conditions have improved for African Americans. About one-third of males and 25% of females stated there should be no special treatment in the form of government aid to African Americans. In responding to whether affirmative action hurts Whites, 16% of men and women felt it was very likely. Close to half of males and over half of females felt somewhat likely that affirmative action could be harmful to Whites. Lastly, in conducting an independent samples t-test, there were statistically significant differences between the group means for males and females on how likely Whites would be hurt by affirmative action by annual family income ($t = 2.345$, $p = .019$), political party affiliation ($t = 2.232$, $p = .026$), and Black shouldn't push themselves where they are not wanted ($t = -2.379$, $p = .018$).

In general, attitudes toward affirmative action efforts directed toward African Americans did reveal some variations relative to the subsample for each year of the GSS survey (i.e., 1994, 1996 and 1998). Eighty-four percent of those responding in 1994 and 1996 opposed racial targeting in the hiring of African Americans while 92% of the 1998 subset of traditional college aged respondents were opposing. Roughly three-fourths of Whites from each subset felt that African Americans should overcome prejudice without favors. Intriguingly, when asked if conditions for African Americans improved, in 1994 51% felt conditions had improved, 59% felt similarly in 1996 and 63% of those answering in 1998 responded that times were better for African Americans.

Of greater interest are the differences in the perceived threat of affirmative action to Whites. When asked if Whites are hurt by affirmative action, 81% of the 18-24 year olds replying in 1994 felt it was somewhat or very likely that affirmative action could be harmful to them. There was a small decrease in 1996 as 78.7% felt that affirmative action hurt Whites and two-thirds of the 1998 respondents echoed the same sentiment. Also, there was some variation in the responses to Blacks shouldn't push themselves where they are not wanted by GSS year. In 1994 30% agreed strongly or slight with the previous statement, while in 1996 those in agreement dropped to 22.2% and in 1998 those agreeing strongly or slightly rose to 32.4%. Finally, increasing numbers of Whites felt things were good for African Americans and while disfavor for affirmative action targeting African Americans grew from 1994 to 1998 the perceived likelihood of affirmative action hurting Whites was not as great with each separate administration of the GSS during this period.

As the intentions of the researcher were not to manipulate any of the variables, the research design of this exploratory study utilized correlational analyses to determine the association of the variables. The correlation coefficients showing the degree to which the variables are related yielded produced some statistically significant relationships that reflect weak-to-moderate measures of association (See Table 1 for the correlation matrix containing all pairs of correlations of the set of variables).

The Salience of Race and Affirmative Action: Implications for Campus Climate

National opinion surveys have found that the overwhelming majority of Whites oppose government programs that provide special assistance to African Americans (Bobo & Kluegel, 1993). With regard to a college student population, roughly 50% of college freshmen agree with abolishing the use of affirmative action in college admissions

(Sax, Astin, Korn, & Mahoney, 1996). As issues surrounding race become increasingly pronounced at institutions of higher learning, student attitudes regarding important social policies may relate to tensions assessing campus climate (Yang, 1992; Chang, Witt, Jones, & Hakuta, 1999).

The climate at the vast majority of college campuses needs significant improvement to meet the growing number of students from racially/ethnically diverse backgrounds. In the next decade students of color will comprise approximately one-quarter of those under age 18 (Carter & Wilson as cited in Hurtado, Milem, and Clayton-Pedersen, 1999). Therefore, I contend that diversity on campus does not simply equate to the numerical representation of racial/ethnic group members but should move beyond mere student statistics to encompass inclusive learning environments, an institutional culture that supports diversity, broadens access, fosters cross-cultural interaction and achieves equitable educational outcomes for a multi-ethnic student populace.

As campus climate affects educational outcomes of students, a primary concern of educators ought to include constructing campus environments that permit each student to self-actualize while receiving the multiple benefits of a multicultural college community (Hurtado, Milem, and Clayton-Pedersen, 1999). With the demographic shifts in American society, the traditional age college student population at colleges and universities, institutions of higher learning have gradually began placing more focus on the increasing racial/ethnic, cultural and economic diversity among those enrolled by formally assessing campus climate (Morrow, Burris-Kitchen, Der-Karabetian, 2000; Ponterotto, 1990). Campus climate assessments have been conducted utilizing various questionnaires such as the Multicultural Assessment of Campus Programming (MAC-P) and the Kettering Climate Scale as well as qualitative forms of inquiry through focus groups interviews (Johnson, Johnson, Kranch, & Zimmerman, 1999; McClellan, Cogdal, & Lease, 1996; Morrow, Burris-Kitchen, Der-Karabetian, 2000).

Overall, campuses that are proactive in attending to campus climate can for the most part steer improvement in the race relations, racial antipathy and sense of community. San Jose State University was recognized for installing a comprehensive campus climate plan that reformed the culture of the institution from a school plagued with racial tensions to one that is more accepting of difference, appreciates diversity, and openly nurtures all students. The campus climate plan outlined 10 goals for improvement and as a result of implementation

Table 1. Correlation Coefficients for Variables of Interest

	Gender	Highest year of school completed	Mother's highest level of education	Father's highest level of education	Annual family income	Subjective class	Political party	Liberal Conservative
Blacks shouldn't push	.130*	.167*	.152*	.081	-.065	.038	-.038	-.118*
	N=332	N=332	N=302	N=256	N=299	N=332	N=329	N=316
Favor race targeting in hiring Blacks	-.074	.117*	.084	.035	.050	.030	.009	.118*
	N=323	N=322	N=289	N=252	N=289	N=322	N=323	N=308
Blacks should overcome prejudice without favor	.034	.190*	.122*	.142*	-.105	.016	-.115*	-.190**
	N=338	N=338	N=300	N=261	N=302	N=337	N=338	N=332
Conditions for Blacks have improved	.037	.032	.039	.065	-.143*	-.096	-.009	-.101
	N=335	N=335	N=296	N=257	N=300	N=334	N=334	N=316
Whites hut by affirmative action	-.001	.092	.102	.134	-.038	.013	-.142*	-.070
	N=212	N=212	N=192	N=157	N=195	N=212	N=211	N=199

* Correlation is significant at the .05 level (two-tailed).
** Correlation is significant at the .01 level (two-tailed).

the campus is perceived by employees and students as a place that values diversity, promotes student involvement and cross-cultural communication (Simmons, 1999).

A recent survey reported that almost 90% feel it is critically important to have racially/ethnically diverse students in higher education while roughly 81% of people stated it is important that people from different races and cultural backgrounds are included in the workplace (Yates, 2000). However, there is a misnomer in that Americans egalitarian responses to Gallup polls and other surveys often fail to translate into support for affirming diversity via affirmative action. One way that colleges and universities have been responding to the importance of multiethnic relations has been in the form of establishing diversity requirements. An estimated 62% of colleges and universities have existing or pending diversity requirements illustrating that at long last diversity is something that students of all backgrounds can benefit from (Conciatore, 2000).

In closing, public opinion of affirmative action has several implications for campus climate relative to the representation of people of color and the embedded institutional values of colleges and universities the majority of which are predominantly White institutions that reflect Eurocentric cultural norms (Ponterotto, 1990). Improving the interaction between majority and minority students calls for acknowledging how vital cross-cultural communication and socialization are in achieving one value system that is supportive of all its participants.

Creating, maintaining and valuing diversity on college campuses is a questionable undertaking as the use of race-targeted forms of affirmative action was recently struck down at the University of Georgia; soon following, the University of Michigan argued in favor of affirmative action at the undergraduate and graduate levels before the U.S. Court of Appeals (Hebel, 2001). The two University of Michigan cases will have historical significance as both will set the precedent for the use of affirmative action in admissions policies for every institution in the Sixth Circuit (i.e., Michigan, Ohio, Tennessee, and Kentucky). Conversely, after eliminating affirmative action based on race and gender six years ago, the University of California Board of Regents in a 13-to-2 vote ruled in favor of adopting a new policy which would broaden factors considered for admissions (Whitaker, 2001).

While Proposition 209 prohibited the use of race and sex in hiring decisions it sparked the dismantling of affirmative action for admitting students. The number of non-Asian students of color plummeted to an all time low. As a result, the UC system is revisiting how to extend opportunities while redefining merit to include overcoming economic hardships and educational disadvantages with standardized test scores, class rank and grade point average. Finally, as the world outside of academe is culturally pluralistic, it is essential that institutional leaders are cognizant of students' racial attitudes and perceptions of affirmative action. It is imperative that educational administrators and policymakers recognize that demographic realities clearly suggest the future success of the U.S. will greatly depend on having well-educated people of color in the workforce.

Limitations of the study and Conclusions

The descriptive nature of this study provides only small portraits of traditional-college age Whites feelings relative to special considerations to increase opportunities for African Americans. As the purpose of this exploratory investigation was to describe responses to race-based forms of affirmative action targeted toward African Americans and measures of association among the variables of interest, caution must be used in reporting the correlational analyses. The correlations yielded do not infer causation of affirmative action attitudes.

The subsample examined in this chapter concurs with previous research regarding the vast majority of Whites opposing assistance in the form of race-specific programming (Bobo & Kluegel, 1993; Tuch & Hughes, 1996a; Tuch & Hughes, 1996b). It has been argued that race-targeted initiatives are less likely favored in lieu of income-targeted programming efforts that are economic/need-based which is perhaps due to the competitive individual and group self-interest of Whites (Bobo & Kluegel, 1993). Although self-interest measures were not investigated they have been found relevant as race-targeted policies may be considered threatening to Whites as they assert self-interested positions and pursue ways of protecting their advantageous racial status (Stoker, 1996). This could be particularly relevant with a college-age sample with regard to agreement or disagreement with considerations of race/ethnicity in admissions or hiring.

Additionally, the findings of this exploratory examination are limited as a split-sample approach was employed in which a rotation of GSS items that reflect views on race-targeted social policies/programming for African Americans appeared on only two-thirds of the surveys. Therefore, future inquiry employed with a more robust sample size and utilizing multiple methodologies that seek to predict relationships between additional variables and views regarding race-based programs and policies is recommended. Continued research is needed to grasp a clearer understanding of social policy acceptance particularly with respect to opposition when assistance is race-targeted versus need-specific increases. As majority students and the larger population-at-large find difficulty supporting affirmative action, the quality of interaction will suffer at American institutions as a result of becoming more homogenous and less racially tolerant. Should the pendulum of opportunity enhancement continue to swing backwards, the campus environment at many colleges and universities will literally and figuratively reflect the "ivory towers".

References

Ancis, J. R., Sedlacek, W. E., and J.J. Mohr. 2000. "Student perception of campus cultural climate by race". *Journal of Counseling and Development*, 78 (2): 180-185.

Arnold, C. L. 1995. *Chabot College campus climate survey results: Fall 1994*. Hayward, CA: Chabot College. (ED 402 982)

Barnes, E. 1996. "Community college becomes battleground for complaint about privately funded scholarship." *Black Issues in Higher Education*, 13 (16): 8-10.

Bobo, L. and J.R. Kluegel. 1993. "Opposition to race-targeting: Self-interest, stratification ideology or racial attitudes?" *American Sociological Review*, 58: 443-464.

Bobo, L. and R. A. Smith. 1994. "Antipoverty policy, affirmative action, and racial attitudes." In Danziger, Sandefur, and Weinberg (Eds.), *Confronting poverty: Prescriptions for change*, 365-395. New York: Russell Sage.

Bonacich, E. 1975. "Abolition, the extension of slavery, and the position of free Blacks: A study of split labor markets in the United States, 1830-1863." *American Journal of Sociology*, 81: 601-628.

Bonacich, E. 1989. "Inequality in America: The failure of the American system for people of color." *Sociological Spectrum*, 9: 77-101.

Boris, E. 1998. Fair employment and the origins of affirmative action. Nwsa Journal, 10 (3): 142-51.

Cabrera, A. F., Nora, A., Terenzini, P. T., Pascarella, E., and L.S. Hagedorn. 1999. "Campus racial climate and the adjustment of students to college." *The Journal of Higher Education*, 70 (2): 134-160.

Chang, M., Witt, D., Jones, J. and K. Hakuta. 1999. *Compelling interest: Examining the evidence on racial dynamics in higher education*. CA: American Educational Research Association and the Stanford University Center for Comparative Studies in Race and Ethnicity.

Chatman, S. P. and K.M. Smith. 2000. "Economic affirmative action and race-blind policies." *College and University Journal*, 76: 3-14.

Chideya, F. 1995. *Don't believe the hype: Fighting cultural misinformation about African Americans*. New York: Penguin.

Clegg, R. 2000. "The bad law of disparate impact." Public Interest, 138: 79-90.

Cohen, A. M. 1998. *The shaping of American higher education: Emergence and growth of the contemporary system*. San Francisco: Jossey-Bass.

Collison, M. N. K. 1992. "Young people found pessimistic about relations between the races." *The Chronicle of Higher Education*, 38 (29): A1-32.

Conciatore, J. 2000. "Study shows more than half of American colleges now have diversity requirements." *Black Issues in Higher Education*, 17 (20): 22.

Conley, V. M. and P. B. Hyer. 1999, November. *A faculty assessment of the campus climate for diversity*. Paper presented at the Annual Meeting of the Association for the Study of Higher Education, San Antonio, TX. (ED 437 010)

Crosby, F. 1994. "Understanding affirmative action." *Basic and Applied Social Psychology*, 15: 13-41.

Davis, J. A. and T. W. Smith. 1994. *The General Social Survey: Cumulative codebook and data file*. Chicago: National Research Opinion Center.

Dietz-Uhler, B. and A. J. Murrell. 1993. "Resistance to affirmative action: A test of four explanatory models." *Journal of College Student Development*, 34: 352-357.

Dovidio, J. F. and S. L. Gaertner. 1996. "Affirmative action, unintentional racial biases, and intergroup relations." Journal of Social Issues, 52 (4): 51-75.

Dovidio, J. F., Gaertner, S. L., and A. J. Murrell. 1994. *Why people resist affirmative action*. Paper presented at the 102nd Annual Convention of the American Psychological Association, Los Angeles, CA.

Dovidio, J. F., Mann, J. A., and S. L. Gaertner. 1989. "Resistance to affirmative action: The implication of aversive racism." In F. A. Blanchard & F. J. Crosby (Eds.), *Affirmative action in perspective*, 83-102. New York: Springer-Verlag.

Farley, R. 1984. *Blacks and Whites: Narrowing the gap*. Cambridge, MA: Harvard University.

Feinberg, W. 1996. "Affirmative action and beyond: A case for a backward-looking gender- and race-based policy." *Teachers College Record*, 97: 362-399.

Feldman, S. and J. Zaller. 1992. "The political culture of ambivalence: Ideological responses to the welfare state." *American Journal of Political Science*, 36: 268-307.

Fleming, J. E., Gill, G. R., and D. H. Swinton. 1978. *The case for affirmative action for Blacks in higher education*. Washington, DC: Howard University Press.

Gillett-Karam, R., Roueche, S. D. and J. E. Roueche. 1991. *Underrepresentation and the questions of diversity: Women and minorities in the community college*. Washington, DC: American Association of Community and Junior Colleges.

Grahnke, L. 1999, July 5. "Group threatens race bias suit: Objects to local universities' affirmative action programs." *Chicago Sun-Times*, 13.

Hebel, S. 2001, November 12. "U. of Georgia won't ask Supreme Court to reverse decision striking down use of race in admissions." *The Chronicle of Higher Education*,
    http://chronicle.com/daily/2001/11/2001111201n.htm.

Hinich, M. and M. Munger. 1994. *Ideology and the theory of political choice.* Ann Arbor, MI: University of Michigan Press.

Hurtado, S. and D. F. Carter. 1997. "Effects of college transition and perceptions of the campus climate on Latino college students' sense of belonging." *Sociology of Education*, 70: 324-345.

Hurtado, S., Dey, E., and J. Trevino. 1994, April. *Exclusion or self-segregation? Interaction across racial/ethnic groups on college campuses.* Paper presented at the Annual Meeting of the American Educational Research Association, New Orleans, LA.

Hurtado, S., Milem, J. F., and A. Clayton-Pedersen. 1999. *Enacting diverse learning environments: Improving the climate for racial/ethnic diversity in higher education.* Washington, DC: ASHE-ERIC Higher Education Report.

Johnson, W. L., Johnson, A. M., Kranch, D. A., and K. J. Zimmerman. 1999. "The development of a university version of the Charles F. Kettering Climate Scale." *Educational and Psychological Measurement*, 59: 336-350.

Kee, A. M. 1999. *Campus climate: Perceptions, policies and programs in community colleges.* Washington, DC: American Association of Community Colleges. (ED 430 597)

Kelly, J. 1996. "Who benefits from affirmative action?" *Black Issues in Higher Education*, 13 (7): 78.

Kinder, D. R. and L. M. Sanders. 1990. "Mimicking political debate with survey questions: The case of White opinion on affirmative action for Blacks." *Social Cognition*, 8: 73-103.

Kluegel, J. R. 1990. "Trends in Whites explanation of the Black-White gap in socioeconomic status, 1977-1989." *American Sociological Review*, 55: 512-525.

Kluegel, J. R. and E. R. Smith. 1986. *Beliefs about inequality: Americans' views of what is and what ought to be.* New York: Aldine deGruyter.

Lederman, D. 1997, October. "New briefs to high court take opposing views on key affirmative action case." *The Chronicle of Higher Education*, 24: A28.

Mack, D. E. and E. L. Pittman. 1993, October. *The quality of life: Asian, Black, Latino, and White students.* Paper presented at the Annual Conference of the Association for University and College Counseling Center Directors, Keystone, CO.

Mack, D. E., Tucker, T. W., Archuleta, R., DeGroot, G., Hernandez, A. A., and S. Oh Cha. 1997. "Interethnic relations on campus: Can't we all get along?" *Journal of Multicultural Counseling and Development*, 25: 256-268.

Mackay, K. A. and G. D. Kuh. 1994. "A comparison of student effort and educational gains of Caucasian and African American students at predominantly White colleges and universities." *Journal of College Student Development*, 35: 217-223.

McClellan, S. A., Cogdal, P. A., and S. H. Lease. 1996. "Development of the multicultural assessment of campus programming (MAC-P) questionnaire." *Measurement and Evaluation in Counseling and Development*, 29: 86-99.

Meader, E. W. 1998, November). *College student attitudes toward diversity and race-based policies.* Paper presented at the annual Meeting of the Association for the Study of Higher Education, Miami, Florida.

Morrow, G. P., Burris-Kitchen, D., and A. Der-Karabetian. 2000. "Assessing campus climate of cultural diversity: A focus on focus groups." *College Student Journal*, 34: 589-602.

Nettles, M. T. and L. W. Perna. 1997. *The African American education data book: Higher and adult education* (Vol. 1). Fairfax, VA: Fredrick D. Patterson Research Institute.

Perna, L. W. 2000. "Differences in the decision to attend college among African Americans, Hispanics, and Whites." *The Journal of Higher Education*, 71 (2): 117-141.

Ponterotto, J. G. 1990. "Racial/ethnic minority and women students in higher education: A status report." *New Directions for Student Services*, 52: 45-59.

Rendon, L. I. and H. Garza. 1996. "Closing the gap between two- and four-year institutions." In L. I. Rendon and R. O. Hope (Eds.), *Educating a new majority: Transforming American's educational system for diversity*, 289-308. San Francisco, CA: Jossey-Bass.

Redon, L. I. and R. O. Hope. 1996. *Educating a new majority: Transforming American's educational system for diversity.* San Francisco, CA: Jossey-Bass

Tharp, M. 1998, November. "Copying California." *U. S. News & World Report*, 9: 34. Riordan, C. A. 1991. *The campus climate for minorities at the University of Missouri-Rolla.* Rolla, MO: University of Missouri-Rolla Press.

Sax, L. J. and M. Arredondo. 1999. "Student attitudes toward affirmative action in college admissions." *Research In Higher Education*, 40 (4): 439-459.

Schwitzer, A. M., Griffin, Oris, T. A., Thomas, J. R., and R. Celeste. 1999. *Journal of Counseling and Development*, 77 (2): 189-197.

Sears, D. O. and T. Jessor. 1996. "Whites' racial policy attitudes: The role of White racism." *Social Science Quarterly*, 77 (4): 751-759.

Shingles, R. D. 1992. "Minority consciousness and political action: A comparative approach." In A. M. Messina, L. R. Fraga, L. A. Rhodebeck and F. D. Wright (Eds.), *Ethnic minorities in advanced industrial democracies*, 161-184. New York: Greenwood Press.

Simmons, J. 1999. "A campus climate plan relaxes racial tension." *Education Digest*, 65 (4): 33-38.

Smith, W. A. 1996. *Affirmative action attitudes in higher education: A multi-ethnic extension of a three-factor model.* Unpublished doctoral dissertation, University of Illinois, Urbana-Champaign.

Sniderman, P. M. 1993. *Prejudice, politics, and the American dilemma.* Stanford, CA: Stanford University Press.

Stoker, L. 1996. "Understanding differences in White's opinions across racial policies." *Social Science Quarterly*, 77 (4): 768-777.

Tierney, W. G. 1997. "The parameters of affirmative action: Equity and excellence in the academy." *Review of Educational Research*, 67 (2): 165-196.

Trent, W. T. 1991. "Student affirmative action in higher education: Addressing underrepresentation." In P. G. Altbach and K. Lomotey (Eds.), *The racial crisis in American higher education*, 107-134. NY: SUNY.

Tuch, S. A. and M. Hughes. 1996a. "Whites' racial policy attitudes." *Social Science Quarterly*, 77 (4): 723-745.

Tuch, S. A. and M. Hughes. 1996b. "Whites' opposition to race-targeted policies: One cause or many?" *Social Science Quarterly*, 77 (4): 778-788.

Van Dyke, V. 1995. *Ideology and political choice: The search for freedom, justice, and virtue.* Chatham, NJ: Chatham House Publishers.

Whitaker, B. 2001, November 15. "University of California moves to widen admissions criteria." *New York Times*, http://www.nytimes.com/2001/11/15/education.

Wright, S. W. 1997. "Private scholarships for minorities challenged." *Black Issues in Higher Education*, 14 (5): 14-16.

Yang, J. 1992. *Chilly campus climate: A qualitative study on White racial identity.* Washington, DC: U. S. Department of Education, Office of Educational Research and Improvement.

Yates, E. L. 2000. "Survey shows support for diversity in colleges and business." *Black Issues in Higher Education*, 17 (2): 17.

Zamani, E. M. 2001, June. *Community college students' attitudes toward affirmative action in college admissions.* Paper presented at the Annual Meeting of the Association for Institutional Research, Long Beach, California.

Article 11

African American Male Students at Predominantly White Female Institutions of Higher Education

Amitra Hodge

I began my college career in the fall of 1990 with my heart set on majoring in psychology; I was going to be a psychiatrist. I quickly noticed that I was one of the few "persons of color" on a predominantly female campus; I'm an African American female. The emphasis on empowering women, small class sizes, and the location of the school lured me to this particular state-supported campus. By the time I graduated with a Bachelor of Science degree in psychology in the summer of 1993 I was used to seeing white females filling up most of the seats in the classrooms, in the library, in the lounge area, and in the lunch cafeteria. After seeing the light and realizing that counseling was not the job for me, I started my Master's degree in sociology in the fall semester of 1993. At this time, I noticed a few white American males mostly taking college courses at this predominantly female university. I saw a few black males walking across campus with books and book bags. They were headed towards class. During the fall of 1995, the semester I graduated with my Master's degree, I continued on with my studies and taught as a graduate student and as a qualified mental health professional at a non-profit organization until I earned a Ph.D. in sociology in the fall of 1999.

When I think back to my last years at the University, I can remember when I first saw a group of African American males sitting in the student union at the University. These individuals were under 25 years of age and they appeared to enjoy themselves as indicated by their laughter and their ability to draw in a small crowd around their table. Sure, I had seen one or two African American male students at the University before, but those one or two students were in graduate school; they were often seen on campus during evening hours. In addition I saw groups of undergraduate and graduate white male students hanging out at the student union. Seeing five African American male students laughing in a student union eating area should not have caused eyebrows to raise. I found it interesting that my eyebrows did lift up at the time. I remember thinking to myself "what are these guys doing here? They must be here just to party and have fun." Strangely enough, I don't ever recall thinking this way when seeing white American males or older "non-traditional" African American males on the campus. If I as an African American female graduate student instructor and had these preconceived stereotypes, I can only imagine what others felt, especially fellow graduate student instructors responsible for giving African American males a good education. Confronting my own biases and stereotypes of African American and white American male students at a predominantly female university sparked my research interest. I wanted to know why these males chose a predominantly female university. I wanted to learn about their experiences and their perceptions at the University as told by them.

Two areas were considered while I formulated my research topic. The first area concerns the history of formal education for African American and white American males. In the United States, access to and benefits received from formal education were different for African American males when compared to white American males. Wealthy white males were able to receive formal education while African Americans were forbidden to learn how to read and write from the time that they entered this country. After emancipation, the United States did not encourage a widespread literacy program for African Americans resulting in a game of catch-up for African Americans. African Americans taught their children at predominantly black schools (albeit due to segregation and widespread discrimination) and created their own black colleges and universities. Advancements in access, quantity, and quality have been hampered because of discrimination and segregation even with measures such as desegregation, Title VI of the Civil Rights Act of 1964, and affirmative action programs.[1]

The second area of focus concerns gender. Gender refers to the social significance and role expectations a society attaches to the biological characteristics of male and female. Gender does not just encompass society's definition of masculine, feminine, or androgynous traits. It involves a power structure as gender affects the opportunities that men and women face.[2] In the larger society some men occupy the dominant position; they seek to protect privileges, such as the access to socially valued resources. Males, because of their gender, are accorded more power, privileges and rights than women. Women, in the United States, were excluded from formal education by admission policies, by tracking into sex-typed fields as a way of keeping women from higher education. Women received less education than men did even if they went beyond primary studies and women received different lessons in academic programs. Studies for women emphasized how to be a good mother or a good wife or a teacher.[3] As a result, colleges for women largely came into existence in the early nineteenth century.

Besides the two areas, 1) formal education for African American and white American males and 2) gender, a change in the University's policy peaked my interest even further. In 1994 the Board of Regents voted to admit male students in all undergraduate programs. Two years after the decision, the following quote appeared in a local newspaper,

> As a male nursing student. . . .I'm glad to know now that I am a second-class student at this school; it helps to explain many things that go on there in the way males are treated.[4]

This statement was made by a white American student in response to an article, which reaffirmed the mission of the University. I found it interesting that college and local newspapers have taken notice of male students' perceptions about their experiences in a predominantly female university when it was "newsworthy." Empirical research examining the perceptions and experiences of male students entering predominantly female colleges has not been conducted. Research, instead, has largely been conducted with females in higher education and has largely focused on self-esteem, on math and science ability, and on gender-role acquisition. Studies, follow-ups, and indicators report the "progress" and achievement of women in higher education.

Text and readers describe the experiences of females in various settings in higher education. The attention given to female students is due to the fact that female students are at a disadvantage in higher education because of sexism.[5]

The chief concern of this article is to focus on male students rather than female students. More specifically, the experiences and perceptions of black and white students at a predominantly female university will be described. The parameter of this article is determined by the following research question: What is Life Like for African American and White American males at a predominantly female university?

Characteristics of Respondents

During the spring of 1999, this researcher mailed out a survey to undergraduate male students (N=261) enrolled at Texas Woman's University. Sixty (forty-nine white males and eleven black males) completed and returned the mail-out survey. Of the sixty, seventeen (ten white males and seven black males) agreed to participate in the in-depth interview. See Table 1 for characteristics of those who responded to the survey.

TABLE 1. Demographic Characteristics of Respondents[a]

Characteristics	Blacks N	%	Whites N	%
Classification				
Freshman	2	18.2	5	10.2
Sophomore	1	9.1	6	12.2
Junior	1	9.1	12	24.5
Senior	7	63.6	26	53.1
Total	**11**	**100.0**	**49**	**100.0**
College/School				
Arts and Sciences	7	63.6	28	57.1
Education and Human Ecology	1	9.1	1	2.0
Library and Information Studies	0	0	0	0
Health Sciences	2	18.2	4	8.2
Nursing	1	9.1	6	12.2

TABLE 1. Continued

Characteristics	Black N	%	White N	%
Occupational Therapy	0	0	6	12.2
Physical Therapy	0	0	0	0
Non-declared Majors	0	0	4	8.2
Total	**11**	**100.0**	**49**	**99.1**
Course Load[b]				
Full-time	5	45.5	27	55.1
Part-time	6	54.5	22	44.9
Total	**11**	**100.0**	**49**	**100.0**
Age				
18-24	6	54.5	18	36.7
25-31	1	9.1	19	38.8
32-38	2	18.2	7	14.3
39-45	0	0	3	6.1
46 and over	2	8.2	2	4.1
Total	**11**	**100.0**	**49**	**100.0**
Start Date				
1994	0	0	1	2.0
1995	2	18.2	4	8.2
1996	2	18.2	11	22.4
1997	2	18.2	16	32.7
1998	5	45.5	17	34.7
Total	**11**	**100.1**	**49**	**100.0**
Current Residence				
On Campus	3	27.3	7	14.3
Off Campus	2	18.2	10	20.4
With Parents	2	18.2	2	4.1
With Other	4	36.4	30	61.2
Total	**11**	**100.1**	**49**	**100.0**

[a] Due to rounding, percentages may not add up to 100.
[b] An undergraduate is considered full time if enrolled in 12 semester hours during the fall of 1998, and part time status is if enrolled in less than 12 hours during the fall of 1998.

Reasons Why Males Chose a Predominantly Female University

There are over 100 colleges and universities in the state of Texas with eight being historically black. The University is located in North Central Texas where another state-supported university is located. With many colleges and universities to select from, why would African American males and white American males choose a predominantly female university? When thinking about males who attend a predominantly female university, the image of sex, parties, and fun immediately comes to mind. Are males choosing the school to satisfy their social and personal needs? Do male students think that a predominantly female university is an easy route to obtaining a degree? Using a list of reasons provided (including an open-ended one) respondents ranked the top three reasons for choosing the University. Table 2 presents these reasons rank-ordered from high to low for black and white male students. The overall ranked scores suggest that major, location, and size are the top three reasons for choosing the University for black males while major, location, and reputation were the top three reasons for choosing the University for white males. According to this, these males did not decide to enroll at the predominantly female university because they wanted to party but because majors/programs were offered in a convenient area.

Table 2. Distribution of Responses: Reasons for Choosing the Predominantly Female University

Reasons	Black N=11	White N=49
Major	17	82
Location of School	14	52
Reputation	6	45
Size	9	34
Other (Cost)	4	24
Family/Friends Attended	4	22
Raise Grades	3	16
Female Population	4	6
University is Easy	0	6

To compute the rank score, the frequencies for each rank were weighted (rank 1=3, rank 2=2, and rank 3=1) and summed.

Respondents also described how they explain to family and friends if asked, "Why do you go to Texas Woman's University?" Based on the responses, five categories were formed as can be seen in Tables 3 and 4.

Table 3. African American Males Respond to Family and Friends

Responses	Family N	%	Friends N	%
Reputation	4	36.4	6	54.5
To Get an Education	4	36.4	4	36.4
Convenience	2	18.2	0	0
Focus on Females	0	0	0	0
Not Applicable	1	9.1	1	9.1
Total	**11**	**100.1**	**11**	**100.1**

Table 4. White American Males Respond to Family and Friends

Responses	Family N	%	Friends N	%
Reputation	30	61.2	30	61.2
To Get an Education	10	20.4	13	26.5
Convenience	2	4.1	3	6.2
Focus on Females	0	0	1	2.0
Not Applicable	7	14.3	2	4.1
Total	**49**	**100.0**	**49**	**100.0**

For both black and white males, the reputation of the school (including department and faculty) are reasons explained to family and friends as why they attend. The one individual, who stressed the focus on females when responding to family members stated,

> It's a great school. . .I concentrate more on how women think or view the business world. I think it is an opportunity to experience that.

However, when responding to friends, he claims to go because it is convenient. He added, "I'd rather not tell friends I am going [to the predominantly female university]." Convenience refers to cost and location of the school.

If males are indeed coming to the University for academic reasons, what is life like for them? Do these males perceive that they are being treated unfairly?

What is Life Like for Black and White Male Students?

In 1994, the Board of Regents voted 6 to 1 to admit all qualified applicants (male and female) to all undergraduate programs. An outrage followed. According to local newspapers students and faculty "angrily protested," "quietly wept," and "occupied the office of admissions."[6] The school newspaper featured articles with titles indicating anger among those who opposed the decision. "Texas Woman's and Man's University: Regents Pull Sneak Play, Angry Students Protest" and "Sold Out: Campus Outraged by Backdoor Politics" are examples. Some students and faculty felt betrayed by the regents; many felt that the regents deliberately made the decision at the end of the semester (when students were occupied with final exams and some had already left) without taking anyone's feelings into consideration. The Coalition, a group of students, faculty, and alumnae, filed a lawsuit against the Board of Regents and the Regent's secretary. Students, faculty, and administrators took an active role (their strategy included establishing a hotline, erecting a tent city, and encouraging a girlcott of the University's Bookstore) in expressing their dissent over the Regent's action until the Court's verdict was rendered.

Do these male students feel comfortable attending the University after hearing about, reading about, and/or witnessing the resistance for undergraduate males to enroll in all programs? What is Life Like for black and white males?

Respondents answered a series of Likert-type questions on the mail-out survey, described the best and worst things in an open-ended question on the mail-out survey, and described a typical day at during the in-depth interview. This section presents the findings.

Overall responses to the Likert-type items suggest that both blacks and whites: feel comfortable in class; feel safe on campus; feel proud to be at the University; feel their experiences are positive at the University; receive the same treatment in and out of class; and support the concept of the University. A majority of black (72.7%) and white (67.3%) respondents disagree that they will wear special clothing. One white respondent wrote on his survey, "I doubt it," and another wrote, "I just don't wear those types of shirts."

TABLE 5. Responses to What-is-Life-Like Items

	Blacks (N=11) N %	Whites (N=49) N %
Comfortable in Class		
SA/A	9 81.8	46 93.9
NO	0 0	1 2.0
D/SD	2 18.2	2 4.1
Safe on Campus		
SA/A	10 90.9	49 100.0
NO	1 9.1	0 0
Participate in Campus Activities		
SA/A	5 45.5	21 42.9
NO	3 27.3	12 24.5
D/SD	3 27.3	16 32.7
Wear Clothing with the University Name		
SA/A	3 27.3	9 18.4
NO	0 0	7 14.3
D/SD	8 72.7	33 67.3
Experiences Positive		
SA/A	9 81.8	46 93.9
NO	1 9.1	2 4.1
D/SD	1 9.1	1 2.0
Proud to Be at the University		
SA/A	8 72.7	42 85.7
NO	2 18.2	7 14.3
D/SD	1 9.1	0 0

TABLE 5. Continued

	Blacks (N=11) N %	Whites (N=49) N %
Feel Lonely on Campus		
SA/A	3 27.3	7 14.3
NO	1 9.1	1 2.0
D/SD	7 63.6	41 83.7
Same Treatment in Class		
SA/A	8 72.7	32 65.3
NO	0 0	2 4.1
D/SD	3 27.3	15 30.6
Same Treatment Out of Class		
SA/A	7 63.6	33 67.3
NO	0 0	7 14.3
D/SD	4 36.4	9 18.4
Understand What It's Like To Be a Minority		
SA/A	7 63.6	35 71.4
NO	1 9.1	4 8.2
D/SD	3 27.3	10 20.4
Support Concept of University Primarily for Women		
SA/A	7 63.6	36 73.5
NO	4 36.4	4 8.2
D/SD	0 0	9 18.4
Bothers if Only Male or One of Two or Three Males in Class		
SA/A	3 27.3	3 6.1
NO	0 0	5 10.2
D/SD	8 72.7	41 83.7

TABLE 5. Continued

	Blacks (N=11) N %	Whites (N–49) N %
Often Thinking about the School As Predominantly Female		
SA/A	7 63.6	8 16.3
NO	2 18.2	10 20.4
D/SD	2 18.2	31 63.3
Bothers when People Tease		
SA/A	1 9.1	8 16.3
NO	2 18.2	7 14.3
D/SD	8 72.7	34 69.4
Become Androgynous		
SA/A	2 18.2	7 14.3
NO	2 18.2	9 18.4
D/SD	7 63.6	33 67.3

Interestingly, a majority of black (63.6%) and white (71.4%) respondents agreed that they understand better what it is like to be a minority even though men are considered to comprise the dominant group in the larger society. The term dominant group refers to "all groups participating in a pattern of discrimination against a particular minority."[7] When examining the history of higher education in the United States, one quickly realizes that white men in higher education received rights, benefits, privileges, and rewards whereas men of color and women in higher education have received limited options. This suggests that women and men of color (because of their race) comprise a minority group, not white men. There is no significant difference between black and white respondents on this response. One black male strongly disagreed with the item and wrote, "I'm Black." Another black explained during the in-depth interview that he believed being a numerical minority is different than a minority based on color.

> Many females here have power. Being a black minority is different than a numerical minority. Different type of discrimination. Different type of experience.

One white respondent stated that he now knows what it must be like for blacks.

Respondents indicated the best and worst things about the school. Responses were categorized and are presented in the following table.

TABLE 6. Distribution of Responses: The Best Thing

Responses	Blacks N	%	Whites N	%
Academic Quality	4	36.4	30	61.2
Female-Centered Environment	5	45.5	1	2.0
Atmosphere (non-academic)	1	9.1	12	24.5
Convenience	1	9.1	6	12.2
Total	11	100.0	49	99.9

$X^2=18.97$, df=3, p<.001

It should be noted that when respondents listed more than one "best thing," the first response was used and analyzed. Over half the white respondents, 61.2 percent, and 36.4 black respondents perceive that the quality of academic programs is the "best thing." The variable "academic quality" includes reputation of departments, professors and their styles of teaching, and the staff. One student remarked,

> The profs take an interest in each individual and there is an opportunity to voice questions and concerns in class.

Another stated,

> The level of courtesy and professionalism extended by the faculty and staff.

For the majority of black respondents (45.5%), the best thing is the female environment. Typical responses include the following: (1) educated females and (2) the emphasis on females in courses and course work. One respondent claimed, "The women are usually friendly."

Atmosphere refers to beauty of the campus and the "friendly-type" feeling and experiences. One white respondent wrote,

> It is a very friendly school. I feel much more comfortable and at home than in other schools I have attended.

One black male student reported,

> If you need assistance with any aspect of your academic or personal life it's available. It's nurturing.

Typical responses for convenience include the following: (1) nice commute from the DFW area, and (2) good location in Denton.

Table 7 reports the distribution of responses to the question asking for the "worst thing."

TABLE 7. Distribution of Responses: The Worst Thing

Responses	Blacks N	Blacks %	Whites N	Whites %
Atmosphere (non-academic)	2	18.2	23	46.9
Academic Quality	2	18.2	10	20.4
Bias	3	27.3	8	16.3
Loneliness	4	36.4	6	12.2
No Response	0	0	2	4.1
Total	11	100.1	49	99.9

$X^2=5.98$, df=4, p=.20

When the responses are ranked ordered, atmosphere (46.9%), academic quality (20.4%), and bias (16.3%) are the top three "worst things" for white males. For black males, loneliness (36.4%) and bias (27.3%) are the top two "worst things." For blacks, atmosphere (18.2%) and academics (18.2%) tied for the third worst thing. "Atmosphere" refers to the lack of facilities/products and inadequate services. For example, one white respondent complained about the contents in the University Bookstore. He indicated that the clothing and hats do not fit most male students. The complaint of inadequate service was directed towards support staff (i.e., housing and advising staff). Typical "worst thing" responses include the following: (1) finding a parking space, (2) lack of men's restrooms, and (3) run down facilities.

Complaints about academic quality on the part of respondents refer to limited class choices, poor departments, instructors' styles of teaching, and the limited course times (e.g., not enough evening courses).

Examples of bad styles of teaching include the following (1) taking the women's rights issue to the extreme, and (2) the instructor's teaching information only from the textbook. Individuals who reported a specific course as being the "worst thing" mentioned Women's Studies. "Male bashing" is a typical phrase used when Women's Studies courses were mentioned. One student wrote,

> Women's Studies--the course is mainly male bashing and lamentation over inequality. The same issues get rehashed over and over, i.e., women make less money than men.

Another respondent stated,

> Having to take a women's studies class. Having some dyke force her opinion on you is not what I thought [the University] was about.

More blacks (27.3%) than whites (16.3%) reported bias as being the "worst thing." "Bias" includes discrimination against males, sexism, and stereotypes associated with a male going to the University. Some responses blamed faculty and staff (e.g., the police department) for being sexist. One white male stated,

> Being ignored by professors in class discussions, also being cut off mid-statement.

Another white male reported,

> Sometimes I am overlooked in class and other school situations because I am male.

Some respondents viewed the name, Texas Woman's University, and the meaning associated with the name as a negative. One black male stated,

> The name. . . . I don't mind being the minority. However, it is hard to tell other people (without an explanation) why I chose to go to [the University]. I would consider a compromise name. No gender bias.

Another black male remarked,

> It is negative being a man here--rather my diploma not say Texas Woman's University.

One who remarked about the "meaning" associated with the University stated, "I want to wear a sign everyday that says I'm not gay and come talk to me."

Blacks (36.4%) and whites (12.2%) reported feelings of loneliness which includes the feelings of isolation, the lack of activities for males, and the feeling of being the center of attention all the time. One white respondent wrote, "The loneliness I feel on campus," which was a typical response. Another typical statement is, "The number of males in my classes and/or that I encounter on campus." Another student maintained that it is negative to be the center of attention. He stated,

> Being the center of attention. It would be nice to blend in every once in awhile.

Survey respondents indicated how they perceive that females at the University treat them by filling in the blank "Females treat me _____." The following table presents the distribution.

TABLE 8. Treatment by Females

Responses	Blacks N	%	Whites N	%
Positive	10	90.9	32	65.3
Negative	0	0	2	4.1
Indifferent	1	9.1	14	28.6
No Response	0	0	1	2.0
Total	**11**	**100.0**	**49**	**100.0**

Typical response for the category labeled positive include the following: fine, equal, part of the family, well, nice/good, okay, and friendly. Responses for the negative category include "second-class citizen" and as a "minority. Typical statements categorized as neutral include: indifferently, as a peer, and as a person.

Typical Day Responses

During the interview respondents were asked to describe a typical day at the University. The theme of socializing with peers emerged from responses and was coded into very social, somewhat social, or non-social as shown in the following table. Five out of the seven black males and two out of ten white males indicated that they are very sociable. These individuals indicated that they talk to other students in and out of class, have no problem walking on campus outside of school hours, and frequently participate in campus activities. An African American male reported that he loves to socialize. When asked if he socializes on this campus and whether he perceives initiating a conversation with unknown female students as problematic, the student responded that he has encountered a few problems.

> I get oh disgusting male look, oh foxy male look, or oh I'm a lesbian look. Sometimes white women make you look like you don't exist. I am tired of jumping off the sidewalks when you [white females] kick me and I'm the one who says I'm sorry. I prefer to be called a nigger than to seem like I don't exist. I will never be able to change my mind about not existing.

The four who reported that they were somewhat social at the University described themselves as someone who did not actively seek a conversation. Also, outside factors, such as family obligations and/or jobs, kept these male students from participating in campus activities after school hours. One respondent who resides on campus described his day as such:

> I wake up at seven in the morning, go to my classes. I sit in the front. I have my classes spread out so I can do my homework in between. After my classes, I go to my room and relax for about an hour then I do homework for the rest of the evening.

This respondent indicated that he has a girlfriend and a few male friends who also reside on campus. He also stated that he rarely leaves campus during the week unless he needs to get something. He doesn't belong to any clubs or participate in activities unless he has to for a class.

Two blacks and four whites reported not having any friends on campus, not having time to socialize because of work, and not wanting to socialize with the student population. Individuals who reported not wanting to socialize indicated that they are here for an education and not to party. An extreme example of a typical day for one black participant, who has a fear of being labeled gay, is:

> I walk to my classes. . . .If I see females I don't want to be looked at. I will say hi to the girls if they are close enough. Most of the time I am alone.

When asked why, the respondent stated:

> I walk to class alone. I don't like hanging out in the halls. The scariest place for me is the student center. I don't want to be called gay. I feel intimidated. I feel people look at me because of all the women. . . .I usually eat by myself. If there is not a big crowd I will go to the student center [and eat there].

TABLE 9. Typical-Day at the University

Responses	Blacks N	%	Whites N	%
Very Social	5	71.4	2	20.0
Somewhat Social	0	0	4	40.0
Non-Social	2	28.6	4	40.0
Total	**7**	**100.0**	**10**	**100.0**

During the interview respondents answered the question, "In general, what does it feel like for you as a male at the university?" Responses were coded into "positive," "mixed," and "negative."

Table 10. General Feeling at the University

Responses	Blacks N	%	Whites N	%
Positive	5	71.4	8	80.0
Mixed	1	14.3	1	10.0
Negative	1	14.3	1	10.0
Total	**7**	**100.0**	**10**	**100.0**

A majority of blacks (71.4%) and whites (80%) indicated that they have positive feelings at the University. Typical phrases include: "rewarding," "fun," "it's cool," and "I feel special." One individual reported that he is grateful to come to the University.

> I feel fortunate and honored. I am lucky to be able to hear the female perspective. I would not trade this experience. I would do it again. . . and tell boys graduating from high school to come here.

Two interviewees indicated uncomfortable feelings. One respondent stated that he does not like to be made the example for all men. The other male reported his fear and the stress of contact with individuals.

> I feel alone pretty much. I don't want to associate with males because I will be labeled gay. I can't associate with females here on campus because I don't want to start a relationship.

Individuals stating a sense of mixed feelings indicated that their feelings depend on the situation. One stated that his feelings are affected by others' actions as well as by his own.

> Depends, sometimes feel good and sometimes feel bad. I'm surprised how a "hello, how are you" changes your day. It is a give and take thing.

Concluding Remarks

This descriptive research was conducted to determine who these male students are and to provide at least a partial description of what their life is like in this predominantly female environment. Overall, the undergraduate males at the University perceive their experiences to be positive, both in and out of class. Few report feeling lonely or being bothered because they are the numerical minority. A majority of the respondents perceive their life to be good because the college offers quality education, opportunities for interaction with peers, and a nurturing and supportive environment. After conducting this research, I realized that these male students were at the school to learn although the school that they happened to be at was a predominantly female university.

Notes

1. Pinkney, A. 1999. *Black Americans* 5th ed. New York: Prentice Hall.
2. Riley, N. 1997. "Gender, Power, and Population Change." *Population Bulletin* 52(1).
3. Eshbach, E. 1993. *The Higher Education of Women in England and America: 1865-1920*. New York: Garland Publishing
4. *The Dallas Morning News* April 2, 1996
5. Nieto, S. 1996. *Affirming Diversity: The Socio-Political Context of Multicultural Education*. New York: Longman Publishing Co.
6. *Fort Worth Star Telegram* (December 10, 1994)
7. Davis, F. 1978. *Minority-Dominant Relations: A Sociological Analysis*. Illinois: AHM Publishing Co.

Article 12

Interaction Patterns between Black and White College Students: For Better or Worse?

Jas M. Sullivan, Ashraf M. Esmail and Raymond S. Soh

Introduction

For many years now, colleges and universities around the nation have tried to build more welcoming climates on their campuses for students of color. In 1998 the Association of American Colleges and Universities (AAC&U) launched "Racial Legacies and Learning: An American Dialogue" in an attempt to foster campus/community discussion while addressing issues of racism, urban development, school reform, and race relations. With the advent of new technology, we see an increasing number of websites dedicated to multicultural issues and communication. For example, the *DiversityWeb Listserv* was set up primarily to discuss diversity in higher education. One might expect that communication between different cultural groups to increase significantly.

A reality check

A number of universities have conducted campus climate surveys in an attempt to determine how a diverse campus community benefits all students. The general findings were:

- Students of color have similar reasons for attending university as their White counterparts do, namely, strength of academic programs, location and proximity, previous friends, and social activities.
- Many students of color have different social experiences than White students. Black students felt more isolated than White students. When asked about the quality of social relationships, 50% of Blacks students reported that they were satisfied with their social relationships, compared to 75 % of Whites. (Report on Campus Climate Survey, Indiana State University, 1998).
- Black students were more likely to say that they made friends with students who differed in terms of interests, family background, and race.

Research on Interracial Interaction

Past research has examined racial prejudice in the United States. Condran (1979) found that from 1963 to 1972 that there was evidence of generally liberal racial attitudes in our society. However, by the mid-1970s, there was evidence that racial liberalism among Whites was slowing its growth and even reversing in some cases, most notably housing and intrusion. Monteith and Spicer (2000) found that among Blacks and Whites, that positive socialization and intergroup experiences, along with the recognition that prejudice and stereotyping are unjust, appeared to form the basis of positive intergroup attitudes. However, there was evidence of the notable divide between Blacks and Whites. Despite the change of prejudice throughout time, it appeared to be largely rooted in antiegalitarianism. Whites expressed resentment about the supposed special favors that Blacks obtain. They also maintained that discrimination against Blacks in the United States was not a problem for them in the United States. In contrast, the attitude of

Blacks towards Whites appeared to be strongly related to discrimination, stereotyping, and prejudice.

More recent studies have indicated that racial prejudices may occur more often among White attitudes toward Blacks in various institutions in the United States. Dovidio, Kawakami, and Johnson (1997) conducted three experiments examining automatic and controlled processes in racial prejudice. The study revealed that Whites demonstrated implicit negative racial attitudes toward Blacks that were largely dissociated from explicit self-reported racial prejudice. The authors speculated that Whites who reported that they are non-prejudiced on traditional measures of prejudice might have unconscious negative feelings toward Blacks. Schaefer (1986), drawing on a nationwide survey data gathered 1942-1985, found that there has been consistent and growing support among Whites for racial integration. At the same time, the resistance to the American Creed is evident in White hostility to affirmative action.

However, Jacobson (1983) gathered survey from a national survey of US Blacks. It was found that Blacks as a whole gave strong support for affirmative action programs. More important as predictors of Black attitudes were feelings of powerlessness and views of the effectiveness of Black leaders in achieving equality for Blacks. Also significantly related were the amount of contact Blacks had with Whites, the amount of discrimination experienced by Blacks, their support of integration in general, and their view of how much race relations have changed in the past and in the future.

Krivo and Kaufman (1999) found that there were still strong prejudices of Whites against Blacks and Whites' preferences for living in neighborhoods with few Blacks. The authors noted that in metropolitan areas, desegregation would not be possible until there were enormous changes in Whites' toleration for living with Blacks. Goodman and Streitwieser (1983) concluded that Black retention, attributable to actual or anticipated racial discrimination against Blacks, is responsible for most of the White-Black gap in rates of city-to-suburb movement. Finally, Hwang, Fitzpatrick, and Helms (1998) found no significant class differences in Blacks' attitudinal orientation toward Whites.

Sociologists have refocused their interest in race toward the interaction of minority groups in a White society (Jones, 1990). Wilson (1986) using a national sample collected from the National Opinion Research Center's General Social Survey, collected in 1980 and 1982, found that Blacks prefer much less distance from Whites than Whites do from Blacks. Sigelman, Beldsoe, Welch, and Combs (1996), in a more recent study, conducted a survey with 1,124 Black and White residents from Detroit to explore to what extent and in what manner interracial contact has changed over the past quarter century and is shaped by propinquity and personal characteristics. Analysis indicated that interracial contact is more common than it was during the late 1960s, especially for Whites, but still consisted primarily of brief, superficial encounters. For Whites, the quantity and quality of contact with Blacks was determined by propinquity. For Blacks, place of residence mattered less, and early childhood experiences mattered more.

Racial prejudices that occur in our society may be significantly related to the interactions patterns that Blacks have with Whites. Extensive research has been done looking at various interaction patterns between Blacks and Whites. Studies have shown that there is a significant relationship between the interaction patterns of Blacks and Whites and the contact hypothesis – i.e., contact between members of different races fosters positive racial attitudes (Sigelman and Welch, 1993; Ellison and Powers, 1994). Sigelman and Welch (1993) obtained data in a 1989 nationwide telephone survey of adult Americans. Their analysis reveals that in several instances interracial contact is associated with more positive racial attitudes, especially among Whites. Ellison and Powers (1994) using the National Survey of Black Americans explored the relevance of the contact hypothesis for the distribution of racial attitudes among Blacks. The results indicated that interracial friendship is among the strongest predictors of Blacks' racial attitudes.

Interracial contact, especially when it occurs early in life, enhances the likelihood that Blacks will develop close friendships with Whites. Jackman and Crane (1986) used national survey data to address the central postulates of the contact theory. The analysis of the interview data on racial beliefs, policy views, feelings, and social dispositions of 1,648 Whites who have contact with Blacks as friends, acquaintances, or neighbors suggested that personal interracial contact is selective in its effects on Whites' racial attitudes, that intimacy is less important among contacts, and that any effects are in relation to the relative socioeconomic status of Black contacts.

Interactions of Blacks and Whites in the Public School System

Studies have been done looking at the interaction patterns of Whites and Blacks in the proper environment will undermine unreasonable prejudice. Bullock (1978) conducted a study in which a survey was administered to approximately 5,800 students throughout Georgia in urban and rural schools. Data were collected from Black and White students, males and females, in 1974 and early 1975. On the racial tolerance scale, the most tolerant group was segregated Whites, followed by desegregated Blacks, segregated Blacks, and desegregated Whites. Correlations between tolerance and the biracial friends measurement vary little with sex and grade differences and with urban White youth, although they did play a slightly larger role with rural White students. Outside contact was more strongly related to tolerance among urban Whites than rural Whites. Biracial friendships and school contact with Blacks became increasingly strong correlates of tolerance by Whites in schools with 70% Black enrollment. The correlation coefficient dropped in schools with greater than 70% Black enrollment. Both the friendship and school contact variables showed that correlations with tolerance are highest in schools with the least number of Blacks in attendance. Correlations using outside contact as the independent variable were small and except for students in schools with 61-70% Black enrollment, the coefficients indicated that out-of-school contact was associated with less tolerance.

Other studies have looked at the interaction patterns of Blacks and Whites in the public school system and findings have not generated conclusive results. Silverman and Shaw (1973) looked at the extent to which Blacks and Whites interacted socially on school grounds and their attitudes toward each other were ascertained across time during first semester of an integration program in three secondary schools, in Gainesville, Florida. They found that interracial interactions remained sparse throughout the semester and over time showed no significant increases approaching significance though attitudes did become more tolerant.

Rainwater's (1966) asserts that Blacks have low self-evaluations because they receive more negative evaluations from other Blacks than Whites receive from other Whites. However, P. Heiss and S. Owens (1972) had evidence to suggest that negative self-evaluation among Blacks was limited to work- & school-related traits. These were areas in which Whites had control over Blacks and could impose White evaluative standards. On traits relevant to intimate primary-group interaction, Blacks' self-evaluations did not differ from those of Whites.

Muir and Muir (1988) provided questionnaires to 475 White and Black eighth graders at an Alabama middle school. They found that the majority of respondents of both races approved of casual social interactions between Whites and Blacks. However, Whites tended to be more rejecting of Blacks at more intimate levels of interaction, while Blacks accepted Whites not only publicly but also socially. The results suggested that although the public school system has been desegregated, it has not been integrated. Finally, Dickinson, Holifield, Holifield, and Creer (2000) looked at elementary magnet school students' interracial interaction choices. They found that Whites tended to interact across racial lines more than Blacks. Black female students tended to interact less across racial lines. This could be attributed to the lack of Black female role models in the curriculum.

Interaction of Black and White Students on College Campuses

Few studies have looked at the interaction patterns of Black and White students on college campuses. Muir (1989) did a local time-series measure of White attitudes towards Blacks at the University of Alabama in the quarter century since desegregation. Data showed that there was a consistent increase in public and social acceptance of Blacks except for 1982. Changes in attitude were consistent with the sociological theory predicting that interaction leads to positive sentiments. The study found that over nine out of ten "white" students accept "blacks" in classroom and campus situations, and over eight out of ten accept them as eating companions. It was found that over four out of ten "whites" are now willing to room and double date with "blacks". However, less than one of six "white" males and one of ten "white" females accept "blacks" as dates.

Longshore (1979) found conflicting results. In a questionnaire survey of racial attitudes among Black and White college students, Whites' ratings of "white people" were more favorable than their ratings of "Negroes," which in turn were more favorable than their ratings of "black people". This suggests that negative connotations of the color Black negatively affect Whites' attitudes toward Blacks. Blacks' ratings of "white people" were less favorable than their ratings of "black people," especially among Blacks who more strongly supported a Black power ideology. This suggested that the Black power movement, in its emphasis on Black pride and independence from White values and culture, may have reversed the connotations of the color Black among power adherents.

This study attempts to answer two important questions through social network analysis, focus groups and interviews: One, though studies demonstrate that Whites accept Blacks in the classroom, what is the interaction pattern of Black students at a predominantly White college? Two, what are the factors that may cause weak relationships between Black and White students?

Design and Methodology: Social Network Analysis

The setting for this study is at a large Mid-Western University. The undergraduate population is around 25,000, with a 4 percent Black population and the graduate enrollment is roughly 12,000 students. Though students from various states attend this university, an overwhelming majority are students from within the state. To understand the interaction pattern of Black students, social network analysis was used. This research will apply the "realist" framework. This framework will be set from the perspective of the individual who is actually in the situation. Another term for this framework is called "egocentric" social network analysis, which looks at the connections around a particular point in the network. The attributes of people being studied ("attributes of nodes") are Blacks and their interactions with those around them. This will be an egocentric social network study.

Twenty-four Black undergraduate students participated in the study. Students were solicited through a university e-mail list serve. The first twenty-four students who replied to the e-mail were selected to participate in the study. Of those who participated in the study, ten of the students were female and the other fourteen were male.

These students were asked to keep track of whom they talked with for a week. All citations were to be marked. E-mails and Internet conversations were not to be recorded in this study. Participants were asked to mark several items: the person's gender, ethnicity, who initiated the conversation, and how long the conversations lasted. It is important to make clear that it is possible that not all Black students' interaction pattern at this particular university will be consistent with those twenty-four students included in this study.

To analyze the interactions a matrix was employed. Agents will be shown in the rows and whom they interacted with according to race will be in the columns. Race will further be sub-divided into: Whites, Blacks, and other. All raw numbers are then converted into percents. Race, gender, time, and initiating contact were included in the analysis in order to understand the interaction pattern of these students. Several questions were analyzed through the use of network analysis: 1). Who are Black students most frequently interacting with? 2). Duration of total time Black students spend with their own group, Whites, and others. 3). Were Black students more likely to initiate contact with other Blacks, Whites, and other minorities? Network analysis will allow for identifying the pattern of interaction of Black college students. After clearly identifying the pattern of interaction, focus groups and interviews were utilized to determine Black students' attitude towards Whites, their own group, and interaction with Whites.

Focus Groups and Interviews

In trying to understand the factors that create weak relationships, focus groups and interviews were utilized to understand Black college students' attitude toward Whites, their own race, and interacting with Whites. Seventy-five interviews and six focus groups were conducted. Each of the focus groups included four participants and each session lasting about two hours. Three of the focus groups consisted of two females and two male, two consisted of all females, while one included all males. The seventy-five interviews lasted between twenty five to thirty minutes. Thirty-eight males and thirty-seven females were interviewed. Students who participated in this portion of the study were also selected in order of their response to an e-mail solicitation. It is possible that not all Black students in this study will have the same feelings and attitudes as found from the group of students interviewed in this sample.

Three questions were asked of the Black students in the focus groups and the interviews, namely, 1) what are the words that come to mind when they hear the mention of White people? This question was asked to understand the feelings and attitudes these students have towards Whites. Next, what are some words that come into mind when people of their own color are mentioned? This question was raised to see if Black students perceived their race to be superior to that of Whites. These two questions are important because one could compare the overall attitude that Black students have about their race and that of Whites.

Finally, Black students were asked if they interacted with Whites. This question allows us to assess the students' associations or interactions. If they said "no", they were further asked about the reasons for the lack of interaction? All three questions as mentioned above assists us in understanding the barriers that may exist that blocks positive interactions with Whites.

Findings: Social Network Analysis

The scenario that Black students' confront on this particular campus is that their chances of seeing someone White is much greater than running into someone who is Black or in another minority group. Therefore, you would assume that the likelihood of interaction is much greater between Whites and Blacks. However, the data gathered from this study indicates that Blacks tend to interact more with other Blacks than with Whites.

When assessing for the frequency of interaction of Blacks by race (and not the amount of total time spent interacting but on the number of interactions with different racial groups), all those in the sample interacted most often with their own group. Two of the twenty-four students in the analysis interacted a 100% with other Black students; seventeen students interacted between 90-99% of the time with other Black students. The other four students in the sample interacted between 80-89% with other Black students. Ultimately, when we compare all of these students (in terms of the number of interactions with different racial groups and not total time spent on those interactions), their interactions conclude that they interacted far more with other Blacks—between 80-100%. The flip side to this is that Blacks had minimal contact with Whites and other minorities. Just about three of the twenty-four students in the sample interacted between 10-16% of their time with Whites and other minorities.

Black females not only interacted more frequently with other Black students, but they interacted more frequently with other black females, as seen in Table 1.

Table 1. Black Female Students: Contact by Gender and Race

Characteristics	White Male	White Female	Black Males	Black Female	Other Males	Other Females
Average (%)	2.6	2.8	44.2	49.2	0.5	0.7

When examining for their interactions within gender groups, four of the ten Black females interacted more frequently with Black males, while, the other six interacted more frequently with other Black females. Each of the ten Black females interacted with at least with one White male and one White female. Further, Black females were more likely to interact with other minority females than with other minority males.

Black males also interacted more frequently with other Black students. Further, in assessing for their interaction pattern within gender groups, Black males were more likely (see Table 2) to interact with other Black males than with Black females. When looking at the interactions with Whites and other minorities, Black males interacted at least with one White male and one White female.

Table 2. Black Male Students: Contact by Gender and Race

Characteristics	White Male	White Female	Black Males	Black Female	Other Males	Other Females
Average (%)	2.6	2.4	48.8	44.4	0.6	1.2

Black male students' were more likely to interact with other minority females than with other minority males. When looking at the interaction pattern of the whole sample by race and total time spent interacting, Black students spent most of their time interacting with other Blacks—between 90-100%. The total time spent with Whites and other minorities was 1-4%. When examining Black female students' total time spent interacting by race and gender, Black females spent most of their time with other Black males as illustrated in Table 3.

Table 3. Black Female Students: Interaction by Race, Gender, and Time

Characteristics	White Male	White Female	Black Males	Black Female	Other Males	Other Females
Average (%)	1	1.3	51.1	46.1	0.3	0.2

Black females spent minimal time with Whites and other minorities. However, they were more likely to spend greater amount of time interacting with Whites than with other minorities.

Black males spent more time interacting with other Blacks. In assessing for gender and time, Black males spent about equal time interacting with other Black males and females. In general, they spent minimal time interacting with Whites and other minorities. However, when they did interact with Whites, Black males spent about equal time with both White males and females (See Table 4).

Table 4. Black Male Students: Interaction by Race, Gender, and Time

Characteristics	White Male	White Female	Black Males	Black Female	Other Males	Other Females
Average (%)	1.6	1.1	49.2	46.2	0.3	1.6

Black students had no problem initiating contact with other Black students. Furthermore, Blacks as a collective had no problem initiating contact with Whites and other minorities if interaction took place at all. More often than not, Blacks were more likely to initiate contact with Whites and other minorities. If further broken down by gender, Black females are more likely to initiate contact with Black males. Unlike Black females, Black males were more likely to initiate contact with other Black males. Black males initiated contact more frequently with White females, other minority males and females.

Social network analysis has allowed for the understanding of the interaction patterns of Black students. It has revealed that there are low levels of interaction between the two groups. If interactions did take place with Whites particularly, it was within the confines of the classroom or structured educational or work environment where the dependence on students and staff was detrimental in completing group assignment, understanding something that was discussed in the class, or carrying out a task at a particular place of employment. Very little interaction took place outside of the educational and work structure. Meaning, after leaving class, black and white students did not generally go to parties, eat out together, or interact socially.

The next question that has to be investigated is: What barriers are causing this low level of interaction between the two groups. Focus groups and interviews are utilized to understanding the reasons that cause this low level of interaction between Blacks and Whites.

Focus Groups and Interviews

The interviews and focus groups yielded a substantial amount of information on Black students' attitudes toward Whites, their own race, and interacting with Whites. When asked Black students what they thought about Whites, most possessed a negative attitude. Black students viewed Whites as being: racists, suspicious, paranoid, conceited, hypocritical, untrustworthy, and manipulative." A Black male student expressed: "…..When I hear the word White people, it upsets me…." Another Black male noted:

> "…. I think paranoid. I think conceited. They are always paranoid around Blacks. They look out of place….. The conceited part is that you can tell when White people think they are better than anyone else. They give these little vibes and try to get jazzy with you while you are with other White people. I think that we are not equal and don't have anything in common. We can basically understand where they are coming from, but they can't understand where we are coming from. I think that they are always trying to label us….."

However, the next step is to understand the reasons why they had such negative attitudes toward Whites. The theme that occurred over and over is "slavery." Most of the Black students argued that slavery and history caused them to have such negative attitudes toward Whites even today because Whites failed to understand the long-term consequences of slavery.

Many of the Black students argue that they "can't trust" Whites. Still, some point out that "Whites think they are too good." A Black student notes: ".....They first took over the Indian land and forced them to grow stuff and they could not survive. Then they bring African over here to do the labor so they won't have to do anything but sit back and relax....." Statements like the one previously mentioned demonstrate the sentiments that the majority of those in the sample expressed. Another Black male stated:

> "......Basically when I think of White people, I just think White people. I just think fuck them because of slavery and they hold us down and do so much to us. They are bogus people. How can someone just put down a whole culture like that? How can White people build their whole government around us and suppress other cultures and shit."

Another student points out: ".....I think of them as being slick. Honestly, when you think about it, the whole scheme of slavery and the different places they have been to and taken over is sad." It would seem very difficult for two groups (Whites and Blacks) to interact if one group has a negative perception of the other and visa versa. At the same time, Black students have positive and negative attitudes towards their own race. Black students described their race as: "beautiful, equal, hard working, powerful, having a rich heritage, jealous, lazy, strong, not understood, and spiritual." A Black female states:

> "Some of the words are negative in my list about Black people, but it's like below......I think of a lot of positive words. The negative words do occur, but they are at the bottom, unlike for the Whites, they're at the top."

Blacks see their race as being negative, but as being less negative than that of Whites.

Further, majority of the Black students interviewed stated that they did not interact with Whites. These students refuse to interact with Whites due to: "history, slavery, lack of similar interests and values, comfort zone, and trust factor." A Black male argues:

> ".....I just hate that they consider us lazy and violent. I mean, as far as I am concerned, when we were slaves, they were the ones that were lazy and violent. They had us doing all of the work."

This is a classic example of how slavery has an effect on Blacks today. The past wounds still fester. These statements may help in understanding why Blacks do not interact with Whites: "don't know each other, White people and Black people are different, are they calling me a "nigga" in their minds, do they want me to be their slave, feel more comfortable around Blacks, they tell so many lies, and you never know what they are thinking." Blacks' attitudes toward Whites come from historical evidence and empirical observation of their experiences in post-segregation institutions such as school and workplaces. However, given their experiences in the post-segregation era, the students have negative attitudes toward Whites and positive attitudes toward Blacks.

In conclusion, focus groups and interviews show that there is real disparity in the way Black students' view Whites. Also, Whites have similar negative attitude toward Blacks. For Whites, they fear Blacks, they feel incompetent when they are in racially mixed situations, and they fear interracial friendship (Tatum 1997: 14). Thus, it is not just Blacks who have negative attitudes toward Whites, but Whites also fear Blacks. From this study, we discover that Blacks' negative attitudes come from past and present conditions. However, Whites' negative feelings come from fear of Blacks and the fear that one-day that the power that the Whites have will be diminished. Tatum explains that "White people are paying a significant price for the system of advantage. The cost is not as high as for Whites as it is for Blacks, but a price is being paid" in perpetuating racial advantage (1997: 14). As a consequence, little progress has been made in increasing interaction on the primary level of education, housing, churches, social gatherings, and relationships.

Discussion

Source of problems

Despite the efforts to promote diversity on college campuses, students of color have not benefited from these efforts as the programs had hope for. These could be due to:

 1. *Lack of coordinated effort of various programs*

Most campus activism tends to be fragmented and issue-specific. Programs tend to be reactive with activities scheduled around current political issues. Ironically, there appears to be a lack of communication among various cultural groups. Each group seems to have their own political agenda, which can defeat diversity appreciation. More importantly, there is a need to connect student activists and link campus groups around more central themes of cultural communication.

2. *Lack of evaluation research of diversity initiatives.*

Some universities have taken cultural diversity seriously. However there is insufficient data gathered on the efficacy of diversity programs. There is a need to create local, campus-specific assessments of diversity initiatives to help universities improve programs and convey research about what they have and have not achieved. We cannot assume that by putting out programs students are necessarily communicating.

3. *Lack of staff involvement*

Faculty and academic departments are just as important as outside-class personnel and activities in shaping the cultural climate for students of color. Many students would welcome greater numbers of direct contacts from faculty in areas of academic advising as well as cultural education. Virtually all university and community activities play a role in shaping students' sense of belonging especially for minorities. Everything is important, from courses and faculty to student support programs to community organized events.

Suggestions for change

1. *Be aware of the search of pathology in racism.*

As we see from the current study there is a tendency to blame others for the lack of communication. Racism comes from the *lack of information* between groups and *misinformation* about the other group. This is where negative racial stereotypes originate. While there may be some validity in the way blacks feel about the way they are treated, growth in cross-cultural communication will take place only when we adopt a systems view of diversity.

More specifically, *both* whites and people of color are adversely affected by racism. Some whites are also not comfortable with affirmative action programs. These programs, they argue, were created to undermine a system where factors such as race and ethnic background were more important than merit. Affirmative action worked by forcing the opposite: instead of giving preference to whites, employers were required to give preference to minorities. The argument against Affirmative Action takes this line of reasoning: Instead of being judged on merit, nonwhites were secured of jobs even when they were less qualified.

One very obvious implication of this study is that we have a long way to go in the area of cross-cultural communications. The blocks to communication are not external. It is not "them making it hard for us". Instead, if we are to be honest, and it is painful to admit this, the problem lies within us, blacks, and whites. To survive in a multi-cultural world, one has to adopt a systems view of communication, which includes a "win-win" attitude in fostering communication. For example, it is easy to interpret being passed over in class as a deliberate effort by the white majority classmates to "gang up" against one or two blacks in class.

It would be advantageous to reframe one's perceptions and break the "pathology of racism" by realizing that self-selection may not necessarily be a bad thing. According to social psychologists, individuals tend to group around those who share similar features and interests. *Being around other students "like me" is important to all students.* For many students "like me" most often means "from my racial/ethnic group." This concept extends to other groups as well, such as married students, Christian students, or fraternity students.

In order to promote cultural communication, Universities can help students find and link with others with *similar* interests. This should be helpful in improving the situation for students of color. Structured activities, which encourage interaction across racial/ethnic groups, can also help improve the situation for students of color. Students should be taught skills in cultural communication in their daily interactions. It cannot be presumed that students have the capacity of such communication by just attending cultural activities.

2. *Be critical viewers of Hollywood racial stereotypes.*

What you see is not what it is. Media generates and perpetuates negative stereotypes of minorities. Most of what we know about other cultures is manufactured by Hollywood. Through history, minorities have been cast in unfavorable roles. In both television and film, domestic laborers, such as maids and housekeepers, are portrayed as members of racial minorities.

In addition, the role of the "sidekick" is assigned to a stereotypical minority figure. These portrayals get into people's minds, and many start believing all of the stereotypes that they see. For some people, television images become the default value of life. In her video documentary, *Cultural Criticism and Transformation*, Bell Hooks illustrates how white male supremacists intentionally create certain images in an effort to discredit people of color.

In *Gangsta Rap*, we see the theme of black violence and sexism. Women are presented as 'bitches' and 'whores' and young black men kill each other for sport. Anger and rage at women is expressed through music. To survive in this harsh world, viewers are told that it is acceptable to use violence. Killing is necessary for survival. The producers of *Gangsta Rap* would like other black aspiring entertainers to know that audiences would buy their music if it contained violence, profanity and aggression towards women. Media consistently legitimizes and glamorizes violence against women. Hooks argues that *Gangsta Rap* is about the demonizing of black youth designed and manipulated white racist producers.

In *Hoop* Dreams, we see the stereotype of a minority group choosing sports over education. The movie is about two inner-city Chicago youths who display a natural talent for basketball and who are encouraged to pursue the American Dream, which in this case, means aiming for a professional basketball contract. Both boys, who come from poor families, see basketball as their chance to make it out of the ghetto. In fact, they have other tickets available to them, such as education. However, they chose basketball. *Hoop Dreams* continues to reinforce the stereotypical image of minorities who are more interested in pursuing athletics rather than intellectual pathways.

Currently there is a lack of critical black presence in higher education. In her work with black youths, Hooks found that most of them were bright. However the street youths did not believe that they were entitled to a different form of life. Where did the negative messages come from? It comes from the producers of Hollywood. Minority youths watching Hollywood will get the wrong impression that athletics, not education, will empower them; the media shapes shape social reality. The more critical we are of negative racial stereotypes in the media, the more we will be able to challenge them instead of accepting them as truth.

Conclusion

The intention of this study is to examine the extent of communication between African American students and their White counterparts. It would be wrong to conclude that efforts of diversity initiatives have been of no avail. According to social psychologists, individuals tend to group around those who share similar features and interests: Birds of a feather flock together. *Being around other students resembles them is important to all students.* One tends to associate with individuals from one's racial/ethnic group. This concept extends to other groups as well, such as married students, graduate students, or fraternity students. Such self-selection can be preserving and important for one's self-esteem especially the need of belonging to a particular group.

In order to promote cultural communication, efforts must be made to help students find and link with others with *similar* interests. This should be helpful in improving the situation for students of color. Structured activities, which encourage interaction across racial/ethnic groups, can also help improve the situation for minority students. Finally, students should be taught skills in cultural communication in their daily interactions. It cannot be presumed that students have the capacity of such communication by just attending cultural activities.

References

Bullock, III, C. S. 1978. "Contact Theory and Racial Tolerance among High School Students." *School Review* 86, 2, 187-216.

Condran, J. G. 1979. "Changes in White Attitudes Toward Blacks: 1963-1977." *Public Opinion Quarterly*. 43, 4, 463-476.

Dickinson, G. B., Holifield, M. L., Holifield, G. and D. G. Creer. 2000. "The Elementary Magnet School Students' Interracial Interaction Choices." *The Journal of Educational Research*. 93, 6, 391-394.

Dovidio, J. F., Kawakami, K. and C. Johnson. 1997. "On the Nature of Prejudice: Automatic and Controlled Processes." *Journal of Experimental Social Psychology*. 33, 510-540.

Ellison, C. G. and D. A. Powers. 1994. "The Contact Hypothesis and Racial Attitudes among Black Americans." *Social-Science-Quarterly*. 75, 2, 385-400.

Goodman, J. L. and M. L. Streitwieser. 1983. "Explaining Racial Differences: A Study of City-to-Suburb Residential Mobility." *Urban-Affairs-Quarterly*. 18, 3, 301-325.

Heiss, P. and S. Owens. 1972. "Self-evaluations of Blacks and Whites." *American Journal of Sociology*. 78, 912:935.

Hwang, S. Fitzpatrick, K. M. and D. Helms. 1998. "Class Differences In Racial Attitudes: A Divided Black America?" *Sociological Perspectives*. 41, 2, 367-380.

Jackman, M. R. and M. Crane. 1986. "Some of My Best Friends Are Black…": Interracial Friendship and <u>Whites</u>' Racial Attitudes." *Public Opinion Quarterly*. 50, 4, 459-486.

Jacobson, C. K. 1983. "Black Support for Affirmative Action Programs." *Phylon*. 44, 4, 299-311.

Jones, C. 1990. "Sociological Research in Racial Theory, 1960-1998". *International Journal of Group Tensions.* 20, 1, 91-98.

Krivo, L. J. and R. L. Kaufman. 1999. "How Low Can It Go? Declining Black And White Segregation in a Multiethnic Context." *Demography.* 36, 1, 93-109.

Longshore, D. 1979. "Color Connotations and Racial Attitudes." *Journal of Black Studies.* 10, 2, 183-197.

Monteith, M. J. and V. C. Spicer. 2000. "Contents and Correlates of Whites' and Blacks' Racial Attitudes." *Journal of Experimental Social Psychology.* 36, 2, 125-54.

Muir, D. E. and L. W. Muir. 1988. "Social Distance Between Deep-South Middle-School "Whites" and "Blacks." *Sociology and Social Research.* 72, 3, 177-180.

Muir, D. E. 1989. "White" Attitudes toward "Blacks" at a Deep-South University Campus, 1963-1988." *Sociology and Social Research.* 73, 2, 84-89.

Rainwater, L. 1966. "Crucible of Identity: the Negro Lower-class Family." *Daedalus.* 95, 172-217.

Schaefer, R. T. 1986. "Racial Prejudice in Capitalist State: What Has Happened to The American Creed." *Phylon.* 47, 3, 192-198.

Sigelman, L. and S. Welch. 1993. "The Contact Hypothesis Revisited: Black-White Interaction and Positive Racial Attitudes." *Social Forces.* 71, 3, 781-795.

Sigelman, L., Bledsoe, T., Welch, S. and M. W. Combs. 1996. "Making Contact? Black-White Social Interaction in an Urban Setting." *American Journal of Sociology.* 101, 5, 1306-1332.

Silverman, I. and M. E Shaw. 1973. "Effects of Sudden Mass School Desegregation on Interracial Interaction and Attitudes in One Southern City." *Journal of Social Issues.* 29, 4, 133-142.

Tatum, B. D. 1997. *Why Are All the Black Kids Sitting Together in the Cafeteria?* HarperCollins.

Tierney, W. 1993. *Building Communities of Difference: Higher Education in the Twenty-First Century.* Westport, Conn.: Bergin & Garvey.

Turner, B. F. and C. B. Turner. 1974. "Evaluations of Women and Men Among Black and White College Students." *Sociological Quarterly.* 15, 3, 442-456.

Wilson, T. C. 1986. "The Asymmetry of Racial Distance Between Blacks and Whites". *Sociology and Social Research.* 70, 161-163.

III

Interaction

Article 13

Black Professor/White Students: The Unique Problems Minority Professors Face When Teaching Race/Ethnicity to Majority Group Students

George Yancey

For whatever reasons students sitting towards the front of my classes tend to do better than those who sit in the back. I discovered this correlation from my early experience teaching Introduction to Sociology courses. However, I did not really take note of this tendency until it was violated. That violation happened the first semester that I taught a Race/Ethnicity course. The class began with the normal amount of interaction between the students. Thus, I subconsciously assumed that my better students were the vocal ones sitting towards the front of the room. However, as I gave back the first test, I noticed that many of the A's and B's in the course were going to students who sat at the back of my class. These students tended to be white males who did not speak up in class. I might never have noticed these students except that their scores were violating the correlation of seating and grades that I had noticed in other classes. It was this contradiction that began my process of examining how effective I have been in teaching my white students issues of race and ethnicity.

Why were some of my better students sitting in the back of the class when they had not done so in the past? I have come to the conclusion that there were two factors that led to this anomaly. The first factor is that because I was teaching a Race and Ethnicity course, the students were constantly dealing with controversial subjects. That by itself is not a sufficient explanation since in other controversial courses my better students still sat closer to the professor. Yet with courses concerning race there were students who are less likely to want to participate in the controversies surrounding racial issues than other types of controversies. Some of them merely wanted to sit in class, get a good grade, and meet the requirement of the university. Judging by their scores on my first test, they were doing just that. Nevertheless, I feared that all those students were going to get from that class was a grade and without gaining any further insight into dealing with the problem of race, nor would they gain critical thinking skills from the course.

The second reason I believe that this anomaly exists is that I am African-American. As an African-American, and especially as a social scientist, it is very clear that there are certain stereotypes that some majority-group students have developed which they may use to nullify whatever I attempt to teach. Imagine what may happen when certain white students take a diversity course that they do not want to take. On their first day of class they discover that their professor is black. At this point the students may accept contemporary American mythology about the competence of black professors, believing that we are "affirmative action" hires, or the radical black myth about the professor who seeks to push a brand of Afrocentrism to the class. Some of them undoubtedly decide what they need to do to get a decent grade is to not "rock the boat" even if they dismiss any of my arguments as being "biased." Thus I have students who are solid academically and have much to add to the class discourse, but who choose to merely sit in the back of the class and "play it safe" with their African-American professor.

Am I biased? Of course I am biased because everyone is biased. Is it fair that students dismiss what I may have to say because of my bias? No, because if they are consistent then they must also dismiss what their parents, peers, clergy, co-workers etc. say because of their bias as well. But this unfairness does not eliminate the fact that some of them are going to dismiss my teaching as "biased" anyway. Therefore, rather than worry about whether it is fair or right that this process takes place, it is important to find ways to overcome the barriers that many of my majority group students have put up against the lessons I want to present.

These barriers are particularly problematic because I emphasize class interaction and discussion in my courses. Students who sit in the back of the class, keep quiet and make good grades are not a problem for a professor who merely desires to give a lecture during the entire class time. I do not wish to criticize those who utilize this as their main teaching style. In fact there are topics that I cover in my Race/Ethnicity classes when I focus more on lecturing than class interaction. Nevertheless, I have chosen to emphasize interaction throughout most of my course because I believe classroom discourse is the best method for allowing students to explore issues of race and ethnicity in multiracial America. Because of this commitment students who refuse to contribute to the class discussion operate as a roadblock to the educational goals for my courses.

To deal with this dilemma, I have altered the way I teach Race and Ethnicity with these realities in mind. I believe that the challenge for the African-American professor who teaches courses in race/ethnicity is how to help students to confront their own preconceived notions about racial issues and to become self-reflective about those issues.[1] If we take that challenge seriously then we may realize just how daunting a task it may be. What I will discuss is some of the insights that I have gained from taking on this challenge as well as some of the strategies that I have found to be useful. While I do not make a claim of having solved this problem, I do contend that there are some steps that can be taken that may enable minority professors to overcome at least some of the biases they face in the classroom.

Types of Students

To understand the problems that African-American instructors face, one has to comprehend the type of majority-group students in Race/Ethnicity classes. I have classified five different types of white students I have encountered in those classes. As I have taught those courses at several different academic settings, it has become clear to me that the percentage of these types easily varies from school to school and even among different classes in each school. Nevertheless, it is my belief that in every Race/Ethnicity class that has a reasonable number of white students I will find some of each of these different types of white students.

The first type of student is the "GPA" student. This student's interest in taking the class is limited only to what the class will do for his/her GPA. The student does not desire to learn more about other races or how to handle racial issues but only how to get an "A" in the course. As such the student is not normally interested in participating in class discussions or group projects unless the instructor can tie such participation to the student's grade. Naturally such a student can be found in other classes as well, and the frustrations that African-American instructors feel with such students is one that majority-group instructors may feel as well. Nevertheless, it is my experience that students are even more withdrawn about participating in the discussion in race/ethnicity courses than classes of other subject matter. This tendency may be related to the student's fear that the African-American instructor is more punitive than non-black professors, especially when dealing with issues of race. Thus for black instructors who desire to create an understanding for the racial issues that have a profound effect upon their lives, this student can be particularly confounding.

Closely related to the "GPA" student is what I call the "Prisoner" student. This student perceives the class as a necessary evil. Often the student is taking the class to meet a diversity requirement and as such has little interest in learning about racial issues. The student is hesitant to participate in classroom discussions. In this way the Prisoner student is similar to the GPA student. Nevertheless, unlike the GPA student the Prisoner student does not have as much interest in his/her grade. The dominant goal of the GPA student is a good grade. The primary goal of the prisoner is often to get out of the class with his/her previous belief systems intact. Thus, this student is even less likely to participate in classroom discussions since the threat of a bad grade may not provide enough incentive for this student to risk those previously held beliefs. The white students, I described earlier, who did not engage in the discourse of the course, are generally a combination of GPA and Prisoners students.

The third type of student is what I would call the "Rebel." Unlike the first two students, this majority-group member has no qualms about participating in class discussions. In fact, such participation may seem enjoyable to the student since this student is often determined to show how "politically correct" the class is. The social and political outlook of this student may be similar to that of a Prisoner; however, unlike the Prisoner this student is also determined to change the attitudes of others in the class and often is not afraid of challenging the professor. While I have no empirical evidence to support this, it is my suspicion that these students challenge African-American professors more openly than white professors who teach Race/Ethnicity because they perceive that black professors as more biased than white professors.[2] Furthermore, one can argue that he or she may see black professors as "affirmative action" hires, and thus not as qualified as white professors. This loss of legitimacy makes the job of minority teachers more difficult since they have to spend time earning respect automatically given to white instructors.

The fourth type of student is the "Progressive." These are students who previously have progressive racial beliefs. They may be taking the course to supplement their current knowledge of racial issues or to bolster their own progressive beliefs. The fifth type of student is the "Seeker." This student may not have a progressive orientation but he/she is relatively open-minded to learning more about racial issues. They may not accept the perspectives of the African-American instructor, but they are not automatically hostile to that teacher's position. Many African-American instructors tend to enjoy the presence of the latter two types of students in their class since these students tend to make the most useful contributions to classroom discussions.

Some minority professors are able to handle at least one of the first three types fairly well. I personally have enjoyed dealing with Rebel students in my class while I have generally struggled with the teaching of GPA and Prisoner students. Indeed it is the presence of all of the first three types of white students that give African-American professors so many problems. Most Race/Ethnicity classes have a significant number of white students and generally have all five of these types of students. It is important that black instructors find ways to teach their classes so that all five of these types of students can participate fully in the class.

Dynamics of Minority Teachers of Race and Ethnicity

There are two important dynamics that must be taken into account when minority professors teach race and ethnicity classes. The first dynamic is the tendency of majority group members to protect their own racial rights. Professors of color must find ways to overcome this barrier if they are going to intrinsically challenge white students. The second dynamic is the institutional power that minority professors have over majority group students. Institutional power creates a relationship of status inconsistency and must be taken into effect when minority professors address issues of race and ethnicity.

Several studies have indicated that European-Americans have tended to adopt a social and racial philosophy that protects their racial group interest (Bobo and Hutchings 1996; Bobo, Kluegel, and Smith 1997). This statement is not meant to disparage whites since members of all groups tend to protect the interest of their groups, but we would be naïve to not take into account this attempt at protection when we teach on race/ethnicity issues. This means that, to some degree, it is against the utilitarian interest of majority group students to understand the effects of institutional discrimination, white privilege, new forms of prejudice, or other important racial issues.[3] This cognitive resistance should be expected and anticipated by minority professors. While we will not be able to help all white students gain a full understanding of American racism, we must develop techniques that best enables us to overcome this resistance.

Racial minorities still have lower social status than majority group members do. Nevertheless, all professors hold power over their students in that they can make demands upon the students, which the students must adhere to if they want the desired goal – a class grade. This has created what Weber calls "status inconsistency" (Gerth and Mills 1946). When a minority professor teaches a class, he/she likely does not get the same respect given to majority-group professors. This deficit may be enlarged when minority professors teach race/ethnicity courses since white students may believe that the professor is plagued with racial bias. Yet the professor still has formal power over those students' grades. Thus, minority professors have the challenge to find a way to use their institutional power to overcome the status deficit created by their racial identity.

These two dynamics indicate that minority professors who teach race/ethnicity courses have special barriers to overcome. We must think about how we can fashion teaching strategies that overcome these barriers. My experience in dealing with these barriers is the focus of the next section.

Teaching Strategies

I am the first one to admit that I have not found all the answers to this problem. But I have found some strategies that have helped me to serve this variety of students. My thoughts upon how to engage majority group students in the study of race and ethnicity begins with a decision that instructors of such courses have to make. That decision is what do we believe white students should receive from our course. One legitimate perspective is that students should learn to support the interests of racial minorities. If we can show students how historical and structural racism continues to effect racial minorities then majority group students will be more supportive of measures that help racial minorities. I believe that while this is a laudable goal, it is not my goal. I want students to critically test their own assumptions about racial reality and to consider, even if they do not accept, alternate explanations for understanding racial issues. For example, if a white student comes into my course with a strong tendency to make individualistic attributions to the problems of the black community, it is not my goal that he or she stop making such attributions altogether. Rather, my more modest goal is that they stop automatically making these attributions and begin to ask deeper questions about the role of social structure and historical racism in the social dysfunctions suffered by African-Americans. If they then continue to hold on to individualism as the way they understand racial issues, I may be disappointed, but at least I encouraged them to think through the issues in ways that they have not thought about before.

This goal may seem limited, but I would argue that the GPA student, the Prisoners and the Rebel usually do not even think about challenging their own assumptions on racial issues unless they are strongly prompted to do so. Therefore, these students do not even accomplish the limited goal of considering alternate attributions or understandings of racial problems that differ from the ideology they possessed when they entered the class. Thus, even my more modest target is one which professors miss on a regular basis. (I believe that) if I can reach even this modest goal, and encourage more of my students to test some of their individualistic assumptions, then I am hopeful that many of them will become more sensitive to the concerns of racial minorities.

The first major principle that I use to meet my goals is based upon research by Sherif et. al. (1961). They have found that members of previous out-groups can learn to develop primary relationships if the principles of the contact hypothesis can be applied. Those principles are the development of intergroup relationships that are 1) fairly intimate, 2) based on cooperation instead of competition, 3) supported by relevant authority figures, and 4) equal in status.

The best way I have found to apply these principles is through small groups. Thus, early in the semester I divide the students into small interracial groups. I give these groups academic tasks so that they have to work together, and thus get to know each other. During the course of the semester I pose questions to the class. But rather than have individual members answer the questions I have the students go into their groups to discuss the answers to these questions. The purpose of these groups is twofold. First, in small groups individuals cannot hide from each other, as some do in the general classroom discussions. Therefore, the GPA and Prisoner student is forced to express him/herself to at least some members of the class. Ideally, this forces them to think more critically about their ideas about race since they will have to express those ideas and defend them to a group in which some of the students are minorities. Second, I allow the principle of the contact hypothesis go to work. Rather than see members of other races as strangers, the students are forced to interact with those strangers. I have found that begins to ease some of the stereotypes and preconceptions that have often developed among all of my students.

The second principle that is required to help me reach my goal is to conduct class discussions in such a way so that the majority group students feel free to express their opinions. This is no small task. Certain European-American students tend to either be silent when confronted with a minority professor or try to challenge the professor's authority. The way a professor handles students who challenge him/her, whether that student is a "seeker" or a "rebel," will set the tone for the rest of the class. To this end I announce the first day of class that there are no "taboo" opinions in my class and that everyone, including the professor, is expected to treat the other students with respect even, no especially, if one does not agree with that person's opinion. Students are free to disagree with the opinions of other students, but they must never be allowed to personally denigrate the worth of that person because of his/her opinion.

I have taught long enough to now be comfortable with my authority in the classroom. Therefore, it is not threatening when I hear someone quote Rush Limbaugh in their defense of color-blindness as the solution to racial inequalities. In fact, I can jump all over that student and point out many fallacies in him/her arguments. But if I readily do so then that student will never say another word that he/she thinks I will disagree with in my class again. I may turn a "seeker" student into a "prisoner" if I do not handle classroom discussion carefully. Worse still, I can also signal to the other majority group members that they had better not challenge me. What I hope to turn into an open discussion turns either into a monologue by me or a conversation between me and the "progressive" European-American students and minority students.

There is a fear we have that if we do not challenge uncomplex thinking about racial issues as soon as it happens, then we run a great risk of allowing students to leave our classroom misinformed. I used to believe that, but now I do not for three reasons. First, some students are going to leave my class with the wrong ideas about race. Not every majority-group member student wants to develop such an understanding, and there is no way to reach some of the students. The best we can do is reach the most students that we can. Second, we sometimes forget that there are other students in the classroom who will not agree with a Limbaughian view of the world. If I have created an atmosphere where students of all types of beliefs feel free to discuss, I find that there will be minimal need for you to allow a shallow interpretation of racial issues go unheeded. Other students can generally do an admirable job of pointing out cognitive fallacies. In some ways such correction can better come from their peers than from the "old guy" standing in front of the class.

The third, and I believe the most important, reason I do not feel I have to immediately respond is because there is nothing I can say in 30 seconds that cannot be stated better over the course of my class. If a class is organized to illustrate time and time again how historical discrimination deprives racial minorities of equal opportunities then there is less of a need to immediately confront a student. If one illustrates several ways contemporary racism still exists and is powerful then there is less of a need to challenge the notion of color-blindness. If the class gives the students multiple ways to understand the notion of racial constructiveness then ideas about biological and racial distinctions tend to collapse under their own weight. I am not comfortable in dealing with complex social issues through a "soundbite" technique. Such a method often produces an answer that is as shallow as the student's original statement. I construct a class where the concepts I believe are most important are taught many times over. I eliminate the urge to engage in that level of discourse.

Conclusion

I identified two basic problems that minority teachers of race/ethnic relations run into when they teach classes of predominately white students. Those problems are the defensiveness of majority groups students and the alienation created by the power of the minority professor. I am not arrogant enough to suggest that I have solved these problems, but I do contend that I developed pedagogical approaches that target those issues. By adopting these approaches I have noted a qualitative improvement in the classroom discussion of my classes. Allow me to express why I think the quality of interaction has improved.

Since I have started using small groups for discussion, I have noticed that some students who may be "Prisoner" and/or "GPA" students interact fairly freely within those small groups. As a result I have noted that some majority-group students who do not speak up early in the course tend to start speaking up later that semester. Although I have not tested this possibility, I believe that white students who learn how to discuss racial issues in relatively safe small groups then feel more confident about expressing their ideas to the entire class.

Another reason why students may feel more comfortable discussing racial issues is my attempt not have any "taboo" subjects and to respect all opinions. Often a critical time comes in the class when I am tested to see whether or not I welcome all opinions. This time may occur when a minority student personally insults a white student.[4] Or it may occur when a student engages in "victim-blaming" or falls upon stereotypes. On the former situations I believe that I must immediately clarify that we are not to insult each other although we can critique each other's ideas. In the latter situation I may throw a question or two at the student who is engaging in sloppy thinking, but I do not attempt to show the student up. I have found that most of the time such sloppy thinking occurs only at the beginning of the semester as I think that the student realize his/her errors during the course of the semester. The student may then be free to change his/her opinion without being embarrassed by the professor. In either situation I must allow the students to see that I am not going to penalize them for not accepting what I believe. In doing so I think that I can facilitate a rich conversation that will have more long-term positive effects than any short-term confrontation or correction of a student can bring.

Of course, this leaves me with the possible problems that the "rebel" students may bring. They may use the relative freedom in my class to distract the class from the issues that I wish to cover so that they can push their point of view. If my only restriction is that students are respectful of one another, what is to stop a student who is a white supremacist, or an adherent to some other nonsensical ideology, from pushing a brand of racism in my class? Before I explain how I deal with this dilemma, I first must state that one must be careful not to quickly label a student as a rebel when that student may truly be a seeker. Given the ideological background of some of my majority-group students, it is not unusual for some of them to unintentionally advocate racially insensitive ideas. In fact, I believe that one of the best ways to teach students about being sensitive to the perspectives of other races is through dialogue with their peers, not a professor from an older generation. This is what I hope to generate through open classroom dialogue.

Nevertheless, there are rebel students who come into our classes. I differentiate them from the seekers in that I see such students as entrenched in their ideology and not really wanting to learn from other students or the professor. Surprisingly, I have had very few problems with rebel students. The reason for this is that I believe that such students thrive in environments which individuals with institutional power are attempting to squelch their opinions. They correctly assert that they have the right to have their opinion heard. So, in my class they get that opportunity. But because my students know that they are allowed to critique the comments of other students, rebel students soon find that it is their peers, not the larger authority figure, they have to deal with. I contend that when they cannot make the claim that they are being robbed of their opportunity to speak, their mind that they often either find more productive ways to contribute to the conversation, or stay relatively silent during the remainder of the course.[5] Contrary to what one might predict, I found that openness in classroom discussions does not encourage rebel students; it tempers them.

These methods have helped me to create an atmosphere in my classroom that encourages, rather than discourages, discourse among the students. Of course, I still have my fair share of majority group students who still refuse to utter a word in classroom dialogue. But I have noticed a higher percentage of white students willing to speak out on racial issues and that not all of these students are those with progressive worldviews. Discussion is enriched discussions between radical minority students and relatively conservative majority group students. I count these sorts of discussions a victory since I believe that racial understanding cannot develop in American society until there is honest conversation between the members of different races.

I do not know if a classroom is the best place for such a conversation. The power of the professor and the demand of grades can often stifle this discussion. But there probably is not a perfect place to begin this conversation. However, it is my hope that my classroom can be one of the places that this conversation can begin. I tell my students in the beginning of the class that I want them to get more than a grade out of this class. One of the things I want them to gain is the opportunity to learn about members of other races, the opportunity to meet members of those other races and to understand more of the social reality those individuals have to live within. While there are lessons that minorities can learn from majority group members, clearly whites would do well to learn about the pain and frustration that many racial minorities have experienced. It is a long process for white students to learn of this racial alienation, and I look to my class as one place where this process can start. Of course, many white students escape my class with the same racial perspective they had prior to taking the class. They do not take the time and energy to challenge their racial preconceived notions. However, I believe that in promoting a classroom where there is more open dialogue I can maximize the number of majority-group students who will be open to new ideas about race/ethnicity and learn from students of color.

Given the changing multicultural nature of American society, Race and Ethnicity courses are becoming one of the most significant classes students take. This class is vital because all students, but particularly majority-group students, have to learn to operate in an atmosphere that is multiracial. As such, many universities now require students to meet a diversity requirement. I have taught in situations where the course meets a diversity requirement and in situations where it did not meet this requirement. Ironically, I tend to find a more cooperative majority-group students in those situations where the course does not meet a diversity requirement, due to the lack of incentive for prisoners or GPA students to take the course. Nevertheless, because of my commitment to preparing students to succeed in our multicultural society, it is important to advocate for diversity requirements that have substance and to shape our Race/Ethnicity courses in such a way that we can reach all various types of majority group students.

My goal is to create an atmosphere whereby students might challenge their preconceived notions of race and privilege. It is relatively easy to convince students to write the proper answer on an exam. It is a great deal harder to influence them to leave the class with a transformed perspective on racial issues. Unfortunately, I have yet to assert whether the dynamics I witness in my class are temporary or permanent. One of the areas that I have not yet investigated is how much of a long-term effect my class has had on my students. An extension to this work would be the development of a methodology to assess whether or not attendance in such a course produces stable changes in students' cognitive perceptions about race.

Notes

1. This is not to state that there are not challenges for majority group professors as well. They may have a more difficult time earning the trust of minority students than minority professors. However, the challenges are clearly different since white professors may be seen as less biased and more authoritative then a minority professor by white students.

2. Moore (1997) finds that the gender of the professor influences how accepting students are of feminist ideology. She found that male instructors faced less resistance than female professors. Likewise one should suspect that white professors face less resistance in discussing racial issues than minority professors.

3. One can make the argument, which I would agree with, that it is in the humanitarian interest of whites to recognize these concepts. I believe that it increases our humanity to recognize social ills and to work to combat those ills. In doing so one can find some measure of purpose and fulfillment. Nevertheless, we would be remiss to not recognize that when any group that has had power surrenders some of that power to previously disadvantaged individuals, this group generally pays economic/social costs. At least some of our white students understand this loss and are going to resist attempts to understand dynamics of race and ethnicity because of the moral demands such an understanding can bring.

4. To my knowledge I have yet to have a white student openly insult a minority student in a class discussion. White students have expressed opinions that minority students find insulting, but we should not confuse that with an overt attempt to insult. I believe that since I am an African-American professor, white students are less likely to insult a minority student than vice versa. Of course, my experience may be unique, and other minority professors in

different educational situations might have to deal with obnoxious majority group students more than I do.

5. Of course, my preference is that they are not completely silent but that they enter into honest discourse with the rest of the class. Nevertheless, if they are not willing to look at alternate ideas and have as a main goal disruption of the class then silence is not the worst thing to happen. But note that this silence is not because they do not have an opportunity to discuss issues but because they are not willing to defend their ideas from their peers. Thus such students have lost their legitimate claim against "political correctness" and helps me to overcome the idea that this class is biased against those who do not agree with the professor.

References

Bobo, L., and V. L. Hutchings. 1996. "Perceptions of Racial Group Competition: Extending Blumer's Theory of Group Position to a Multiracial Social Context." *American Sociological Review* 58:443-464.

Bobo, L., J. R. Kluegel, and R. A. Smith. 1997. "Laissez-Faire Racism: The Crystallization of a Kinder, Gentler, Antiblack Ideology." In *Racial Attitudes in the 1990s: Continuity and Change*, ed. S. A. Tuch and Jack K. Martin, 15-41. Westport, Co: Praeger.

Gerth, H. and C. W. Mills. 1946. *From Max Weber: Essays in Sociology.* New York: Oxford University Press.

Moore, M. 1997. "Student Resistance to Course Content: Reactions to the Gender of the Messenger." *Teaching Sociology* 25 (2):128-133.

Sherif, M., O. J. Harvey, J. White, W. Hood, and C. Sherif. 1961. *Intergroup Conflict and Cooperation: The Robber's Cave Experiment.* Norman: University of Oklahoma, Institute of Intergroup Relations.

Article 14

Interracial Dating and Marriage: Fact, Fantasy and the Problem of Survey Data

Charles A. Gallagher

The U.S. Census reports that interracial marriages increased by 800 percent between 1960 and 1990.[1] This rather spectacular percent increase in the number of interracial marriages is supported by any cursory or anecdotal look at American popular culture as presented by the media. Tiger Woods "Cablinasian" mixed racial ancestry was nothing less than a media obsession when he was initially establishing himself as the world's greatest golfer. Many daytime soap operas, like the *Young and the Restless* and *All My Children* have featured at least one interracial romance subplot. Prime time television drama and situation comedies like *Dawson's Creek*, *West Wing*, *ER*, and *Sex in the City* are sprinkled with interracial relationships and plot turns. The 1990s saw a number of successful mainstream movies address various aspects of interracial romance including *Jungle Fever, Mississippi Masala* and *Bullworth*. It is practically impossible when consuming MTV not to see a cast of handsome, twenty-something, interracial hip-hoppers dancing, flirting or v-jaying. Within the world the media constructs for us it would appear that marital assimilation, the last stage of assimilation as intially outlined by Milton Gordon, has arrived. Gordon predicted as cultural differences between groups diminished a large number of individuals from different ethnic and racial backgrounds would date, fall in love and marry across the color line.[2]

The above narrative describing a society where interracial marriages are both socially accepted and becoming more common place ignores, however, a more complicated story. In 1998 interracial marriages accounted for only about 4% of all marriages in the United States even though 83% of blacks and 67% of whites approved of such pairings.[3] What individuals support in survey questions or allege they would do in the hypothetical situation offered in a survey is often quite different from what people actually do. In his now classic example of how attitudes are a poor predictor of behavior LaPiere found that restaurant and hotel owners who expressed discriminatory intent by indicating they would not serve Chinese patrons did serve them when placed in face-to-face situations with Chinese customers.[4] Given the inconsistency between thought and action it is not surprising that indication of support or willingness to enter into an interracial relationship is not matched by the actual rates of interracial marriage. This chapter attemps to draw on a number of key cultural and sociological theories to explain the disjuncture between what individuals indicate they would do and the broader patterns of interracial dating and marriage we observe in society. It will examine who marries whom and how we can explain the differences in rates of interracial marriage between groups. Finally, if racial differences in mate selection exist within and between groups to what extent do these trends reflect racial stereotypes?

Race, Ethnicity and Marriage

Within the assimilationist perspective, marriage between different ethnic and racial groups is viewed as the final stage of assimilation. As the sons and daughters of these immigrant groups gradually blend into the cultural mainstream, assimilation theory predicts their acceptance into the dominant culture and the structural mobility which that acceptance insures for future generations. Now thirty years old, Milton Gordon's predictions about marital assimilation have proven surprisingly accurate for patterns of interethnic marriage among the non-Hispanic white population. Some clarifications are needed however regarding how the meaning and salience of ethnic and racial identity has changed over time and how these changes reflect current trends in interethnic and interracial marriage. The process of assimilation and convergence of cultural differences among whites several generations removed from the immigrant experience has altered dating and marriage patterns. Two-thirds of the white children born during the 1970s had parents of mixed ancestry compared to one-third of the whites born in 1920.[5] These hybrid ethnic families create for their children social situations which involve "more ethnic heterogeneity in their social networks and may possibly lead to a diminution or dilution of ethnic identity".[6] The "unmeltable ethnics" that Robert Novak described some time ago appear to have, at least in terms of interethnic marriages, melted smoothly into the "pot" through interethnic amalgamation.[7] It often comes as a surprise to whites born after 1980 that crossing the ethnic boundaries to date or marry had social consequences in recent American ethnic history. The dating and marriage of, for example, an Italian-American and an Irish-American forty years ago not only raised eyebrows in each community but often brought disappointment and even estrangement from family members.

Gordon's theory of marital assimilation does not however, describe rates of marriage between whites and non-whites. The 1992 census found about 2% of marriages in the US were interracial.[8] Comparatively, 66% of the white families with children born in the 1970's were "interethnic." In 1970, 7/10 of one percent (.007) of all couples in the United States were interracial families. One might argue that there has been almost a 300% increase between 1970 and 1990 in the number of interracial marriages; at that rate and holding other things equal, the percent of interracial marriages would matched the current percent of interethnic marriages somewhere around the year 2065, some seventy years from now.

White and black respondents' expressed desire to enter into or avoid close interethnic and interracial relationships presents us with the interracial dating and marriage paradox; Why is it so few individuals cross the color line for romance when in surveys they say they would? A non-random purposive sample was conducted of 335 white and 105 black college students at a large urban university in 1993. The survey illuminates these questions: is dating or marrying within ones' ethnic group markedly different from dating or marrying inside ones' racial group? If there are discrepancies between the two, how should they be interpreted? Finally, what do these differences suggest about the salience of ethnic groups versus racial groups? Tables 1 and 2 examine the dating and marriage preferences of white and black respondents. See appendix "A" for the exact wording of the questions used in the survey.

The white respondents who felt it was very important to date or marry someone from their own ethnic group was quite small, about 13% and 18% respectively. The middle category "yes but would/could" can be interpreted to mean that respondents may have a preference for someone with a similar ethnic background but if they were so moved by romance, would date or marry someone from a different background. Combining columns "B" and "C" from Table 1 results in over 87% of the respondents willing to date someone from a different ethnic group, with 83% ready to consider marrying outside their ethnic group.

Table 1. Interethnic and Interracial Dating and Marriage Preferences: White Responses

	(A) Yes, Very Important To Date/Marry Within My Group	(B) Yes, But Would Date Marry Outside My Group	(C) Not Important Either Way
1. Date Same Ethnic Group:	12.8	21.5	65.7
2. Marry Same Ethnic Group:	17.1	21.0	62.0
3. Date Same Racial Group:	31.0	25.4	43.6
4. Marry Same Racial Group:	39.8	20.1	40.1

n=335

These findings are consistent with assimilation theory as it applies to interethnic marriages; respondents appear quite willing to date and marry outside of their ethnic group. Their responses should be viewed as a larger, albeit projected trend; as I mentioned previously, the 33% mixed families in the 1920's eventually grew to 66% mixed families in the 1970's. In 1980 only 25% of married couples were from the same ethnic background.[9] If student responses are to be believed, when this group reaches the typical marrying age around the year 2000, about 85% will form ethnically mixed families. As the "ethnic heterogeneity" of family networks increases predictions about the "dilution of ethnic identity" will be realized. It may be that white identities will become so diluted and Americanized through the assimilation process that young white ethnics will be culturally indistinguishable from one another, if they are not that already.

The veracity of student responses is evidenced by the ever growing pool of potential mates that are from mixed backgrounds. The sheer ethnic mixing that has taken place in the last seventy-five years supports the assertion that single ethnic identities will become an anomaly for whites as a group. If the majority of respondents come from mixed ethnic backgrounds, then the dating and marriage pool will also contain an growing population of mixed or hybrid ethnics. It will be increasingly difficult to search out a "pure" white ethnic because their pool has steadily been decreasing while that of "mixed" ethnics has been increasing exponentially. As maintenance of single ancestry becomes increasingly difficult statistically, so the majority of whites, at least in this sample, put no particular weight on the ethnic background of a potential mate. Of course, it is possible for an individual to claim five ethnic backgrounds but identify with only one, but the literature as well as this survey suggest a watering down of ethnic salience takes place.

What is of particular note in Table 1 is the significant difference between the ethnic and racial questions on marriage. Almost 40% of the respondents replied that it was very important for them to marry someone from their own racial group. Comparatively, just over 17% answered that it was important for them to marry someone from their own ethnic group. Combining columns "B" and "C" as a measure of those that are do not care the race or the ethnicity of their potential mates, 83% of respondents would marry out of their ethnic group while just over 60% say they would marry out of their racial group. The findings among this mostly traditional age college sample is consistent with national polling data. Among whites between the 18 and 34 82.7% expressed approval of interracial marriages. Note that the question in the white college sample asked if *they would* marry someone from a different race. Given that 60.2% of whites replied that they would enter into an interracial marriage it is likely that those who would approve of such relationships would be significantly higher.

Combining columns "B" and "C" (from rows one and two) Table 2 suggest that a majority of black respondents would date (68.3%) or marry (57.7%) someone from a different ethnic background. Methodologically this questions creates a validity problem for both

Table 2. Interethnic and Interracial Dating and Marriage Preferences: Black Responses

	(A) Yes, Very Important To Date/Marry Within My Group	(B) Yes, But Would Date/Marry Outside My Group	(C) Not Important Either Way
1. Date Same Ethnic Group:	31.7	37.5	30.8
2. Marry Same Ethnic Group:	42.3	30.8	26.9
3. Date Same Racial Group	41.3	33.7	25.0
4. Marry Same Racial Group:	51.9	25.0	23.1

n=105

white and black respondents. Does this question ask, for instance, if someone who defines herself as African American would date or marry a man from Afro-Carribean from Jamaica or might it also mean the same African-American would be willing to date or marry a self-defined white Italian-American. The same understanding of ethnicity being synonymous one variation of racial identity could apply to white respondents as well. Typically within the social sciences racial groups are understood as being distinguishable on the basis of physical, ascribed characteristics. These traits are rooted in physical traits even though it is a social process that makes these arbitrary physical differences, such as skin color hair texture or eye shape important. Physical characteristics associated with racial categories are the cultural "givens" from which our everyday understanding of race is derived. Someone is "black" or "Asian," because social convention has so defined them. Members of racial groups internalize that definition, and are in turn viewed by others as being members of that racial group.[10] Ethnic groups are distinguished by sociocultural heritage or ethnic markers such as nationality, language, customs or religion but are subsumed under the larger, less mutable social category of race. For example the racial category "Asian" encompasses many Ethnicities: Korean, Filipino, Hmong, Japanese, etc., all of whom presumably share some physical race based similarities. Like race, ethnicity is socially constructed; unlike race, ethnic identity can change in response to various social pressures. Race and ethnicity are not mutually exclusive categories, nor is it difficult to find examples in which they seem to overlap or merge. The purpose of a definition which treats race and ethnicity as distinct and conceptually different facets of social identity is to suggest that individuals can construct, resurrect, ignore or abandon ethnicity, but race is generally fixed. As the saying goes, you can change your ethnicity, but you can't change your race.

An almost equal number of black respondents, slightly over 48% responded that they would date or marry someone from a different racial background. While this is somewhat lower than the whites' responses it is important to note the trend for both groups. As the questions implied more intimacy (from dating to marriage) and greater social implications (family response, the wedding, having children) the percent willing to enter into an interracial relationship and marriage decreased. The need for greater social distance appears to increase as relationships move from casual interactions to intimate relationships. However it is important to note that like the white respondents, the 48.1% of blacks who said they would marry across the color line (adding columns B and C in row number 4) stands in stark contrast to the fact that among even younger cohorts only 8.5% of black males and 3.7% of black females marry outside of their race.

Understanding the Cultural Contradictions of Race and Romance

There is a wide gulf between what respondents say and what they actually do. Respondents may think they are willing to be in white/nonwhite relationships, but find that willingness mediated by many seen and unseen social obstacles. One such obstacle is residential segregation and the resulting lack of exposure to other racial groups. If proximity and exposure to racially different groups is one possible condition for intermarriage, there is little doubt that white ethnics will increasingly be involved in relationships with other whites where it is not uncommon to find a mix of six or more Euro-ethnic ancestries.

The overwhelming majority of white respondents in the university survey described their neighborhoods as ethnically "mixed." However, and predictably, the ethnic makeup of neighborhoods stands in stark contrast to the racial makeup. Both black and white respondents described attending high schools that were primarily racially segregated. If proximity is a significant factor in mate selection, it also means that whites will be less likely to intermarry non-whites due to the high degree of racial segregation throughout the US. Almost 65% of white respondents describe living in neighborhoods that are at least 95% white. Another 24% live in neighborhoods they describe as 65% to 94% white. It is also likely that the 24% living in mixed neighborhoods live in the white section of a mixed area. Townships or even neighborhoods may have a sizable non-white population but these communities are usually quite segregated. Communities with whites and non-whites dispersed evenly from block to block and house to house are an anomaly. The metropolitan area in which this study was conducted has the dubious distinction of being ranked tenth among cities considered "hypersegregated", that is an isolated, clustered, unevenly distributed white and non-white populations.[11]

The respondents in this university study mirror larger housing trends in the United States. Census data from 1990 found that in nearly half of the counties in the United States blacks comprised less than half of 1% of the population. The suburbs are even more segregated with over 86% suburban whites living in of communities having a population of less than 1% black.[12] Racial segregation means there will be little sustained interpersonal contact with individuals from different racial backgrounds. The extent to which a racially segregated society and the resulting lack of prolonged social contact influences the likelihood of interracial dating or romance can not be overemphasized. You can not flirt, date or marry across the color line if residential and educational segregation restricts social interaction. Due to past and present patterns of discrimination in the housing market and whites' preference to live in neighborhoods that are overwhelmingly white maintains the centuries old caste like quality of US race relations and high rates of endogamy.

What makes racial residential segregation all the more suspect as a primary influence in on the low number of interracial marriages is the general liberalizing of attitudes towards interracial relationships and the percent of blacks and whites who claim close cross race friendships. A 1997 Gallup poll found that 75% of blacks had a "close" white friend and 59% of whites claimed to have a close black friend.[13] Both blacks and whites do not attach the same stigma to interracial marriages and interracial personal interaction appears to have increased. Given these two trends in the national survey data it is ponderous that we do not see more interracial marriages. Where a high number of interracial marriages occur does however tell us about the role of sharing interracial social space and the propensity to date and marry across the color line. Those individuals who serve in the military provide an important example of what happens when individuals are placed in an environment that promotes, at least in theory, a truly color blind institution. White men in the military are three times as likely to marry black women then white civilians and black men and white women seven times more likely to marry black men then women not in the military. As a total institution the military is able to de-emphasize race and promote a philosophy based egalitarianism and a camaraderie based on defending the flag.[14] The high rates of interracial marriage among the men and women in the armed services is perhaps another example of why the military is defined as the most integrated institutions in our nation.

Michael Lind points out the association between race, space and intermarriage by noting that "white men in California in 1990 were more than six times as likely as Midwestern white men to marry outside their race. Overall, interracial marriages are twice as common in California (1 in 10 new couples) as in the rest of the country (1 in 25)."[15] Whites in California now account for about 50% of the states' population. Given that Asians, Blacks and American Indians account for the other 50% it not surprising that California leads the nation in interracial marriages.

Media Mediating Marriage

The comparatively high percentage of respondents who declare themselves willing to enter an interracial relationship in the university survey may reflect an exaggerated response stemming from media exposure to non-whites. Black street culture (or more accurately the mass marketed aesthetics of black youth culture) has made significant inroads into the culture of white youths. A quick survey of fashion on campus or in the malls tells a story of many whites "dressing black." The largest consumers of rap and hip-hop music are white suburban teenagers. MTV (Music Television) once void of non-white entertainers now has a large share of videos featuring black performers. Snoop Doggy Dog, Dr. Dre and Lauryn Hill have wide appeal among young whites. BET (Black Entertainment Television) with an all black format that no doubt taps both black and white youth markets, is part of basic cable in this metropolitan area. As Robert Staples points out "Three of the five wealthiest entertainers in America are black, the biggest box-office starts and the highest-rated TV shows have, in the past, been black, and the largest sales of a record album are by a black performer."[16] Fox network has been dubbed by some young whites I've talked with as the "black" network. In a similar way professional sports has also produced media heroes that have crossed racial lines. Seventy-four percent of the NBA and 62% of the NFL are black.[17] Magic Johnson, Michael Jordan, Emmitt Smith, Barry Bonds, to name just a few, are black sports superstars who are idealized by both blacks and whites. If Nielsen ratings, Grammies and Billboard magazines' buying charts are to be believed, then blackness, at least for a segment of young whites, may be what is considered "cool". Of course, appropriation of black culture by whites is not new but what appears different at this particular moment is the sheer magnitude of this trend. Interracial couples dancing to black entertainers and the ersatz racial harmony young whites see repeatedly on TV, especially MTV, may make interracial dating, which has historically been off limits, not only desirable, but to some degree a measure of "hipness."

If this is indeed the case then the idealized, TV constructed image of "otherness" may create a generalized willingness on the part of white respondents to be involved in an interracial marriage but only with a very specific type of racial "other". Whites may not want to be romantically involved with Snoop Doggie Dog or Sister SoulJah but Chris Tucker, Halle Berry or any of the Cosby kids might do.

Viewing the media and popular culture as interracial matchmaker, is highly speculative, however, the extent that media images are able to construct both positive and negative stereotypes of racial groups can not be ignored. Over 71% of households in the East Coast City metropolitan area have cable service. It would be difficult to argue that the 23 hours of TV 18 to 24 year olds watch a week have <u>no</u> influence on how this group constructs its social reality. [18]

Being a Certain Color Still Matters

While young whites are in large part responsible for the bulk of rap and hip-hop music sales and white Americans routinely list Colin Powell or Bill Cosby on various lists of greatest or favorite Americans, whites' fascination with black America does not, however, result in the kind of dating patterns one might expect given the huge cultural exchange which takes place between these groups. If, as trend data suggests, attitudes towards interracial marriage have become more tolerant over past decades and if the implicit assumption of this openness is that we are moving towards a color-blind society it is logical to conclude the pairings of interracial marriages would be similar between racial groups. In other words, if race has declined in social significance for a sizable part of the population then one might expect that all groups would have roughly equal rates of interracial marriage. This is however, not the case. Whites (particularly men) and African Americans (particularly women) are less likely to engage in endogamy then Asian or Latinos. What is particularly striking is how these rates vary by gender. Reynolds Farley review of marriage data of couples between 25 and 34 found that more than half, 54.5% of native born Asian American women married men that were not Asian. Native Asian American women were almost as likely to marry a white man (45.1%) as they were to marry an Asian man (45.5%) where as 96.7% of white women married white men. As a general pattern Asians, Native Americans and Latinos marry out of their group at a higher rate than blacks or whites but again important gender qualifications must be made. Within this age cohort Black men are more likely (8.5%) to marry out of their group than are black women (3.7%).[19]

How do we explain the high rates of marriage between native born Asian American women and white men and tendency for black men, when they do marry out of their own race, to marry white wives? Why are the rates of interracial marriage among blacks, particularly black women so low relative to other groups? Military service, living on the west coast and increased levels of education are strongly associated with higher rates of interracial marriage but these variables do not explain why, for example, a native born Asian American female is more likely to marry an Asian or white man rather than a black man and Asian females and black males are a rare pairing.

The answer to this question may be, at least in part, a reflection on the extent to which racial stereotypes influence mate selection at various levels. Beauty may be in the eye of the beholder but a society dominated by Euro-Americans will unsurprisingly privilege a standard of beauty and cultural styles that is a mirror image of itself, even if that image is a media distortion. Sue Chow found in her interviews of Asian men and women that a sizable minority of respondents preferred whites as potential or current mates because of their preference for "European" traits including "tallness, round eyes, "buffness" for men and "more ample breasts" for women.[20] In addition to these physical attributes Euro-Americans possess positive personality traits that, as her respondents put it, other Asian males and females lacked. If whites in this study have personality traits that are highly valued it appears that much of white America views African Americans in a much more negative light. A 1991 National Opinion Research Center study found that 78% of whites believed blacks were more likely to prefer to live off welfare, 62% believed that blacks were less hardworking, 56% believed blacks were more violent and 53% believed that blacks were less intelligent.[21] Contrast this rather disheartening list of racial stereotypes towards blacks with another; the Asian "model minority." This equally stigmatizing label of Asians who are hardworking, good at math, family centered, natural entrepreneurs, and among Asian women, demur and exotic becomes a form of marriage capital as stereotypes seep into the dominant groups' collective consciousness.

How then do we make sense of the tendency for individuals to say they would marry outside of their racial group but typically do not? The answer may in part reflect how the dominant group views race relations. The color blind narrative of contemporary, post-civil rights race relations asserts the social, economic and political playing field has been leveled. Equal opportunity for all, regardless of race, has been achieved. A 1991 poll found that whites believe that blacks now had "equal or greater opportunity" than whites in education (83%), job opportunity (60%) and "opportunity for promotion to supervisory or managerial jobs" (71%).[22]

If one embraces a color blind view of society where it is believed that individuals who delay gratification, work hard, and follow the rules will succeed, irrespective of color it becomes a contradiction to suggest that color does matter within the context of a survey question. This point is underscored by the fact that there is absolutely no social cost, no stigma from friends or family, no stares from strangers in the street by indicating you might marry across the color line. On the contrary, given the various social pressures not to appear racist in a color blind society where equal opportunity is now presented as the norm, survey responses to interracial marriage questions may reflect a socially acceptable answer rather than a response that is an actual predictor of future behavior.

Acknowledgements

I would like to express my gratitude to those who have helped shape my views on the cultural and political meaning of interracial dating and marriage. Abby Ferber's work on white supremacy discourse and sexuality Heather Dalmage's on interracial relationships has be invaluable. Charlie Jaret, Ralph LaRossa and Alexia Chororos have been a constant source encouragement and sociological insight.

Notes

1. Michael Lind. The Beige and the Black. *New York Times Magazine*, September 6, 1998 p 28.

2. Milton Gordon, *Assimilation in American Life: The Role of Race, Religion and National Origin* (New York: Oxford University Press, 1964). See Abby L. Ferber, *White Man Falling: Race, Gender, and White Supremacy* (New York: Rowman and Littele Field, 1998) and Heather Dalmage , *Tripping the Color Line: Blackwhite Multiracial Families in a Racially Divided World* (NJ: Rutgers University Press, 2000).

3. Howard Schuman, Charlotte Steeth, Lawrence Bobo and Maria Krysan, *Racial Attitudes in the America: Trends and Interpretations* (Cambridge MA: Harvard University Press, 1997)

4. R. T. LaPiere, "Attitudes vs. Action", Social Forces 13:230-237.

5. Richard Alba, *Ethnic Identity: The Transformation of White Identity* (New Haven, CT: Yale University Press, 1994).

6. Stanley Lieberson and Mary Waters, *From Many Strands: Ethnic and Racial Groups in Contemporary America* (New York: Russell Sage Foundation 1988).

7. Michael Novak, *The Rise of the Unmeltable Ethnics: Politics and Culture in the Seventies*, (New York: Macmillan Co., 1973).

8. Statistical Abstracts of the U.S., 1993.

9. See Alba.

10. See Michael Omi and Howard Winant, *Racial Formation in the United States: From the 1960's to the 1980's*, 2d ed. (New York: Routledge, 1994), Michael Banton, *Racial and Ethnic Competition*, (Cambridge: Cambridge University Press) and Frederik Barth, *Ethnic Groups and Boundaries*, (Boston: Little, Brown Publishing).

11. Douglas S. Massey and Nancy A. Denton, *American Apartheid: Segregation and the Making of the Underclass* (Cambridge: Harvard University Press, 1993).

12. George Lipsitz, "The Possessive Investment in Whiteness: Racialized Social Democracy and the "White" Problem in American Studies," *American Quarterly*, Volume 47, September 1995, Number 3.

13. Cited in Orlando Paterson, *The Ordeal of Integration: Progress and Resentment in America's "Racial" Crisis* (Washington, D.C. : Civitas Press) p. 45.

14. Tim Heaton and Cardell K. Jacobson, "Intergroup Marriage: An Examination of Opportunity Structures," *Sociological Inquiry*, Vol. 70, No. 1, Winter 2000, 30-41.

15. Lind.

16. Robert Staples, "The Illusion of Racial Equality: The Black American Dilemma, " p. 229 in *Lure and Loathing: Essays on Race, Identity and the Ambivalence of Assimilation*, Gerald Early (ed.), New York: The Penguin Press, 1993). Michael Jackson's *Thriller* is the album Staples is referring to. Some might argue that Michael Jackson has moved from being black to being racially ambiguous.

17. Staples.

18. Statistical Abstract of the United States, 1993.

19. Reynolds Farley, "Racial Issues: Recent Trends in Residential Patterns and Intermarriage" in *Diversity and Its Discontents: Cultural Conflict and Common Ground in Contemporary Society*, Neil J. Smelser and Jeffrey C. Alexander (ed.) , Princeton: Princeton University Press, 1999).

20. Sue Crow, "The Significance of Race in the Private Sphere: Asian Americans and Spousal Preference," Sociological Inquiry, Vol 70, p. 2

21. New York Times, 1/10/91.

22. Jennifer Hochschild, *Facing Up to the American Dream* (Princeton, NJ: Princeton University Press 1995), p. 63.

Article 15

Do Undergraduate College Students Self-Segregate?

Bette J. Dickerson, Kianda Bell, Kathryn Lasso, and Tiffany Waits

Introduction

In an increasingly global society, there is general consensus that individuals must develop cross-cultural understanding and tolerance. Such understanding and tolerance is most easily cultivated through natural friendships and associations, rather than through other means. However, despite nearly fifty years of legislated school integration in the United States, even in settings with high levels of ethnic diversity, Buttny (1999 p. 247) reports "a climate of separateness, or a 'new segregation' on college campuses". Is this segregation self-imposed by students who, of their own free will, separate themselves by race or ethnicity? In this study we examine racial/ethnic integration among college students at the level of friendship formation, describe how self-segregation manifests itself, and identify possible underlying causes.

This study provides important information for those seeking to create and maintain race and ethnic diversity on campus. Because it was conducted at one of the most diverse campuses in the United States, it provides insight about the realities of race and ethnic relations and friendship formation in an environment that publicly embraces cross-cultural understanding. This study also provides recommendations to begin and guide the process of change. It sheds light on areas in need of future related research and, hopefully, will inspire you, the reader, to further examine this important issue.

Rationale for the Study

Are the effects of mandated and institutionalized integration of college campuses felt on an individual level? Does recruitment of diverse student bodies translate into a college experience characterized by diverse interactions and friendship circles? These have long been important questions in the United States and are best illustrated in the 1954 *Brown vs. Board of Education* case when the Supreme Court declared that separate is not equal, ushering in an age of conscious efforts to desegregate schools. Contemporarily, debates have moved beyond the quality of the formal classroom education into an examination of college as a microcosm of an increasingly pluralistic society. The college experience, therefore, has achieved a significant role in exposing individuals to cross-cultural experiences in an attempt to create mutual tolerance and understanding. Such exposure can be obtained formally in the classroom or informally through friendships. In this study, we observed patterns of friendship formation on a racially and ethnically diverse college campus in order to examine whether undergraduate students self-segregate based on race/ethnicity when forming friendships. There are clear benefits to the support that comes from associations based on common culture, beliefs, and identity, but do the benefits of these associations tend to direct students towards forming friendships overwhelmingly within their own racial/ethnic in-group?

Literature Review

College is often the first time that most young people have been away from their families and familiar surroundings for an extended period of time. Friendships become an important way for students to "anchor" themselves in their new environment, serving as an affirmation of identity as well as providing a framework in which students can "'make sense' of their own behavior and the behavior of others" (Ting-Toomey 1981 p. 384). During this important new stage of maturation, friendships also help young adults work through issues such as the need for independence, developing social skills, and conflict resolution (Marcus 1996). Naturally, college students seek to form friendships with others based upon perceived commonalties which facilitates the development of a sense of intimacy. Among all characteristics differentiating individuals, ethnicity, the "cultural characteristic of the self" may be the most important contributor, at least to initial friendship pairings (Ting-Toomey 1981).

Yet identity consists of a hierarchy giving order to various components of self in relationship to group. For example, gender or language (related to ethnicity) may be the salient factors that prescribe where we fit into some group situations, while race (equated with ethnicity) may be more important in other situations (Jackson 1998). Furthermore, Doane (1997 p. 375) found that the "ethnic identity of dominant groups ... assume[s] ... a position of dominance shape[ing] the nature of group ethnicity" within a social system composed of several ethnic subgroups. He defines a dominant group "as the ethnic group in a society that exercises power to create and maintain a pattern of economic, political and institutional advantage, which, in turn, results in the unequal (disproportionately beneficial to the dominant group) distribution of resources" (Doane 1997 p. 376).

Adler (1996) distinguishes between two complementary elements in the hierarchy of identity, which she calls *status*, prescribing popularity or relative dominance over others, and *relationship,* characterized by trust and freedom from loneliness. She states "Together, these two elements combine to stratify groups and their members along the identity hierarchy" (Adler 1996 p. 137). This hierarchical layering emerges through a process of "competing discourses" between individual self perception, perceptions of one's core subgroup, and perception of the larger social system outside of one's own subgroup, prescribing both status and relationship between and within groups and between individuals (Buttny 1999). Cohesion within the social system, then reflects both inter- and intra-group stratification, as social rules, especially as developed by more dominant individuals or subgroups, reflect acceptable attitudes towards individuals and subgroups belonging to the social system. Alternatively, less dominant individuals or subgroups, may resist the role prescribed to them by more dominant members and form "counstergroups" (Yeh and Huang 1996).

Intergroup relations theory (Buttny 1999 pp.249-250) suggests that, across groups, "the greater the perceived dissimilarity, the greater the subjective intergroup distance....Perceived difference may result in increased levels of uncertainty and anxiety, which leads individuals to avoid contact with out-group members." Communication between groups becomes vital for inter-group understanding and for decreasing uncertainty and anxiety.

With regard to friendship formation between individuals, several studies confirm that, as with inter-group relations, the most salient factors in strengthening friendships relate to frequency and quality of communication (Buttny 1999). Bliesszner and Adams (1992 p. 64) state that "As people get to know each other better, they discover and respond to each other's unique personality characteristics; stereotypes become less influential in the relationship." The more we communicate with our friends, the more we understand and trust them, and the greater intimacy we feel with them. As frequency and quality of communication between persons increase, the level of trust between those persons increases, and the feelings of uncertainty decrease while similarities between persons emerge (Ting-Toomey 1981). In an environment of low levels of inter-group familiarity and understanding and low levels of friendship pairings across ethnic divides, one would expect higher levels of stratification by ethnicity, with high risks associated with and more rigid barriers to crossing those divides.

Buttny (1999 pp.249-250) contrasts two different views about segregation versus integration. The *social support model* suggests that students segregate themselves in search of "the support of their own cultural groups and organizations to succeed in higher education." Intergroup integration can cause a loss of social identity, which can be more important for minority groups than dominant groups. On the other hand, the *integrational model* posits that if children of different backgrounds could get to know each other, they wouldn't develop racial/ethnic prejudices and stereotypes. His research also distinguishes between three distinct attitudes that can lead to self-segregation: *nonassertive segregation, assertive segregation,* and *aggressive segregation.*

Nonassertive segregation occurs when students are interested in having more interracial contact but don't know how to achieve it. Chavous' (2000) research suggests that pre-college backgrounds may contribute to a student's ability to manage his/her surroundings on campus, especially when coming from an ethnically homogenous neighborhood. This type of segregation could be related to uncertainty and inexperience with inter-racial groups. In addition, it is important to note that in an environment where one subgroup (such as Whites) is numerically dominant, that subgroup can more easily avoid contact with minority subgroups, while minority subgroups must make conscious decisions to avoid contact with the dominant group.

Assertive segregation occurs when students consciously seek out others with whom they have common ethnic traits. Assertive segregation is related to feelings of pride of one's own heritage as well as an expression of individuality. This may be especially important for minorities surrounded by cultural expressions reflecting the social identity of a dominant group.

Aggressive segregation is related to conscious racial separation, based upon a rejection of "other." Principal reasons for rejection stem from feelings of threats. Chavous (2000 p. 80) found "In entering mainstream college settings, ethnic minority students often face unique challenges regarding the meaning or value of their ethnic identity, which may represent threats to their identities." These feelings of threats may come from inter-group tension, where one group feels threatened by another, or intra-group pressure, where the culture of one's own group expresses rejection of other groups. "This construct taps into individuals' beliefs that they cannot express their cultural values in school settings, that their ethnic culture was incompatible with their college environment, causing them to engage in self-protective strategies in order to enhance self-esteem" (Chavous 2000 p. 80). While we often think of ethnic minorities engaging in aggressive self-segregation, Buttny (1999 pp.249-250) notes that "Whites often tell racial narratives structured around a complication that is not resolved by the end of the story, suggesting continuing problems with minorities. ... These can be characterized as an ideological dilemma, with Whites being critical of minorities on one hand, but not wanting to appear prejudiced on the other." Chavous (2000 p. 83) argues that "ethnic-related organization[s] may serve as a protective or supportive factor," while "students who identif[y] less strongly [with their ethnic backgrounds are] more likely to experience feelings of threat and have lower levels of collective self-esteem."

Ethnic segregation may occur for several reasons, including uncertainty about how to cross racial divides, accompanied by inexperience. It may result from a strong sense of "acceptance" and celebration of one's own ethnicity; or from a sense of perceived threat from others, and a need for self-protection. What becomes important, then, is to discover not only the relationship between individuals, but to understand the dynamics of group relations within the social system in which those individual relationships occur.

Related to this is the *contact hypothesis*, a popular view which assumes that people of diverse race/ethnic backgrounds living in close residential proximity will "get to know, understand, and like one another, leading to long-standing cross-cultural understanding" (Bochner, Hutnik, and Furnham 1984 p. 690). This hypothesis was tested by Bochner, Hutnik, and Furnham (1984) by looking at the friendship patterns of overseas and host students in an Oxford, England, student international house. Their findings indicated that while these students had a great deal of contact with one another because they shared a dorm, most of the English students' friends were also English, and most of the foreign students' friends were other foreign students, although not necessarily from their same home country. It seems that the factor of being a "foreigner" in another country served as a commonality that brought foreign students together, perhaps because of the shared experience of being the "other."

The amount of racial homogeneity and heterogeneity also affects the salience of ethnic roles. This was examined by Bochner and Ohsako (1977) who were interested in examining the factors that contributed to a heightened awareness of another person's ethnicity. Although their study examined three societies (Japan, Australia, and Hawaii), the findings are useful as a theoretical model and can be applied to other situations, including a university campus. The authors found that in segregated societies, "the perception of another's racial role will have a direct and exaggerated effect on interpersonal behavior; whereas, in integrated societies, the effect will be more indirect and muted" (Bochner and Ohsako 1977 p. 490).

Research Methodology

This study explores whether undergraduate students segregate themselves based on race/ethnicity in the process of friendship formation. Ting-Toomey (1981 p. 391) suggests forming friendships within ethnic groups is easier "because of congruent cultural beliefs and values, [creating] a stronger degree of intimacy for each other than friends belonging to different ethnic groups." Blieszner and Adams (1992) found that when people first meet, they naturally differentiate others based on physical traits, which can lead to stereotyping – and possibly to self-segregation in friendship formation. To the extent that self-segregation exists, we describe how it manifests itself and suggest preliminary ideas about why it may occur.

We hypothesized that undergraduate students would tend to segregate by racial/ethnic similarities when forming friendships. Hypothesized reasons for self-segregation included the following: resisting opportunities to form friendships across ethnic divides because of a need to maintain a level of comfort; self-segregation as means to maintain peer support networks; resisting forming friendships across ethnic lines because of negative perceptions of racial out-groups. We also considered the possibility that self-segregation could be indirectly and unintentionally encouraged by university institutions.

In this study the unit of analysis is the individual within the population of undergraduate students at a major university. Information was collected with regard to differentiation by ethnicity/race, gender, language, and age. Three methods of qualitative data collection (observation, interviewing key informants, and administration of a survey questionnaire) were used.

Before discussing the sample selection and the methodology used to conduct the study, it is important to point out a central assumption. In order to determine if students were self-segregating themselves by race/ethnicity when forming voluntary friendships, we had to assume that the students that we saw together during the observations were indeed friends. A subjective determination was made that if the students were not studying together, which might indicate "forced" association arising from classroom assignments, then they were with a group of voluntarily chosen "friends."

Definitions of Key Concepts

Although the concept of *race* is associated with physical traits and *ethnicity* with cultural traits (Doane, 1997; Yeh and Huang, 1996), in this study, the two concepts are recognized as social constructs, with essentially the same meaning (Buttny, 1999; Doane, 1997; Ting-Toomey 1981; Yeh and Huang, 1996). *Ethnic identification* is a "feeling of membership with others ... based on a sense of commonality of origin, beliefs, values, customs, or practices of a specific group of people" (Yeh and Huang 1996 p. 645). *Friendship* is based "in part on perceived similarity of personality, values, attitudes, beliefs, needs, or, social skills between partners" (Blieszner and Adams 1992 p. 65). In fact, "[p]ersons belonging to similar ethnic backgrounds because of congruent cultural beliefs and values, possess a stronger degree of intimacy for each other than friends belonging to different ethnic groups" (Ting-Toomey 1981 p. 391). Lastly, *self-segregation* is defined as arising from the intent of the individual to preserve race/ethnic separateness in the process of forming friendships.

Sample selection

As mentioned earlier, the target population for our study is university undergraduate students. This group was chosen for several reasons. First, it was a group whose higher education socialization process was more likely to be grounded in on-campus experiences. Contrary to many graduate and professional degree students (who are typically non-traditional students), undergraduates are likely to spend more time at the university (most live on campus) and, therefore, their on-campus relationships are likely to be a formative part of their socialization. Second, since our study is qualitative and exploratory, a more homogeneous population increases the ability to generalize our results. Lastly, the study sample varied because three data collection methods were used (i.e., observations, key informants, and surveys). This triangular approach strengthens the total research project because each method contributes information essential to understanding the topic.

In a sense, this is an exploratory study, due to the lack of previous research on the topic of self-segregation by race/ethnicity on college campuses. There is enough literature, however, on the various aspects of this study (e.g., race/ethnic relations in the United States, friendships and friendship formation, particularly its importance at college) to guide the study in such a way as to provide useful analytical data as an end result.

Study Location

The study was conducted on the campus of a university, that will be referred to as Mid-Atlantic University (MAU), located in a highly diverse city. MAU prides itself on its diverse student population and was praised by a representative of President Clinton's Initiative on Race for its programmatic efforts to increase and improve linkages among the many diverse groups on campus. In a recent communication to students, MAU president cited the University's Strategic Plan as identifying "the quality, diversity, and inclusiveness of the university community as a priority." With regard to diversity, the strategic plan commits the university to recruiting, hiring and retaining diverse faculty and staff members as well as the recruitment, acceptance, and retention of students from all demographic groups, with consideration of race, gender, ethnicity, nationality, disability, and sexual orientation. In this respect, MAU provides rich insight into whether a public institutional commitment to diversity yields private diversity on the level of friendship formation among the students.

Study Methodology

As an exploratory and qualitative study, the following three methods (i.e., observations, key informant interviews, survey questionnaires) were chosen because they would yield descriptive, cross-sectional data.

Observations

The first method of data collection was through observations taken at one point in time, from 7:00 p.m. to 8:00 p.m. on a weeknight, and at one field site, the student center building (SCB) on the campus of MAU. The SCB was chosen because of the high number of undergraduate students who frequent the building. It houses the main dining area downstairs, a small food court upstairs, and a lounge area upstairs. The time of observation was chosen because that was when dinner was served, and students could be observed eating together and engaging in other social activities. All students who were sitting at tables or couches were observed.

The observational methods design used in this study is based on that of a previous study conducted in a school cafeteria (See Greene and Mellow 1998). Students were coded as being segregated if all the people directly next to, across from, and diagonal from one another appeared to be of the same race/ethnicity. Conversely, if just one person appeared to be of a different race/ethnicity than the other members of the group, all those sitting together were coded as integrated.

Other variables of importance were also coded, such as demographics (gender and age) and variables that may have caused the formation of the group, such as the activity the group (studying or other) and language spoken. These variables were coded because it was hypothesized that some students might be grouped together because of a class assignment. These groups were not included because they were not considered to be voluntary friendship groups but, rather, that they were in a sense "forced" together. Language was also coded because language is a key aspect of ethnicity.

Key Informant Interviews

Three interviews with key informants were conducted. Informant 1, an Asian American female, was MAU's Assistant Registrar and also chaired MAU's Diversity Committee, charged with monitoring progress on issues related to diversity, in accordance with the university's strategic plan. Notably, this diversity committee reported directly to the MAU President. Informant 2, an African American female, was the chair of a social science department, immediate past Chair of MAU's Diversity Committee, and a recognized advocate for diversity. Informant 3, a European American female, had been MAU's Ethnic Clubs Advisor. Each of the informants had expertise in issues involving race and ethnicity. They also had direct experience in counseling students, expert knowledge about cultural diversity at the university level, and extensive and intensive direct contact with undergraduate students.

One standardized interview guide was established. This uniform approach minimized interviewer bias and facilitated the analysis of the responses. Each of the three interviews lasted 30 minutes and consisted of 17 open-ended questions and 6 demographic questions. The interview guides followed the general rules for sequencing, beginning with non-controversial topics and descriptive dialogue and then moving into more sensitive topics surrounding race/ethnic interactions at MAU. Our objectives were to learn about the respondents' role(s) on-campus, determine whether they thought self-segregation occurred at the university and, if so, find out what they perceived the causes and effects to be.

The respondents were given a full statement of disclosure that informed them that the interview focused on themes of race/ethnicity and student interactions that might be construed as being controversial in nature. They were also informed that their participation in the interview was voluntary, that they could choose to discontinue at any time, and that their responses would be kept confidential. Detailed notes were taken during all three interviews and were later coded into themes related to the research question(s).

Survey Questionnaires

A one-page self-administered survey questionnaire was developed. The survey was pre-tested on a pool of five students. The pre-testing was designed to catch errors, unclear questions, and to judge the overall flow of the interview.

Fifty surveys of undergraduates were selected for analysis, using proportional stratified sampling to approximate the racial/ethnic profile of MAU's undergraduate student population. MAU reported a total undergraduate student population of 5,161 students for the Fall 1999 semester. The race/ethnic breakdown of students for that semester was 57% White, 17% International, 5% Black, 4% Hispanic, 3% Asian/Pacific Islander, 13.7% Unknown, and .3% American Indian.

Students in and around the SCB on a Saturday afternoon, and in the library and the international dorm on a Sunday afternoon, were asked to fill out the one-page, self-administered questionnaire. The respondents were largely chosen by convenience. However, in order to achieve the total numbers needed to match the percentages of the university, some of the respondents were also purposefully chosen by the appearance of their race/ethnicity and then the respondents' self-identification of race/ethnicity was used to match the university percentages. All respondents were told that their participation was voluntary and their identities would be kept confidential. A total of 60 surveys were collected in order to achieve the desired sample of 50 respondents that represented MAU's undergraduate student body proportionally.

Limitations of the study

As mentioned, the research design for this study included triangulation, or the use of the three types of research methods, to ensure validity and reliability. In addition, the study was grounded in the body of previous research on similar themes in order to build upon the work of others. However, limitations do exist.

The first limitation surrounds the approach to measuring integration. Attempting to accurately identify a student's race by visual appearance is prone to error, if not impossible. Race and ethnicity are not visibly observable because they are social constructions. Our observations students categorized as White, Black, Asian… could have actually been observation of students from many different ethnic and cultural backgrounds all of which greatly influence social interaction. Greene and Mellow (1998) faced similar problems in their observations of elementary school lunchrooms.

Their method involved matching the observed characteristics of the student to the official self-reported information on race in the schools records. Because the proportions matched, they postulated that their observations were somewhat accurate. We attempted to replicate this logic. Our sample, however, did not consist of the entire school population, as did Greene's. Rather, a sample was used of only 115 students present in the SCB dining hall at that particular time. Further, race/ethnic minorities were not over sampled, and a very small number of specific race groups were represented in the survey results. Though the proportion of the races observed did match the proportions given by the schools statistics, the level of external validity arrived at by this method is limited and caution should be exercised in generalizing the results to a larger population.

In addition, it is important to keep in mind that race/ethnicity is only one construct that can divide students; other important sources of differentiation include economic status, gender, and sexual orientation, for example. The survey data instructively reminds us that student identity is, indeed, hierarchical, with a myriad of considerations and components. Any future attempts to address self-segregation by race/ethnicity must include an awareness of how that may be affected by intersections with other aspects of identity.

Though the principal limitations of this study relate to the data collection processes, the primary goal of this study was to provide exploratory data that would inform the design of a more in-depth follow-up study. Toward that end, this study offers preliminary ideas about whether and why segregation occurs among undergraduates. To increase the levels of validity and reliability, future studies of these preliminary findings could consist of a series of observations over a longer period of time, a stratified simple random sample based on a complete list of a university's undergraduates, and focus group conversations about the motivations behind the observed patterns.

Findings

Description of Observations

The findings of the observations are discussed by the variables observed.

Self-segregation of students

The overall findings of the observations showed that of the 209 students observed, 135 (64.6%) of these met the definition of being segregated, 40 (19.1%) were considered to be integrated, and 34 were not classified (16.3%) (Graph 1).

Graph 1. Percent of segregated and integrated students during observation period at SCB.

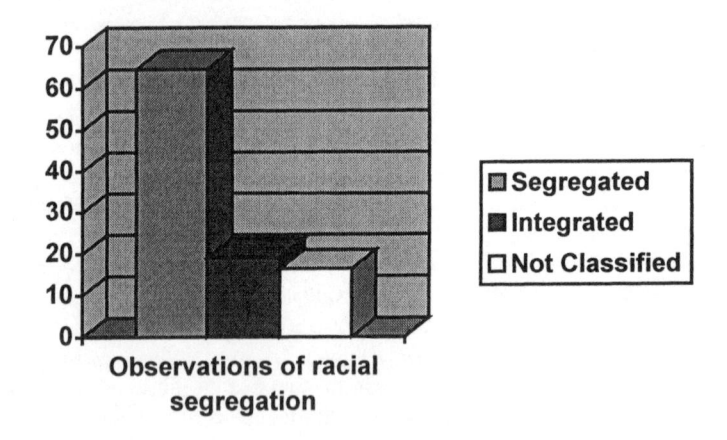

Activity

The observations can be divided into 2 groups: (1) those conducted in the dining hall, where the activity of all the students was "eating," and (2) those conducted upstairs where the activities varied. As noted in the methodology section of this paper, the activity of the students is important in determining whether students are coming together voluntarily, or if they are in a sense forced together by a class assignment. Because all of the students in the dining hall were eating, the activity of the students was noted only in the upstairs area. The following activities were taking place upstairs; out of a total of 45 students observed at 18 tables and couches (people sitting alone were not counted), students at 7 tables were studying, and students at 11 tables were doing some "other activity." Since our assumption is that study groups are not formed voluntarily, rather, professors mandate them, this means that students at 11 of the 18 tables were not voluntary social arrangements, and were therefore excluded from the analysis. Of these 11 tables that were not studying, 2 of these were integrated and 9 were segregated.

Race

Overall, the racial breakdown of the students observed in SCB was as follows: 156 White/Caucasian students, 31 Black/African American students, 13 Asians, and 9 others, for a total of 209 students. The percent of each group observed in this observation is higher than the total percent of each group total at the university.

Gender

The variable "gender" was also coded and the overall breakdown, of the 209 students observed, was 105 males and 104 females.

Age

Age was coded as either above or below 30 years old. Because these are observations, it is likely that some error on the part of researchers guessing age occurred. However, because the researchers in the dining hall did not observe anyone who appeared to be near 30 years of age, it is unlikely that error exists here, and if so, it is very minor and does not affect the results of the observation. The total age breakdown of those observed was 3 persons who appeared to be over 30 years and 206 students who appeared to be under 30 years of age.

Language

The variable language was also observed. Segregation by language was not observed in the downstairs dining hall; however, upstairs, each table or couch was given a language code of either "English" or "Other language." The results for upstairs only with regards to language were of the 18 total couches and tables observed 14 had groups that were speaking in English, 3 groups were coded as "Other language," and one group was coded as "don't know" because the members of the group were not speaking.

Key Informant Interviews

After coding the interviews with the three key informants, several patterns emerged. The topics can be grouped and discussed in the following manner: (1) university environment, (2) friendship formation, (3) self-segregation, (4) university encouragement/discouragement of self-segregation, (5) self-segregation and the quality of the university experience, and (6) responsibility for promoting desegregation.

University Environment

All three informants agreed that MAU is ethnically diverse and is located in an ethnically diverse city. Calling it a "global university," Informant 2 pointed out that university students represent 150 countries and all 50 of the United States. Informant 1 asserted the proximity of diversity automatically exposed university students to much more diversity than would be found in a small town in the Midwest, for example. At the same time, Informant 2 lamented that the ethnic composition of the university did not reflect the city's diversity: "the tragedy of the ethnic composition at [the university] is compounded by sitting in [this city] and having so few African Americans at [this university]." Informant 2 also emphasized that the university's diversity is "selective", meaning that the predominant racial composition of students is white American, with virtually no Native Americans and relatively few Asian or Latino/a Americans on campus. Informant 3 suggested that the level of diversity found at the university can be directly linked to an aggressive campaign to recruit international students, while its American students are virtually all whites. In addition, Informant 3 suggested that the students do not reflect economic diversity that most of the undergraduate students, including the "ethnic kids," come from privileged backgrounds, which Informant 2 called the "economic class factor."

Friendship Formation

The key informants were asked to talk about the primary factors in friendship formation on campus. All three informants agreed that friendships are formed based on commonalties between students, creating a sense of comfort, familiarity, and mutual support. Key Informant 1 felt that economics, language, race, and ethnicity were all things that led to students' friendship formations with one another. These commonalities create a feeling of "comfort," a term that was used by each key informant and was also an important finding in the survey data analysis. The second key informant mentioned that language and culture are two critical factors in friendship formation. Culture also can mean shared values and religion, and a sharing of the same experience. The third key informant noted that friendship formation is based on where the students live. She noted that the dorms are highly segregated (for example, international dorm versus Greek fraternities and sororities). She added that students tend to think in terms of race, not ethnicity, and that race is a factor. She also mentioned that students become friends with people in the same academic program because they share classes together.

Next, the key informants discussed what they noticed about students forming friendships with other students from a different race or ethnic background as themselves. The first key informant noticed those students of different races or ethnic backgrounds were usually seen studying together. This indicates that separation begins in the classroom, but she also noted that it doesn't seem to continue outside the walls of the classroom. The second key informant said it is very important that students are forced to intermingle in the classrooms and the dorms. She mentioned that having class assignments designed to force students to do group work is important. Informant 3 said that separation is a problem and is very difficult.

Self- Segregation

The second topic surrounds the voluntary self-segregation of students at the university. All three informants agreed that undergraduate students self-segregate, citing the support that students receive from others similar to themselves as the primary reason. Informant 3 believes that international students are especially prone to stay within their own ethnic groups because most will be returning back to their country after earning their degree here. She also noted that white Americans self-segregate because they have never been exposed to students from diverse backgrounds, while ethnic Americans may self-segregate because they are "just tired of being teachers," educating others about their culture and beliefs.

The key informants were asked if students appeared to self-segregate themselves by race or ethnicity. All three informants agreed that self-segregation occurs at the university. Informant 1 said that the bonding element is the economic class factor. She went on to say that self-segregation is not necessarily a bad thing. For instance, Latin Cultural Awareness week or Black History Month is not based on discrimination or exclusion. Outsiders can participate. She noted that "self-segregation is necessary for people who have had their cultures and history obliterated." Informant 2 also believed students self-segregate by race and ethnicity. Like informant 1, she does not see this as a negative, as long as they are forced to integrate in other situations. She felt that self-segregation is extremely important because it provides students with a source of support and shared experiences. Informant 3 differentiated between "unconscious" and "conscious" self-segregation. She believes that students engage in unconscious self-segregation because it provides an "ethnic comfort zone," and it is easy to go with what is familiar. She also noted that there is also some intentional self-segregation occurring and cited the student government as an example. However, it is important to note that all three informants expressed concerns about self-segregation. They felt that spending too much time in one's "ethnic comfort zone" was not desirable because it limited opportunities to be exposed to other cultures.

The informants were asked why students engage in self-segregation. Informant 1 believes that it is "due to similarity, the ability to talk uncoded, and relax after a long day of being 'the other.'" Informant 2 mentioned commonalties such as economics and regional similarities and Informant 3 said, " ethnic comfort zone."

University Encouragement and Discouragement of Self-Segregation

The next topic examines the structural level and how it affects self-segregation on campus. The key informants were divided on this issue. Informant 1 said that the university did not overtly encourage self-segregation of students, but because it is a microcosm of society, and self-segregation occurs in society, it naturally will occur there. She noted that incidents can occur that encourage self-segregation, but that the focus of MAU is on diversity. Informant 2 also said that the university focuses on diversity and wants to be known for that, so they would have no reason to segregate students. She felt that self-segregation was largely voluntary on the part of the students and that everyday there is an opportunity for students to be involved in some form of a diverse activity on campus. It is their choice whether or not to participate in the multicultural programs MAU has to offer. Informant 3 believed that the university consciously segregated students through dorm assignments. She also noted that the active Greek system was highly segregated. For example, there were actually three separate governing bodies: one for white fraternities, one for white sororities, and one for race/ethnic fraternities and sororities. She argued that because the university does not discourage such structural segregation it, therefore, informally encourages it.

The informants were then asked to discuss how the university encourages integration of the students. Informant 1 mentioned activities such as extra-curricular student services, interdisciplinary and diversity committees, as well as a wide variety of groups and themes. However, she noted that the effectiveness of these activities was debatable. Informant 2 said that MAU promoted itself as a "global university," and students came for this diverse experience, so it was very important to "student satisfaction" that they get it. She mentioned that clubs, the international dorm, international music, food fairs, and craft shows are available to all students, for example. Informant 3 felt that the university was in denial that segregation exists on campus, and mentioned that she noticed that most people in the clubs are not there because they are looking for new friends, rather it is a group of people who are already friends that join the club together.

Self-Segregation and the Quality of the MAU Experience

Informant 1 felt that self-segregation does not affect the quality of the university experience. She believed that there needed to be both pluralist and self-segregation movements. Although she noted the importance of assimilation, she also mentioned that:

> The society at [this university] being a microcosm of Society, an environment 75 percent European descendant intentionally or unintentionally there will be self-segregating among Whites constantly, every day, everywhere. So if we don't have a problem with that, which is not problematic because it is just indicative of daily existence, then I clearly know its okay for people of color to self-segregate. Until it is not okay for that larger model then it's okay for all groups. I have no problem with disenfranchised groups coming together when they need to, and they need to. The chipping away at negative aspects of self-segregation has to occur on the dominant side. More responsibility has to be put on the dominant group.

She also noted that the students who are interested in diversity are the ones who are involved, and they already have open minds to it.

The ones who need it the most are not getting it. The suggestion of informant 3 was to require all incoming students to take a 1-hour course on cultural differences and understanding, and this would affect all students. She noted that, "self-segregation is sad. Students miss out on the opportunity to see the global view." Informant 2 said that it wasn't self-segregation that negatively affected students, but rather limited access to diversity. She noted that pressure from students and faculty who want changes within the university is forcing administrators to look at policies and make those changes. Students want this because they realize that they must be prepared to work in a "global society," and the university should prepare them for that work.

University Responsibility

The key informants all agreed that the university has some responsibility for the desegregation of students. This is done through the faculty, who need to teach it and promote it through group assignments both inside and outside the classroom. Informant 2 noted that MAU needs to "recruit, hire, and retain more Latino, Asian, and African-American faculty." Informant 3 believed that a mandatory one-hour course for freshmen, stratified to reflect the university's ethnic composition, and designed as "an understanding and embracing of differences" would help break down ethnic divides. Key informant 1 concurred, stating that a curriculum "with more group work, which forces students to integrate" would be effective, "because if forced or mandatory integration is not done, then the students will naturally segregate themselves."

Survey Respondents

The results of the 50 surveys overall indicated that students tend to self-segregate themselves by race and ethnicity when choosing friends. The respondents also justified this self-segregation, while noting the importance of having friendships with students from a race or ethnicity different from their own.

Demographics

The gender of the survey respondents included 28 (56.0%) who were female and 22 (44%) males. The racial/ethnic breakdown was 3

Black/African-Americans (6.0%), 2 Hispanics (4.0), 2 Asians (4.0%), 7 International students (14.0%), 7 mixed race (14.0), and 29 (58.0%) students who were White/Caucasion. The age of the respondents ranged from 18 to 25, with the majority of respondents (47 or 94.0%) between the ages of 18-21 years old. Regarding their standing, 20, or 45.5%, were freshman, 10 (22.73%) were sophomores, 9 (20.45%) were juniors, and 5 (11.36%) were seniors. Of the 50 students surveyed, 15, or 30.0%, lived off campus and 35, or 70.0%, lived on campus.

Friendships

The students surveyed were asked about their friendships with other students at the university and their participation in multicultural activities. Students were first asked to think of their closest friends at the university and check off the characteristics they had in common with them. Table 2 describes the responses to this question.

Students also responded to the question, "Among your friends at this university, what percentage would you say are of a different race or ethnic background from yourself?" Of the 49 students who answered this question, 8 (16.33%) said 'None', 8 (16.33%) said 1-20% of their friends were of a different race or ethnic background from themselves, 12 (24.49%) said 21-40 %, 8 (16.33%) of the students surveyed said 41-60%, 6 (12.24%) said 61-80%, and 7 (14.29%) said that 81-100% of their friends at the university were of a different race or ethnic background than themselves (see Table 3). Respondents often felt it important to emphasize that this was true of their friends "at [this university]", and that overall the characteristics of their friends were more ethnically diverse. This was actually written in on several questionnaires. Respondents seemed uncomfortable reporting low numbers with regard to this question, and this could have had the effect of underreporting in the "none" category. Depending on one's definition of "friend," it is also possible that individuals perceived The students were asked whether they participate in any multicultural activities on or off campus. Of the 45 who answered this question, 17 (37.78%) said 'Yes' and 28 (62.22%) responded 'No' to participating in these types of activities.

Table 1. Demographics of student survey respondents.

Variable	Total N	Percent
Gender		
Male	22	56.00
Female	28	44.00
Total	*50*	*100.00*
Race/Ethnicity		
Black/Afro-American	3	6.00
Hispanic	2	4.00
Asian	2	4.00
International	7	14.00
Mixed	7	14.00
White/Caucasion	29	58.00
Total	*50*	*100.00*
Age		
18	13	26.00
19	12	24.00
20	15	30.00
21	7	14.00
22	1	2.00
24	1	2.00
25	1	2.00
Total	*50*	*100.00*
Program Year		
Freshman	20	45.45
Sophomore	10	22.73
Junior	9	20.45
Senior	5	11.36
Total	*44*	*100.00*
Live On/Off Campus		
Lives on campus	35	70.00
Lives off campus	15	30.00

Table 2. Common characteristics survey respondents have with their university friends.

Response	Total N	Percent
Same year in school	29	15.43
Same first language	29	15.43
Same dorm	28	14.89
Same race	22	11.70
Same gender	21	11.17
Same sexual orientation	19	10.11
Same political beliefs	12	6.38
Same major	10	5.32
Same religious beliefs	7	3.72
Member of same Fraternity/sorority	5	2.66
Knew before coming to the University	5	2.66
Other	1	.53

themselves as having friendships across ethnic boundaries, but the number and quality of these friendships could be limited compared with those within their ethnic in-group.

Table 3. Surveyed undergraduate students and their percentage of friends from a different race or ethnic background than themselves.

Percent of friends from different race/ethnic background	Total N	Percent
None	8	16.33
1-20%	8	16.33
21-40%	12	24.49
41-60%	8	16.33
61-80%	6	12.24
81-100%	7	14.29
Total	49	100.00

The University Environment

Students were also asked about the environment at MAU with regards to race and ethnicity. When asked if they thought it was a culturally diverse campus, 31 (58.49%) responded 'Yes,' 3 (5.66%) responded 'No,' 18 (33.96%) said 'Somewhat,' and 1 responded 'Not Sure' (N=53). Students were also asked if they thought that the university encouraged cross-cultural understanding. Of the 45 students who answered this question, 26 (57.78%) said 'Yes,' 6 (13.33%) said 'No,' and 13 (28.89%) said 'Somewhat.' None of the respondents answered 'Not Sure.' We asked students if they agreed with the statement, "Some students think that the dorms are segregated by race/ethnicity." Nine students (20.93%) strongly agreed with this statement, 12 students (27.91%) agreed, 9 students (20.93%) disagreed, 1 strongly disagreed (2.33%), and 12 (27.91%) were not sure (N=43). The last question was "What could [this university] do to foster better understanding across racial/ethnic groups?" Because this was an open-ended question, the responses varied. However, patterns emerged and the responses (as can be seen in Table 4) were as follows: 8 (27.59%) suggested desegregating the international dorm, 7 (24.14%) suggested cross-cultural activities, 6 (20.69%) suggested more cross-cultural classes, 3

(10.34%) recommended recruiting and retaining more minorities, 2 (6.90%) felt that things were fine as is, and 1 person each (3.45 % each) suggested getting rid of the fraternities and sororities, forced integration of the dorms, and providing more money for multicultural affairs.

Table 4. What the university can do to foster better understanding across racial/ethnic groups (student responses).

Suggestion	Total N	Percent
Desegregate the international dorm	8	27.59
Cross-cultural activities	7	24.14
More cross-cultural classes	6	20.69
Recruit, retain minorities	3	10.34
It's good enough	2	6.90
More money for multicultural affairs	1	3.45
Forced integration of dorm	1	3.45
Get rid of fraternities/sororities	1	3.45
Total	29	100.00

Personal Beliefs

The last group of questions surrounded personal beliefs about friendships with people of the same race or ethnic background as oneself. Students were asked why they thought that some students preferred to spend time with students from the same race or ethnic background as themselves. Table 5 shows the responses.

Table 5. Why students prefer to spend time with other students from their same race/ethnic background.

Reason	Total N	Percent
Comfort	15	40.54
Things in common	6	16.22
Knowledge	3	8.11
Avoid culture shock	2	5.41
It's easier	2	5.41
No effort to bridge gap	2	5.41
Don't deal with stereotypes	1	2.70
Language barrier	1	2.70
No previous exposure	1	2.70
Scared of differences	1	2.70
Ethnicity isn't important	1	2.70
May get along better	1	2.70
Similar upbringing	1	2.70
Total	37	100.00

Next, students were asked if they thought there were benefits to having friends from the same race/ethnic background as themselves, and then asked to explain their answer. Thirty-nine respondents answered this question, of which 28 (68.29%) said that 'Yes' there are benefits. Two (4.88%) responded 'No' it was not important, and 11 (26.83%) were not sure. The respondents mentioned that having friends of the same race/ethnic background as yourself was important because of common interests and experiences (n=12, 44.44%), shared thoughts (n=6, 22.22%), and similar beliefs (n=4, 14.81%). Other responses mentioned by the respondents included identity, more understanding, language, and fewer visual barriers (Table 6).

Table 6. Common reasons identified by respondents for having friends of the same race/ethnic background as oneself.

Response	Total N	Percent
Common interests/exp.	12	44.44
Share thoughts	6	22.22
Similar beliefs	4	14.81
Other	5	18.5
Total	27	99.97

Lastly, students were asked if they thought there were benefits to having friends from a different race or ethnicity as themselves, and to explain their answer. Of the 43 who responded, all 43 (100%) believed there were benefits to having friends from a different race/ethnic background than themselves. The open-ended explanations fell into 4 categories. The majority (n=26, 60.47%) noted that it was important in understanding others. Next, 14 students (32.56%) said that the benefit is that it gives you a different perspective. Two (4.65%) said that the world was not homogenous, and 1 student (an international student) said, "practice English."

The findings of the survey data can be grouped by responses related to friendships, university environment, and personal beliefs.

Friendships

The descriptive data collected from the 50 surveys found that the most common characteristics survey respondents have with their friends at the university are: year in school, same first language, same dorm, same race, same gender, and same sexual orientation. Many students also had the same political beliefs and the same major in school as their closest friends at the university. There was a good amount of variation in the responses to "Among your friends at this university, what percentage would you say are of a different race or ethnic background from yourself?" The variation showed responses evenly distributed across categories. Lastly, most students surveyed do not participate in any multicultural activities either on or off campus, although over 1/3 of the students do.

The University Environment

The surveys found that while over 50% of the students thought that MAU had a diverse campus, almost 50% thought that it was either somewhat or not at all a diverse campus. Also, most students believed that the university encouraged cross-cultural understanding, although 19 of the 45 respondents who answered that question felt that it somewhat encouraged or did not encourage cross-cultural understanding. Regarding the segregation of students by dorms, nearly half of the students agreed or strongly agreed that the dorms were segregated by race/ethnicity, while 23.33 disagreed or strongly disagreed and 27.91% were not sure. This is a particularly important finding, especially when coupled with the number of students whose closest friends at the university were in the same dorm as them. In order to foster better understanding across racial/ethnic groups, student responses mainly suggested desegregating the international dorm, increasing cross-cultural activities, and providing more cross-cultural classes.

Personal Beliefs

The findings about students' personal beliefs echoed much of what was said by the key informants. Over 50% of the students said that students prefer to spend time with students from the same race or ethnic back ground as themselves because of comfort and things in common. Nearly 70% of the respondents said that it was important to have friends from the same race/ethnic background as oneself, and the most common reasons for this were common interests and experiences, shared thoughts, and similar beliefs. On the other hand, 100% of the students said that it was important to have friends from a different race/ethnic background as themselves (n=43). Over 60% felt it was important in order to understand others and the next reason mentioned by 1/3 of the respondents was that having friends from a different race/ethnic background from yourself gives you a different perspective.

Conclusions and Recommendations

The data gathered during this study both contradict and confirm elements of previous research and of our hypothesis that undergraduate students tend to segregate themselves by racial/ethnic similarities when forming friendships. Overall, our data confirm that self-segregation occurs among undergraduate students at MAU. This could be attributed to several things, including conscious or unconscious segregation by the university regarding dormitory assignments, students feeling more "comfortable" with students of their own race/ethnic background, common language (especially in the case of international students), reinforcement of race/ethnic identity, and replication of the larger society, which segregates itself by race/ethnicity. Using Buttny's (1999) framework the data suggest that this segregation can be classified primarily as *nonassertive segregation*, where students are uncertain about how to form cross-cultural relationships and/or *assertive segregation*, where race/ethnic minority groups, due to their relatively small numbers, form groups in order to preserve their own sense of identity. Although the information gathered does suggest that some level of *aggressive segregation* may exist on the campus studied, this influence appears to be minimal. Indeed, during the course of our work, we found both an institutional commitment to cross-cultural understanding as well as an openness on the part of the students to learn about and benefit from the richness of alternative perspectives afforded by divergent cultural expressions.

However, as opposed to assumptions made in much of the literature, self-segregation occurred overwhelmingly on the part of Whites in our sample. As shown by our observations, the proportion of Whites in integrated settings was significantly lower than the proportion of non-Whites. Similarly, Whites self-reported having fewer friends from ethnic backgrounds different from their own. Insights from the key informant interviews support the importance of this dynamic. As a numerical majority, Whites are constantly self-segregating in every day situations. This, however, is seldom perceived as separatist or cliquish behavior. As a sociological majority, Whites are powerbrokers in society who have higher degrees of social mobility. With the greater ability to move within and about the social arrangements in society comes a responsibility to challenge oneself to cross race/ethnic boundaries that can cause negative forms of self-segregation.

Another important conclusion derived from this study is that not all forms of self-segregation are negative. Self-segregation based on *similarity attraction*, likeness of kind based on cultural and identity, is natural and can provide the necessary support system one needs to "make it" at MAU. This is particularly true for disenfranchised groups who have had their "histories obliterated." This moves us to a discussion of why self-segregation occurs, and what positive and negative effects can ensue.

Self-segregation can occur as a means of support for marginalized groups or groups in culturally unfamiliar circumstances. This type of cohesiveness can be essential to a successful college experience. Likewise, "comfort level" can be an important factor in coping with pressures and feelings of detachment often felt by new college students. The latter mentioned type of support applies to all different race/ethnic groups, minority and majority. In no circumstances was self-segregation observed or self-reported to be practiced as a result of negative racial/ethnic outgroup sentiment.

The students in this study overwhelmingly reported feeling that cross-cultural understanding is important; however, this belief does not seem to be acted on by students. This study has found that friendships with persons of one's same race and ethnic background serves a purpose, namely "comfort." Yet, students acknowledged that friendships with students of other race and ethnic backgrounds were of importance. Perhaps what we see is a separation between what students are being taught versus the reality of living in a society where racism continues to exist, despite the talk of encompassing diversity and multiculturalism. It could also be that students are providing the socially acceptable answers to a sensitive topic. It is difficult to determine from the data at hand whether or not students are suffering from a subsequent lack of cross-cultural understanding and respect for difference.

Based on the conclusions, several recommendations can be offered. First, self-segregation should not be treated solely as a phenomenon occurring primarily among non-White groups. Nor should the practice be perceived as entirely negative. Secondly, support groups and cultural groups that celebrate different race/ethnic identities should be encouraged. A cultural celebration that is inclusive of many different racial/ethnic elements could facilitate cross-cultural experiences and foster greater understanding and respect for difference. A third recommendation is to include mandatory curricula, for all students, which address diversity issues and encourage cross-race/ethnic interactions, particularly those universities with relatively low numbers of race/ethnic minority students. At MAU, one of the informants even referred to herself as a "token Black female faculty member." To construct a genuinely diverse environment, a strong effort must be made to recruit racially/ethnically diverse students, faculty, and staff. However, professors may also tend to slip into their own race/ethnic "comfort zones." At the same time, they hold a visible position of authority and influence and their curriculum design must therefore reflect the institutional commitment to race/ethnic diversity. Therefore, the university should look at ways to provide in-service training to its professors to ensure that they are consciously representing its commitment to cross-cultural understanding to students, and to help professors design their class curricula in ways that provide increased opportunities for course-related cross-cultural interaction.

The final recommendation involves increasing the amount of interaction among students on an individual level. Evidence from this study suggests that rigidity between ethnic groups does still exist, yielding levels of nonassertive segregation, where students are unsure about how to successfully integrate and therefore retreat into "ethnic comfort zones," where they have a higher probability of experiencing success in social situations. This rigidity can then easily create social stratification on campus -- and dominance of one group over another --

by race/ethnicity, especially when one subgroup is numerically dominant. We see hints of dominance of the white undergraduates over multiethnic undergraduates manifested in the hierarchy of the student government, which may serve to heighten minority students' sense of alienation, resentment and powerlessness.

In this respect, more ways must be found to coax -- and push -- undergraduates into situations where they will be exposed to students who are different from them, making the unknown more familiar and more comfortable to be around. Data suggest that the willingness to integrate and learn is there. At the same time, ways must be found to "guarantee success," so that this exposure leads to acceptance and not rejection, so that when self-segregation does occur, rather than reflecting a rejection of other (aggressive self-segregation), it is assertive, reflecting an acceptance, an embracing, a celebration of self.

The university is in a good position to take further steps to become the global university that it envisions in its strategic plan. As Bochner and Oshako (1977 p. 480) argue, "a social system with a heightened awareness of ethnic differences may be a necessary condition for racial integration...." Institutionally, the university has made an overt commitment to fostering cross-cultural understanding and has incorporated that commitment into its strategic plan. Administratively, it has set up several bodies that support its integrated vision, such as its Diversity Committee and its support of multi-ethnic clubs.

In closing, it is important to acknowledge that almost everyone asked felt that cross-cultural understanding and respect for difference is important and that the university plays an important role. If self-segregation characterizes much of the actual interactions among students then this diverse interaction may not be occurring. If the university fails to prepare students to interact in a society that is increasingly multi-racial/ethnic, society on the whole will feel the negative effects. If the university is, indeed, a microcosm of the larger society, lack of cross-cultural understanding among its students will in turn translate into the same for this nation's future educators, leaders, and general public. While all of the causes and effects of self-segregation are not negative, it is important that the directive of fostering a diverse environment not be lost.

References

Adler, P. 1996. "Preadolescent clique stratification and the hierarchy of identity." *Sociological Inquiry* 66 (2): 111-142.

Adler, P. and P. Adler. 1994. "Social reproduction and the corporate other: the institutionalization of afterschool activities." *The Sociological Quarterly* 35 (2): 309-328.

Asante, M. K. and Al-Deen. 1984. "Social integration of Black and White college students: A research report." *Journal of Black Studies* 14: 507-516.

Babbie, E. (2000). *The practice of social research* (6th ed). Belmont, CA: Wadsworth.

Blieszner, R. and R. G. Adams (1992). *Adult friendships*. Newbury Park, CA: Sage Publications.

Bochner, S., N. Hutnik, and A. Furnham. 1984. "The friendship patterns of overseas and host students in an Oxford student residence." *The Journal of Social Psychology* 125 (6): 689-694.

Bochner, S. and T. Ohsako. 1977. "Ethnic role salience in racially homogenous and heterogeneous societies." *Journal of Cross-Cultural Psychology* 8 (4): 477-491.

Buttny, R. 1999. "Discursive construction of racial boundaries and self-segregation on campus." *Journal of Language and Social Psychology* 18 (3): 247-268.

Chavous, T. M. 2000. "The relationship among racial identity, perceived ethnic fit, and organizational involvement for African-American students at a predominantly white university." *Journal of Black Psychology* 26 (1) February: 79-100.

Crain, R. with R. Mahard and R. Narot (1982). *Making desegregation work how schools create social climates*. Cambridge: Ballinger Publishing.

Doane, A. 1997. "Dominant group ethnic identity in the United States: the role of "hidden" ethnicity in intergroup relations." *The Sociological Quarterly* 38 (3): 375-397.

Duncan, O. and B. Duncan. 1955. "A methodological analysis of segregation indexes." *American Sociological Review* March 20: 210-217.

Gay, G. 1985. "Implications of the selected models of ethnic identity development for educators." *Journal of Negro Education* 54: 43-55.

Grant, C. 1990. "Desegregation, racial attitudes, and intergroup contact: A discussion of change." *Phi Delta Kappan*. Special Section on School Desegregation September.

Greene, J. P. and N. Mellow. 1998. *Integration where it counts: a study of racial integration in public and private school lunchrooms*. University of Texas September.

Greenberg, M.T., Siegel, J. and C. Leitch. 1983. "The nature and importance of attachment relationships to parents and peers during adolescence." *Journal of Youth and Adolescence* 12 (5): 373-386.

Jackson, L. 1998. "The influence of both race and gender on the experiences of African American college women." *The Review of Higher Education* 21 (4): 359-375.

Klaczynski, P. 1990. "Cultural-developmental tasks and adolescent development: theoretical and methodological considerations." *Adolescence* XXV (100) Winter: 811-823.

Kurtines, W. and R. Hogan. 1972. "Sources of conformity in unsocialized college students." *Journal of Abnormal Psychology* 80: 49-51.

Marcus, Robert. 1996. "The friendships of delinquents." *Adolescence* 31 (121) Spring 145-158.

Martinez, A. A. 2000. "Race talks: undergraduate women of color and female friendships." *The Review of Higher Education* 23 (2): 133-152.

Steitz, J. and T. Owens. 1992. "School Activities and Work: Effects on Adolescent Self-esteem." *Adolescence.* 27 (105) Spring: 37-50.

Taylor, D and A. Rickel. 1981. "An analysis of factors affecting school social integration." *Journal of Negro Education* Spring 50 (2): 122-133.

Ting-Toomey, S. 1981. "Ethnic identity and close friendship in Chinese-American college students." *International Journal of Intercultural Relations* 5: 383-406.

Yeh, C. and Huang, K. 1996. "The collectivitistic nature of ethnic identity development among Asian-American college students." *Adolescence* 31 (123) Fall: 645-661.

Zack, N. (1995). *American mixed race: the culture of microdiversity.* ed. Lanham, MD: Rowan and Littlefield

Article 16

Student Tolerance Levels Within a Four-year Institution

Elliott Anderson

> Being born here in America doesn't make you an American. Why if birth made you an American you wouldn't need any legislation, you wouldn't need any amendments to the constitution. No, I'm not an American, I'm one of the 22 million Black people who are the victims of Americanism. One of the 22 million Black people who are the victims of democracy, nothing but disguised hypocrisy. And I see America through the eyes of a victim. I don't see an American dream, I see an American nightmare...—Malcolm X

Introduction

Americans have had reservations about accepting non-English immigrant groups. At SUNY Maritime College in the Bronx, twenty-one Arab students fled after a series of assaults and harassment. At

Brown University, Rhode Island, a Black senior is beaten by three White students who tell her that she is nothing more than a "quota." At State University in Binghamton, New York, three students are charged with a racially motivated assault that left an Asian-American student with a fractured skull (Potok 2000, 8). If education is thought to broaden an individual's outlook on different racial/ethnic groups and to increase levels of tolerance (Hyman 1954; Brooks 1973; Gaasholt 1995; Kuh 1995; Pascarella 1996), why do events such as these occur in an area where cultural enlightenment should be the mindset of the students?

The purpose of this research is to examine the racial and ethnic stereotypes, attitudes, and behaviors held by students of a small, residential, rural-based college. This research will seek to determine if a relationship between the individual respondents' student rank (*i.e.* freshmen, sophomore, junior, senior), and their views towards other racial and ethnic groups, exists. Does education have any impact upon the diminution of racial or ethnic stereotypes, attitudes or behaviors? It is hypothesized that the higher the education level of the individual, the lower the accepted number of stereotypes about a different ethnicity outside of the individuals own group.

Literature Review

Ernest Pascarella, *et al.,* proponents of the education-tolerance theory, sampled a total of 3,910 college freshmen from eighteen different four-year institutions. They administered a pre-college survey examining the students' openness to learning and their openness to diversity. A follow-up test was given to the same sample in the spring of 1993. Pascarella concluded that, "… during college… students tend to change in the direction of greater openness" and that, "From freshmen to senior year, students become less authoritarian… and ethnocentric… They (the students) also demonstrate statistically significant shifts in the direction of greater support for individual rights" (Pascarella 1996: 17).

Table 1: Scale of Respondents' Openness to Diversity

I enjoy having discussions with people whose ideas and values are different from my own.
Learning about people from different cultures is a very important part of my college education.
I enjoy taking courses that challenge my beliefs and values.
I would support a friend involved in a romantic interracial relationship.
I would date someone from a racial group different from my own.
I would support a family member involved in a romantic interracial relationship.
I would marry someone from a racial group different from my own.

Table 2: Scale of the Respondents Rating Diversity Within the Institution

Gilmore College has an environment which fosters cultural diversity.
At Gilmore College there are many opportunities to socialize with people different from myself.
Gilmore College is placing too much emphasis on achieving cultural diversity. *
Cultural diversity at Gilmore College should be actively promoted by its administrators.

*Recoded for consistency

Table 3: Scale of Respondents Rating Tolerance of the Student Body

Gilmore students of different ethnic backgrounds socially interact harmoniously with one another.
Whites tend to separate themselves socially on this campus.
Blacks tend to separate themselves socially on this campus.

Table 4: Scale of Respondents' Interaction Levels with Different Racial/Ethnic Groups

People often interact with individuals of a different race or ethnic group from themselves in many situations. Please indicate how often you interact with individuals of a race or ethnic group different from your own...	
As classmates	At sporting events
In dating	In campus organizations and their events
As majors in the same department	At parties

Oystein Gaasholt and Lise Togeby concluded that, "... education stands out as a critical factor" in the reduction of ethnocentric attitudes (Gaasholt 1995: 267). Gaasholt and Togeby claim that there is a positive relationship between an individual's education level and their tolerance for social "outgroups." They note that in America, a high school graduate holds more tolerant attitudes towards these social "outgroups" than does a high school dropout. The same holds true for the college graduate who holds higher levels of tolerance for "outgroups" than does the high school graduate (Gaasholt 1995). This study was an examination of the relationship between education and political tolerance levels. "It seems beyond dispute that Danish society education is a powerful variable behind interethnic attitudes. In all, people with an academic-oriented education are dramatically more likely than people without such a background to hold tolerant attitudes toward ethnic outgroups" (Gaasholt 1995: 270).

George Kuh has argued that "in-class" learning is not the only part of what influences an individual's tolerance of outgroups. He believes that "out-of-class" experiences also play a major role in shaping students' perceptions on diversity. Two questions guided Kuh's research, "(1) To what activities, events, and people do the students attribute their intellectual, social, and emotional development?" and, "(2) Do the types of out of class experiences associated with various outcomes differ by type of institution attended and such characteristics as sex and ethnicity?" (Kuh 1995: 125). Kuh interviewed 149 undergraduate students between January and June of 1989. The participants were asked to answer questions concerning their most significant college experiences, major surprises and disappointments at the institution, changes within the student, and to what the student attributed these changes (Kuh 1995). Kuh concludes that students

Table 5: Scale of the Rejection of Racial/Ethnic Stereotypes

Asians tend to remain a foreign element in American society to preserve their old social standards and to resist the American way of life.
I believe that individuals who live in poverty are there by their own doing (*i.e.* laziness, criminal behavior, etc.)
I believe that Whites are generally more manipulative of others in obtaining what they want as compared other racial/ethnic groups.
Since Blacks have their own interests and activities, it is best that they engage in their own fraternities and sororities, just as Whites get along best in all White fraternities.
The best way to eliminate the drug menace is to control the Hispanic element which guides it.
One trouble with White businessmen is that they stick together and connive, so that a non-white doesn't have a fair chance in competition.
The Hispanic districts in most cities are results of the clannishness and stick togetherness of Hispanics.
Blacks keep too much to themselves, instead of taking proper interest in community problems and good government.
When Whites create large funds for educational or scientific research, it is mainly due to a desire for fame and public notice rather than a really sincere scientific interest.
The trouble with letting Blacks into a nice neighborhood is that they gradually give it a typical Black atmosphere.
On the whole, Native Americans have probably contributed less to American life than any other racial/ethnic group.
We are spending too much money for the pampering of criminals.*
One main difficulty with allowing the entire population to participate in government affairs (voting, jobs, etc.) is that such a large percentage is intellectually deficient.*
Affirmative action at Gilmore College leads to the admission of under-qualifies students.

*Recoded for consistency.

of "color" more frequently mentioned that out-of-class experiences influence their levels of tolerance of different ethnic and political backgrounds than Whites, as women reported that their education and out of class experiences affected their reflective judgement and application of in-class knowledge outside of class more than men (Kuh 1995).

In a recent study conducted by Debra Kelley, she summarizes a few key findings concerning a survey administered on student subculture. A portion of the survey was directed towards racial attitudes and tolerance. One set of questions asked whether or not the respondent had ever challenged derogatory comments made against other races, the opposite gender, or homosexuals. The second set of questions asked if the respondent had ever felt uncomfortable being alone in the presence of members of another race, the opposite gender, or members of another sexual preference.

For the index of challenging derogatory statements, Kelley reported that, "The majority of students indicated that they had rarely if ever challenged derogatory comments" (Kelley 1999: 2). Only a minority of the respondents ever challenged derogatory comments against other races, the opposite gender, and homosexuals. Kelley also found that a significant relationship between student rank and the likelihood to challenge derogatory remarks, showing a positive relationship between student rank and tolerance levels. Juniors and seniors were more likely to challenge derogatory statements than were freshmen and sophomores.

For the index of ever feeling uncomfortable being alone in the presence of another race, the opposite gender, or another sexual preference, Kelley notes that a majority of the students indicated feeling uncomfortable alone with members of another race and members of another sexual preference at some point in time. However, Kelley also states that there is no statistical relationship between student rank and comfortability levels (Kelley1999).

In a final set of questions on tolerance, the indexes examined the respondents' attitudes towards interracial relationships. The questions asked if interracial relationships were fine for others, if the respondent would consider interracial involvement, and if the respondents' family would support an interracial relationship. Kelley stated that 88% of the respondents stated that interracial relationships were fine for others, while only 50% indicated that they would consider involvement in an interracial relationship. This becomes an even smaller percentage. Kelley reports, only 41% of the students indicated that their parents would be supportive of an interracial relationship. Finally, Kelley notes that there is no significant relationship between student rank and openness to interracial relationships (Kelley 1999).

Proponents of the Education-Tolerance theory are often criticized because the findings are weak with no strong levels of association. There are even several instances where the highly educated were measured to be even more prejudiced than the general public. C.H. Stimber argued that the highly educated were more likely to, "... hold certain highly charged and derogatory stereotypes, favor informal discrimination in some areas of behavior, and reject intimate contacts with minority group members" (Stimber 1961: 168).

John Duckitt argues that higher education does not increase an individual's prejudiced attitudes, however, it may produce a superficial commitment to democratic norms and principles. "The educated may show greater support for abstract democratic principles, but be no more willing to apply these principles to specific situations. Education merely polishes and qualifies a person's negative attitude expressions" (Duckitt 1992: 183).

Richard Schaefer states that, "An often replicated finding in post-1980 studies of white prejudice is that it remains pervasive despite the significant increase in educational levels" (Schaefer 1996: 6). He also points out 25 to 50 percent of all minority college students are victimized for reasons of prejudice annually (Schaefer 1996). Schaefer argues that the percentages for racial incidents are high for an educational institution that supposedly increases multicultural tolerance and understanding with higher education. He cites previous research that makes the claims of increased education having a direct association with decreasing interpersonal prejudice. However, Schaefer makes the argument that, "... the experience of a university education not only does not reduce inter-group hostility, but as presently constructed, may indeed promote it" (Schaefer 1996: 7).

To support his position, Schaefer uses four pieces of data. He argues that predominantly White colleges, even though they have experienced an influx of minority applicants, still remain predominantly White. The small number of minority faculty, or minority faculty being placed in part-time lower paid positions, is a second indicator. Third is the "balkanization of campus life" in the call for separate hall space of both on and off campus housing where students keep the housing situation segregated. Finally is the "insularity of colleges from their surroundings," where the racist ideals on campus are completely oblivious to the surrounding social impact (Schaefer 1996).

Knud Knudsen also believes that increased education does not increase multicultural diversity tolerance. Knudsen does not belittle the need for education but states that, "... highly educated individuals have a better understanding of which opinions are less socially acceptable and will tend to hide their true reactions when certain items are brought up in survey interviews" (Knudsen 1995: 319). Knudsen maintains that individuals who are more educated are more likely to give socially accepted responses. "The well educated... are more sensitive to social-desirability pressures..." (Knudsen 1995: 320). Thus, those not educated will tend to score higher on racist statements not because they are more racist, but rather because they have not learned the socially approved responses.

The research publications that were the most beneficial in the formulation of the survey are actually classic survey designs concerning social distance and authoritarian personality. The first is the research conducted by T.W. Adorno, Else-Frenkel-Brunswik, Daniel J. Levinson, and R. Nevitt Sanford in their research titled *The Authoritarian Personality*.

T.W. Adorno, Else-Frenkel-Brunswik, Daniel J. Levinson, and R. Nevitt Sanford researched many different factors in inter-group prejudices. In a statement made on anti-Semitism, Levinson states:

> The irrational quality in anti-Semitism stands out even in casual everyday discussions. The fact that people make general statements about 'the Jew' when the Jews are actually so heterogeneous—belong to every socio-economic class and represent every degree of assimilation—is vivid evidence of this irrationality. This striking contrast between the Jews' actual complexity and their supposed homogeneity has suggested the hypothesis that what people say against Jews depends more upon their own psychology than upon the actual characteristics of Jews (Adorno 1950: 57).

To measure anti-Semitism, Levinson created the F-scale, which was subdivided into four distinct scales. The first subscale measures the respondents' reaction to various stereotypical traits of a group that are considered offensive, unpleasant, or disturbing. The second subscale measures the respondents' reaction to various stereotypical traits of a group with the group viewed as threatening to the respondent, dangerous to majority society, or corrupt. The third subscale measures respondents' reaction to various negative and hostile statements made against a group. The statements in the third subscale vary in their degree of hostility, and are measured on various levels ranging from simple avoidance to suppression and attack. The final subscale in the Levinson instrument examines seclusive and intrusive ideologies of individuals. For the seclusive ideology, the statements claim that Jews are too foreign and unassimilated, and not taking part with other groups in social functions. For the intrusive part of the scale, the statements refer to Jews as being over assimilated and participating too much in the goings on of society.

The Adorno research however, comes under a great deal of criticism. Especially in light of the writings of Mary Jackman who questions some of the more common measurements of discriminant behavior. Stating that while many of the common indexes seek to measure discriminant behavior, the instruments may fall short of measuring the behavior, and may in-fact skew results to make individuals seem more prejudiced than they are.

Jackman raises several reasons as to why some questions may be misleading. An example of one reason is the examination of the statement, "Jews are aggressive," which the respondent would rate on a Likert scale. The first criticism Jackman makes is that this instrument overlooks the fact that this statement may not have a negative connotation, unless a negative value is placed on the statement (Jackman 1977).

The second criticism Jackman makes is that the problem with measuring beliefs alone, concerning inter-ethnic attitudes, is that some negative beliefs may actually be shown as empirically true, or at least have an empirical basis. Therefore, the individual may sound prejudiced when agreeing with the statement "Jews are aggressive," however, they may just be agreeing with literature that portrays Jews as aggressive businessmen (Jackman 1977).

The third critique that Jackman makes in questioning the adequacy of beliefs as indicators is the commonplace nature of many beliefs about certain ethnic groups. "Some stereotypical beliefs have such a platitudinous element that respondents may adhere to them in an unthinking fashion with very little intellectual or emotional involvement" (Jackman 1977: 149).

Jackman also criticizes social distance scales such as those developed by Emory Bogardus. Jackman asserts that a person may answer a question a certain way, however, the orientation of the individual's actions are unknown. An individual may act or show that he or she may like someone of another group simply for reasons of personal gain or avoidance of conflict. Furthermore, Jackman cites the predisposition of individuals in their tendency to conform to the norms of society, and that often the intensity of feelings toward an ethnic group may be attributed to other stimuli not presently measured by the indicator (Jackman 1977).

Finally, Jackman comments on the interpretations of the measures, stating that even though we assume an individual's positive feelings are related to their rejection of negative stereotypes, individuals may actually interpret some stereotypes in a positive manner and accept the stereotypes while still feeling positive towards an ethnic group. "Although we assume that everyone with a negative affect toward a group will hold more negative than positive beliefs about that group, a measure of affect alone will not tell us how many or what kinds of beliefs the respondent based his or her feelings on" (Jackman 1977: 154).

Jackman also examines the two arguing sides of the study conducted by Adorno *et al* of *The Authoritarian Personality*. After the Adorno study, researchers proclaimed that education allowed an individual to look past personal prejudices. Jackman argues that the arguments that the Adorno F-Scale does not show that the uneducated hold fast to anti-Semitic beliefs. Rather, Jackman argues, the uneducated individual may have been caught in a response set. The phrasing of the items may have coerced the respondents to respond in such a manner, responding more so to the form of the indicator as opposed to the content.

> Since all items on the F-Scale are phrased as abrupt 'authoritarian' statements with which the respondent may agree or disagree, it has been argued that many respondents may score high on the F-Scale because they will say 'yes' to any questionnaire statement, regardless of the context (Jackman 1973: 329).

Jackman further asserts that increased education allows the respondent to better ascertain the meaning of the question or statement. Thus statements concerning anti-Semitism are evaluated more cautiously by those who have a higher education.

> Thus two factors, low general knowledge and low cognitive sophistication, contribute to the greater tendency of the poorly educated respondent to acquiesce to any agree-disagree item, regardless of content... we can argue that this tendency to substantive content of the item becomes more ambiguous and the respondent reacts more and more to the form rather than to the certain content of the item in his search for cues (Jackman 1973: 330).

Jackman also presents arguments supporting the F-Scale, claiming that the F-Scale does indicate a form of authoritarian syndrome in that those who comply with any of the statements regardless of the contents, have submissive personalities and therefore, will follow any form of authoritarian and dictatorial regimes. However, Jackman argues that in a study of her own, the F-Scale did not survive the replacement of her own scales, which were comprised more of social distance questions. Where Jackman pushes the argument that the relationship between education and authoritarian attitudes is weakly related to true anti-Semitism.

Mary Jackman seeks to dispel the relationship between education levels and tolerance. Examining tolerance studies completed in 1964, 1968, and 1972, Jackman claims that while students of higher education showed higher tolerance levels with abstract and ambiguous question types, their scores were only slightly higher than the scores of the uneducated (Jackman 1977). Jackman continues by stating that as the questions become more specific in their content, and focus on the actions of supporting integration programs in the surveys, the answers of the educated at every level, even though scoring higher in tolerance that the uneducated, the difference between the two scores was "trivial and nonexistent." Jackman goes even further in stating that, "... the relationship between education and policy orientation toward Blacks is considerably weaker, rather than stronger, as one moves from general principles to more specific policies" (Jackman 1978: 310).

In her critique of the studies reviewed, Jackman states that the primary problems in these studies are the assumptions that: (1) Commitment to democratic norms does not develop spontaneously, but must be learned, and (2) that the major institutions in society project democratic cues (Jackman 1978).

Emory S. Bogardus in his research examined a concept he termed as social distance. Bogardus' theory of social distance is best described as a series of concentric circles. In the very center of these circles, we find ourselves and our loved ones. Outside of that circle are our regular friends, which gives way to the third circle that encases our speaking acquaintances. Within the fourth circle we find the non-speaking acquaintances, and inside the fifth circle there are what Bogardus calls "Strangers of a Different Culture". The seventh circle holds what is considered as individuals of intolerance, which inevitably leads into the eighth and final circle holding our enemies (Bogardus 1959).

Bogardus developed a foundation of several types of social distance. Bogardus states that social distance may be active or passive. An active nearness or farness is where an individual actively pursues a friendship, or actively demonstrates intolerance for and another individual. An example of passive nearness would be two friends who live far apart and rarely correspond. However, should one of them be in any amount of trouble, one would literally fly to be at the aid of the other. An example of passive farness is where an individual will have nothing to do with another individual. This includes mentioning them, and even going so far as to avoid any events that the other may be in attendance. Bogardus also states that social distance can take on a pseudo-character. An example of this would be where an individual is nice to another individual even though they may despise the individual they are being nice to. The pretending individual is using the other in order to obtain some gain, whether it be monetary, power, position, etc. (Bogardus 1959).

Finally, Bogardus states a theory concerning distancing that applies directly to this research. Bogardus states that social distancing is a dynamic phenomenon as it takes on three different forms.

> One is found in the common behavior of persons in maintaining distances from other persons, in order to protect status, safeguard security, and to defend self-identity. Another type is called 'existential distancing,' which is the maintaining of distance due to a person's inner nature, his temperament, his moods, without reference to social factors. A third expression of distance is designated 'self-distancing.' It may be called intra-self distancing, for it refers to 'being beside oneself' and 'not being myself today' (Bogardus 1959: 13).

Bogardus' measurement of social distance was explored through a survey instrument. Bogardus prepared a list of sixty descriptions that could all be heard within the context of the everyday conversation in which an individual would express about other individuals. All of the statements on Bogardus' list represented various levels of social relationships such as, "… contacts within the family, within social or fraternal groups, within neighborhoods, within churches, within schools, within play groups, within transportation groups, within occupational groups and business groups, and within political or national groups" (Bogardus 1933: 265).

After the creation of the sixty statements, Bogardus assembled a panel of one hundred judges and asked them to rate the statements in accordance to the amount of social distance that the judges felt the statement represented. The judges would rate the social distance that they thought existed between the person making the statement and the individual that the statement was referring to. The judges narrowed down the statements to seven social situations that Bogardus referred to as "the seven equidistant social situations." These statements were then supplied with a list of different racial and ethnic groups asking the respondents if they would consider any of the following with the listed groups.

1) Would marry...
2) Would have as regular friends...
3) Would work beside in an office...
4) Would have several families in my neighborhood...
5) Would have merely as speaking acquaintances...
6) Would have outside my neighborhood...
7) Would have live outside my country...
(Bogardus 1933: 269).

The survey was administered at three different intervals in 1926, 1946, and 1956. Bogardus found that current politics and world events strongly influenced the responses on the surveys. For example, in 1946, the social distance for Japanese and Japanese-Americans skyrocketed (meaning people were placing a greater distance between themselves and the Japanese). The Germans were another ethnic group that experienced an increase in social distance during the aftermath of World War II. In 1956, Bogardus found that the growing civil rights movement might have actually spawned a decrease in the social distance that respondents placed between themselves and African-Americans (Bogardus 1959).

In commenting on international distance, Bogardus states that distance between nations was originally started as a defense, and to build unity within a particular culture. In order to more effectively promote unity, education and propaganda built patriotism, which helped to develop a barrier against other nations. Language differences keep individuals from understanding one another and even when two countries do understand the same language, semantic and cultural differences are still working against them. Thus, Bogardus asserts that a world community cannot be attained in a "single bound". That there are too many cultural and ideological differences even between those who are geographic neighbors to escape extreme social distancing (Bogardus 1959).

In order to understand a social phenomena, it must first be defined. Mary Jackman provides one definition of tolerance as, "... competing groups in society [who] accommodate one another in spite of openly conflicting goals and interests" (Jackman 1977: 145). Michael Walzer argues that there is a difference between tolerance and "mutual respect." Walzer defines tolerance as, "... the peaceful coexistence of groups of people with different histories, cultures, and identities" (Walzer 1997: 2). However, Walzer continues in implying that tolerance is a hierarchy of power, that is, "... a relationship of inequality where the tolerated groups or individuals are cast in an inferior position. To tolerate someone else is an act of power; to be tolerated is an acceptance of weakness" (Walzer 1997: 52). Mutual respect, however is an attitude that is beyond toleration. It is the opening door towards an enculturation attitude, however it is not always likely to develop. Thus, tolerance becomes the more easily developed of the two concepts within society. Toleration does not include the acceptance of an individual's beliefs or ideologies, however it does include the rejection of negative impulses (*i.e.* prejudice, discrimination, etc.). Walzer states that intolerance is at its worse when difference of culture, ethnicity, or race coincide with class differences.

Methods

The research site is Gilmore College (An alias for the actual institution). Gilmore college is located in a rural area of Southern Virginia. It is a small, residential, public college with a current student population of approximately 3,300. The average class size is about twenty students, with a faculty-to-student ratio of one faculty member to every fourteen students. The racial makeup of the survey sample closely resembles the Gilmore College population that is primarily Caucasian students who are 87% of the student population. African-American students are 9% of the student population. Asian-American students are approximately 2%. Hispanic/Latino students make up about 2%. While Native American students constitute less than one percent of the entire student population (*All information received through the college's Registrar's Office*).

The survey instrument had questions about demographics, social class, primary major, GPA, student rank, age, gender, race/ethnic group, and religion. The research question was based on the literature search. The survey instrument was based on work by Ernest Pascarella,

T.W. Adorno, and Emory Bogardus. The instrument was a forty-four question survey with eleven demographic questions. The rest of the questions included a five-item Likert scale, that ranged from strongly agree to strongly disagree (See Appendix A).

The respondents were selected from a random class list chosen through a table of random numbers. All classes of honors, internship, practicum, and short-term courses were excluded from the list. In total, a list of 15 classes were sampled for survey administration. Professors were notified in advance and their permission was requested for survey administration. The surveys were administered to the classrooms after all instructions concerning voluntary participation, confidentiality and anonymity were given. The ideal sample size for this research was 380 students. However, due to a disaster that directly affected the college, the survey sample fell short of the goal of 380 participants, and only 214 administered surveys were collected.

Levels of association between dependent and independent variables are measured through use of the chi square statistic. The independent variables were age, gender, race/ethnic group, and student rank. All questions were collapsed into scale groups, which consisted of (1) openness to diversity, (2) levels of interaction, (3) institutional rating, (4) student cohort rating, (5) stereotypes, and (6) effects of knowledge in the classroom. All negatively worded questions created to avoid response sets were recoded for consistency.

Conclusion

A few individual survey items did, however, show rather high levels of strong statistical significance despite being unable to determine any strong significance in the relationship between the measures and the chosen independent variables based on the scales used. With the strongest of the statistical relationships being the independent variable age and the survey item "I enjoy having discussions with people whose ideas are different from my own," and the independent variable race and the survey item "Gilmore students of different ethnic backgrounds socially interact harmoniously with one another."

In summary of what can be derived from the individual responses tends to support the reviewed literature. Males are less likely to be open minded than females in that they are more likely to shun the idea that school curriculum includes learning about different ethnic groups and cultures outside of their own. Males are also more likely to place blame within the individual than on the external factors of society, less likely to be open to or supportive of new and different cultural experiences, and more likely to disagree with being opposed by different ideas and beliefs. An explanation for this may be that in American society, males are expected to be less emotional and more callous in their dealing with others. An emotional male is often taken for weak, therefore, males may feel the need to take a slightly more harsh tone on some issues than females.

In the student ranks, while Upper-classmen were more likely to be open to new cultural experiences and new ideas, surprisingly, they were also more likely than lower classmen to see daily occurrences as having a negative racial overtone, and less likely to actually interact with different racial and ethnic groups. An explanation for this may be that as students progress through their academic careers, the broad range of classes they once experienced narrows down as they select their major. They then interact less with different people and ethnic groups, as they are more likely to interact with the same people consistently until their graduation. Also as students progress through academia they become more aware of social situations and their consequences. Possibly noticing any racial or ethnic unrest where a Lower-classmen would not.

As for age, younger students tended to be more open minded in experiencing new cultures and ideas. Younger students also were more likely to either support or accept a romantic interracial relationship in themselves or someone they know. An explanation for this may simply be the changing times. Where older individuals may have matured in a society where Whites and Non-Whites were separated, or older students may be more tenacious to their beliefs and values than younger students. Older students also were less likely to view any racial difference on campus. An explanation for this may be that many of the older students were possibly commuter students, and were not as exposed to campus life as the on-campus students.

In terms of race, Non-Whites were more likely to remain open to new ideas, beliefs and values than Whites. Both ethnic groups were near even on responding that they feel either Whites or Blacks separate themselves socially on campus. However, Non-Whites were more likely by a large margin over Whites to disagree with the statement that different ethnic groups interact harmoniously on campus. Non-Whites tend to perceive prejudice or racial discourse where Whites are either completely oblivious to the occurrence of the these events, or unintentionally causing racial unrest.

Non-Whites are more supportive of romantic interracial relationships, and are more likely to see Whites as manipulative, however, they are less likely to agree to the statement that White businessmen connive together so others do not have a fair chance. In interaction levels Non-Whites are more likely to have interacted with ethnic groups outside of their own in dating, inside their department, as the same majors, and within campus organizations and campus event. A likely explanation for this is that since the Non-Whites are a minority population on campus, they would really have no choice but to interact outside their own ethnicity. However, for such interactions as dating outside their own ethnicity, shows an open mindedness not demonstrated by Whites. However, Non-Whites were also more likely to state that they do not attend an integrated church, as more Whites than Non-Whites claimed to attend an integrated church. While Non-Whites are more likely to consider interracial relationships, Sunday morning still continues to be the most segregated time for many of these Non-White respondents.

Several factors prevented this research from holding more exact indicators. One such limiting factor is that this survey was conducted as a cross-sectional examination of the Gilmore College student body. The only real way to know if education is the principle factor in changing an individual's prejudiced or narrow minded attitudes and beliefs is to follow an individual throughout the course of their student career in a longitudinal study. Another stigmatizing factor in this research is with the survey, there is now way to take into account personal history, or events outside of the college experience that may shape or change the way a student acts or thinks. An individual who exhibits traits of an Authoritarian personality may attribute this to their higher education, while an open minded individual may attribute this to experiences in high school.

Recommendations in directions for taking this research would be to expand on the views of how the students rated each other. Results showed that while individuals were confident in themselves that they did not hold any prejudiced or discriminating beliefs, they were a little less sure about their peers and classmates, and were more hesitant to identify the student body as a tolerant network. The majority of the respondents rejected the stereotypes, however, they felt that other students were separating themselves ethnically, or that the college does not support ethnic diversity.

Another direction for the research is examining if the respondent is a commuter student and a resident of the community or a resident on-campus. The slight oversight by the researcher by not placing this variable into the survey may have been at the cost of several explanations of behavior. Where residency within the community may have made a difference in certain variables as community may influence they way an individual may have responded.

Another recommendation would be administering a similar survey to a sample of the faculty and staff of Gilmore College. The students are the products of their instructors. If education is to have a profound effect on the students, then it comes from the direction of the professors and administrators. Perhaps learning more about the professors will give a better idea as to what the students are learning and applying to their daily actions and behaviors.

There should also be a closer examination of the survey measures. Some of the measures may have been misunderstood, or not taken in the connotation that the measure was written in. An example of this is the survey measure, "Since Blacks have their own interests and activities, it is best that they engage in their own fraternities and sororities, just as Whites get along best in all white fraternities." While this measure was grouped into the stereotype category, those who agreed with the statement may have viewed the statement as Blacks should have the right to have separate fraternities rather than Blacks should be made to have separate fraternities. The interpretation of the statement could make a difference in how the respondent answers the survey, thus corrupting the scale. While the answer of the individual can be recorded, the actual intent of the individual in their answering is still unattainable.

In conclusion, while this research was unable to reject the null hypothesis, there were several other avenues that this research might take for future research. This research was unable to find any strong correlation between student rank and overall diversity tolerance and acceptance of different social outgroups. This research could go on to support the argument that higher education increases an individual's ability to place themselves in a socially desirable position, and therefore portray less bigoted attitudes when asked directly or indirectly about them. Or, these findings may be indicators that the intolerance in today's society is itself towards prejudice, discrimination, and bigotry.

References

Adorno, et al. *The Authoritarian Personality* New York: Harper & Brothers. 1950.

Bogardus, E. S. *A Social Distance Scale Sociology & Social Research* 17. (February 1933): 265-74.

Bogardus, E. S. *Social Distance* Yellow Springs: Antioch Press. 1959.

Brooks, L. M. *Racial Distance as Affected by Education Sociology & Social Research* 21. (1973): 128-33.

Duckitt, J. *The Social Psychology of Prejudice* New York: Oxford University Press. 1978.

Gaasholt & Togeby. *Interethnic Tolerance, Education, and Political Orientation Political Behavior* 17. (September 1995): 265-85.

Jackman, M. R. *General Applied Tolerance: Does Education Increase Commitment to Racial Integration American Journal of Political Science* 22. (May 1978): 302-24.

Jackman, M. R. *Education and Prejudice or Education and Response Set? American Sociological Review* 38. (1973): 327-29.

Jackman, M. R. *Prejudice, Tolerance, and Attitudes Toward Ethnic Groups Social Science Research* 6. (1977): 145-69.

Kelley, D. S. *Issues of Tolerance & Diversity at Longwood College*: http://web.lwc.edu/assessment/Final%20Tolerance%20Report.pdf (July 1999).

Knudsen, K. *The Education—Tolerance Relationship: Is It Based On Social Desirability? Scandinavian Journal of Educational Research* 39. (December 1995): 319-34.

Kuh, G. *The Other Curriculum: Out of Class Experiences Associated With Student Learning and Personal Development. Journal of Higher Education* 66. (March 1995):123-50.

Pascarella, et al. *Influences on Students' Openness to Diversity and Challenge in the First Year of College. Journal of Higher Education* 67. (March 1996): 124-95.

Potok, M. *Hate Goes to School Intelligence Report* 98, (ed). (Spring 2000): 6-15

Schaefer, R. T. *Education and Prejudice: Unraveling the Relationship The Sociology Quarterly* 37. (1996): 1-12.

Schaefer, R. T. *Racial and Ethnic Groups* New York: Longman Publishing. 1998.

Stimber, C. H. *Education & Attitude Change* New York: Institute of Human Relations Press. 1961.

Walzer, M. *On Toleration* New Haven: Yale University Press. 1997.

Article 17

Understanding the Margins: Marginality and Social Segregation in Predominantly White Universities

Will Tyson

Introduction

The university setting is a rare opportunity to study the interaction of diverse peoples as one of the few settings where individuals from different racial, ethnic, socioeconomic status, and cultural backgrounds come together as peers for an extended period of time (Smith and Moore 2000). Modern research on race and higher education is actually a peculiar place for classic sociological theory. From a historical perspective, black students are relatively new at predominately white college and university environments that have evolved in this century of great social change. There was little need to address social issues in higher education among classic theorists. However, several early theoretical traditions have emerged for use in this new sociological milieu. Theory provides a general framework and agenda for research, yet it can be strengthened using personal experience as an impetus for research. As individuals, researchers seek out problems to address from the more objective perspectives of quantitative and qualitative methods guided by a coherent research agenda constructed from previous research and guiding theory.

This chapter examines classic and current research on marginality and developing research on race and higher education to examine how marginality expands understanding of the experience of African American students on predominantly white campuses. These perspectives are strengthened by my personal experience as a black student at two small elite private predominately white institutions, Wake Forest University (Winston-Salem, NC) for undergraduate and Duke University (Durham, NC) for graduate school. The personal narrative is key in guiding research. Preston (1995) cites the role of minority and women scholars and writers like Virginia Woolf and Audre Lorde in questioning dominant philosophical and theoretical perspectives about the lives they lead. "Theoretical language passes over and distorts the differences it would understand. Theory more attentive to difference needs to gain access to the meanings that circulate within different lives, especially as reflected in literary writing of those who, themselves, speak and write from sites of difference" (Preston 1995). While I do not compare my writings or experience to those of Woolf and Lorde, I do recognize that as a young black male scholar, I must balance my narratives with theory and the research method in order to increase the effectiveness of research. While "the master's tools will never dismantle the master's house," (Lorde 1984) theoretical perspectives must adopt experience to both speak and change the language of theory.

Marginality

Chicago scholar Robert E. Park introduced the concept of the "marginal man," one with a personality affected by their relative status and position in society. Park and Burgess (1921) conceptualized marginality within the process of migration where people may find themselves in between an in-group and an out-group with antagonistic relationships between both and loosely defined relationships within each. Park (1928) describes the marginal individual as a "mixed blood" who "finds himself striving to live in two diverse cultural groups" (881). While Park conceptualized marginality as a personality construct, one of Park's students, Everett Stonequist (1937) expanded on this idea by introducing the role of social change and cultural conflict into the psychological uncertainty this plurality may cause.

The marginal individual is self-conscious, yet observant and critical of dominant culture, thus they may feel inferior in social situations where they are made to feel inferior or uncomfortable within the societal context. This unrest causes them to search to areas within the plurality of marginal existence where they can excel. While acknowledging these personality traits are problematic, Stonequist (1937) did not conceptualize them as such, instead focusing on society instead of the individual as the source of unrest, creating a macrolevel examination of society through the reaction of the marginal individual. Being restricted to a marginal place within a difficult social climate causes such personality conflict.

This marginal status creates barriers that increase the gap between marginal peoples and the mainstream (Preston 1995). Areas of comfort within the margins and the gap that creates distance introduce the role of social place in understanding the marginal experience, especially in predominantly white universities. Solórzano and Villalpando (1998) interpret marginality as "complex and contentious location and process whereby People of Color are subordinated because of their race, gender, and class" (212). Subordination and location in the margins prevents marginal peoples from designating and obtaining the valuable social and cultural capital in the larger society. Gossett, Cuyjet, and Cockriel's (1998) conceptualization of marginality further asserts the concept of distance to stress the utility of this theoretical perspective. Marginality as a "permanent way of life for students when pulled between two cultures" (23) truly represents an experience African American students face at predominantly white universities.

Current State of University Research

This increased diversity in American colleges and universities has had and will continue to have several important implications for future research on the impact of campus life on students. Pascarella and Terenzini (1998) identify three specific areas of conflict and interest in new millennium colleges and universities. First, research is more difficult. Ethnic and cultural heterogeneity brings new backgrounds and new cultural norms. Standard assumptions in early foundational research may not apply in new university social settings. Second, additional culture norms mandate further exploration of interaction effects. Past studies examine the main effects of a particular experience such as college choice, Greek affiliation, or extracurricular participation. Examining interaction effects acknowledges that different experiences can affect different individuals and peoples in different manners and magnitudes. Third, this necessitates that research expand the conceptualization of outcomes of postsecondary education past previous research based on narrow views of desired outcomes and effects. Research typically focuses on traditional values of liberal education in residential settings, such as critical thinking, intellectual flexibility, and liberalization of social attitudes. Other areas, such as personal growth and adjustment in the transition to college, have not been a focus of research.

Acknowledging the need for expanded research goals identifies theoretical areas that better address issues of race in higher education. Marginality helps establish theoretical cultural baselines for black students as well as provide a starting point for the interaction of cultural background and race on college experience. Understanding the marginal college student and life in the margins is necessary to expand the research plan. Research can then move beyond limited theoretical perspectives and limited research outcomes into a new paradigm that truly represents the increasing multicultural look of predominantly white colleges and universities. As we understand that the values and ideals of liberal education in a residential setting may not be experienced or desired to be experienced the same in all populations, marginality becomes useful in conceptualizing difference. With this heightened accountability, research of university settings has become more complex. "If there was ever a time when we needed a broad repertoire of approaches to inquiry in research on the impact of college, it is now" (Pascarella and Terenzini 1998:155). Marginality can be a cornerstone perspective in studying the impact of college on minority populations.

Marginality and Higher Education

In its classic form, marginality is a good fit for research on minorities in higher education. Park's (1928) original conceptualization of the marginal man as a product of migration is helpful on two particular levels. Historically, one can easily understand the process of desegregation through all levels of education as migration. As *Brown v. Board of Education* (1954) ripped through American elementary and secondary educational systems, black students were forced to merge with a culture with which they were not familiar in social situations that were often hostile. Second, on predominantly white college and universities campuses, black students continue to be "strangers in a strange land" when confronted with the personal, environmental, and institutional conflicts of college life (Douglas 1998; Smith and Moore 2000).

Understanding the marginal African American student as a product of migration emphasizes the process and journey of desegregation, while acknowledging the demographic change taking place in predominantly white colleges and universities. While assimilation was a desired outcome of Park's (1928) marginal man, a theoretical basis that accounts for personal narratives and individual difference within research on university systems and structures is helpful in restructuring understanding of the issues. Race and the marginal experience interact with several areas of the college experience and university setting to increase the set of possible personal experiences and outcomes for the black student.

Marginality and Transition into College

For African American students, the migratory process of transition into college may bring feelings of insecurity as marginality sets in before they can establish connections and relationship at the university (Schlossberg 1989). Douglas (1998) quotes a black student in his first year on a predominantly white campus, "When I was in high school thinking about getting ready to come to [name of school], I was like, "Yeah, it's a predominantly White campus, but I've been going to predominantly White high schools my whole life. So that's not going to be a big deal. When I got here, it was, like, totally different. I had never seen this many White people in one place at one time...." This quote speaks to differences between mostly white high schools and college. Life in high school is a small subsection of life in the larger society. The typical high school student goes to school from 8:00 to 3:00, then returns to neighborhoods, family, and activities in their larger neighborhoods, communities, and cities. For most college students at small private residential universities, the campus is the larger world. They live and work away from family and loved ones and must create a familiar world within the campus bubble that becomes their home within the new larger society.

The small campus life that attracted me to Wake Forest presented difficulties related to the small number of black students within a seemingly homogeneous general population. I got my first impression of Wake Forest at a one-week summer program for black students entering their 10th grade year. Even a mild introduction to the limited

Wake Forest experience left me thinking, I could not attend Wake because there were not enough black people. I remember my dad looking at me wearing the free Wake shirt I received at the program and telling me I looked very comfortable in that shirt and that it fit me well. With time, I fell in love with Wake Forest, yet I recognized the unique task ahead of me in attending a university with a very small minority population. When I enrolled, Wake Forest was approximately 89% Caucasian in an undergrad population of 3,600 students. I could have chosen to run from these problems, but I chose to address them. I had fallen in love with Wake Forest and I knew that for the university to progress in minority campus life, I had to accept the challenge I was presented.

Part of this challenge is to understand what it means to be black in a small campus environment. African American students used to mostly black surroundings and sensitive to racial issues may find that attending a predominantly white university may heighten their awareness of differences between themselves and the white majority, thus forming their personal identity as a black person. Smith and Moore (2000) argue that black students raised in mostly white areas who are used to being one of the few blacks in their social setting, may find that expectations from their black peers in values, attitudes, dress, speech, and other areas may make race more salient to their college experience. Marginal individuals evaluate their position by deciding how the social norms, values, attitudes, and personal attributes important to them compare to that of the majority group (Marsden and Campbell 1984; Smith and Moore 2000). By assessing these differences, black students understand their social place within the margins of the larger campus society. Whether it be clothing styles, choice of music, social tastes, or vernacular, campus culture interacts with race to increase the salience of these racialized expectations and differences. Entrance into the university setting brings the onset of a complicated set of adjustment processes as all students attempt to find their proverbial niche. For the marginal individual, locating that niche may be more difficult and wrought with more personal conflict.

Marginality and Institutional Structure

While individual students bring their own set of expectations and personal values, the climate and culture of the predominantly white university setting indirectly interacts with the marginal student through traditions, cultural norms, rules, and mores of predominantly white universities were developed before black students became a part of the campus. While black students interact with white students in academic, social, and residential settings, they also interact with the institutional setting through policy and faculty and administrative influence on social and academic life as well as general expectations set forth by the university. The quality and presence of institutional support systems effect the academic achievement and success of black students as well as their social adjustment (Allen 1992).

Black administrators are invaluable to these social processes in what can be a small isolated campus environment. Whether or not the effects can be felt through policy and institutional direction, it is good to know there is someone up there who can represent a black perspective. Black administrators who have an open door let black students provide an important link from the institution to the margins. On a small campus like Wake Forest, incoming black students often know a few black administrators before they enroll through visits, recruitment, minority weekends, and scholarship interviews. Unfortunately, no matter the size of the university, institutional structures formed in response to desegregation, such as minority life offices, cultural centers, and advising for black Greek organizations may also be marginalized within the organizational framework of the university. Support mechanisms and the individuals who run them may be searching for their proper place in what are often unstable institutional arrangements. While black students search for support, it is likely black administrators and faculty are searching for institutional support as well.

Even with the support these mechanisms provide, person-environment interaction may be a stronger contributor to marginality than person-person relationships between black and white students. Using marginality scales on four predominantly white campuses, Gossett, et al (1998) found significant differences in perceptions of marginality between black and white students. African American students feel more marginalized by institutional structure, while white students fail to perceive the person-environment conflict faced by their black peers. In this respect, person-environment conflict may breed person-person conflict as black and white students interact differently with the larger university. Differential person-environment conflict faced by black students and their white counterparts must be understood in order to address institutional support, policy implications, and programs that seek to create a welcoming environment for all students.

While a person-environment analysis is beneficial to understanding the perspectives of marginalized students, it is important for black students not to view their marginality within an oversimplified dichotomy. Black students may view white students as part of an "anonymous other" linked to structural components of the university, thus breeding "us vs. them" conflict. Through the lens of conflict, black students may not see an accurate view of the struggles their white counterparts face within the college "bubble." While black and white students do face different problems in this unique social climate, black students may not feel it is possible for a white student to be distanced and marginalized from what they perceive to be a "white world." While black and white students may get to know each other as individuals, this person-person dynamic may be mutually exclusive from group-group dichotomy. A person-environment analysis is key to realizing the role race plays in one's perceived and actual social distance from what is considered the mainstream in their college society.

Negative feelings about university life and campus culture among black students are generally related to social transitions (Douglas 1998). The same is true for white students, but the social transitions faced by black students are more racialized and seem to include a more critical critique of social structures as predicted by Stonequist (1937). White students may feel more comfortable with the campus cultural norms of the university as their population has long been the focus of policy and development of the traditional and modern campus scene. Like their black counterparts, white students must adjust to person-person social transitions, but may feel more comfortable than black students with person-environment social transitions. By focusing on how students negotiate the new university environment, marginality theory views the college environment as an active mediator in the lives of black college students.

Conceptualizing marginality in the university setting as a "normal situation that relies on institutional and associational proximity" (Goldberg 1941; Grant and Breese 1997) allows black students to believe that they can overcome the racial barriers between themselves and the predominantly white university structure. It is important to understand this idea in order to counter the fatalistic dichotomy that can cause a black student to believe they have no chance for success against these barriers simply because they are black and the system is white. Such an approach also allows black students to view their social transitions in college life as a struggle they share with white students who also have person-environment interaction with the institutions. This balanced approach to the concept of marginality places emphasis on personal and social factors along with the unique factor of race, to account for variables of academic, personal, and social success in college.

The above highlights key areas where marginality intervenes with person-environment and person-person dynamics as black students navigate the predominantly white university environment. Transition into college and the corresponding transition into adulthood for traditional students is a difficult life progression only made more difficult by marginal status. Black students must balance their personal entrance into college with a racialized social dynamic that requires them to establish relationships with two distinct societies intertwined in one social setting. Finding a social place in both the black community and the larger university community is a difficult task that requires immediate attention upon arriving to campus while learning to live as a marginalized individual. With the social distance that often exists between mainstream social spheres and marginalized areas, a dichotomous social environment may be difficult to negotiate.

Marginality and Interpersonal Relations

While addressing macro-level concerns, it is important to remember that marginality is a shared struggle with individual outcomes. Different people respond differently to marginal status. Grant and Breese (1997) identify possible individual responses to marginality under the assumption that the individual reacts to marginality using a range of possible reactions and interpretations of their situation. Four key processes form individual responses to marginality: (1) social structure creates marginality by restricting equal access to resources and opportunities, (2) marginality limits full participation in the social environment, (3) this limited participation causes social psychological reactions, and (4) these reactions to marginality influence behavior.

The importance of social psychological reactions to marginal status emphasizes the role of individual difference. Smith and Moore (2000) stress that a common flaw in college effects studies is an assumed homogeneity of African American campus populations. Three demographic trends force research to account for diverse reactions of black students to marginal status on predominantly white campuses. First, growth in the black middle and upper-middle classes has created an increased bifurcation of blacks by class and socioeconomic status (Wilson 1978; Jaynes and Williams 1989). Along with that observation, the number of black Americans living in racially diverse or predominantly white neighborhoods and attending mostly white schools continues to rise, thus increasing the numbers of young black students with interracial contact before college (Massey and Denton 1988; Frey and Farley 1996; Sigelman, Bledsoe, Welch, and Combs 1996). Within black populations, the number of foreign-born blacks has grown, along with the number of individuals identifying themselves as biracial or multiracial (Root 1996; Smith and Moore 2000). Demographic heterogeneity within black populations at predominantly white universities makes it necessary to consider a diverse set of responses to marginal status.

It is important to remember that black students must choose how to integrate and situate themselves into this heterogeneous black campus community as they work to clarify their identity as black individuals while understanding blackness on the college campus. Being black at home amongst family is different than being black on a small college campus. While blackness in a family setting may be based on a familiar set of expectations that interact with upbringing within a set of regional, religious, and other demographic factors, blackness in a small, intimate society of young adults takes on a complex meaning. For me, my blackness at home was reinforced in family life and the black church within a rural Southern Christian perspective. In college, blackness takes on diverse forms and expectations within an age-graded heterogeneous black community of individual who bring their own versions of blackness to college life.

The difficulty or ease of integrating into the black community may play a role in a black student's decision to integrate into the larger campus community. Formal university-supported activities and informal cultural activities targeted at African American students provide social and academic forums where black students can interact with each other to provide a buffer between the black community and the possibly isolating nature of the campus environment. Smith and Moore (2000) report that African American students view participation in cultural activities as a measure of integration into the black community and closeness to other black students. Sitting at the "black table" in the cafeteria, attending black Greek functions, and general immersion in the black community are indicators of an individual's connection to the black community as perceived by others.

Marginality and Social Segregation

Understanding heterogeneity within the African American student body within the context of marginal status is important in discussing interpersonal and social relationships between black and white students on college campuses. Marginality addresses many of the core issues surrounding so-called "self-segregation" by black students, a common trend on predominantly white college campuses that has generated attention in research over the past decade (Douglas 1998; Fisher and Hartmann 1995; Hurtado, Milem, Clayton-Pedersen, and Allen 1998; Smith and Moore 2000). To study social segregation, group identification must be separated from racism. It is easy to assume that black and white students are racially motivated to socialize separately. However, group identification for black and white students can be based on strong in-group identification along with a strong desire not to identify with the out-group, which can be called "racism." Either or both motivations can lead to "self-segregation" by white or black students. The actions and behavior of black students draw more attention because black students are small in number and often seen as having "special" circumstances surround their presence at the university, such as being student-athletes or benefiting from affirmative action or quotas (D'Souza 1991).

Due the heterogeneity of black and white communities, we cannot assume homogeneous social relations between all black students and all white students. Any study of social segregation and social distance by race must examine the factors that contribute to social segregation in both black and white university communities. Further study of these areas of interest can allow researchers to formulate questions about the role of white students in social segregation. Even accounting for the numbers and simple majority status of white students, closeness and social interaction between black and white students remains a two-way street. The question is how far down the street black and white individuals must go in order to meet each other. Research must assess the social distance between black and white students and examine how institutional factors contribute to this distance.

It is assumed that black students who integrate themselves in the larger campus community choose to represent themselves in ways consistent with white people in order to establish closeness. Smith and

Moore (2000) hint that pre-college factors may influence closeness to white students as well as closeness to black students. Looking at racial identity formation for black students can yield a great deal of information about how minority students choose to negotiate in-group/out-group dynamics in predominantly white, but still often multicultural university settings. Social distance and institutional conflict interact with pre-college factors to account for individual social distance and position in the university society. Further study of these factors for white students would provide a more balanced perspective on racialized social adjustments.

Comfort in the Margins

The idea of black "self-segregation" is quite peculiar when viewed both in the context of history and the current struggle. The black students are marginalized within the college setting, yet criticized for building security and developing relationships within the margins. Instead of letting the majority determine marginal identity, marginal peoples create space in which to determine their own identity. Solórzano and Villalpando (1998) suggest that many black students choose to remain in the margins in order to empower themselves and determine their own status instead of entering the mainstream and letting the larger society determine their worth. Through cultural activities on campus and work in black communities, black students can redefine the margins as an area of strength and a home base from which they can succeed. Collins (1991) asserts that instead of rejecting marginality it can be used as a position of strength to gain understanding and influence in the larger community.

Much of the benefit of using marginality as a theoretical position of strength is that this perspective realizes the situation black students face in higher education and fights the battle from the academic bunker of the marginal reality. Perspectives that assume we have overcome or underestimate the challenges of the social adjustment do no justice to the struggle, in theory or in everyday practice. We cannot bridge the gap until we know the dimensions of the gap itself. Extending this gap analogy reinforces the internal strength of the margins. Only from within the margins can one truly assess the magnitude of the gap that must be crossed to effectively integrate into a society that cannot clearly see the full reality of the gap or the margins. The margin must be used as a safe haven and base of operations for understanding the task at hand. Blindly stepping into the gap without a plan of action may be detrimental to the true progress of the individual and the marginal group. Forsaking one's position within the safety of the margins may risk personal security, thus sacrificing one's strength in the margins. Re-conceptualizing the margins by "distinguishing between a dominated marginal status imposed by an oppressive and contradictory higher education system, versus an empowering and self-defined marginal site" (Solórzano and Villalpando 1998:216) adds human agency in the margins to transform marginal experience (Giroux 1983; Solórzano and Villalpando 1998).

Conclusion

This chapter has highlighted the role of the sociological concept of marginality in identifying areas of segregation in predominantly white colleges and universities. As a theoretical starting point, marginality sets up the marginal existence as the baseline from which black students can participate in the larger community. For African American students, the margins, not the mainstream, are a cultural norm. Marginality does not admit defeat in the struggle for truly open social, academic, and structural realms in our colleges and universities. This approach simply allows research to use a clearer lens for examining the same processes that have been the focus during decades since desegregation began. This lens from the margins allows us to focus on problems previously missed by viewing university life through the rose-colored lens of the "universal" ideals of liberal education.

For every "success" story in our predominantly white universities, there are battles fought, barriers overcome, and a long way to fall from the tightrope one must walk to continually cross the gap between the margins and mainstream. Simply stated, marginalized African American students need a different set of tools than white students to succeed on the college campus. The marginality approach makes this clear.

Racial identity formation and personal growth and maturing that may occur due to marginal status should gain due consideration in campus life research. Growth of racial identity and other related areas are not generally considered in campus life research. Assimilation is no longer a goal of the "marginal man." Assimilation requires the marginalized individual to lose his or her own identity. As the margins become a stronger position in university, the goal of higher education should be to make both the mainstream and margins equally accessible to all students with no sanctions from either realm for joint participation, thus welcoming all identities in a true multicultural and diverse university setting.

References

Allen, W. R. 1992. "The color of success: African American college student outcomes at predominantly white and historically black public colleges and universities." *Harvard Educational Review* 62:25-43.

Collins, P. H. 1991. *Black feminist thought: Knowledge, consciousness, and the politics of empowerment.* New York: Routledge.

D'Souza, D. 1991. *Illiberal education: The politics of race and sex on campus.* New York: Free Press.

Douglas, K. B. 1998. "Impressions: African American first-year students' perceptions of a predominantly white university." *Journal of Negro Education* 67:416 431.

Farley, R. and W. H. Frey. 1994. "Changes in the segregation of whites from blacks during the 1980s: Small steps toward a more integrated society." *American Sociological Review* 59:23-45.

Fisher, B. J. and D. J. Hartmann. 1995. "The impact of race on the social experience of college students at a predominantly white university." *Journal of Black Studies* 26:117-133.

Fordham, S. and J. Ogbu. 1986. "Black students' school success: Coping with the burden of acting white.'" *Urban Review* 18:176-205.

Frable, D. E. S. 1993. "Being and feeling unique: Statistical deviance and psychological marginality." *Journal of Personality* 61:85-110.

Frey, W. H., and R. Farley. 1996. "Latino, Asian, and black segregation in U. S. Metropolitan areas: Are multiethnic metros different?" *Demography* 33(1):35-50.

Giroux, H. A. 1983. "Theories of reproduction and resistance in the new sociology of education: A critical analysis." *Harvard Educational Review* 53: 257–293.

Goldberg, M. M. 1941. "A qualification of the marginal man theory." *American Sociological Review* 6:52-58.

Gossett, B. J., M. J. Cuyjet, and I. Cockriel. 1996. "African Americans' and non-African Americans' sense of mattering and marginality at public, predominantly white institutions." *Equity & Excellence in Education* 29:37-42.

_____. 1998. "African Americans' perception of marginality in the campus culture." *College Student Journal* 32:22-32.

Grant, G. K. and J. R. Breese. 1997. "Marginality theory and the African American student." *Sociology of Education* 70:192-205.

Green, A. W. 1947. "A re-examination of the marginal man concept." *Social Forces* 26:167-171.

hooks, bell. 1992. *Black Looks: Race and Representation*. Boston: South End Press.

Hurtado, S. 1992. "The campus racial climate: Contexts of conflict." *Journal of Higher Education* 63:539-569.

Hurtado, S. and D. F. Carter. 1997. "Effects of college transition and perceptions of the campus racial climate on Latino college students' sense of belonging." *Sociology of Education* 70:324-345.

Hurtado, S., J. F. Milem, A. R. Clayton-Pedersen, and W. R. Allen. 1998. "Enhancing campus climates for racial/ethnic diversity: Educational policy and practice." *The Review of Higher Education* 21:279-302.

Jaynes, G. D. and R. M. Williams, Jr. (eds.). 1989. *A common destiny: Blacks and American society*. Washington, D.C.: National Academy Press.

Lorde, A. 1984. *Sister outsider*. Trumansburg, NY: Crossing.

Marsden, P. V. and K. E. Campbell. 1984. "Measuring tie strength." *Social Forces* 63:482-501.

Massey, D. S. and N. A. Denton. 1988. "Suburbanization and segregation in U.S. metropolitan areas." *American Journal of Sociology* 94:592-626.

Park, R. E. 1928. "Human migration and the marginal man." *American Journal of Sociology* 33:881-893.

Park, R. E. and E. W. Burgess. 1921. *An introduction to the science of sociology*. Chicago: University of Chicago Press.

Pascarella, E. T. and P. T. Terenzini. 1998. "Studying college students in the 21st century: meeting new challenges." *The Review of Higher Education* 21:151-165.

Preston, L. M. 1995. "Theorizing differences: Voices from the margins." *American Political Science Review* 89:941-953.

Rimstead, R. 1995. "Between theories and anti-theories: Moving toward marginal women's subjectivities." *Women's Studies Quarterly* 23:199-218.

Root, M. P. P. 1996. "The multiracial experience: Racial borders as a significant frontier in race relations." In *The multiracial experience: Racial borders as the new frontier*, ed. M. P. P. Root, xiii-xxviii. Thousand Oaks, Calif.: Sage Publications.

Schlossberg, N. K. 1989. "Marginality and Mattering: Key Issues in Building Community." In *Designing campus activities to foster a sense of community*, ed. D. C. Roberts, 5-15. San Francisco: Jossey-Bass.

Sigelman, L., T. Bledsoe, Welch, S. and M. W. Combs. 1996. "Making contact? Black-white social interaction in an urban setting." *American Journal of Sociology* 101(5):1306-1332.

Smith, S. S. and M. R. Moore. 2000. "Intraracial diversity and relations among African-Americans: Closeness among black students at a predominantly white university." *American Journal of Sociology* 106(1):1-39.

Solórzano, D. G. and O. Villalpando. 1998. "Critical race theory, marginality, and the experience of students of color in higher education." In *Sociology of Education: Emerging Perspectives*, ed. C. A. Torres and T. R. Mitchell, 211-224. Albany, NY: State University of New York Press.

Stonequist, E. V. 1937. *The marginal man: A study in personality and culture conflict.* New York: Charles Scribner's Sons.

Wilson, W. J. 1978. *The declining significance of race: Blacks and changing American institutions.* Chicago: University of Chicago Press.

Article 18

Race, Gender and Intimacy on a College Campus

Robert M. Moore III

Almost thirty years ago William Cross proposed that African Americans experience stages of identity development that are different from those experienced by many white Americans (Cross, 1995). Positive re-affirmation of self is considered difficult to achieve in a society where African Americans have considerably less power than white Americans to affect a positive identity (ibid). For example, standards of beauty more often reflect physical characteristics of white Americans and not African Americans.

Janet Helms proposed a model to explain the development of an identity for whites - one that masked privilege (Helms, 1995). College and university campuses should be ideal locations for African Americans and whites to affect and enhance a more realistic identity (Gordon, 1954; Blumer, 1958; Bobo, 1999).

In very few instances in the literature has the researcher found an emphasis on the possibility that whites could understand what it means to be African American. DuBois "veil" or double consciousness idea implied that African American groups must learn about the dominant culture to survive (DuBois, 1996). But little has been written about the possibility that whites could or should learn about the life experiences of African Americans (ibid). It is the premise of the researcher that certain situations do exist that will enable whites to feel and experience what many African Americans feel quite routinely - a sense of difference.

The researcher believed that a significant romantic involvement between an African American and a white college student, would force the partner who is white to come to grips with a reality that he or she had probably not experienced before interracially dating (Festinger, 1957). The new reality would be experienced not because the person who is African American would tell his or her partner what it means to be a person of color. But because whites who date interracially would be subject to similar environmental cues experienced by African Americans, especially by other whites such as stares, comments and more. The researcher does not believe a similar change would occur for African Americans since most African Americans are already very aware of the characteristics of the dominant culture (Reuter, 1969).[1]

Love between the races has been shunned in many areas of the country. Emmett Till, a fourteen-year-old African American teenager from the north visiting Mississippi in the early 1960's, was lynched because he spoke to a white female on a dare from his friends (Bennett, 1982; Lewis, 1998). Countless others have been lynched based on fear of sexual contact between the two races.

Interracial dating can lead to marriage. The exploitation and advantages accrued by many white Americans via slavery and segregation, economic relationships, could not have been accomplished without the social barriers that were erected both formal, laws, and informally, social pressure. Marriage between two people, each of a different race, can mean the sharing of the resources each family has in its possession. It is only recently that attitudes about interracial dating have started to substantially change.

Colleges and universities are places where students often interact in primary settings such as clubs, dormitories or group projects. Students often claim to enjoy and value the social interaction that occurs during their college years. The researcher recognized that other institutions, such as the military, probably would be more ideal settings to study interracial dating because of the expressed commitment to equality

---

[1] It should be noted here that the term culture is not being used in the sense that African Americans may have different traditions, tastes, values or beliefs than white Americans. This is not being examined here. Culture is being used here to denote life experiences that members of each race are likely to have with members of another race.

between different racial and ethnic groups (as well as women) in our society. But because of the increasing importance a college education has in our society the researcher feels our campuses are significantly important settings to study this particular social behavior.

There are twenty-five million people between the ages of 18 to 24 (Wilds, 2000). Nearly half of all high school graduates will attend college (Wilds, 2000).[1] Of those who presently attend college, nearly one and half million are African American (ibid). It is safe to say that both African Americans and whites, given current educational requirements by employers, a "credentialized" society, will continue to place a high value on a college education and continue to attend. Gordon believed that structural pluralism, or the inclusion of minorities into clubs, social cliques, and the same educational institutions would increase the chance of interracial marriage (Gordon, 1964).

Implications of the research

Surprisingly only a handful of studies have been done on intimacy between African Americans or whites on college campuses (Davis, 1941; Merton, 1941; Bernard, 1966; Porterfield, 1982; Spickard, 1989; Tucker and Mitchell-Kernan, 1990; Kouri and Lasswell, 1993; Gadberry and Doddler, 1993; Williamson, 1995). Perhaps this reflects an emphasis that began in the 1960's to place more emphasis on same-race couples rather than inter-race couples as a result of the Black Power movement which criticized previous assimilation and integration social movements (Mills, 1999). College campuses are a good place to study interracial dating because more people are attending given the increasing importance of a college education in a post-industrial economy.

Methodology

The college selected for the study, River University (fictitious name) was located in a rural area with a substantial Amish and Mennonite presence close by – communities very different from the backgrounds of almost all students. There was a heavy reliance on farming in the immediate as well as surrounding area. The immediate county had 36,261 whites and 149 African Americans, or less than a half of one percent (U.S. Census, 1990). The adjacent three counties were similar. Two were less than one percent African American and the third was three percent (ibid). The opportunity for students to meet other young people in the surrounding communities was limited.

The size of the student body during the two years the study took place was approximately fifteen hundred. According to an official list from the college, there were 75 minority students (five percent). African Americans made up two percent of the student body, approximately thirty.

Students as well as alumni, who had dated interracially, participated in the study. Forty-two people over a two-year period were interviewed. Over two-thirds of the African American students participated in the study. African American students who had not dated interracially were also interviewed.

The study was conducted using a semi-structured interview. The areas of interest to the researcher included personal feelings about dating interracially, the reaction of family and friends, family social history, involvement in campus activities and the goals and aspirations of each participant in the study.

A snowball sampling technique was used to locate and interview students and alumni for the study. Students were initially contacted through electronic mail. Almost all of the students had access to e-mail and most checked it on a regular basis. Interviews were conducted in person although one interview with an alumnus was conducted through electronic mail and another interview with an alumnus took place by telephone.

The process of identifying individuals dating interracially was made easier because of the size of the school. Students were able to identify others who dated or were dating interracially. There was a feeling of solidarity (some said "family") among African American students. Many participated in an affinity group, the Black Student Union, or one of two other groups, one for African American men and the other for African American women. It was common for an African American student to know the identity of the dating partner of another African American student.

Intimacy was defined as two people involved in a relationship to the exclusion of others. The researcher was interested in relationships whereby each person considered the other a boyfriend or a girlfriend, respectively. Surprisingly there was little ambiguity in determining if two people were in a relationship based on the criteria used to define dating for the study. All of the participants who were dating, or had dated, had done so for a significant period of time, ranging from four months to two years.

Results and Discussion

Friendship before Romance: African American Males as Non-Aggressive

Interracial dating did occur. In fact, more than half of the African American males on campus had dated interracially or were currently doing so. Repeated chance encounters in public spaces rather than "chasing" led to interracial dating. This defied stereotypes some may have held of African American males as aggressive. Dormitories, cafeterias and the library were common places for an initial series of contacts. For example, Jack (African American) saw a woman (white) in the lobby of the library wearing a jacket with the insignia of a high school that was in his hometown.[2] He asked her if she knew some of his friends who had attended that particular high school. It turned out she did and in fact had attended the high school. They shared rides home out of convenience during school breaks. During the rides they became friends and eventually dated. Although she was younger than Jack, they continued to date after he graduated.

In another situation, both students, African American male and white female, after they had finished practice with their respective athletic teams, ate meals in a nearly empty cafeteria. Rather than eat alone they began to eat with each other. They became friends first and then dated. Another couple met through a roommate because he (African American male) had befriended the roommate (white). In another situation, the individuals met because they lived in the same dormitory and often sat in the same common area. They used to return to this area, a lounge, after dates and tell each other how bad their evenings had been. A semester went by before they finally decided that perhaps they should try dating each other.

Kouri and Lasswell, as well as Porterfield's work, both on non-college populations, showed that the primary determinants of interracial dating were meeting in integrated settings and holding similar values (Porterfield, 1982; Kouri and Lasswell, 1993). Love at first sight may explain why some people date. It was not the case for interracial couples at River University. Frequent contact by chance is a better explanation as well as feelings that each had something in common with the other. As discussed below, students who dated interracially did not seek to purposively date outside of their race. The findings call into question stereotypes that may exist to explain interracial dating for reasons other than feelings of commonality and romantic love such as rebellion or to fulfill sexual fantasies.

In fact African American men expressed caution when interacting with white females:

> **Jack** - I couldn't take as many chances as my white male friends. I made very sure about the signals I received. I knew the consequences could possibly be much greater for an African American male than for a white male if my behavior was perceived as being aggressive or forward.[2]

The consequences Jack, a senior, spoke of were related to the possibility of being falsely accused of harassment or even worse sexual assault. Jack had been called as a witness in a student judiciary inquiry in an alleged attempted rape by one of his white fraternity brothers. He vividly remembers the hearing even though several years had passed. He felt sure that if the alleged perpetrator had been an African American male the call for judgement would have been swift, more harsh and handled by the local police instead of university staff. Although written over forty years ago, Merton expressed similar ideas about social distance between African Americans and whites:

> ... the contacts between members of different racial castes are regulated by codes of racial etiquette so that there are few opportunities for relationships not involving considerable social distance. (Merton, 1941)

To summarize this section, African American and white students who dated interracially met by chance. Friendship was usually a precursor to dating. In fact, some African American males, similar to DuBois' concept of a "double consciousness," expressed caution when interacting socially with white females on campus, perhaps aware that society held numerous stereotypes of African American male behavior (DuBois, 1996; Anderson, 1990). In only one interview did the researcher find that the initial contacts were based on "chasing." In that case, an African American male saw a picture of a white female in a yearbook of incoming first-year students and decided, based only on the picture, that he wanted to meet her. "Chasing" was not a factor in the other relationships. Given the caution expressed by African American males, it is the researcher's opinion that "chasing" probably leads to more same-race dating than interracial dating.

---

[2] The names of those interviewed are fictitious.

African American Women: Openness to Date White Males

More African American women were open to interracial dating than African American men. This may be contrary to what some might think. This would follow social dominance theory. White males were most resistant to interracial dating whereas African American females least resistant (Sidanius and Pratto 1993; Sidanius, Pratto and Rabinowitz, 1994). More research is needed given the low number of white males interviewed.

African American women were at the bottom in terms of a perceived willingness to date and marry interracially when ranked by all participants in the study - even though most expressed a willingness to do so. White males were ranked next to last, white females second from the top, and African American men at the top. Although African American women expressed a greater openness to the possibility of dating and marrying interracially, interracial dating among white males and African American women was almost non-existent. African American women, although more open to the possibility, felt a greater social distance than that felt by African American males with white females. African American women felt white males to be too culturally distant:

> **Barbara** (African American)– I don't always want to be constantly teaching someone. My mother always said you want to date someone from the same background as you. I never understood that. Now I do.
>
> **Keisha** (African American) – I think we [as] Black women are more mature [than] white men. [They] can't relate to our needs and values, some of them not at all. When we observe white men...they see things that are totally different.

African American women perceived white males to be more interested in being able to tell others they had had sex with an African American woman than in having a relationship:

> **Tara** (African American) – I know a lot of white guys if they see an attractive Black female probably would like to say I slept with a Black girl.

Although most African American males had interracially dated by the end of their senior year at River, more African American males were initially (when they arrived at River) opposed to interracial dating than

African American females. William (African American) was a transfer student who played basketball for River. He was initially against interracial dating. At his previous university, one day he visited his best friend (African American). His friend called for the woman upstairs to come down so he could introduce her to William. His friend's new girlfriend was white. William was shocked and angered. He couldn't believe his friend was dating interracially. Feeling betrayed he did not talk to his best friend for over a year.

After William transferred to River, his feelings about interracial dating began to slowly change, given time and repeated exposure to other African American men who were dating white females. At the time of the interview he was dating a white female from the surrounding community.

African American men and even African American women were more likely to have dated interracially prior to college compared to white students. African American men were more likely to date interracially while in college than African American women. Interracial dating prior to college for African American men did not predict whether they would date interracially in college. But dating experiences for African American women prior to college did predict if they would date interracially while in college. If an African American woman did not date interracially in high school she was very unlikely to do so afterwards. If she did date interracially before college she was likely to continue to do so. This may speak profoundly to the different social situations available that may potentially enrich college social experiences for African American men and women and perhaps to all men and women on college campuses.

Because white females who dated interracially had little exposure to African Americans before college, it is doubtful they had a predisposition to date African American men. Only one expressed the feeling that she specifically liked dating interracially. In fact many women came from neighborhoods where friends and family were opposed to it. Bobbie, white, explained how her grandfather refused to talk to her after learning the racial identity of her boyfriend. Her parents cut her off financially. Amanda, white, spoke of the extreme negative and open hostility people in her town (rural) expressed when they saw a person of color (Brown, 1995). Students who dated interracially at River did not do so for reasons of social experimentation. Their relationships developed because of propinquity.

Feeling comfortable on campus dating interracially

Almost every white female who had dated or was dating interracially told a story about an incident at a party on campus where a white male, usually after drinking, would comment: "so you are down with the brown," or "what's wrong, a white man, isn't good enough for you?" But almost all of the students who interracially dated felt very strongly that the campus atmosphere was quite tolerant regardless of these comments.

White females who dated interracially were not rebelling against their parents and most had loving relationships and good communication with their parents. Only one of the women considered race to be a variable that attracted her to her partner. It is hard to make a case that rebellion or a predisposition to date interracially based on cultural or physical attraction to African American men was relevant in explaining why white females dated interracially. While in college almost all considered dating white males and most had. Kouri and Lasswell found no evidence of rebellion as a determinant of interracial marriage in their study of Los Angeles married couples (Kouri and Lasswell, 1993).

Students who dated interracially were aware that the surrounding rural communities were not as tolerant as the campus. African American men tended to be more idealistic and optimistic than white females about the level of tolerance for interracial couples in society. White females expressed more pessimism.

White females who dated interracially were not loners. They were socially well adjusted. None of the women felt a sense of estrangement from social gatherings before or after they began interracially dating. They attended campus social functions as well as Greek sponsored parties. Most had friends who were members of a fraternity or sorority. Some were in sororities but most were not (discussed below). When asked if they thought of themselves as popular on campus they indicated that they had not thought about it.

Merging of in-group and out-group within the Individual

It became evident that one of the important side effects of dating interracially was that white females, as well as white males that dated interracially, became more sensitive to issues related to race. Dawn, a white female, became more aware of intolerance when expressed in social situations. Only two white males were located who were or had dated interracially. Robert, a white male who was an alumnus, said he was much more conscious of race as a result of dating an African American woman, still a student at River. They were engaged to be married at the time of the interview. He talked about walking into various offices while traveling on business and seeing managerial levels all with white employees and lower levels predominantly staffed by minorities. He said he had never noticed before dating interracially. Whites who dated interracially also became aware of stares they received away from campus while in stores. One couple amusingly indicated that they purposively showed more affection with each other in local stores when they became aware of someone looking at them in what they perceived to be a disapproving manner.

Similar changes were not noted among African American men and women who dated interracially. Jane Elliot, famous for her films showing people in workshops divided on the basis of eye color, argues people of color are forced to know what it means to live in a "white world" for purposes of survival but the opposite is rarely the case. More research should be done on processes related to social identity and the emergence of an awareness of whiteness that occurs among whites that have dated interracially.

The research uncovered situational contexts that profoundly altered the way individuals think about race (Blumer, 1958). There was a reconsideration of a group's position in our society as Blumer indicated or at least a new awareness (ibid). Students were more aware of "racial formation" processes (Omi and Winant, 1986). Situations of "acculturation," as described by Redfield, Linton and Herskovits, occurred brought on by primary contact between members of two different groups (1936).

Acculturation is usually thought of as occurring when a minority group adopts the culture of the majority society. In this case white females and white males that interracially dated adopted ways of seeing and experiencing society from the perspective of many African Americans. For African Americans who dated interracially and for many that had not, this had already occurred – part of the socialization process while growing up. Thus there was no noted change in their racial awareness.

Creating Myths: Maintenance of group boundaries

When asked about interracial dating, the majority of African American women believed African American men were using white females for a variety of reasons including for sex, to do laundry, or to obtain access to a nice car and more. When asked how they came to have these feelings, many responded that African American men had told them so. African American men who refused to date white females voiced similar feelings about African American men who did. The findings indicated that the propagation of these ideas served to maintain a feeling of solidarity or community among African American students. These feelings, myth making, served to mask the true nature of interracial dating between African American males and white females. Interracial-dating partners really did care about each other and these myths served to perhaps sustain a positive self-identity (Willie, 1975; Tajfel and Turner, 1986; Tatum, 1997) This echoes Goffman's work on face saving (Goffman, 1993).

Gordon speaks of "marginal people" or people who straddle two groups (Gordon, 1964 p56). He discusses assimilation (Gordon, 1964 p 62) as a process whereby people take on "memories, sentiments, and attitudes of other persons or groups, and, by sharing their experience and history, are incorporated with them in a common cultural life." For whites that date interracially this is what occurs. The results suggest that whites that date interracially are subject to understanding the cultural norms, values and ways of looking at the world that are similar to African Americans. They find themselves experiencing feelings related to the marginal man concept or straddling a world they once knew and the world of their significant other. They have obtained what DuBois called a "double consciousness," able to see and feel their society from two perspectives, one African American and one white, even when not in the presence of their significant other (DuBois, 1996).

African American men made a distinction between dating and "casual" sex whereas African American women saw dating and sex more intricately intertwined. William, when he was opposed to interracial dating, was not opposed to having sex with a white female. He made a clear distinction between having sex and dating. These findings echo those by other researchers on differences between men and women concerning sex and love regardless of race (Collins and Coltraine, 1995). Although some African American men and women chose not to date interracially, most did not object to those who did. Their objections were limited to their own lifestyles and thus they felt what other people of color did was their own business.

White Females did not Join Sororities

One third of all female students on campus were in a sorority. Most of the white females who dated interracially were not members of a sorority. A common feeling was that joining a sorority was akin to buying friends.

Samantha (white) - I don't know why you need a sorority to be a name [on campus].

Joanna (white) - No desire not at all to join a sorority. I think it is kind of retarded and I don't have the money – not worth buying your friends.

It is possible that white women who dated interracially were more socially independent – many did not seek out or join formal social groups. Economic variables emphasizing the class background of students – since most sororities and fraternities ask members to pay dues – did not explain why these women did not join a sorority. According to Gavazzi, people from rural areas are more independent than people from suburban backgrounds (Gavazzi, 2000). It is possible that some people who join sororities do so to reduce feelings of social alienation. Sororities do reduce social alienation significantly (Lane, Daugherty, 1999). Being more independent there may be less of a need to join. There is also tremendous conformity of behavior. Incidence of heavy drinking increases in sororities after joining (Wechsler, Dowdall, Maenner, 1998). Eating disorders, desire for a more thin body, issues related to appearance and higher dissatisfaction with ones body in general are far more prevalent in sororities than in non-sorority members (Hamilton 1999; Schalken, Pinciaro, Sawyer 1997). It should also be noted that Greek members are more concerned about what their peers will think about their behavior and are less likely to date interracially than non-Greek members (Campbell, 1988).

More women who dated interracially were from rural backgrounds. Their greater level of independence compared to suburban women may allow them to engage in more non-conformist behavior such as interracial dating. It isn't clear why more rural white males did not show up in the study. It is possible that rural white males are more similar to suburban white males than white rural females and white suburban females. Men as a group tend to show higher feelings of social alienation than women (Lane and Dougherty, 1999).

The majority of white females who dated interracially were from rural backgrounds. It may be that many rural women had not been exposed to stereotypes and thus when an opportunity to date came about, and the person happened to be of another race, they were more likely to proceed with dating that person (Merton and Rossi, 1968).

More research is needed on those who date interracially. Dating interracially may also suggest personality differences such as those hypothesized by Adorno (Adorno, Frenkel-Brunswick, Levinson and Sanford, 1950). There were no predominantly African American fraternities or sororities on campus – the number of African American students on campus was too small to support these organizations.

Further Discussion

Status within the Student Body

There was often a feeling among African American males who played a school-sponsored sport that they were popular on campus. Over half did play a sport. African American women also thought that many African American men on campus were popular.

> **Janice** (African American) – Just here at school most Black males are football players and they look really good. African American males who don't play sports tend to socialize with African American females and they don't tend to have white females swooning over them.

Although interracial dating was almost always a result of frequent contact and friendship (and not limited to those who played school sports), African American men often discussed their popularity in terms of being able to potentially "be with" a particular white female on campus. Certain women were considered more desirable than others on campus. Being popular provided the opportunity to imagine or fantasize that one could have a "chance." These fantasies were linked to having sex not dating. Some African American men expressed frustration that although popularity was there, they knew race would still be a factor in the eyes of the particular woman they fantasized about and would prevent fulfillment. These fantasies were comparable to what some might label in common parlance "locker-room talk." Research needs to be done on non-dating interracial relationships, i.e., sexual, on college campuses.

Sex Ratio

An increase in the number of African American students as well as an increase in the number relative to the overall size of the student body might actually decrease the percentage of interracially - dating couples (Monahan, 1971; Blau, 1977; Blau, Blum and Schwartz, 1982). Research by Monahan in upstate New York on interracially - married couples reached a similar conclusion. As the number of non-whites in an area increased, the number of interracial marriages actually decreased (Monahan, 1971). This suggests that when there are relatively few African Americans in a given area in proportion to the white population, African Americans have more contact with whites (Monahan, 1971; Blau, 1977; Blau, Blum and Schwartz, 1982). It may also suggest that whites may feel more threatened in some ways when the number of African Americans reaches a certain level.

These ideas may lead to intriguing future hypotheses about "race ratios" or trying to quantify a "critical mass" theory in regard to race relations in a given area. African American men in the current study expressed feelings of having little choice but to date white females. An increase in the number of African American students would allow African American men and women to have more choices of potential dating partners who are African American. This may increase social pressure against interracial dating.

Contrary to the stereotypes some may hold, African American men did not favor dating white females over African American females. Jonathan, an African American male, thought dating an African American female on campus to be "like dating someone in your family." Although there were slightly more African American women than men on campus, very few dating relationships had developed between African American men and women. Again, since African Americans made up approximately two percent of the student body, there may have been too few to provide choices for dating partners intra-racially.

African American men expressed a willingness to date African American women and almost all had done so before college. Many more African American women than African American men said they were either not dating or dating someone off campus, "back home." Almost all African American men and women interviewed expressed pride in being African American with one exception. Don, for example, believed white females to be more "refined" and "cultured" than African American women. He didn't identify with being African

American but with the West Indian roots of his parents. Perhaps this was a factor in his beliefs.

Summary

Is College a Man's World?

The findings may suggest that African American females are having a different college experience than African American males. Or, white males are having a different college experience than some white females since more white females dated interracially. It would seem that African American males and white females are having "richer" college experiences, perhaps more meaningful and life changing, than white males and African American females. Based on who dates interracially more African American men and white females are experiencing what Park called a marginal man (woman) existence.

African American women may not be as included in the life of River University as African American men. The "social distance" (an abbreviated version of a Bogardus social distance scale was given) as expressed in the interviews, between African American women and white males was greater than that between African American men and white females. These findings further suggest that, especially in regard to a feminist perspective, African American females and white females have different life experiences and that it may be appropriate to consider what Boca Zinn calls a "multiracial feminist" perspective (hooks [sic], 1992; Zinn, Dill 1996). But the findings also suggest that white females can experience marginal identities. In fact two white females who had dated interracially joined an affinity group for African American women.

American standards of beauty may also influence white males to seek only white females. Future research should give attention to more casual relationships such as sexual encounters. It is quite possible that African American females and white males are "hooking up" (term used by student population where the research took place to indicate having sex) but do not date. Hooking up could be seen as safer and therefore not a challenge to ones feelings of social identity and social status. This would fit with social dominance theory in that groups could maintain positions of dominance by how they perceive their social behavior. This would also imply that it is white males who are more reluctant to date African American females rather than vice versa since they would have more to lose (Merton, 1941). This may seem eerily similar to the days of slavery when it was common in many localities to define the race of a child by the mother's race. This allowed for the confluence of patriarchy and race. White males could have sex with African American females without any of the social obligations or ramifications that would accompany white males having sex with a white female (Williamson, 1995; Davis, James F., 1997). This reasoning adds a new dimension as to how one perceives racial segregation on college campuses (Tatum, 1997). It is not uncommon to blame African Americans by indicating "they are self-segregating" or "choosing to segregate." In reality, supporting social dominance theory, whites, particularly white males, may be equally or more resistant (Bobo and Zubrinsky, 1996).

From the researcher's perspective, the existence of so many interracial relationships on a small college campus, although predominantly African American male-white female, can be viewed as a good reason to believe "race relations" were good at the university. There was some dating between white males and African American females but certainly not to the extent of that between African American males and white females. It may be that African American females and white males are not integrated in the life of the college in ways that allowed for intimate relations to develop between them. Even so the college experience at River affected African American men in a different way than African American women. Bobo has extended social dominance theory to show the similarity with Blumer's group position theory (Bobo, 1996). From a social dominance theoretical perspective, the groups with the most power are less likely to have a marginal man identity. Groups at the top actively try to hold onto their social positions. Although this article does not prove that white males were reluctant to date interracially, it is interesting that so many African American females expressed a willingness to date interracially. Out of the four groups, African American males and females and white males and females, African American females have less power in our society.

Many River Universities exist and it is safe to conclude that similar social behavior occurs - interracial dating occurs and couples feel comfortable on campus to do so. Partners at River felt a sense of commonality with each other that deepened as the relationship progressed and affected how one perceived one's "racial identity" or "racial space." White partners, in this case mostly white females, were able to identify more with a "Black experience" (Frankenburg, 1997). So often we only hear about the great divide between African

Americans and whites. Research on interracial couples is cause for celebration and could lead to policies that promote more meaningful college careers for all students regardless of race and gender - the promotion of more marginal identities.

The researcher does not know of viable contemporary theories or research that attempt to explain why there are fewer white male-African American female couples dating or married than African American male-white female. Merton proposed, almost sixty years ago, that there were greater incentives for the formation of African American male-white female couples than vice versa. He hypothesized that African American males by marrying white females gained social status by marrying someone who is white. White females could gain economic status because, according to Davis and Merton, white females were more likely to marry "up" (Davis, 1941; Merton, 1941). Thus it was a mutual trade so to speak. The same could not be said for white males marrying African American females. One could not speak of a mutual trade.

Other research besides the one at hand has refuted Davis and Merton's theories (Bernard, 1966; Porterfield, 1982). Those who date interracially expressed feelings of shared similarities as a primary reason for dating each other. African American males did not show any indications that dating interracially was motivated by wanting to increase social status on campus. White females did not give any indication that they dated interracially as a way of improving their economic status.

It is true that American men regardless of race are more prone than American women to initially value physical attraction in perspective dating partners (Collins and Coltraine, 1995). But the evidence in this research suggests that contrary to popular opinion, physical attraction is less important as a mechanism that promotes the formation of interracial couples than it is for same-race couples. The evidence from this research also supports, provides evidence to the origins and existence, of marginal or fractured identities among white students as a result of interracially dating.

References

Adorno, T. W., Frenkel-Brunswick, E., Levinson, D. J. and R. N. Sanford. 1950. *The Authoritarian Personality*. New York: Harper and Row.

Allport, Gordon W. 1954. *The Nature of Prejudice*. Boston, Mass: Beacon.

Anderson, E. 1990. Streetwise. Chicago: University of Chicago Press.

_____ 1999. *Code of the Street: Decency, Violence, and the Moral Life of the Inner city.* New York: W. W. Norton and Cpy.

Bennett Jr., L. 1982. *Before the Mayflower: A history of Black America.* New York: Penguin.

Bernard, J. 1960. "Note on Educational Homogamy in Negro-white and white-Negro Marriages, 1960." *Journal of Marriage and the Family.* Vol 28. 274-276.

Blau, P. M. 1977. "A macrostructural theory of social structure." *American Journal of Sociology.* 83 #1. 26-54.

Blau, P. M., Blum, T. C., and J. E. Schwartz. 1982. "Heterogeneity and Intermarriage." *American Sociological Review.* 47: 45-62.

Blau, P. M. and J. E. Schwartz. 1982. "Heterogeneity and intermarriage." *American Sociological Review* 47: 45-62.

Blumer, H. 1958. "Race Prejudice as a Sense of Group Position." *Pacific Sociological Review.* 1 #1. 3-7.

Bobo, L. D. 1999. "Prejudice as Group Position: Microfoundations of a Sociological Approach to Racism and Race Relations." *Journal of Social Issues*, 55 #3: 445-472.

Bobo, L. D. and V. L. Hutchings. 1996. "Perceptions of racial groups competition: extending Blumer's theory of group position to a multiracial social context." *American Sociological Review.* #61: 951-972

Bobo, Lawrence D. and C. L. Zubrinsky. 1996. "Attitudes on Residential Integration: Perceived Status Differences, Mere In-group Preference, or racial Prejudice?" *Social Forces* 74 #3 (March). 883-909.

Brown, R. *1995. Prejudice: It's Social Pscyhology.* Cambridge: Blackwell.

Collins, Randall and S. Coltraine. 1995. *Sociology of Marriage and the Family.* Chicago: Nelson - Hall, chp. 9.

Cross Jr., W. E. 1995. "The Psychology of Nigrescence: Revising the Cross Model." In *Handbook of Multicultural Counseling.* Ed Joseph g.

Ponterotto, J. Manuel Casas, Lisa A. Suzuki and Charlene M. Alexander. Thousand Oaks, Ca.: Sage. 93-122.

Davis, F. J. 1997. *Who is Black? One nation's definition.* University Park, Pa.: Penn State University.

Davis, K. 1941. "Intermarriage in Caste Societies." *American Anthropologist.* 43: 376-395.

DuBois, W. E. B. 1996. "The Souls of Black Folks." In *Oxford W. E. B. DuBois Reader.* Ed. Eric J. Sundquist. New York: Oxford University Press. 97-241.

Festinger, L. 1957. *A Theory of Cognitive Dissonance.* Stanford:Stanford Univ. Press.

Frankenburg, R. 1993. *The Social Construction of Whiteness: white women, race matters.* Minneapolis: University of Minnesota Press.

Gadberry, J. H. and R. A. Doddler. 1993. "Educational Homogamy in Interracial Marriages: An Update." *Journal of Social Behavior and Personality. Vol* 8: 155-163.

Goffman, E. 1993. "On Face-work." In *Social Theory: The Multicultural and Classic Readings.* Ed. Charles Lemert. Boulder, Co.: Westview Press. 199-204.

Gordon, M. M. 1964. *Assimilation in American life: the roles of race, religion, and national origins.* New York: Oxford University Press.

Helms, J. E. 1995. "An Update of Helms' White and People of Color Racial Identity Models." In *Handbook of Multicultural Counseling.* Ed Joseph g. Ponterotto, J. Manuel Casas, Lisa A. Suzuki and Charlene M. Alexander. Thousand Oaks, Ca.: Sage. 181-198.

hooks, bell. [sic]. 1992. *Ain't I a woman: black women and feminism.* Boston: South End Press.

Kouri, K. M. and M. Lasswell. 1993. "Black-white marriages: social change and intergenerational mobility." *Marriage and Family Review.* 19 #3-4. pp. 241-

Lane, E. J. and T. K. Dougherty. 1999. "Correlates of social alienation among college students." *College Student Journal.* 33 #1 (spring). 7-9.

Lewis, J. and M. D'Orso. 1998. *Walking in the Wind: A Memoir of the Movement*. New York: Simon and Schuster.

Massey, D. S. and Denton, N. A. and I. Luckey. 1995. "American Apartheid: Segregation and the Making of the Underclass." *The Social Service Review*. Vol 69· p 773.

Merton, R. K. 1941. "Intermarriage and the Social Structure: Fact and Theory." *Psychiatry* Vol 4: 361-374.

Merton, R. K. and Alice Kitt Rossi. 1968. "Contributions to the theory of Reference Group Behavior." In *Readings in Reference Group Theory and Research*. Ed. Herbert Hyman and Eleanor Singer. London: Free Press.

Mills, C. 1999. *The Racial Contract*. Ithaca: Cornell University

Monahan, T. P. 1971. "Interracial Marriage in the United States: Some Data on Upstate New York." *International Journal of Sociology of the Family*. Vol 1, special issue, 49-58.

Newcomb, T. M. , Koenig, K.E., Flacks, R., and Warwick, D.P. 1967. *Persistance and Change: Bennington College and its students after twenty-five years*. New York: Wiley.

Omi, M. and H. Winant. 1986. *Racial Formation in the United States: From the 1960's to the 1980's*. New York: Routledge and Kegan Paul.

Porterfield, E. 1982. "Black-American Intermarriage in the United States." *Marriage and Family Review*, Vol 5 #1: 17-34.

Redfield, L. and M. Herskovits. 1936. "Memorandum for the study of Acculturation." *American Anthropologist*. 38 #1 (Jan-March).

Reuter, E. B. "The Personality of Mixed Bloods." 1969. In *Personality and the Social Group*. Ed. Ernest W. Burgess. Freeport, NY: Libraries Press. 55-63.

Schaefer, R. T. 1996. "Education and prejudice: unraveling the relationship." *The Sociological Quarterly*. 37 (Winter), 1-16.

Schulken, E. D., Pinciaro, P. J., and R. G. Sawyer. 1997. "Sorority Women's body size perceptions and their weight-related attitudes and behavior." *Journal of American College Health*. 46 (Sept). 69-74.

Sherif, M and Harvey, O. J., White, B. J., Hood, W. R. and C. W. Sherif. 1961. *Intergroup Conflict and Cooperation: The Robbers Cave Experiment.* (Norman: University of Oklahoma Book Exchange.

Sidanius, J. and F. Pratto. 1993. "Racism and Support of Free-Market Capitalism: A Cross-Cultural Analysis." *Political Psychology, 14 #3: 381-401.*

Sidanius, J., Felicia P. and M. Mitchell. 1994. "In-group identification, social dominance orientation, and differential intergroup social allocation." *Journal of Social Psychology.* 134 #2: 151-168.

Sidanius, J., Pratto, F. and J. L. Rabinowitz. 1994. "Gender, ethnic status, and ideological asymmetry: a social dominance interpretation." *Journal of Cross-Cultural Psychology* 25 #2. 194-217.

Spickard, P. R. 1989. *Mixed blood: Intermarriage and Ethnic Identity in Twentieth-Century America.* Madison: University of Wisconsin Press.

Tajfel, H. and J. C. Turner. 1986. "The social identity theory of intergroup behavior." In *Psychology of Intergroup Relations.* Ed. Stephen Worchel and William G. Austin. Chicago: Nelson-Hall. 7-24.

Tatum, B. D. 1997. *"Why are all the Black kids sitting together in the cafetaria?"* New York: Basic. 75-90.

Tucker, M. B. and C. Mitchell-Kernan. 1990. "New Trends in Black American Interracial Marriage: The Social Structural Context." *Journal of Marriage and Family*, Vol 52 (February): 209-218.

U.S. Census. *1990 Census Database C90STF3A Summary Level State-County.*

Wechsler, H., Dowell, G. W. and G. Maemer. 1998. "Changes in binge drinking and related problems among American college students between 1993 and 1997: results of the Harvard School of Public Health Alcohol Study." *Journal of American CollegeHealth.* 47 #2. (Sept) 57-68.

Wilds, D. J. 2000. *Minorities in Higher Education 1999-2000: Seventeenth Annual Status Report.* American Council of Education: Washington D.C.

Williamson, J. 1995. *Miscegenation and Mulattoes in the United States.* Baton Rouge: Louisiana State University Press.

Willie, C. V. 1975. *OREO on Race and Marginal men and women.* Wakefield, Mass.: Parameter Press.

Zinn, M. B. and B. T. Dill. 1996. "Theorizing difference from multicultural feminism." *Feminist Studies*, vol 22 (Summer) 321-31.

Index

Adler, P., 256
administrators, 313
affirmative action, 163, 164, 168, 173, 178, 219; and policies, 161
African American: student heterogeneity, 317; thoughts about white students, 216; women and willingness to date white males, 329
American Association of Community Colleges (AACC), 168
Appalachianism, 6
Aptheker, H., 39
Asian ethnicities, 246
Assimilationist perspective, 241
Association of American College and Universities (AACU), 204
authoritarian personality, 294

Baldwin, J., 22
Beastie Boys, 48
Berry, H., 249
biracial friendships, 208
Blumer, H., 323
Bobo, L., 323
Bogardus, E., 103, 297
Bonachich, E., 150

Brown vs. Board of Education, 43, 244
Buttny, R., 254, 257, 258

California and interracial marriages, 248
Carter, M., 128
Civil War, 6
Cliff, Michelle, 24-27
college friendships, 256; and commuters, 19
Cosby, B., 249
Cross, W., 323

Dalton, H., 130
Delta State, 1
DiversityWeb Listserv, 204
Dixiecrats, 3
DuBois, W.E.B., 147, 156, 323, 333

Edwards, H., 44
Ellison, R., 151

families in the 1920's, 243
Feagin, J., 147
Federal Bureau of Investigation and bias-motivated crimes, 127
Free Enterprise, 25
Freedman Bureau, 36

Gallup polls, 176
Gangsta Rap, 220
Gates, H., 16
General Social Survey (GSS), 169
Gordon, M., 241-242
Gould, S., 152
Gramsci, A., 54
Greek system, 49
group boundaries, 332

Helms, J., 323
homophobia and internalization, 136-137
Hispanics, 15
Hoop Dreams, 221
Horne, G., 147
Hughes, E., 125
Human Resource manager, 111
Hurston, Z., 145, 151

institutionalized oppression, 62
interracial romance and television shows, 240

Jackman, M., 295
Jim Crow, 9, 38

Ketering Climate Scale, 176
Kent, N., 149
Kid Rock, 48
King, M., 6, 144, 149, 151; and father, 152
Ku Klux Klan, 151

Lee, H., 9
Limp Bizkit, 48

marginal individual, 308
Marriage between Italian-American and Irish-American, 242
McIntosh, P., 147
Merton, R., 325
minority youths, 221
Mississippi, 1
Moody, A., 9

Morrison, T., 145
MTV, 60, 72, 249
Multicultural Assessment of Campus Programming (MAC-P), 176
Myrdahl, G., 147

National Civil Rights Museum, 144
National Collegiate Athletic Association (NCAP), 34-35
National Opinion Research Center (NORC), 169
New Jersey State Normal School, 18
North Carolina and cotton belt, 143
Novak, R., 242

Oberlin College, 36-37
Owens, J., 42

Park, R., 308
Phi Beta Kappa, 39
Philadelphia College of Pharmacy, 110
Poussaint, A., 132
Promoting Minority Education in Graduate Schools (PMEGS) and funding for at Notre Dame, 163

race targeting, 172
racial segregation and aggressive segregation, 258; and language, 267; self-segregation, 248, 269-272; and society 259; and nonassertive segregation, 257
racism and adversely affected, 219; and southern, 21
Robeson, P., 39-40
rednecks, 14
role models, 209; and contact with African American males,

214; interaction patterns, 212
rural white females, 334

Schultz's Fundamental Interpersonal Relations Orientation Questionnaire (FIRO-B), 85
Second Morill Act of 1890, 36
sex, 333
Shepard, M., 128
Sherif, M., 232
slavery, 215
Social Learning Theory, 95-96
Spin City, 133\
social status, 231; and subordinate, 135
Staples, R., 132, 249
standards of beauty, 251
students and interaction patterns, 213

Tatum, B., 333
Teaching: feeling comfortable, 226; and challenging preconceived notions, 237; and power in the classroom, 231; strategies, 231-234
Tony Brown's Journal, 132

United Negro College Fund, 42
University of Kansas, 41

Vanderbilt University, 4
Vietnam War and protests, 109

white supremacist, 73
Wild, D., 325
Williams, P., 23
Wilson, W., 147
Woods, T., 240
Woodward, C., 5
Wright, R., 145

About the Contributors

Elliott Anderson recently completed his graduate work in sociology at Longwood College.

Tim Baylor is currently an Assistant Professor of anthropology and sociology at Missouri Western State College where he teaches cultural anthropology, introductory sociology, and sociological theory. His interests are in Native American cultures, religion, and comparative ethnic studies using anthropological, historical, and sociological perspectives.

Kianda Bell is a Ph.D. student and Graduate Fellow in sociology at The American University.

Wanda Collins (see footnote at bottom of article on first page, she passed away)

Eddie Comeaux Eddie Comeaux is a Ph.D. student in Higher Education at UCLA. His research interests include urban identities in education and sport, African American male student athletes and their socialization, and faculty and student-althlete relationships at major universities.

Bette J. Dickerson is a Professor and the Chair of the Sociology Department at The American University. She has received Meritorious Service to the Organization Award and the American University Faculty Member of the Year Award from the Student Confederation Association. She is current President of the Association of Black Sociologists and chaired its 1999 Program Committee. She also chaired the American University's Diversity Committee, and was named a

1998 Chesapeake Regional Scholar in African American Studies of the Carter G. Woodson Institute, University of Virginia. She has edited two books and authored a number of chapters in these and other works. Her latest book is *African American Single Mothers: Understanding Their Lives and Families*. Her interests include the social construction of race and identity in American society, collective memory and public history, Africentric and Black feminist socio-historical research.

Ashraf M. Esmail is a doctoral student in sociology at the University of Southern Illinois, Carbondale and is an instructor in the Department of Sociology. Ashraf is also an instructor and the assistant to the Academic Coach Coordinator in the Department of Basic Skills. His research interests include homicide studies, Sociology of the Family, and Race and Ethnicity.

Natalie Fasnacht is currently studying whiteness in the Cultural Studies Ph.D. program at the University of California Davis.

Charles A. Gallagher is Assistant Professor and director of the race and urban studies concentration in the Department of Sociology at Georgia State University in Atlanta and Associated Faculty, Jean Blumenfeld Center for Ethics. He teaches classes on urban sociology, social inequality and race and ethnic relations. He has written numerous articles on racial and ethnic assimilation in the United States. He has been honored with three teaching awards, most recently the 2001 Outstanding Teacher of the Year, College of Arts and Sciences, Georgia State University. He is editor *of Rethinking the Color Line: Readings in Race and Ethnicity* (Mayfield Press). His recent work focuses on the political and cultural meaning whites attach to their race. His book, *Beyond Invisibility: The Meaning of Whiteness in Multiracial America*, will be published by New York University Press, forthcoming.

Larry J. Griffin was born in the Mississippi Delta and, for much of his life, educated there. In 1977, he received a Ph.D. in sociology from Johns Hopkins University in Baltimore, Maryland. After teaching at Indiana University and the University of Minnesota for 14 years, he returned to the South to teach at Vanderbilt University. He has received both research and teaching awards and published widely on the U.S. South. Currently Director of Vanderbuilt's Program in

American and Southern Studies, he also teaches in African American Studies, history, and sociology programs.

C. Keith Harrison is a former student athlete and coach. He teaches race relations, cultural images and sport and social sports history at the University of Michigan. Harrison has published several research articles and chapters on media images of African American athletes. He is Assistant Professor of kinesiology in the department of sports management and communication. He is also founder and director of the Paul Robeson Research Center for Academic and Athletic Prowess. Harrison is currently working on a book titled, *Image, Race, Sports and Society*.

Amitra A. Hodge received her Ph.D. in sociology at Texas Woman's University. She is currently an Assistant Professor in sociology at Buffalo State College. She also serves as the Coordinator of the Women's Studies Interdisciplinary Unit and Minor Program. Dr. Hodge is the author of a book to be published later this year by Mellon Press on men who attend predominantly female colleges.

Sara Dalmas Jonsberg is Assistant Professor of English and Coordinator of English Education at Monclair State University. She attended Mount Holyoke College, Johns Hopkins University and the University of Massachusetts Amherst.

Kathleen Korgen is an Assistant Professor of Sociology at William Paterson University. She is author of *From Black to Biracial* (Praeger, 1998, 1999) and is currently writing *Crossing the Racial Divide: Close Friendships between Blacks and Whites*, which will be published by Praeger.

Kate Lasso is a Ph.D. student in sociology at The American University. She holds a Master's in Applied Development from Tulane University and in International Studies from the American University. Ms. Lasso earned undergraduate degrees in International Relations and Economics from Miami University of Ohio.

Sharon Anderson Lewis is an Assistant Professor of English at Montclair State University where she teaches Black American literature and first-year writing courses.

Contributors

Robert M. Moore III is an Assistant Professor of Sociology at Frostburg State University, Maryland. He recently edited a book, *The Hidden America: Social Problems in Rural America* (Susquehanna University Press, 2001). Although many of the courses he teaches deal with issues of race, ethnicity and gender, he maintains diverse interests. Some of his work has focused on the creativity of small groups. He has been published in the *Journal of Social Psychology*, *International Social Science Review*, and *Sociological Viewpoints*. He is the immediate past president of the Pennsylvania Sociological Society. His current interests include research on interracial dating on college campuses.

Douglas Neil is a doctoral candidate in the Counseling Psychology at Michigan State University who is currently an intern at the University of Missouri Columbia university counseling center. His primary areas of interest are multicultural counseling training and the influence of racial and ethnic identity on ego development, and counseling and supervision process.

Joseph W. Ruane is a Professor of Sociology and Health Policy at the University of the Sciences in Philadelphia. He received his Ph.D. from the University of Delaware in 1978 and his M.A. from Temple University in 1971. He is a past president of the Pennsylvania Sociological Society and has served on committees of the Eastern Sociological Society. He is also undergraduate dean of Global Ministries University.

Wanda Rushing is Assistant Professor of Sociology and an affiliate of the Center for Research on Women at the University of Memphis. She received her Ph.D. from the University of Tennessee in 1998. Her primary research interests include racial and ethnic inequality, the political economy of development, and education and economic development in the U.S. South. She has published articles in *Current Sociology*, the *Journal of Poverty*, and *Race Ethnicity and Education*. Her current research includes a study of power elites in agro-industrial hog farming in North Carolina (her home state) and a study of the education of Southern women. The Oromo Studies Organization awarded an excellence award to Dr. Rushing in July 2000 in honor of her work with the organization and *The Oromo Studies Journal*, an African Studies journal.

Raymond Soh, Ph.D., is a psychologist who has taught in the U.S. and overseas. He has been involved with human resource development training with various corporations. His professional and research interests include: Learning Problems and Strategies and Organization Development and Training.

Robbie J. Steward is an Associate Professor in Counseling Psychology and the Coordinator of the M.A. Counseling Program and the doctoral Counselor Education program at Michigan State University. Her primary areas of interest are multicultural counseling training, counseling supervision, and the academic persistence of racial/ethnic minorities on predominantly White university campuses.

Jas M. Sullivan is the Associate Director of the Upward Bound Program and is currently a doctoral student in the School of Education pursuing training in School Psychology at Indiana University. His research interests include: race and ethnicity, the sociology of education, and emotional intelligence.

Will Tyson is currently a graduate student in Sociology at Duke University. His research interests include race, gender, education and sport.

Tiffany Waits is a Ph.D. student in Sociology at The American University. Ms. Waits works for Westat, a local social science research company.

Gabe T. Wang is Assistant Professor of sociology at William Paterson University, New Jersey. He received his Ph.D. in sociology from Brigham Young. Gabe's research interests include socioeconomic development, juvenile delinquency, and cultural values.

George A. Yancey Ph.D., sociology, is an Assistant Professor at the University of Texas. He teaches undergraduate and graduate courses on race and ethnicity as well as a course on the multiracial family at the University of North Texas. He has recently helped develop a Race and Ethnic Relations program at the University of North Texas. He is currently conducting research on multiracial churches and cross-racial social attitudes. He has published in several scholarly journals including *Journal of Family Issues, Sociological Imagination, Sociological Spectrum and Sociological Perspectives.*

Eboni M. Zamani is an Assistant Professor in Higher Education Administration in the Department of Leadership and Counseling at Eastern Michigan University. Her Ph.D. was received from the University of Illinois at Urbana-Champaign in Higher Education Administration. Her research interests and publications have examined retention and transition among two and four-year students, college readiness and remedial programs, and the changing context of attitudinal responses toward affirmative action in higher education.